LIT ED

Anthony Curtis

LIT
ED

on reviewing and reviewers

CARCANET

First published in Great Britain in 1998 by
Carcanet Press Limited
4th Floor, Conavon Court
12–16 Blackfriars Street
Manchester M3 5BQ

A CIP catalogue record for this book
is available from the British Library.

ISBN 1 85754 149 9

The publisher acknowledges financial
assistance from the Arts Council of England.

Set in Baskerville by Ensystems, Saffron Walden, Essex
Printed and bound in England by SRP Ltd, Exeter.

To Arthur Crook

... such a price
The Gods exact for song:
To become what we sing.

(Matthew Arnold, *The Strayed Reveller*)

Contents

Acknowledgements

I owe an unpayable debt of gratitude to my wife Sarah for her infinite forbearance and support while the book was being written and for her scrutiny of the text after it was written.

I am sensible of how fortunate I was in my colleagues and reviewers when I was a literary editor and I should like to thank all those who made my life over thirty years such an agreeable one.

While working on this book I asked several people to share with me their memories and their professional knowledge of individual books pages, literary editors and reviewers. I should like to thank the following for their kindness in seeing me and answering my questions:

The Hon. David Astor and E. J. B. Rose (*The Observer*); Arthur Crook and John Gross (*The Times* and the *TLS*); Janet Adam Smith (*The Listener* and the *New Statesman and Nation*); the late Jeremy Potter (*New Statesman and Nation*); Michael Ratcliffe (*The Times* and the *Sunday Times*); Charles McGrath and George Steiner (*The New Yorker*); Derwent May (*The Listener*); the late John Carswell (*New Age*); Peggy Allen (Walter Allen); Merlyn Holland (Rebecca West); Joanna Kilmartin (Terence Kilmartin); Catherine Lambert (J. W. Lambert); Polly Toynbee (Philip Toynbee); John Calder (1962 Edinburgh Writers' Conference). I hardly need add that none of the above-mentioned is responsible for any errors or inaccuracies that may be found in the book; for any such I alone am accountable.

The author and publisher would like to thank the following for permission to quote from unpublished letters and documents:
the Estate of Cyril Connolly c/o Rogers, Coleridge & White Ltd, 20 Powis Mews, London W11 1JN for letters and post-cards from

Cyril Connolly in the Bodleian Library and his published writings copyright © The Estate of Cyril Connolly 1998; Valerie Eliot for a letter and other writings by T. S. Eliot; the late Lady Empson for a letter by William Empson; Victor Gollancz Ltd and the Victor Gollancz Estate for a letter by Victor Gollancz; Francis Greene and Verdant SA for letters by Graham Greene copyright © Francis Greene and Verdant SA 1998; L. R. Leavis for letters by F. R. Leavis; C. S. Lewis Pte Ltd for a post-card from C. S. Lewis; The Rt Hon. the Earl of Stockton for a letter by Harold Macmillan; Lady Marilyn Quennell for a letter by Peter Quennell; Philip Snow for letters by his brother, Lord Snow (C. P. Snow); Peters Fraser and Dunlop Group Ltd on behalf of the Estate of Rebecca West for letters and writings by Rebecca West; The Rt Hon. Lady Falkender and the Bodleian Library for a letter by Harold Wilson; the University Library, the University of Sussex, representing the Estate of Leonard Woolf for a letter by Leonard Woolf.

The author and publisher would like to thank the following for permission to reproduce published work: the late Quentin Bell for quotations from Clive Bell's *Pot-Boilers*; Richard Garnett for quotations from David Garnett's *Flowers in the Field*; Alfred Kazin for quotations from *Starting Out in the Thirties*; Nigel Nicolson for quotations from Harold Nicholson's *Diaries*; Julia O'Faolain for a quotation from a review by Sean O'Faolain; Mark Hamilton as literary executor of the Estate of the late Sonia Brownell Orwell and Martin Secker and Warburg Ltd and Harcourt Brace Inc for the quotation from 'Confessions of a Book Reviewer' by George Orwell copyright © Mark Hamilton; Francis Partridge for quotations from *Memories*; the Society of Authors as agents of the Strachey Trust for a quotation from James Strachey's Preface to *Spectatorial Essays*; Frances S. Toynbee for quotations from *Part of a Journey* by Philip Toynbee; A. P. Watt Ltd on behalf of the Literary Executors of The Estate of H. G. Wells for a quotation from *Boon*; Times Newspapers for a quotation from *The Pearl of Days* copyright © Times Newspapers Ltd 1998; Farrar Straus & Giroux Inc for: excerpts from *The Bit Between My Teeth* by Edmund Wilson. Copyright © 1965 by Edmund Wilson. Copyright renewed © 1993 by Helen Miranda Wilson; excerpts from *Classics and Commercials* by Edmund Wilson. Copyright © 1950 by Edmund Wilson. Copyright renewed © 1977 by Elena Wilson; excerpt from *The Shores of Light* by Edmund Wilson. Copyright © 1952 by Edmund Wilson. Copyright renewed © 1980 by Helen Miranda Wilson; excerpt from *The Twenties* by Edmund Wilson. Copyright

I must also thank for their unfailing courtesy and help members
of staff of the London Library; the British Library at Bloomsbury
and at Colindale; the Kensington and Chelsea Central Library at
Hornton Street; the New York Public Library; the Nuffield College
Library, Oxford, and of the Western Manuscript Division of the
Bodleian Library.

1

Journalist and literary man

Many newspapers and journals carry a member of staff known as the 'literary editor', 'lit ed' for short. Sometimes he is called 'the books page editor' or 'books editor'. Whatever the title the job is essentially the same: to stem the flood of new books and reprints that pour into the office every week and to arrange for some of them to be reviewed. Between a hundred to three hundred titles – September to early December being the peak period – will be submitted for review in any given week of the year.

I was lit ed on the *Sunday Telegraph* from 1961 to 1970 and on the *Financial Times* from 1970 to 1991, when I reached the age of 65. It was much too long for anyone to be lit-eding and remain sane but I confess to having enjoyed it most of the time. Being at the receiving end of every new book of importance and deciding who is going to review it is an addictive occupation. One is educated and entertained simultaneously.

Little has appeared in print about the job of a lit ed yet there is considerable curiosity and confusion about the role. I propose to unfold the nature of the task and to discuss how book-reviewing works, primarily in London but with some comparisons with the United States where I spent a year in 1958/9. I turn from journals on which I have had experience as a member of staff or reviewer to others that have played a part in the formation of taste in the twentieth century and describe the fortunes of their books pages under successive lit eds. I identify moments when through reading the review-columns one can observe a revolution in taste as it is happening.

My approach is selective: I give one former lit ed's view. I also deal from time to time with my own state of mind, extra-curricular activities and travels during the period I was lit-eding. Friendly readers will consider these fragments of autobiography relevant to the main theme: one thing I soon discovered about being a lit ed was that like all journalists you are never off duty. I do not write 'he or she' each time I refer in general terms to the work of literary editors, only 'he'; but it is a job where there has never been a monopoly by male persons and I ask the reader to understand both genders on those occasions when I pontificate on the business of being a literary editor.

The equipment I brought to the work was a consuming love of literature that had survived an honours degree in English – and a stong constitution. The latter proved to be immediately useful. A lit ed is continually invited to receptions and parties to launch books and meet authors. It is as well for him to understand at the outset that his wildfire popularity, the inclusion of his name on all manner of guest-lists from people he has never met, is a form of cupboard-love. His prospective hosts have their eyes fixed on his book-cupboards, where the book they are about to publish may still languish. They invite him to the party not to enjoy the brilliance of his conversation – a mere bonus – but to remind him, to *pressure* him, into sending their book out for review. We lit eds used to insist that our attendance at a launch party was without prejudice.

In Britain the current convention is that the lit ed does not have his own name at the head of his pages, but remains an anonymous presence behind his reviewers. Anonymity for book-reviewers, too, held sway on books pages until the beginning of this century. It began to crumble after the First World War, with the use of initials at the foot of reviews, and by the Second World War was in abeyance except in one or two journals, notably the *Listener* and the *TLS*, which held out until 1974. (Even now anonymous reviews may still be found, regularly, for example, in *The Economist.*) Most readers will be unaware of who chooses the reviewers, and that the entire spread of the books pages is the product of the judgement of a literary editor, even as in the theatre the total effect of what is seen on stage represents the judgement of the director. In my view, readers should be made aware of who the lit ed is and encouraged to see the books pages as the product of his particular taste.

The question I was asked more than any other while I was lit-editing was: 'How do you decide which books you are going to review each week?' And a frequent subsidiary question was: 'Why are the same books reviewed by so many different papers?' I used to have a stock-response along the lines, 'Well, you know, most of the time the books choose themselves', but that answer will only serve here as a preliminary one. These questions will be addressed again; first, though, a look at the lit ed's conditions of work.

The persistence of bulging mail-bags is an eye-opener to the newly appointed lit ed. As Alan Brien once put it, to a friend who had just been made lit ed of the *New Statesman* 'It's rather like being a stoker on the Queen Mary.' As soon as one sack has been unloaded, its contents consigned to their various fates and dispatched to reviewers with laconic instructions – 'About 700 words on this one, if you would.' ... 'Let me know if this interests or contains any fresh material' ... 'News story??' ... 'For your information only' – two or three more full sacks have silently appeared. From early September to early December, the period of the autumn list when publishers release their major titles in time for the Christmas market, the lit ed is likely to disappear completely from view behind the ever-rising inner wall of review-copies that fill his office. However long he has been in the job, he never fails to marvel at such abundance.

The first thing the lit ed notes on the arrival of a book is its 'review slip', giving the book's title, author, price and publication date. Printed on the standard review slip is the request, frequently ignored: 'We ask that no review appear before publication date'.

I must dwell for a moment or two on this thorny, tedious topic of publication-dates and embargoes because it is so important in the working-life of a literary editor. There are in the UK two days of the week when books are published: Monday and Thursday. When I first became a lit ed in 1960, the daily papers published their books pages on Thursday or Friday. That meant that they and the weeklies – *Listener, New Statesman, Spectator* and so on – could have the first opportunity of reviewing the Thursday books; and the Sunday papers, especially then sole heavyweights, the *Sunday Times* and the *Observer*, could have first crack at the Monday books.

From time to time a paper would inadvertently 'jump the gun', as the breaking of the publication-date embargo is known in the trade. Occasionally, however, this would be done quite deliberately as part of a lit ed's calculated strategy to scoop his rivals. It would usually be a book of major importance of which he had organised a review by a famous 'name' of which he was especially proud.

The embargo system, always vulnerable, tottered on the verge of

collapse in the late 1980s when several daily newspapers began to
publish their books pages on Saturday, either instead of, or in
addition to, running books page in the earlier part of the week. I
myself might have been in some small way responsible for the
resulting disregard of embargoes. In 1985 my paper – the *FT* –
pioneered the idea of publishing on Saturday a separate leisure
section, the *Weekend FT.* Our general books page hitherto published on Thursday or Friday was moved to Saturday. From then
on I took it upon myself to extend the Sunday privilege of
reviewing Monday books to Saturday. I was not prepared to seem
to be a week late with books published the following Monday.

Since then many other newspapers have followed the example
of the *FT* and have produced Saturday supplements of which
regular books page are a feature. The main days for book reviews
in Britain are now Saturday and Sunday. The friendly – well,
comparatively friendly rivalry – of yore has become a lethal
struggle as all the papers try to attract more readers. This has
meant that when any book likely to cause a stir for whatever reason
is published the pressure on a lit ed to scoop his rivals has
intensified to the point where the embargo system has become
more honoured in the breach than the observance.

The consequent free-for-all in which any lingering respect for
official publication dates has been abandoned, is in reality in no
one's best interest. It annoys authors by making a mockery of the
publisher's announcement that their books will be published on a
given day; it confuses readers; it puts an intolerable strain on
reviewers. Above all it makes it impossible for a lit ed to plan his
pages carefully. Publication dates are what he has to work with.
They are one of the main reasons why we all appear to be
reviewing the same selection of books: when the system is working
properly those are the important books that are published during
the week when the pages appear.

Journalists are trained to work rapidly in the production of
pages but the book pages benefit from having their main lines
planned and deliberated well in advance. What is the average time
between the arrival of a book in the lit ed's office and its
publication date? Usually it is around three to four weeks. Sometimes it may be more. It is useful to have a mammoth volume –
Vikram Seth's novel, *A Suitable Boy*, say, consisting of almost
fourteen hundred pages – a couple of months in advance; but with
a normal-length book it may be a nuisance. You do not want to
decide that early who is going to review it, so you lock it away in a

cupboard where it gets forgotten and is still there unsent-out on publication. On the other hand, nothing is more maddening than the discovery from the slip in a book that it is published three days' hence or less.

On the day he does his main send-out of books, the lit ed will have a mass of titles to consider, all of which have arrived punctually with a three to four weeks' margin before publication. Surveying these, he will try to work out a schedule of reviews for the next few weeks. The current week and the one after that will already be mainly bespoken but thereafter things will still look quite open. The lit ed will start to cast about for potential leads for those and subsequent weeks. A 'lead' in this context is a book worth reviewing at length. When printed its review will be set across three or more columns of the page, sometimes across all eight. It will usually be illustrated by a photograph or line-drawing known as 'the block' and it will have a double-decker headline with a subsidiary headline – sometimes known as 'the kicker' – aimed at enticing the reader to read the review; for example, VICTORIAN DROP-OUT WHO JESTED AT DEATH (the main headline) under which in smaller type we have 'Tamsin Bloggs looks at the strange life of Thomas Lovell Beddoes and suggests that his poetry needs to be revalued' (the kicker).

Tamsin Bloggs is not, I hardly need to say, the author of the new life of Beddoes. That person's name will appear in much smaller type still with the book's title, publisher, price placed between two thick bars down one column buried in the text of the review. Who, then, is Tamsin Bloggs? Why is she being given such prominence? What are her qualifications for reviewing this particular book? She may be, say, Dr Tamsin Bloggs, of the Victorian Studies Centre at the University of Dorset, who is herself working on a life of Beddoes, in which case she is going to find it desperately difficult to be fair in her review of her rival's book. Or she may be a member of the growing band of professional free-lance literary biographers, not an academic but someone who has published a biography on a subject directly or indirectly related to Beddoes. Or she may be a novelist or poet, one whose reviewing-work represents a significant part of her income from writing. Or she may be a journalist who specialises in reviewing books. The lead-reviewer and his or her qualifications for the task is a role in journalism that I will deal with fully later on, with many examples from both sides of the Atlantic. Let us continue with the lit ed's tasks: he needs to act rapidly in sending out potential lead books, not only to give the reviewers adequate time, but also to secure the services of a particular reviewer before someone else does.

Space is a perennial problem. Most lit eds live in a fool's paradise, imagining they have twice as much space at their disposal as is the case. There are always a number of books that the lit ed cannot resist sending out for review, even if a more ruthless judge might describe them as 'marginal'. The consequence is that the lit ed always has far more reviews subbed, formatted and waiting to be put on the page than can possibly be used in any given week. He groans when the designer, having done her measure of the copy, tells him that X, Y. and Z. on his list will have to be 'held over' (that sinister phrase is like a death-knell). In spite of the lit ed's strenuous efforts to run them, some perfectly good reviews are elbowed out by copy that for one reason or another simply must go in. This is one of the frustrations of the job. Most of these more marginal reviews do get used in the end, but there are always one or two reposing on the 'overmatter' that go out of date and have to be scrapped – 'killed' – and paid off. The reviewer is sent a fee and an apology. Much more rarely, a review commissioned from a hitherto untried reviewer has to be paid for because when it arrived it proved to be too poor to use.

A lit ed is a journalist whose responsibilities cover an area that for most of his colleagues is a source of recreation rather than work. He will be envied by many and despised by some. Even on papers that take books seriously his department does not have the clout of that presided over by the news editor, foreign editor or city editor. He will frequently have to fight hard to preserve the space allotted to him. A last-minute decree from the editor of the whole paper, veiled as a request, may result in the reduction of three pages to two or less. The lit ed is monarch in his own little kingdom of the books page but he will need to consult his editor over the reviewing of certain books of topical importance, the memoirs, say, of a former prime minister, where the review may be taken out of his hands altogether, and published on a news page. The lit ed suffers alternately from harassment by his editorial colleagues and a sense of isolation; this feeling of being ghetto-ised will be lessened if he is invited to attend an editorial conference once a week where the main lines of the paper are laid down.

The conferences of this sort I best remember were those during the early days of the *Sunday Telegraph* in the 1960s chaired by its first editor, Donald McLachlan, held to discuss the proposed contents of the following Sunday's pages throughout all the main sections of the paper. McLachlan had been a schoolmaster at Winchester, then foreign editor of the *Economist* before joining the *Telegraph*, where he had risen to deputy editor before taking on his present job. I shall always be grateful to him because he picked me from the heap to be the new Sunday paper's initial lit ed. But once I was in his clutches he decided I needed to be given a hard time. Possessing authorial ambitions himself, that flowered after his premature retirement, he took particular pleasure in closely monitoring my books page. He was an over-flowing fountain of ideas as to how a Sunday paper's books page should be run. I was expected to put these notions, however wild, into practice.

It was a tradition on the *Daily Telegraph* that the lit ed should prepare a list of the most important books received each week to be circulated to his colleagues and this tradition was adopted by the *Sunday* as soon as it started. At the weekly conference I had to hold forth about the books listed and to take on board suggestions as to their reviewing potential. The editor always pounced gleefuly on a number of titles each week and viva-ed me closely about them. At his right-hand was the managing editor, Brian Roberts, a fiery Welshman who had been news editor on the *DT*. He acted as a corrective to McLachlan's more impractical ideas and made sure that the paper came out each Sunday. Roberts had a reputation for woundingly plain-speaking to his subordinates. However at conference he was polite and often came to my rescue. He would cut short one of McLachlan's arias on the plans for the reviewing of a particular book with, 'I think we can safely leave that to Curtish [Roberts had a lisp], can't we?'

Next to him in seniority was Ralph Thackeray, the features editor with overall responsibility for all the cultural pages, another old *DT* hand, shiningly bald-pated, deceptively gentle-voiced, whose favourite instrument was an eighteen-inch ruler, not to whack his sub-editors with, but to measure the length of copy down to the last millimetre in his eternal quest for cuts. Thack's silences at conference were Pinteresque in the amount of meaning they contained. Then came the leader-writers and assistant editors, chief among them Peregrine Worsthorne, immaculate always in his dress and diction; he might have been appearing in a Wilde play, the wittiest epigrams still waiting to be delivered. His interventions on whatever topic were consistently enthralling however much one might disagree with him. The city editor was Nigel Lawson, his political career all in the future though he often sounded as if it had all been in the past. Treating him unlike the rest of us, McLachlan would listen to Lawson's analyses of the economy and the equity markets respectfully, the pupil-master relationship reversed. Lawson's star-contributor was Jim Slater, then in charge of the pension fund at Leyland, who produced a widely followed share-tipping column under the name Questor.

Among other regulars I remember with affection Lionel (Bobby) Birch, who had worked with Tom Harrisson on *Picture Post*. Birch initiated the light-relief column Mandrake. He had a way of announcing the more bizarre items of his agenda with a Jack Benny-like solemnity that had us all falling about. Then there was Douglas Brown, the foreign affairs leader-writer, George Evans, the news editor and his assistant Desmond Albrow, and Gordon Brook-Shepherd, an assistant editor who combined his work on the paper with the writing of diplomatic history – all of them recipients of my list. Kenneth Rose, whose Albany column appeared in the first issue and continued until recently, never appeared at conference. He was a law unto himself.

The lit ed will go away from such conferences with suggestions for possible reviewers of certain books that have aroused the interest of his colleagues. Most of these suggestions will fall by the wayside but one or two may lead to the discovery of a new reviewer of real worth. The lit ed has an innate tendency to rely on his trusty old faithfuls and it is good that from time to time this habit should be broken. But in the end, when the weekly talking-shop is finished, it is the lit ed who has to decide who is going to review what and decide promptly because the sands of time are always running out due to the imminence of a book's publication-date. A major concern is always to get the book reviewed promptly and not be late with it.

Attendance at the weekly conference alongside colleagues from other departments will serve to remind the lit ed that he is a part of a newspaper. The use of the pronoun 'we' at the conference will remind him of what the aims of his paper are. 'Oughtn't we to be reviewing that one?' they will say to him with the emphasis on the *we*. This will bring home to him his own double nature and the double nature of his books pages. He is both a journalist and a literary man – in that order. This duality lies at the core of his professional being. Any attempt to deny either side of it is likely to prove fatal to his success as a literary editor.

I mentioned just now prime-ministerial memoirs as an instance of where the lit ed would have to defer to those on high in the choice of reviewer. Here, and in a few other such instances that crop up occasionally, this kind of referral is acceptable. What is not acceptable is for the books page to be expected to echo the views of the rest of the paper in the general line it takes. Worsthorne put it to me that the *Sunday Telegraph* books page ought to reflect rather more than it did the right-of-centre outlook that gave the paper its identity. He thought we should have a Conservative books page (if I understood him correctly). Fortunately this idea never got beyond the discussion stage under my period as lit ed. Worsthorne has since explained to me that he took the view at this period (*c.*1960) that most of the liveliest reviewers in London were left-wingers and that we should try to redress the balance. At the time of writing the situation is the reverse of this. Luckily McLachlan wanted all shades of opinion to be represented on the books page. It was at his suggestion, for instance, that I approached Earl. Attlee to review the Earl of Birkenhead's life of Lord Halifax. The review we got from Attlee and printed was typically grey and I have to say unexciting, even if it did have the piquancy of not being politically correct in *Telegraph* terms.

One form of pressure from within the building that the lit ed will have to deal with the whole time is of a technical nature: pressure from the design department. His pages will be required to conform in their appearance to a 'style' imposed on them by the paper's chief designer. From time to time this basic style will be changed quite arbitrarily; 'mock-ups' of the new style will be shown to the lit ed who will be told that that is how his pages will look in the future. In 'making up', as it is called, his pages, the lit ed will have the services of a staff designer. It is the designer who will make the ultimate decisions about type-sizes, shape of headlines, choice and placement of illustrations. Before the designer starts work the lit ed will have had a word with him explaining which reviews are the leads, which ones must be included at all costs, where he wants to put the fiction reviews and so on. He might also – this can be very helpful – make a rough sketch of how he wants his pages to look from which the designer can work.

All this will take place in the early part of the week. Production editors on all national newspapers like to get shot of the books pages as soon as possible. A books page due to appear on Saturday or Sunday will be under way on Tuesday and with luck finalised by Thursday. At the beginning of the week, the designer will receive a layout from the advertising department showing how much of the page is occupied by publishers' advertisements. He will then start to calculate the lengths of the reviews the lit ed plans to use in relation to the total space available, finding as I have said that there is a great discrepancy between the two and that something will have to be held over. Nowadays the designer calls all this material up electronically on a screen, where he can manipulate it rapidly at the click of a mouse-button and experiment with different ways of presenting it until he finds one to his and his lit ed's satisfaction. At present the prevailing view on the design front is that in order to 'sell' book-reviews to readers, they need to be accompanied by enormous illustrations, sometimes occupying as much space as the reviews themselves. Taking the hypothetical case of the review I mentioned earlier, the designer will probably come to the lit ed and say to him: 'Is there a decent picture of Beddoes we can use?' The lit ed will then proudly produce a couple of Victorian portrait-photographs he has dredged up from somewhere. The designer will look at these and say: 'Hm, interesting but I am afraid they won't work, they're far too dark and fuzzy.' Or he might get technical and say instead: 'They're no good. They've got far too much screen on them.' In all my time lit-editing I never discovered what this mysterious 'screen' was, except that it prevented half the blocks I wanted on my pages from being used. Modern printing techniques of half-tone blocks has alleviated this problem but not completely eliminated it. In reluctantly agreeing to the abandonment of his desired block, the lit ed has lost round one to the designer. What he wanted to illustrate the lead Beddoes review was an authentic photograph; what he will get is a caricature drawn by an artist working under instructions from the designer.

Until 1987 the books pages I was running were printed by hot metal. Like other lit eds I would stand by the 'stone' – the metal work-bench in the composing-room where the formes of the pages were assembled – while a compositor, a highly paid member of the National Graphical Association, put the page together under my direction, smoothing the slugs of type as they went in with the palm of his hand, and fitting the last one or two slugs with a pair of tweezers. In that primeval era, the make-up would be done by the lit ed unaided and he would supervise personally the final touches. The compositor – or stone-hand, as he was called – told him how many lines he needed to cut from a review to make it fit; this information would be given usually in the intervals of conversation about football or holiday plans. I am not at all convinced that the end-product was less useful to the reader than the designer-designed pages of today with their elephantine illustrations.

So much for some of the pressures the lit ed may have to contend with within his own newspaper, but what of those from without? Authors do not normally bother him directly; only indirectly through friends who may have the lit ed's ear, which that may well turn out to be a deaf one. Occasionally authors would ring me up to ask when their book was going to be reviewed and I found this a difficult call to take while maintaining a semblance of courtesy. Literary agents sometimes approach a lit ed about forthcoming books by authors who are clients. These approaches are comparatively rare. But approaches from publishers are the staple of the lit ed's life. I mentioned parties earlier. Apart from the cascade of invitations, there are many other forms of approach, direct and indirect, crude and subtle. Every lit ed will have one or more calls of this kind per day.

'Can I speak to Anthony Curtis, please?'

'Speaking.'

'Oh, Anthony, hi! Chaucer Press here.'

'Yes. How can I help you?'

'We wondered if you'd received a book of ours?'

'Which book was that?'

'It's an autobiography of Thomas Lowell Beddoe.'

'Do you mean a biography of Thomas Lovell Beddoes by any chance?'

'Er, yes, that's right!'

'We did receive it, yes.'

'Can you tell me if you're going to review it – and when the review'll be published?'

'No, I'm afraid I can't. All I can tell you is that it's being considered . . .'

'I see, considered . . .'

'Along with dozens of other books that have come in at the same time . . . okay?'

'Yes. Thank you for your help.'

It is sometimes said that no one reads book-reviews any more and that they ought to be dropped altogether in favour of profiles, interviews, diary items. If that is so, why do publishers care about them so desperately? Why do they employ sometimes up to a dozen people to form a publicity machine whose prime target is literary editors? The fact is that reviews are of great importance to

authors trying to establish themselves in a highly competitive world
and to the sales potential of their books. If he stops to think about
it (which he should not), a lit ed has every week the fate of many
authors in his hands. Reviews are the one sure means by which an
author can know whether that long battle he has fought with
himself, his family and the world to get the book written, had any
point at all. The other indicator is sales figures. Whatever they may
tell you about Stephen King, Catherine Cookson and a few others
of that ilk, sales-figures and plentiful, long, laudatory reviews are
closely related.

All the leading publishers employ at least one person as a
member of staff whose main function is to liaise with the literary
editors. By 'liaise' I mean simply to keep him informed about all
forthcoming books, to furnish him with a copy of the spring and
autumn lists, to take him out to lunch twice a year in order to 'go
through the list', and to send him a Christmas card. The lit ed will
soon find he is on friendly first-name terms with most of these book-
publicists. That can be extremely useful when at moments of panic
forthcoming books have to be biked round from the publisher to
the newspaper in a great hurry. The value of the bi-annual expense-
account luncheon (the publisher's expense account) at a trendy
restaurant is more dubious. The list will not usually be produced,
from a tote-bag lying at your hostess's feet – or even mentioned –
until the coffee-stage has been reached. It will then be flipped
through page by page and the exciting merits of each forthcoming
book proclaimed. At the end of the recital an early proof-copy of
one or two of the major titles may be handed over.

On every list there will be one or more books in which a
considerable financial as well as emotional investment has been
made by members of the board of directors of the publishing-
house. The pressure on the lit ed to review such a book from the
publisher will be intense and it may not be left wholly for the
publicist to exert, but could be increased by a call from a senior
editor or even from the company's chairman. I once spent a
mauvais quart d'heure on the telephone with Sir William 'Billy'
Collins in lively discussion as to why the *Sunday Telegraph* had failed
to review a title by Teilhard de Chardin published by a religious
books imprint in which his wife Pia took a close interest, a part of
the Collins empire. The conversation became itself a voyage into
the Noosphere.

It is not only obscure authors like the good father Chardin who
find a firm ally in company chairmen. In the 1960s new books by

Alan Moorehead, Emlyn Williams, Nancy Mitford and other eminent names, would be unlikely to land on the literary editor's desk without a hand-written, personal letter from Hamish 'Jamie' Hamilton commending them for immediate review. Another eminent publisher who would take over some of the functions of the humble publicist was Frederic 'Fred' Warburg, author of a book about the publishing business ironically entitled *An Occupation for Gentlemen*. I can see dear old Fred now, in his beautifully cut houndstooth-check suit, leaning over the table at me, extolling the merits of Julian Gloag or some other young novelist of promise.

Other eminent publishers would also make strenuous efforts on behalf of a first novel. Here is an example:

5th June 1963

My dear Curtis,

May I call your special attention to Caroline Glyn's novel *Don't Knock the Corners Off*, which I am publishing on June 27th? I am sending you a copy under separate cover.

The remarkable facts about this girl are given in the very short 'blurb'. I have refrained from any advance publicity, because I have been anxious the book should stand on its own feet (or whatever the metaphor should be): but I may perhaps be allowed to say now that I think it far and away the most remarkable performance by anyone near her age that I have come across in forty years of publishing. The prose seem to me beautifully clean, the observation extraordinarily acute, and the sense of humour (as well as every now and again, as in the Felias passages, the poetic feeling) most delightful. I would dare even use the word Mozartian to suggest the book's freshness and spontaneity. And there is every evidence that this will not prove to have been a 'flash in the pan', but the beginning of a really distinguished career. She is a very sensible girl, as well as a delightful one: when I begged her not to be in a hurry with a second novel if this one was a success, she replied 'My idea is to wait two or three years: I have to get more experience'.

The novel is also a terrifying exposé of certain aspects of contemporary education.

Yours very sincerely,

Victor Gollancz

Such a letter could easily be counter-productive, although in this instance Glyn's novel received many reviews and marked the start of her successful career as a novelist. She was only fifteen.

A similar arm-twister was the following on the writing-paper of
the Hogarth Press:

Dear Mr Curtis,

I venture to ask you to have a look at *Mrs Mount, Ascendant,* which we
publish on October 24th, by John Goldsmith. This is a first novel by
a young man and might easily escape attention in the torrent of
autumn publishing. It is however a first novel, I think, of exceptional
promise in its originality, directness, exuberant and yet astringent
humour. I know that writers of first novels often become what Alfred
de Musset was said to have become, *un jeune homme d'un bien beau
passé* [a young man with a magnificent past] but there are signs in
Mr Goldsmith's work which give me some confidence that his future
novels will be even better than his first.

Yours sincerely,
Leonard Woolf

These two letters raise a question to which every lit ed has to give
a great deal of thought. What is one to do about all those new
novels?

2

'Because we are too many . . .'

The reviewing of new fiction presents a lit ed with serious problems. I am inclined to think there is no truly satisfactory solution to them. At least I never found one in all those years. It is in this area that the lit ed feels the limitation of his one, two, or even three or more pages most acutely. Yet it is here that reviews could be of the greatest service in alerting the reading public to the emergence of a fresh creative talent or the maturing of an existing talent. The problem was always simply one of abundance, of too many too soon. Almost half the books in the bulging mail-bags were fiction, often fifteen to twenty of them being published at around the same time. How could one deal with them adequately *as well as* giving readers a representative selection of the main non-fiction books also published in that week?

The category of books labelled 'fiction' is a broad one with, from a literary editor's point of view, two main sub-divisions: genre fiction and general fiction. A novel comes into the category of genre fiction when it is clearly written to conform to the requirements of a marketable genre – the hospital novel, the occult novel, the bodice-ripper, the western, the family saga, the historical romance, the romantic novel. The latter has become synonymous with the publishers Mills and Boon, the leading marketer of the genre over many years; this company does not normally send out any review copies of its fiction. It knows from long experience how many copies to print of each title. Reviews – in the unlikely event of their novels receiving any – would not alter that amount significantly. This is a sensible, realistic policy.

All genres of genre fiction are equal but some are more equal than others. Some do get reviewed; some are totally ignored. In other words, some are considered likely to interest readers while others are not. Detective fiction is the prime example of a genre that was always regularly reviewed in quality newspapers, even in highbrow literary journals. In the *Monthly Criterion* for June 1927 we find seventeen detective stories reviewed. Their reviewer was T. S. Eliot, the editor of the journal. He began by warning his readers that: 'The list above does not approach completeness with respect to the detective fiction of the last few months . . .' Nowadays we would take that for granted. Eliot considered S. S. Van Dine's début-novel *The Benson Murder Case* to be the best of the batch. 'The further adventures of Mr Philo Vance, will be worth watching', he concluded, and they were.

Eliot's way with detective fiction – to take an assortment of recent titles and devote a paragraph to each – became standard practice. A lit ed found a skilful writer like, say, Maurice Richardson, a regular *New Stateman* reviewer who was also a crime-story addict. This person became the sole reviewer of this type of book on the paper; every detective story that came in was passed over to him or her, apart from those that were borrowed (or more likely 'nicked') by non-book-page colleagues demanding something to read. Richardson was for two or more decades the occupant of the *Observer's* regular book-page feature, 'Crime Ration'. Many detective-story readers would rely exclusively on his recommendations.

On the *Sunday Telegraph* I was fortunate to have 'Nicholas Blake' – the poet C. Day Lewis – for this job. He was highly efficient at collection and selection as well as at penning terse paragraphs on each book. At that time he lived out at Greenwich and was a director of Chatto & Windus, the publishers. He would plan his Friday visit carefully: it would take in a haircut at twelve, lunch at Chatto at one, and some time after three, the *Sunday Telegraph* literary editor's office to collect the books; then off to the country for the weekend where the books would become available for other guests of the artist Reynolds Stone with whom Day Lewis and his wife often stayed.

When I became lit ed of the *FT* I found another crime-story enthusiast in the music critic and translator from the Italian, William Weaver. Here the books had to make the journey through the post from Bracken House, London, to Monte San Savino in Tuscany, but the reviews were so adroit it was worth the expense. Both Blake and Weaver were prepared to consider any novel that came within the detective fiction definition but they jibbed at reviewing thrillers and espionage novels. These belong to a separate though related genre; they appeal to a different type of reader from lovers of classic whodunits; and require a different type of reviewer. I never succeeded in finding anyone capable of doing them regularly.

Some mystery and espionage novels can pose a delicate problem to the lit ed. What, for example, to do about Len Deighton? Does he go into a batch of thrillers or into the general fiction or docs he have a separate review all to himself? John Le Carré, P. D. James, Dick Francis are similar examples. Nowadays a new novel by any of them would be given a prominent lead-review but this was not always so. Le Carré's early novels were popped into Maurice Richardson's shopping-bag for a succinct paragraph or two. It was *The Spy Who Came In From the Cold* in 1963 that marked the turning-point when Le Carré ceased to be a genre novelist and became a general one. His British publisher, Victor Gollancz, wrought this transformation of Le Carré's work. He not only wrote a personal letter to all lit eds about the book but he sent a copy well in advance of publication to Graham Greene, who wrote back that it was the best spy-story he had ever read. Gollancz had this encomium printed on a band which was placed around the jacket of the book before the review-copies went out.

The pre-publication puff by a famous name is another kind of pressure that used to be directed at a lit ed. Its effectiveness varied; it could sometimes be counter-productive – in his latter years Greene became notorious for his generosity at handing out puffs – but in Le Carré's case it did give some of us pause and may have helped to persuade us to give *The Spy* a solus review. In the end it was the reception of the book in America by reviewers and the public that made it a best-seller and established to writer's reputation as a serious novelist who happened to write in the espionage genre. Robert Harris with *Fatherland* and *Enigma* is a more recent example of the same process.

It happened for a little while to Dick Francis, though he remains quintessentially a genre man. I suggested to C. P. Snow, my lead reviewer on the *FT* books page in the 1970s, that he might like to devote his space one week to an appraisal of Francis. To my surprise Snow, although an avid consumer of crime stories as well as the author of one, had never read a word Francis had written. I asked the publisher to send Snow a complete set of Francis's books in addition to the forthcoming one, something they were only too happy to do. Snow was enthralled by the package. His glowing appreciation of Francis for the *FT* was later reprinted in the

Bookseller as an advertisement. Naturally I was pleased, though in general I hold by the adage that to be quoted at length by a publisher means you are writing carelessly.

In those days when we were so hard-pressed for space the question of whether or not to give a novel a solus review cropped up the whole time when reviewing general fiction, and we were reduced to reviewing much of the new fiction compositely, i. e. in 'batches' ranging from three to six books. Even now, in a more expansive era of fiction-reviewing, this unhappy practice has not completely died out. 'Do you think that next time I could be reviewed *on my own?*' Olivia Manning would wail at me when I met her at a party. Unlike crime fiction, where each title was reviewed in an isolated paragraph, general fiction was reviewed in a piece of continuous prose of between 900 to 1500 words.

The determining factor of what went into each batch was the publication date. The lit ed did his best to make up batches of some thematic coherence but the innate randomness of the procedure in a given week could induce the cohabitation of some strange bed-fellows – say, a tough American novel about a rigged election campaign to Congress, a novel about a lesbian Lancashire schoolteacher, and a social comedy about the elderly members of a seaside bowling-club. The reason for reviewing these three novels together was that they shared the same week of publication and all of them appeared from a cursory glance likely to interest some of the readers of the page; I simply did not have the space to treat each one separately. To try to find common ground between them – experienced fiction-reviewers will not try too hard – could lead to some rather tortuous writing in the linking-passages of the review. On the other hand, a natural binding theme might suggest itself:

> We all have to live in groups that are not entirely of our own choice. My three novels this week are, in their various ways, all concerned with the problem of social adaptability.
> First, smoke-filled rooms in the mid-West . . . etc.

Novelists and publishers of serious fiction became incensed by this method of treating their books. I once heard J. B. Priestley, as guest of honour, inveighing – I think that is the right word – to the Society of Bookmen (a dining-club with a membership of publishers, booksellers, literary agents and some lit eds) about this very practice. 'If there are any literary editors present,' he growled,

'I do hope they will cease this insulting way of reviewing fiction.' Compared, he claimed, to the arduous task of writing a novel, writing a biography that simply involved going to a library and looking up a few facts was 'money for old rope'. Yet, he complained, it was biographies that hogged all the review-space in the daily and Sunday papers. Fiction was given short shrift.

It was perfectly true that lit eds much more frequently led their pages with biography than fiction. The reason lay in the time-honoured journalistic criterion of newsworthiness. The thinking behind it was that a new biography about a famous person of the recent or distant past that contained fresh material, and forced a reassessment of the part played in history or cultural life by that individual, had an inherent news value that was lacking in a new novel by a novelist few readers would ever have read at all widely. The difference was that with the biography the reader's curiosity was aroused *before he or she started to read the review*. Having become thus hooked by the biography review, the reader then went on to read the rest of the page *including the fiction reviews*. That is the way it worked if the lit ed had got the mixture right. Research showed that comparatively few readers turn first to the fiction reviews.

In exceptional cases they would. For example, with a book that had had a news story written about it in advance of publication; or around the time when the Booker Prize was being awarded, and at any time when there appeared a new novel by a novelist as well known as, say, Kingsley Amis or Alison Lurie. Here again it was newsworthiness that was the determining factor. A new novel by either of these two writers was news. A new novel by Hamish Gower-Dunbar or Rose Rossetti-Dickinson was not news. It could be one day, possibly, but it wasn't yet. And if they were as gifted as the publisher claimed, then we – we lit eds and fiction reviewers – had to educate the fiction-reading public into recognising the outstanding nature of their gifts; and the only way we could do that, given the heavy demands on our space, was by putting them in with the batch.

The lit ed on a newspaper daunted by the pile of new autumn fiction that surrounds his desk around Booker-time will look with envy at his colleagues on the *London Review of Books*, the *TLS* and across the water at the *New York Review of Books* and the *New York Times Book Review* supplement where they do have space to give solus reviews to novels in each issue, though even here the selection process can be ruthless. The choice of which novelists to give solus reviews to is an instinctive one in the mind of a lit ed, though there always appears to be a wide measure of agreement among different newspapers about this decision.

Here, off-the-cuff and in no kind of order of merit, are the names of some contemporary British novelists who would in my day be given solus treatment. Many more names could be added (especially if one included American, Latin-American and continental writers). It is a list that is always under revision. No novelist belongs to it as of right and the threat of being put back into the batch for the next novel always hangs over a novelist. Iris Murdoch, Piers Paul Read, Francis King, Elizabeth Jane Howard, Angela Huth, Peter Vansittart, Salman Rushdie, Penelope Lively, Penelope Fitzgerald, Anita Brookner, A. S. Byatt, Peter Carey, A. N. Wilson, Fay Weldon, Rachel Billington, Margaret Drabble, James Kelman, Alasdair Gray, Frederic Raphael, Keith Waterhouse, Martin Amis, Alan Massie, Ian McEwan, Julian Barnes, Barrie Unslow, Muriel Spark, Hilary Mantel, Ben Okri, William Trevor, Julia O'Faolain, Jennifer Johnston, Gillian Tindall.

A lit ed will have in his mind an image of the typical reader of his page. Faced by any given book the lit ed says to himself, does the TR need to be informed about it? If the answer to that is 'Yes', then the lit ed must see that it receives a review. There will be times he will find such a review hard to arrange to his satisfaction. Scientific books are frequently difficult to get reviewed satisfactorily unless the lit ed is fortunate enough to have in-house correspondents willing to take on the task. Most of the experts outside the building are either far too busy to take it on and/or incapable of writing in such a way as to be understood by the TR. Nonetheless with the increasing interest in scientific books of all kinds, a lit ed must somehow overcome this problem. He should always be thinking about how he can get more variety into his pages, and trying to avoid over-concentration on biography.

At one level then the books pages offer a consumers' guide to the TR of newly published books. But they do not by any means stop there. They also have a persuasive and – dare I use the word? – educative role. In addition to giving the TR news of books he or she needs to know about, the lit ed has the scope and to my mind the duty to give them an appraisal of books he thinks they *ought* to know about. That function is one of the great delights of the job. The lit ed is highly privileged in relation to the publishing industry; he has a complete overview of what is going on and almost any new book of importance falls, as we've seen, like a ripe apple into his lap. To justify his privileged position he should have acute antennae tuned to what is new and important. He is a journalist whose special field is literature. It is to literature he hopes to return full-time when he ceases to be a literary editor. For as long as he remains in office he has the opportunity to extend his readers' range of literary appreciation along with his own. There will be weeks when he leads his pages with the predictable book, but there will also be ones when he gives the lead to the unpredictable book.

Let me take that imaginary new biography of Beddoes as a case in point. In those groves of academe where Victorian literature is studied in depth, a new biography of Beddoes would indeed be news; but it can hardly be claimed that it is news for the TR in the way that such biographies as Holroyd on Shaw, Holmes on Coleridge, or Cranston on Rousseau are news. The TR has probably never heard of Beddoes. But the lit ed, prompted by his own curiosity about the author of *Death's Jest Book, or the Fool's Tragedy* (1850), who was a poet and medic living in Switzerland, read the book at an early stage and found it fascinating. And his reviewer, Tamsin Bloggs of the Victorian Studies Centre at the University of Dorset, has done with it just what he wanted her to do – set the scene for the ordinary reader, gone into the merits of the work, the reputation for morbidity and its causes. Was Beddoes the English Baudelaire, as J. A Symons thought? In asking this question Tamsin has made the biography sound so interesting that he has decided to give her review lead-treatment. When the review is published, he may find that several rival books pages have featured the biography with similar prominence. Faced by this sudden flurry of reviews of the same biography on an obscure subject in all the papers, readers may feel they are the victims of collusion over the choice of this particular book by the lit eds, but they would be mistaken in this assumption. It is remarkable how frequently the minds of lit eds think alike without any prompting or prior knowledge.

Alternatively, the lit ed may find when the weekend comes that the Beddoes review he printed on his page was the only one that the book received in any national newspaper or magazine. He has achieved a scoop with it – but was it a scoop worth having? By leading with Beddoes, has he neglected something even more important that everyone else seems to have lead with? If so, he will have a hard task to defend his choice of lead at that week's editorial conference during the post-mortem on last week's paper. Two or more weeks later, the lit ed notices to his delight that long reviews of the Beddoes biography are appearing in the other papers in the wake of his. He will then take some credit for not only having drawn the attention of his own readers to the Beddoes biography but for bringing it to the notice of his rivals too.

Each journal that publishes reviews makes a contribution to a national debate about new books that also nowadays includes discussions and reviews on radio and television. This debate is ultimately transatlantic in its scope, with many British reviewers contributing to the *New York Review of Books* and the *New Yorker*. A lit ed makes his selection on the assumption that his pages will be his readers' only source of information about new books. He hopes that they will find what he offers so useful, stimulating and comprehensive that they will not feel the need to consult other reviews. In practice he knows that this is most unlikely to be the case. He and his team are among a multitude of critical voices all clamouring to be heard. Every reader will have a favourite books page that he or she relies upon for purchases and library-borrowings, but for most people there will be several others that are read in addition.

It is sometimes said that in Britain we have far too many books pages, that we have become a nation of reviewaholics, that no one, however avid a reader of reviews, could possibly read them all. No one possibly can but that is not a reason for reducing their number. At the best of times reviewing is a highly fallible process. Reviewers hope that what they write is accurate and just but a review always remains the opinion of one individual who has all manner of prejudices that may cloud judgement. The more reviews there are of a controversial book the better. Even the most basic requirement of a review, to describe the scope and intention of the book, is a hazardous task. A book will be anything from 100,000 to 400,000 words long. The average length of a review in a newspaper books page is around 800 to 1500 words. Inevitably the reviewer has to compress and curtail in describing the book from a mass of notes he has made on it. He may easily leave something out that the author regards as essential. He may miss the main point altogether. That does sometimes happen. The more reviews the more checks and balances, the more chance that the reader will have of becoming disabused of the received wisdom concerning an author that is always based on past work and be led towards a just appreciation of present work.

The function of a review is to mediate between the book and the reader. This process alternates between the positive and the negative response, the friendly and the hostile. If the message underlying some reviews is: 'Do go out and buy this book or at least get hold of a copy somehow', other reviews have the opposite message: 'Do not on any account waste either time or money on this book'. A book just published is making a claim for the attention of the reading-public. A review is the earliest testing of that claim. Readers of books pages want to know what to read. They also want to know what not to read. An extemely hostile or negative review, a 'hatchet-job', is something a literary editor will have to print from time to time. Before he does so he will need to be sure the reviewer has not been motivated by animus or the desire for revenge.

3

Star wanted

Readers were traditionally drawn to the books pages by a star-turn, a chief-reviewer who performed every week. When they opened the paper they turned to this lead-review to discover what book he was reviewing (by implication one of the most important titles published that week) and what he had to say about it. The success of the method depended on finding someone who combined an omnivorous response to new books with liveliness, taste, judgement, authority; someone who had in addition the ability to make stimulating general observations arising from the particular book.

The 1960s was a period rich in star-turn reviewers. Their weekly verdicts mattered more than those of any single reviewer does today. Cyril Connolly on the *Sunday Times*, and Harold Nicolson and Philip Toynbee on the *Observer*, wrote every week, and reviewers such as Raymond Mortimer, Angus Wilson, Malcolm Muggeridge, Bernard Levin, John Raymond were also under contract to review regularly. How could we on the *Sunday Telegraph*, a paper which started in February 1961, compete with such reviewers?

The editor, Donald McLachlan, believed strongly we should not try. When I arrived for work several weeks before publication started, he told me that the *Sunday Telegraph* would have different aims from its rivals and these aims would affect its books page. Its appeal would be to many readers who found the 'posh' Sundays, off-putting, or beyond their capacity. These papers were too élitist (though we did not use that word then), too obscurantist, too highbrow for the seeker for information about new books who needed something on Sunday that was just as discerning but less demanding. We were going to 'fill the gap' between the *Sunday Times* on the one hand and the *Sunday Express* on the other. The gap-filling aim had come to McLachlan in his bath one morning like a divine revelation. When the paper arrived on the news-stands for the first time on 5 February 1961 it carried a 'box' in the middle of the front-page headed 'The Sunday Telegraph and its Aims' that began:

Today appears the first new national Sunday paper for 40 years.

It is not its aim to improve on some other paper. Instead it is being started in the belief that for educated people there is a sizeable gap in Sunday reading. The Sunday Telegraph *hopes to fill this gap.* [McLachlan's italics].

Where did that leave my books pages? In a difficult bind. The double aim of making the pages more accessible than the opposition's *and* rivalling them in the quality of our reviews (which was what in practice we were aiming to do) was in the end impossible to fulfil. The Fill the Gap campaign, though it sounded feasible when it was first mooted, proved a sad misjudgement from which the paper took a long time to recover. It would make a lot more sense now. All 'quality' Sunday papers have moved many degrees down-market and the gap is now at the top end.

It rapidly became apparent – if not to my editor – that we needed for the books section what our rivals had: one star-reviewer every week to command a loyal following among readers. A first try for this role was J. I. M. Stewart, the English don at Christ Church, Oxford, also known as Michael Innes, a prolific writer of detective stories. He had proved himself to be a wide-ranging judge of literature, an elegant stylist, a reliable deliverer of copy, and he was willing to tackle anything worthwhile in the literary field from Shakespeare on. We were at this time in the wake of the great D. H. Lawrence trial at the Old Bailey from which Penguin Books had emerged triumphantly in the clear. For Stewart to make his début I gave him the book the event engendered, *The Trial of Lady Chatterley*, edited by C. H. Rolph.

Stewart's review appeared leading my book pages in the first issue alongside a review by McLachlan (unlike most editors he was very keen to review) on *The Path to Leadership* by Field-Marshall Lord Montgomery. Stewart's was a good review but not earth-shattering. He was a committed Lawrentian and had lectured on him at Oxford but Lady Chat was rather a problem for the academic Lawrentians. They certainly did not wish to line up themselves up behind the Director of Public Prosecutions; at the same time they were forced to admit that this was far from being Lawrence's best novel. After Stewart's review a memo came down from the 5th floor where the editor-in chief and proprietor, Michael Berry (later Lord Hartwell) resided: could Stewart sign his reviews 'Michael Innes'? 'No, he could not', the reply went back, perhaps not quite in those words.

Useful as Stewart was in mediating interesting books in his field, like an edition of the *Diary* of Philip Henslowe that cropped up a few weeks later, it was at once clear that, whether he was wearing his don's hat or his detective fiction writer's hat, he was never going to become our answer to Cyril Connolly and Philip Toynbee. The two rival quality Sundays had responded to our forthcoming appearance by putting under contract anyone they thought we might take it into our heads to try to poach away from them and it was therefore not easy for us to find reviewers of the strong reader-pulling calibre we wanted. Until I joined the *Sunday Telegraph* I had been working on the *TLS*. In those days all *TLS* reviews were published anonymously. That meant its reviewers *were* potentially poachable; they could continue reviewing for the *TLS* as well as for the new Sunday; but there wasn't anyone in its ranks whom I felt a strong desire to poach for more than occasional reviews.

I had been given leave from the *TLS* in 1958–9 to go on a Harkness Fellowship in Journalism with the aim of studying the state of book-reviewing and arts journalism across the United States. 'That won't take you very long,' quipped an American friend in London before I left. As preparation I had, thanks to Sonia Orwell, been to see W. H. Auden, then living in Oxford as an honorary fellow of Christ Church. He gave me tea he made himself in his rooms across the road from the college. Under scrutiny by the famous face that had already begun to look like pumice-stone I was nervous but soon relaxed. His manner was kindly but sharply focused. How could he help me? Where was I going in America? I sensed Auden was not keen to talk about the state of reviewing. It was, I gathered, something he was forced to do from time to time out of necessity and which he did brilliantly, and that was as far as his interest in it went.

We soon turned to what he wanted to talk about, the poetry of Saint-John Perse which he had been reading with great admiration. Like Auden, Perse was an exile in America. His career as a diplomat under his real name of Alexis Leger had come to a sudden end in 1940 when he had refused to serve under the Vichy Government and had been deprived of his French nationality, since when he had lived in Washington DC. and worked at the Library of Congress. The aspect of his poetry, elegiac in tone and modelled on the long verse-paragraphs used by Paul Claudel, that had so much impressed Auden was the sense it gave of a human society wholly integrated with the natural world; the social structure of this society seen as a living whole. The only comparable poetry Auden could think of was that of Homer and Virgil or *Piers Plowman*. This was a discussion I was happy to have with Auden in lieu of the state of reviewing. In the end, having exhausted his views on Saint-John Perse, he made some practical suggestions about people to see in America. He mentioned Nigel Dennis, one of the regular staff book-reviewers on *Time* magazine. Auden told me what a brilliant chap he thought Dennis was, and advised me to try to see him in pursuit of my programme. In the event my visit to America coincided with Dennis's return to England and I never met him while I was over there. Now Auden's suggestion came back to me. Could I get Dennis to review for the *Sunday Telegraph?*

One day soon after the launch of the paper I was in the deputy editor Peregrine Worsthorne's office for a general chat about the books page. I mentioned Nigel Dennis as a possible reviewer. Perry's face lit up. He not only admired Dennis very much as a writer but knew him personally. 'Good idea!' he said. 'If you like, I'll write to him to see if he is interested.' Dennis *was* interested, it soon emerged. But though he was pleased to be approached, he was chary of signing on to write regularly under contract. He had recently become liberated from the onerous task of having to write a review on a different book each week in the United States. This liberation was not entirely of his own volition but the last thing he wanted now was to become involved in the same treadmill way of life in London. With his reputation as a satirical writer high after the success of his novel *Cards of Identity*, his ambition now was to write plays. He was overjoyed when the English Stage Company at the Royal Court Theatre under George Devine and Tony Richardson asked him to join their new wave of English playwrights. 'Dennis is the modern Ben Jonson,' Richardson, whose idea it was, told me. But Dennis's plays were not as yet bringing him in much money (they never did, alas) and he eventually gave us a hesitant, yes – with the understanding that he should appear only once a month. He was hooked, even if the line was a long one, and would have to be carefully wound in.

First came the problem of finding a book with which he could make a resounding start. After some deliberation I sent him *New Maps of Hell: a survey of Science Fiction* by Kingsley Amis. Dennis's review of it began:

> This book is written in one of the most curious foreign languages imaginable. It is difficult to describe the language exactly but the reader will get some idea of the translation problems that await him if one says that the author appears to be of British stock, an advanced student of American colloquialisms, a non-conformist radical, an enemy of Henry James, George Eliot and William Faulkner, the inventor of those incredible forms that the Government sends us to fill out, and a careless person.

At this time Amis was riding high, not just as a novelist but as a reviewer who paid particular attention to style, and as an iconoclast. He had knocked the idea of going abroad in *I Like It Here* (1960) even as he knocked sacred idols of the academic literary canon in pieces collected a decade later in *What Became of Jane Austen?*. The spectacle of the great putter-down being himself put down on stylistic grounds gave immense satisfaction all round. Dennis's deadpan irony was a refreshingly new tone on my books page, and one that readers soon came to relish.

The editor-in-chief, always referred to by the journalists when not in his presence as Michael, took a keen interest in the way my books pages were shaping. Every three or four weeks I would be bidden to attend one of his working lunches. Michael's view of the function of the books pages did not coincide in all respects with those of McLachlan. His attitude to book reviews had been formed by his experience of the books pages of our parent paper, the *Daily Telegraph*. Its literary editor was H. D. Ziman (known in the office as Zed), a former *DT* foreign correspondent and leader-writer. His deputy was David Holloway, who had been on the *News Chronicle* (the last Liberal daily) until it expired and on Zed's retirement succeeded him. The *DT*'s pages were widely read – the circulation was around a million and a half in those days – and extremely important to the book-trade. A good review there could give a new book a great boost. The pages were not only well edited but also well administered. The highly efficient secretary kept a card-index of every book they received, on which would be entered not only the date of publication but also, for the fortunate few, the date reviewed. This meant that she was able to answer the ceaseless

queries about whether certain books had come in without any
problem or delay. I tried to emulate this filing system on the
Sunday but I never found a secretary devoted enough to keep it
up.

The daily paper had employed Harold Nicolson, Rebecca West,
Malcolm Muggeridge, John Betjeman and Pamela Hansford Johnson at various times as its regular reviewers. The team that was
currently rotating included Anthony Powell and Margaret Lane as
well as Zed and David. With their example before him, Michael
believed that the primary purpose of a books page was to review as
many books as there was room for, as authoritatively as possible;
and he insisted that a review should – whatever else it did – tell the
reader what was in the book. He was keen that we should employ
John Raymond as a reviewer, a desire shared by his wife Pamela,
herself an avid reader of both book-reviews and new books. But
this was frustrated by Raymond's contract with the *Sunday Times*.

Michael's view was in direct conflict with McLachlan's often-
expressed wish to me that we should devote less of the available
space to reviews and print more book-features, profiles of authors,
interviews, caricatures, diary pieces, much that is to be found on
books pages today but – and here came the rub – without offering
me any extra space to accommodate them. The one point on
which both Michael and McLachlan did seem to agree was on the
question of presentation. Lord Northcliffe's prescription for his
editors on the *Mail* of printing as many short items as possible so
as not too daunt the reader, of 'bittiness' in page design, that had
proved to be such a successful formula for selling newspapers in
Edwardian England, had been adopted with enthusiasm by William
Berry, the first Lord Camrose (Michael's father), when he
acquired the *DT* and still held complete sway in the *Telegraph*
building as a prescription for both *Sunday* and *Daily*. This attitude
affected the design and page make-up of the *Sunday* in its vital
teething period. Adversely, in my opinion, and in that of most of
the journalists then on the paper.

Anything said in 1500 words can with a little extra work be said
as effectively in 800, McLachlan told me, and 'Thack', the *Sunday*'s
features editor I mentioned earlier, was always standing by to
prove it, cutting the copy back to the requisite length. He would
give the mangled script back to its author with a mordant smile
and some such remark as 'There, I think that says it all, doesn't
it?' But if we were encouraged to out-do the *DT* in the conciseness
of our writing, we were made equally aware that the *Sunday* was a

separate entity with a separate staff (apart from foreign correspondents), and that the new paper had to discover a distinctive identity of its own. What was never absolutely clear in our minds was what that identity should be. A paper's identity, as a definable concept, is never totally clear to the members of staff. A paper's identity becomes established as the result of an evolutionary process of trial and error, and of trial and success. As the process develops the paper binds readers to it in a bonding of remarkable loyalty. But the paper can never afford to remain static in a belief that it has arrived at a formula for success; readers are always very quick to sense when a paper has become complacent and has begun to lose its way; and then its circulation starts dramatically to plummet. After its initial launch the *Sunday Telegraph* took an unconscionably long time to discover its way forward.

Michael had firmly resisted the idea put out by Ziman that he (Zed) should edit both the *Sunday* and the *Daily* books pages as a literary editor supremo. Knowing this, I was not surprised to detect on my arrival a certain coolness towards me on the part of Zed, a fiercely competitive person. The faint chill emanating from him became a palpable *froideur* when he was informed by McLachlan that Rivers Scott, one of Zed's staff (books pages had staffs in those days), would be joining the Sunday to work with me.

However by the time of my lunches with Michael, Rivers and I were both firmly in place producing books pages with the third member of our editorial trio, Duff Hart-Davis. Had one been able to look into the seeds of time to ten years thence, one would have seen that one day Rivers would succeed me as lit ed (when I departed to the *FT*) and that later still Duff would succeed Rivers. But let me zoom the lens in on Michael turning to face me at lunch. I had been placed next to him, a sure sign that he had important business to discuss.

'Your list . . .' he said with a smile.

'Yes?' A morsel of smoked salmon wrapped around some asparagus stuck in my gullet as I tried to match his smile with one of my own.

'What is the point of it?' he asked.

The list to which he was referring here was not the list of books received circulated to colleagues, but a list of six new titles that we printed above the lead reviews, being the main books published that week. Beside each title was a pithy description – in half a dozen words – of the book. This had been one of McLachlan's pet ideas he had wished on me. The lit ed had to print such a list at

the head of his pages giving the flavours of the week. 'Soon,'
McLachlan chuckled with a demonic grin, 'the publishers will be
fighting like mad to get into it. Just think of the power you'll
wield!'

Here again McLachlan was about fifty years ahead of his time.
In these days of listings (in contrast to reviews), when entire pages
in newspapers are devoted to lists of films, plays, CDs, videos,
musical events, art exhibitions, it makes sense to have among these
recommendations a list of half a dozen of the week's new books.
Such a list will be printed quite separately from the books page
and may well prove useful to a reader who ignores the books pages
altogether. But to put it *on* the books page alongside the ordinary
reviews can lead to confusion, as we soon discovered. Does the
inclusion of a book not yet reviewed imply that its listing is in lieu
of a review? Do you put a book in the list that *is* reviewed that
week but negatively, thus giving an air of critical schizophrenia –
and so on and so forth.

I defended the list as best I could. 'The idea', I explained glibly,
'is to give the reader a quick run-down on the main books of the
week as soon as he opens the page.'

'But can't he get that by simply looking across the page at the
titles of the books reviewed?' came the pragmatic reply.

The short, indeed the only, answer to that was 'yes'. I could see
the irate face of McLachlan who was eavesdropping on this
conversation from midway down the table. It was clear that the list
was not going to be around for much longer, and frankly I was
delighted. Apart from the sweat of compiling it, it was a fiddling
thing to fit in typographically and much loathed by both the subs
and compositors.

The list was item one on the agenda Michael had for me. Item
two was regular reviewers. He had to confess he was not wild about
J. I. M. Stewart. Then he said: 'I should have thought your most
successful reviewer so far was Nigel Dennis.' I forget how the rest
of the conversation went. But I realised at that point the success of
my pages would depend upon my persuading Nigel Dennis to
appear in them on a regular weekly basis. To do that I had still to
convince McLachlan that a weekly star-turn on the books page was
for us a good and workable idea. As I have said, he had resisted it
on the grounds that it was a slavish imitation of our rivals, but
when I mentioned Dennis as my candidate for the role he came
around to it and agreed to a trial trip.

Another thing I had to clear with McLachlan was the fee I could offer Dennis. I knew that that would be a crucial factor in my powers of persuasion. Ordinarily the payment of reviewers is at the discretion of the lit ed. He has an annual budget for his pages within the limits of which he is supposed to keep and which is monitored at regular intervals by the managing editor. The frequency and severity of the monitoring depends on how well the paper as a whole is doing. For payment of free-lance reviewers the lit ed usually has a fixed scale; currently it might be £250 to £300 per lead-review (though this figure differs greatly from paper to paper). There was a special rate for a fiction 'batch' as involving more time and effort than the review of a single book. A lit ed usually also has a contingency fund out of which he can pay someone of great renown considerably more than the standard fee, in order to persuade this great man or woman to do a one-off review of a particular book. With someone you were planning to use on a regular basis, as I was with Dennis, you would offer him a contract stating an annual retaining fee to be paid monthly – for which he would agree to write, say, forty-eight lead reviews in the year – and he would agree, too, that while the contract lasted he would not review for any other newspaper. I told McLachlan I thought we might sign up Dennis on this basis at something in the region of £1800 per annum (multiply by at least ten for today's values) and I was told to go ahead and try.

I invited Dennis to come and have lunch with me and McLachlan. I wanted it to seem as informal as possible, so rather than the neutral setting of a restaurant or club, I suggested to my wife we might have a little lunch party consisting of the four of us at home. I had the good fortune then to be living in a bohemian attic flat at Green Park House, W1. I had occupied it first as a bachelor, now I was in residence as a recently married man with a pregnant wife. The building – at the end of Half Moon Street – was not without its literary associations and that made it seem to me a propitious setting for my first encounter with Dennis. Hugh Walpole had lived there before the war. Harold Macmillan had been a tenant more recently, and Henry James and Robert Ross had had lodgings in a neighbouring street.

A day was agreed in April and Dennis duly arrived – a tall, thin, bony man with a smiling angular face and eyes of penetrating intelligence. His tapering right-hand was raised in greeting, Duse-like, as he introduced himself. The cultured English voice was used in rather a deliberate, somewhat donnish manner. His *bons mots*, as I later discovered, could be quite cutting, but were lobbed at you gently. I had made some lucky hits with the books I had been sending him for review and he claimed to be astonished at my insight into his literary preferences, but in fact it was not at all difficult to guess his likes and dislikes. An acquaintance with his writing suggested that here was someone who loved ironic stylistic elegance. Wilde, Firbank, Wodehouse, Waugh, those English and Irish wits who were incapable of writing an ugly sentence would clearly be blood-favourites.

It was not just a matter of style that drew Dennis to such writers. They were all masters of what Auden defined as a secondary world – an invented world with its own codes of behaviour and coherence that stands at one remove from the real world. Dennis was much concerned as a novelist and a playwright with secondary worlds and their relation to the world we actually inhabit. Out at Broxbourne in Hertfordshire, where he lived in a remote stone house on the edge of a common, Dennis, fanatical about privacy, had tried to create a secondary world of his own without at this time even a telephone link with the outside world. He would call you from the village at a stated time once a week. With spoken dialogue thus reduced to a bare minimum, as his editor one needed to be right on target with the books one sent him.

McLachlan arrived punctually and after a preliminary sherry we sat down to lunch. Sarah, in offering some green salad to Dennis, referred to the dressing as the *huile* – this was a reference to a passage by Ronald Firbank quoted to humorous effect in Dennis's most recent review. 'Sardonic, she stirred the salad ... pouring tarragon, dashing *huile*'. McLachlan did not recognise the reference and we explained it to him. This proved the cue for Dennis to dilate upon the life and times of Ronald Firbank. Dennis was fascinated by the purity of an art that had sprung from such typical middle-class English soil. Firbank's grandfather had been in trade and had made a fortune. Firbank's father had become a Unionist MP and had got through much of his dad's riches. In spite of that Firbank had been left comfortably off when his father died, free to travel abroad and to write novellas without having to descend to the vulgar occupation of regular book-reviewing in order to eke out a living from literature. He had been an aesthete while up at Oxford and had left without taking his degree. His erudition was vast but eccentric, self-taught through unsupervised unexamined reading (like that of Dennis); as a young man he had a passionate addiction to medieval romance and the more recondite saints of the Roman Catholic church. His amorous leanings were homosexual but combined with a strong sense of family. His dominant mother offered a model for those women of a certain age whose utterances give the Firbank *aficionado* such perpetual delight.

Firbank's cv struck many chords of sympathy in the mind of Dennis who, though a great loner by temperament, also had a strong sense of family. He had two daughters by his first wife, who was French. Dennis also had French blood, being related the Bosanquets. The lady to whom Henry James dictated some of his last writings while he was living in Lamb House, Rye, Theodora Bosanquet, had been Dennis's aunt.

Another aunt, and one who had more influence over Dennis's development and outlook was the novelist, Phyllis Bottome, wife of A. E. Forbes Dennis. She was a disciple of Alfred Adler, some of whose works Dennis had helped her to translate into English. Her husband had been British consul in Kitzbuhel, a post that he combined with running a cramming establishment. Dennis's father, an officer in the British army, had died when Dennis was eight, and the boy Dennis was sent out to Austria to his uncle's to be educated. Fellow-pupils included the Fleming brothers, Peter and Ian. The fact that Dennis did not have the customary public school-Oxbridge education for a boy of his background and ability may have had something to do with his refreshingly original approach to literature which he loved. It may also account for the serious gaps in his general reading.

In the pre-war period his family had owned and run a hotel in Chipping Campden where the young Dennis had served as the boot-boy. In Dennis's little book on Swift published in 1964, among his most brilliant pieces of critical writing, he sees Swift's outlook as formed by the reversal of fortune suffered by his family because of the Civil War. History, said Dennis, 'becomes in Swift's eyes, a gloss on his own family's and his grandfather's fate, a clear warning of what may be his own.' Through writing satire Swift sought to recover the status and dignity that should have been his birthright – as did Dennis.

As Dennis spoke even McLachlan became silent, captivated by his discourse. Clearly the lunch was a great success. But what about its main point, to pin Dennis down to a weekly review? Soon after coffee McLachlan departed with warm goodbyes to my wife and Dennis – and a somewhat less warm 'See-you-back-in-the-office' to me. I was now free to pop Dennis the question. It was exactly like a proposal of marriage. What would I do if he turned us down? However when I eventually stumbled out our terms, I received to my great relief an immediately positive response. 'You've saved my life!' said Dennis with a huge smile. His doubts about commiting himself to a weekly performance seemed to be silenced – for the moment anyway. (Later, to my chagrin, they would revive.)

Dennis told us that he had never aimed to be a regular book-reviewer as his profession but that that was what willy-nilly he had become. Regular book-reviewing at this level is something no one ever sets out in life to try to do, in the way that people choose to try to become poets, novelists, singers, dancers, actors. Book-reviewing chooses them and in some cases it is a life-sentence. Dennis told us how when he was in America in the 1940s he had become a book-reviewer on the *New Republic*. 'I married and raised a family on it,' he said. He was for a while in charge of the paper's literary pages. Edmund Wilson, the literary editor in the 1930s, was still a power there. He arranged in January 1941 for Nabokov, recently arrived in America and much in need of remunerative work, to write an article on contemporary Russian literature:

> [Bliven, a member of the editorial board] asked me [Wilson told Nabokov] to tell you not to let it run too long so I'd try to keep it between 1000 and 1500 words. Just go ahead and write one and send it to Nigel Dennis, who is now in charge of the literary department, reminding him that I had arranged for the article with Bliven. I have told Dennis about it.

That is just the kind of by-pass operation that a lit ed absolutely hates. The correct procedure was for Wilson to have told Nabokov to give Dennis a ring and discuss the article with *him* before he started writing. Luckily it did not lead to friction. Nabokov went to see Dennis in the office shortly after that and they 'had a very nice talk', ending with Dennis giving Nabokov a book to review on Shakespeare and commissioning an article on the art of translation.

New York literary life was in those days much enlivened by the presence of writers from Europe uprooted from their native soil and now working in cultural journalism with their American colleagues. Dennis became a friend of not only of Nabokov and Auden but also of James and Tania Stern, like him translators from the German. His superior editors on the *New Republic* seemed to think that Dennis would be a malleable lit ed who would do as he was told. They were mistaken, and after a while he moved with some relief to the literary department of *Time* magazine. Its proprietor, Henry Luce, monster that he may have been, did have the most remarkable flair (plus the power to pay good salaries) for surrounding himself with writers of the greatest distinction. During this period Luce had on *Time* and its sister publication *Fortune,* Dwight MacDonald, Alfred Kazin, Louis Kronenberger, J. G. Cozzens, Walker Evans, Archibald MacLeish, Robert Fitzgerald, Ralph Ingersoll, John Hersey, James Agee and T. S. Matthews, Dennis's immediate boss. The colleague on *Time* who made the most lasting impression on the mind of Dennis was Whittaker Chambers, the American communist apostate who wrote the book *Witness,* triggering off the great *cause célèbre* of modern American history. It was Whittaker Chambers, with his Messianic manner, who provided Dennis with the model for Father Orfe in *Cards of Identity.*

After a while, Dennis's appearances in the *Time* office became less and less frequent. As we have seen, he liked to keep his distance from the mill. *Time* valued his reviews so highly that they were prepared to play along with this affectation – up to a point. When in the mid-1950s Dennis moved back to England to his Boxbourne fastness, they felt with some regret that they would have to let him go and his run of reviews now ceased, *Time's* loss becoming the *Sunday Telegraph's* gain.

I reported the successful outcome of the Dennis lunch to McLachlan, who told Michael and a contract was drawn up. Dennis got into his weekly stride and we too had our star book-critic; we no longer had to fear comparison with anyone, not even Cyril Connolly. After Dennis had been performing regularly for several Sundays, McLachlan went so far as to congratulate me on securing him, as did many people from within and outside the office. This was gratifying but also – let me confess at this distance of time – tinged with sadness. It was not really *my* success. All I had to do was to send Dennis a parcel of books, and back would come an exquisitely entertaining yet thoughtful review. A lit ed is never content. If things are going badly he cannot sleep at night and if things are going well he feels he is wasting his life, subbing other people's copy and getting other people's books reviewed when he should be writing his own.

Still, it was a great step forward. The pressure from Michael was now switched off and though McLachlan never relaxed pressure I had a trump-card in my hand which I could always play when he came up with one of his dottier suggestions for a reviewer of an important book. 'I have given it to Dennis' I could say, eliminating further discussion.

After a while amid the chorus of praise for Dennis's reviews there arose a backlash of dissent. It came mainly from the publishers and authors whose books had been the subject of his more hilarious flights of fancy, and these dissenting voices also included – I need hardly add – that of Zed, who was not above conducting a little smear campaign about my pages. Jamie Hamilton was greatly incensed by Dennis's review of Emlyn Williams's book about the Moors murders, in which Dennis pretended that he was dealing with a book by a twelve-year-old boy. Another non-admirer was Sir Rupert Hart-Davis, then running his own publishing house and about to bring forth his edition of *The Letters of Oscar Wilde*. Rupert was particularly anxious that that volume should not become material for Dennis's satirical pen. His preferred reviewer, he indicated to me through a third party, was J. I. M. Stewart. This was one of those awkward situations that come up from time to time in the life of a lit ed where it would seem he has little choice but to make an enemy of an old friend. I was certainly going to give to give the book to Dennis, who had indeed expressed great interest in it.

To complicate matters further, we were running some extracts from the Wilde letters in the paper in advance of publication. Michael had snapped them up under the nose of the *Sunday Times*. From time to time a literary editor has this problem of arranging for a review of a book that his paper has serialised. First, there is a tricky question of timing: do you overlap the review with the final extract, which usually occurs around publication date, or do you wait until the following week when all the extracts are finished but by which time everyone else has reviewed the book? But even trickier is the choice of reviewer. It does not follow – and other members of staff are sometimes slow to see this – that because the book has been serialised it is going to get a favourable review. This becomes an even more sensitive issue when the book is one written by a member of the staff of the paper. It is only natural for a journalist to feel if amidst all the other pressures he has managed to get a book out it ought at least to be given a rave review in the paper for which he works. Not so! The *locus classicus* is Mary McCarthy's review of a collection of the dramatic criticism of Kenneth Tynan in the *Observer*, the paper of which Tynan was then the dramatic critic, and in which much of the contents of the book had appeared. McCarthy's review was so hostile that though they printed it, they then commissioned a second opinion from someone else and on a succeeding Sunday printed the second, more favourable review. An awkward episode in the history of reviewing. If there were ever to be established a code of practice for book-reviewing it should follow the custom of the *New Yorker*, where books by members of staff and regular contributors are not reviewed but are merely announced as having appeared. In the event Dennis reviewed the great edition of the *Letters of Oscar Wilde* in the *Sunday Telegraph* and made an excellent job of it.

4

Enter the Dame

Having been fanatically opposed to the idea of a weekly star-turn on our books page McLachlan now became a great enthusiast for it. He wanted us to have not just one such reviewer but two. 'Someone to balance Dennis,' he explained, 'but with more *gravitas*, if you know what I mean . . .'

When I said that the *Sunday Times* had bound all their regular and irregular leading reviewers to them with ropes of golden silk there was one exception; and that was Dame Rebecca West, the greatest book-reviewing star of all. She had burst free after a furious row. The row was nothing to do with the *Sunday Times* books page; it was over a feature article she had written about South Africa. There had been a threat of litigation – such threats recurred continually in Rebecca's professional life – and she was very angry at the way the paper had appeared to cave in to the complainer with a printed apology without fully consulting her. Rebecca was so angry that she decided that she would never write for them again – a remarkable decision for any writer to make at that period but she stuck to it, despite persistent attempts by the *Sunday Times* to woo her back.

A meeting was arranged with A D. Peters, her literary agent, in McLachlan's office. Peters explained that reviewing was almost as natural to Rebecca as breathing. She had done it ever since she was a eighteen; and she enormously enjoyed it. Now that she had severed her link with the *ST* she was biddable as a reviewer. He emphasised that Rebecca was more concerned to find a books page that suited her and where she could write regularly, than with the money she might earn from her reviews. That – though not, of course, unimportant – was secondary. (How simply splendid, we said to ourselves under our breaths.) In this case a written contract would not be necessary. We could have a gentleman's agreement settled on the spot. Rebecca would receive a special fee for each review – £50 (about double the usual fee) – and she would agree not to review for anyone else so long as our arrangement lasted. We shook hands and Peters, a no-nonsense individual, left. He seemed well satisfied with his morning's work. McLachlan and I were also delighted by the outcome. 'We must meet her,' McLachlan said, 'and have a chat with her before she starts.' A catch of this magnitude was, he implied, far too serious to be left just to the lit ed.

I had once seen and heard – though not actually met – Rebecca. It was in 1944 when I was on an RAF. cadet course up at Oxford, and she had come to address the English Club. The occasion had left me with a lasting impression of her formidable presence and of the great sweep of her mind. Her theme then was artistic vocation and she cited Paul Valéry, whom she had heard lecture at Sybil Colefax's house, as an example of it. While delivering his address, the *cher maître* had turned over two pages of his script at once and had not noticed the lapse. That had greatly endeared him to her. It showed he was concentrating on his next poem and not on the lecture – a true order of priorities. In speaking to the OU English Club Rebecca made no such error because she spoke impromptu. She also said that Virginia Woolf's *Orlando* had been a liberating work for the women writers of her generation.

The same procedure of a getting-to-know-you lunch was arranged, only this time the venue was McLachlan's flat in Victoria and the hostess his wife Kitty. I made a resolution not to drink too much in case it loosened my tongue. I knew there was one certain topic it was advisable not to broach with Rebecca, her son by H. G. Wells, who lived in the United States and with whom she had a long-running feud. I had read his novel *Heritage* from a copy a friend had brought home from America. (Rebecca's husband was supposed to have paid a large sum for the English rights in order to stop anyone publishing it in the UK.) This novel *à clef* makes bitter comedy out of the plight of its hero, a small boy of illegitimate birth. To the fury of his mother, a famous actress, a darling of the pre-war London theatre, the boy makes contact with his natural father, a famous writer and pundit. The boy's progress into manhood and loss of his virginity, through contact with his alternative family, forms the basis of a beautifully observed and

most entertaining book; one in which the two main characters are
clearly thinly disguised versions of Rebecca and H. G. Wells.

There was a precedent for turning Rebecca into an actress.
When she was seventeen Rebecca had been a student at RADA
and though she soon abandoned thoughts of the stage as a career,
the pseudonym she chose when she started to publish articles and
reviews came from *Rosmersholm*. Ibsen's Rebecca West is a masterful
and manipulative woman, who alienates the ineffectual Rosmer
from his wife and inspires him to become a political activist, with
disastrous consequences. Rebecca always denied that the name
had any significance beyond the fact that she liked the sound of it
much better than the one she was born with. 'I don't think
anybody could really be taken seriously as a writer under the name
of Cicily Isabel Fairfield,' Rebecca said. 'It sounds like something
blonde and pretty, like Mary Pickford.'

Whenever we met or I rang Rebecca up, she seemed close to
breaking-point as she unfolded the catalogue of disaster that had
recently befallen her. The troubles, usually of a domestic nature,
would vary but not her relish for describing them. Here is an
example from a letter she wrote me in December 1961:

> I have had an unpleasing combination of misfortunes – a connec-
> tion of mine whom I liked thought to treat a cold by a large hot gin
> and lemon and double her usual dose of sleeping tablets and did not
> wake up – I then got goat's milk cheese poisoning, which passed into
> severe influenza. I am so wretched we are taking the first sailing to
> the West Indies we could get, which takes us to Barbados on January
> 2.

If I was awed into silence by an equally dire recital at that first
lunch, McLachlan was not. He had been in Germany during the
1930s as a foreign correspondent and had observed the rise of
Hitler. During the war he had worked in the black propaganda
unit with people like Ellic Howe and Sefton Delmer, devising and
broadcasting fake information to undermine German morale. He
was heavily into the murky world of spies and intelligence agents,
and was eager to swap anecdotes with Rebecca. On most topics
concerning celebrities, literature, politics or the arts, you only
needed to give Rebecca the briefest of prompts and she would
respond magnificently, as she did now. Apart from the content of
what she said – drawn from what appeared to be some private

store of knowledge not accessible to ordinary mortals – it was always a pleasure to listen to her wonderful voice. That brief period at RADA had stood her in good stead, while many years of living with a husband whose hearing was seriously impaired, had given her naturally fine diction even more power. Here (from a later conversation) is her recollection of the atmosphere of the war trials:

> There was acre after acre of ruined Nuremberg and you would suddenly be faced – without any explanation – with a vast head of God, cut off at the neck and left lying on the pavement: they had no time to tidy it up. It was the most terrible Last Day Michelangelesque scene of desolation. The trial was quite fantastic in many ways and it was so strange to find that it was overwhelmingly American.

The talk then turned to the Lady Chatterley Trial. Though not an out-and-out admirer of Lawrence, Rebecca had known and liked him; and she had reviewed some of his earliest books in generous terms. At the Trial she had appeared as one of the 'expert' witnesses for the defence.

> I gave evidence but [Rebecca explained] I had 'flu at the time which had strangled my voice, and everbody was very cross with me for one reason or another, and I was very embarrassed because I don't think it's a good book. It's always struck me as showing that Lawrence had no sense of humour.

This touched a nerve in McLachlan. Description by novelists of the sexual act was something that obsessed him to the point of mania. Nowadays his Grundyism is hard to credit. He told me before the paper started that he wanted our books pages to be a 'smut-free zone'. In a very bad mystery story by J. B. Priestley I had reviewed, he came across the sentence – 'Much love was made that night' – which he considered shameful, he told me; but exactly *why* he considered the remark shameful was something he never succeeded in explaining. The nearest he got was when he pointed out to me how Tolstoy had succeeded in conveying the intense eroticism of the affair between Anna and Vronsky without a word of explicit sex. He wanted to know why contemporary novelists could not do the same. Well, precisely because they are contemporary when we no longer need to be prudish; but he could not see that.

Ever since her teens, when she was a ravishingly beautiful young woman, Rebecca had displayed consummate skill in handling her editors. The earliest was Robert Blatchford, the Manchester Fabian who had encouraged her devotion to the feminist cause in his pioneering socialist paper, the *Clarion*, when she was barely twenty. Soon after that Ford Madox Ford recognised her outstanding potential as a journalist-critic.

> I think first-rate editors are rarer than first-rate writers [declared Rebecca]. To have the real feeling where good writing is coming from, and to know how to foster it, is a very great gift, and Ford had it. But he was of course an extraordinary person: he was just a born liar. I've known two very able men who were great liars: one was Ford Madox Ford and the other was Harold Laski. Fantasy took control of their tongues when they spoke, but it didn't impede a lot of quite good intellectual activity.

What had originally drawn her to Ford's attention was a review she had written of a novel *The New Humpty Dumpty* he had published under a *nom de plume* (to avoid the possibility of legal action from his estranged wife). Rebecca made it quite clear in her review that she knew who the real author of the book was. This led to a meeting with Ford and to an invitation to write more reviews. It also led to Rebecca's friendship with Violet Hunt, whose predicament of being the mistress of one of the literary lions of the period (Ford) who was not divorced from his wife, a wife who was not prepared to let him go, was the mirror-image of what Rebecca's predicament was to become in 1914.

It was a book-review, too, that initiated Rebecca's great liaison with Wells. She had reviewed his novel called *Marriage* in *The Freewoman* in 1911 and the review had led to her meeting the author in the flesh, all too literally. This was during the period of Rebecca's sensational début as a reviewer, when her Ibsenite pseudonym was in regular use for the first time over militantly feminist reviews under the editorship of Dora Marsden, a great worker in the cause of women's liberation. It was Marsden who encouraged Rebecca to let herself go as a regular weekly reviewer. The assurance Rebecca showed in the reviews she wrote for Marsden, at an age when many critics are still painfully learning their craft by writing essays for a tutor, is astonishing. Even now they still remain brilliantly readable. Rebecca showed right from the start the essential attribute of a star-reviewer, absolute confidence in her own judgement. She pitches headlong into a national institution like Mrs Humphry Ward, and she is devastating when dealing with the Scandinavian misanthrope Strindberg.

Rebecca's career as a reviewer developed in the 1930s on the *New Statesman* and in many other British journals. Her fame as a critic spread before the war to America, where her editors included H. L. Mencken and Harold Ross, who had had the excellent notion of sending her to Nuremberg. Now in her vigorous third age as a woman and a writer, she had McLachlan (and me). Once we had taken her on board, McLachlan was continually deflecting her from the books page, putting up ideas to her for general articles and features he wanted her to write.

In 1954 John Vassall, a clerk in the British Embassy in Moscow, began to spy for the Russians. A former RAF photographer, he made copies of highly sensitive documents in the Naval Attaché's office and handed them over to his Russian paymasters. After he had been caught, in 1962, he claimed that he had been blackmailed into spying by threats of exposure of his homosexuality. The case raised serious security issues for the Macmillan government, then in its death-throes and also facing the storm unleashed by the Profumo scandal. A Tribunal was appointed to investigate the Vassall Affair. Rebecca attended this and reported on it in the *Sunday Telegraph*, later expanding her articles into a booklet published by the newspaper, with a preface by McLachlan. After McLachlan's untimely death, Rebecca said how much she had liked him and added: 'He gave you ten ideas every time you saw him . . . of which perhaps one was worth taking seriously.' Those of us who were on the paper then would probably agree in principle, though we might wish to lengthen the odds somewhat.

Back in the office I was in my usual quandary about what book to send her for her first review. There seemed nothing quite right 'in our terms' (in that awful constraining phrase of Thack's). In the end I settled for a book of literary criticsm, *The Characters of Love*, by John Bayley, who was then primarily known not for his criticism but for being Iris Murdoch's husband. This was the book that established him as someone in his own right. Before she began Rebecca had been briefed by McLachlan about the *Sunday Tel.* filling the gap. None of that highfalutin' stuff you were able to get away with on the *Sunday Times*, he had hinted. In consequence she was apprehensive that what she eventually wrote about the book might not be what we wanted:

I am worried about this review [she told me in a letter] for the
book is not at all of the popular sort, and I am rather dubious
about whether it is the kind of book you want to review for the
kind of literary page you have in mind. It is in any case the kind
of book which it is verr [sic] hard to review except at length,
because it is so allusive. I could for example have written something that would have been amusing and interesting on the connection between Henry James's *The Golden Bowl* and a very bad but
successful comedy by Henry Arthur Jones called *The Liars* but I
couldn't do that in anything like the length you gave me [1000 –
1200 words]. My review is now about two hundred and fifty words
too long, I think, but if you give me your ideas on cutting I will fall
in with them. I don't say do the cutting yourself, as I am as old as the
oldest carp in the Trianon and have spent much of these centuries
cutting my articles, I have therefore developed a certain low cunning
about it.

As our working relationship developed over the next few years,
harmoniously I am happy to say, I was empowered to do the
cutting. It was nearly always necessary, not only because of the
limited space but because of the richness of Rebecca's mind: great
journalist though she was, she sometimes went chasing after too
many hares and it was necessary to bring her thoughts back to the
direction of the quarry.

Unlike Dennis, who was remote from reach by the office,
Rebecca was readily reachable when not on holiday abroad. She
co-opted you into her domestic orbit and current web of aggrava-
tions. Hence I became quite a friend. She was sometimes ready
with suggestions about what she should review:

I have been looking through some lists and I wondered if I might
be allowed to review Robert Birley's *Sunk without Trace* (Hart-Davis)
as it deals with Young's *Night Thoughts* and *The Rival Queens*, on both
of which I rather fancy myself. Also, if I might, I would like *Lonesome
Traveller* by Jack Kerouac (André Deutsch) and *The Judgment of Joan*
by Lightbody.

I soon discovered that Rebecca was just as choosy as Dennis over
what books she was prepared to review and much more articulate
about her reasons for turning a proposed book down. Here is her
reaction to Charlie Chaplin's *My Life*:

> I have known Charlie for over fifty years and detest him as a
> human being (Scrooge was a sunny little pet compared to him) and
> consider him preposterously over-rated as an artist. This isn't either
> self-revealing or a work of art so I return it (saying 'Steward!').

Sometimes her explanation as to why she would not review a
certain book was almost as long and even wittier than the review
would have been had she written it. I once made the mistake of
suggesting Rose Macaulay's *Letters to a Friend: 1950–1952* edited by
Constance Babington-Smith. The book was rapidly returned to me
with a long note explaining why, from which I quote:

> I really could not bear to review it. I suppose we all have our own
> forms of twaddle that we indulge in when we want to let our hair
> down but I cannot take this form of twaddle; the more that I was very
> fond of her . . .
> It isn't that I object to her religion – it's that it's sheer twaddle,
> and the non-religious part debilitating twaddle, too. All those tea-
> parties with E. M. Forster somehow result in a lot of people meeting
> Apollyon by sitting down in Trafalgar Square and being fined £1.

Recovering the book, I tried to look up what Rose had said
about E. M. Forster and Trafalgar Square. So far as I could
discover Rebecca had invented it. Rose did pay one visit to Forster
at Abinger but it had nothing to do with Apollyon and everything
to do with *Passage to India.*
The great stumbling-block for Rebecca in this case was Rose's
belief in a personal God and her cosy way of referring to Him as if
he were a member of the great Macaulay clan. Rebecca was deeply
into religion but in an entirely different sense from Rose. Rebecca
was into religion in the same way as she was into everything else –
intellectually: religion as a system of thought. Her active involvement in it was shared by my other star, Nigel Dennis, who had
recently written a satirical play about religious fundamentalism,
The Making of Moo, that might be a timely play to revive now.
Dennis viewed religion as a manipulative weapon used by tyrants
to keep themselves in power, matched in ruthlessness only by
totalitarianism and psychotherapy. The one religious thinker for
whom Dennis had undying respect was that fourth-century hereti-
cal monk who believed we are all born in a state of innocence and
that we can live without sin simply by the exercise of our own free
will. 'If we *must* have a religion', Dennis wrote, 'would anyone

object to the erection of a small shrine, dedicated to the worship of Pelagius?'

This Pelagian position was just a little too simplistic to gain Rebecca's full assent though it would, certainly, have been greeted with a squeaky 'Hear, Hear!' from her quondam lover Wells. By contrast Rebecca did believe in the depravity of the human will, especially as manifested in persons of the male gender. This belief was based on wide experience of it, both in real life and in fiction. Although her formal education had ended at around the age of eighteen, Rebecca had a familiarity with theological argument as thorough as her general grasp of most other disciplines. She had learnt much about the ultimate values from her father, a liberal free-thinking journalist, then from Father Matthew Prior, a Catholic priest she had known as a girl, and finally from the sound general training of mind she had had at George Watson's Academy for Young Ladies in Edinburgh.

Rebecca had become so interested in human depravity that she made it the theme of at least two of her books. One was a short volume on St Augustine, who invented most of the theory, and the other *The Court and the Castle*, where she discusses Hamlet as an example of the depraved will and carries her argument through to Fielding. Both these works reveal Rebecca's mind at full stretch. She was able to sustain a complex critical discussion way past the limits of a review. Born a century earlier, Rebecca would have been at her ease writing those viewy review-articles in the *Quarterly* or the *Edinburgh Review* by which the Victorians set such store. Rebecca's most notable performance of this kind was the book she published under the title of *The Strange Necessity*. Here she turns from original sin to consider a more benevolent human activity, that surge of creative energy that results in literary art, especially the art of fiction.

As was typical of her she opens the discussion on a personal note, relating it to her everyday experience. She is visiting the bookshop known as Shakespeare and Co. run by Sylvia Beach in Paris. She purchases a slim volume there – *Pomes Pennyeach* by James Joyce. She walks along the street that leads from the Boulevard St Germain to the Odéon, full of the joys of spring. She quotes in full one of the poems in the book – 'Alone' – and confesses to being delighted by it. What delights her is the discovery that someone whom she regards as a writer of 'majestic genius' should be capable of publishing such a bad poem. She reckons that between the time when the poem was written and the time when it was published in book-form there was plenty of opportunity for Joyce to have destroyed it. That he should have preserved it and given it to the public causes Rebecca to ponder the nature of sentimentality.

Here again she begins with an observation from life – from the game of *pétanque* as played during her visits to Provence. The jarring shock made by the heavy metal *boules* as they cannon into each other is her metaphor to describe the shock in the mind of a discriminating reader when a foreign body disturbs the smoothly homogenous texture of a literary work. In great novelists like Madame de la Fayette, Benjamin Constant, Stendhal, there are no nasty shocks, no sentimental intrusions of this kind; nor are there in two short stories in *Dubliners* – 'A Sad Case' and 'The Dead' – for which Rebecca has the highest admiration. However *Ulysses* is full of such shock-tactics and hence of periodic descents into sentimentality, as are the paintings of that Victorian master of the crowded canvas, Frith.

Ulysses had first been published over a decade ago by Sylvia Beach when Rebecca wrote that, but it had only just become accessible to the reading-public in a 'revised text'. Then there was the Bodley Head edition in 1936 that made it available to the ordinary British reader. As the leading literary journalist of her day, it behoved Rebecca to declare its importance while at the same time exposing its flaws. Rebecca was always among the first to stand up and be counted on any controversial matter. Here she made her quirky but often acute critique of Joyce's *magnum opus* the prelude to a wide-ranging *causerie*. Rebecca goes on to compare the artistic urge that resulted in *Ulysses* to the behaviour of the guinea-pigs under the controlled experiment conducted by Pavlov and described in his book, *Conditioned Reflexes*, another work that made a great popular stir at this time. Rebecca's drift proceeds as always by leaps of metaphor, juxtaposition of texts and flashes of insight.

What she had to say about his novel made Joyce very angry. Not so much her specific criticisms – Bloom seen as a contemporary version of the court jester via the Aldwych farces, Noël Coward, Little Tich, Marie Lloyd – nor even the link with Pavlovian theory. What Joyce resented was the inter-weaving of Bloomsday with Rebecca's day. She devotes almost as much space as she gives to his book to her shopping expedition as it continued along the rue de Rivoli with the purchase of a black lace dress from a leading couturier and three hats from a top milliner; followed by the despatch of some letters concerning her investments to her stockbroker; followed by lunch in 'a divine house on the Isle St Louis'. The only thing she fails to mention is the brief hectic affair she was having at the time with Antoine Bibesco that perhaps contributed most of all to her euphoric mood. As I read, my sub-editorial trigger-finger itches over the delete-button; I wait impatiently for the re-entry of Joyce into the text. But then, I say to myself, why shouldn't she? It is all done with such wit and charm that the dyed-in-the-wool devotee of Rebecca's writing that I soon became would not have a word of it out.

Another contemporary writer to be incensed by *The Strange Necessity* was H. G. Wells. The main piece in the book from which it takes its title is followed by eleven shorter pieces, all from the review articles Rebecca was writing at this time in the United States. Hardy, the Sitwells, H. M. Tomlinson from one side of the Atlantic; Willa Cather, Sherwood Anderson, Sinclair Lewis, Hendrik van Loon on the other, are among people whose work she discusses. Most of these discussions have, like those in most reviews, sunk into oblivion; but one of them passed into literary history, the one entitled 'Uncle Bennett'.

> All our youth they hung about the houses of our minds like Uncles, the Big Four ... [Bennett, Wells, Shaw and Galsworthy]. They had the generosity, the charm, the loquacity of visiting uncles. Uncle Wells arrived always a little out of breath, with his arms full of parcels, sometimes rather carelessly tied, but always bursting with all manner of attractive gifts that ranged from the little pot of sweet jelly that is *Mr Polly* to the complete meccano set for the mind that is in *The First Men in the Moon*.

Wells was prepared to suffer that sort of whimsy, just about; what he did object to violently was what followed:

> His prose suddenly loses its firmness and begins to shake like blanc-mange. 'It was then that I met Queenie. She was a soft white slip of a being with very still dark eyes, and a quality of ... Furtive scufflings ... Waste ... parasitic, greedy speculators [all these elisions are Rebecca's] "Oh, my dear," she said, "my dear ... darn your socks ... squaw." But take him all in all, Uncle Wells was as magnificent an uncle as one could hope to have.

That last sentence did nothing to assuage Wells's fury. It only
served to exacerbate it by emphasising the generation gap that
yawned between him and Rebecca. (When she wrote the article,
she had been his mistress for ten years.) It was the stuff about
Queenie that really hurt the old boy.

> ... the thing [he wrote to her] is a lie and a damned stupid one.
> You can go through all my books and list the woman characters, not
> a bad lot from Aunt Pondervo to Joan and from Ann Pornick to the
> *Meanwhile* women – and you can't find three pages to justify this
> spiteful rubbish. It does me no end of harm; it sets people who
> haven't read me against my books; it will be quoted by all the Lynds
> in the world. And God knows how you benefit!

You could hardly have a better instance of the power at this period
wielded by this reviewer.

By 1961, when Rebecca became a regular reviewer for the
Sunday Telegraph, her affair with Wells was half a century in the
past and she always refused to talk about it, except eventually to
Gordon N. Ray for the authorised account – authorised by her,
that is, – in his book quoted above. After Rebecca was finally
through with Wells she turned to Beaverbrook, most unsatisfacto-
rily. Small, powerfully built, megalomaniac males seem to have
been her type. Then in 1930 she married the banker and Hellenist
Henry Andrews. It seemed to an occasional colleague like me to
be an ideal marriage, despite the recurring domestic crises, but
Victoria Glendinning who had the benefit of talking to Rebecca
right at the end of her life when she wanted to put the record
straight tells us that Henry was an unsatisfactory and philandering
husband.

Be that as it may, the couple looked like the portrait of a happy
marriage; they always showed a united front to the world at large.
When Rebecca went into hospital for a gall-bladder operation,
Henry was deeply concerned. This was in April 1964, by which
time Rebecca was an integral part of my page. She cried off
reviewing for a while:

> After weeks of dreariness I popped into U.C.H. and out of it,
> meditating an operation in May, and had another attack the next
> day so am back again. A dreary prospect. I am to have the operation
> on Friday, and there's not a soul around to whom one could possibly

say, 'Kiss me, Hardy'. I fear I shall be out of commission for some
time, and must be a reader and not a writer. I like today's page ...
Nigel Dennis is always a joy.

In fact she made a very rapid recovery and was soon hard at
work again writing more reviews for me. When she came out,
Henry took a suite at the Ritz for a week where she could
recuperate free of domestic worries. He invited my wife and me to
have lunch with them there. If Glendinning could have been
present on that occasion she would have found them a delightfully
affectionate and supportive couple.

Lunch was the time when Rebecca was at her conversational
best. You can imagine my delight on receiving a note from her in
February 1965, from Ibstone House near High Wycombe, containing the following invitation:

> My dear Anthony,
> Could you and Sarah come out and lunch with us on February
> 14th – 1 o'clock? The Trillings will be here. We would be so glad if
> you could come.
>
> Yours ever, Rebecca.

When the time came we were shown into a large drawing-room
with an expanse of lawn visible through French windows. The
Trillings – Lionel Trilling was Eastman professor at Oxford University nearby – had not yet arrived but there was one other guest
whose name I didn't catch. I gathered he was still an undergraduate at Oxford. Then Lionel and Diana, appeared and we were
introduced to them by Rebecca. After that she turned to the young
man and said, introducing him to them, 'This is Merlyn Holland ...' adding, with impeccable throwaway timing: '... the
grandson of Oscar Wilde.' Holland was then twenty and reading
Modern Languages. He had come to Ibstone on a Green Line bus
as far as Stokenchurch where Henry Andrews, the world's worst
driver, had met him in the car. He had survived the journey and
now shook hands with the Trillings. Lionel seemed completely
checkmated by this superb opening gambit and hardly said a word
throughout luncheon apart from looking up from his roast to bark
out brief gastronomic requests like 'Salt, Rebecca!' Diana, however, more than compensated for his taciturnity. The Warren
Report on the assassination of President Kennedy – one of the

great works of fiction of the period – had just appeared in umpteen
volumes. Both Diana and Rebecca appeared to have read it in full
and were in vociferous agreement about its shortcomings.

Rebecca's cook was on top form that day and we had a good
lunch. Afterwards there was a brief tour of the garden, in which
Rebecca took great pride. From the garden we entered what once
had been the stables but had been made by Henry into a spacious
library where Rebecca could store her books and do her writing.
It was here that the coffee was served, the low table dwarfed by the
high, densely packed bookshelves, many of the books on them
having been sent to Rebecca for review. 'I never know what to
discard,' she explained. 'I never know what I am going to need
next. And you can always reckon when you do discard a book that
the following week you'll need it.'

When she was in London (where she had a flat in Kensington
near the Albert Hall) Rebecca liked to give lunch parties in
restaurants. Boulestins at Covent Garden (before the war, she told
me, she used to go there for supper in the long interval of the
nearby opera) was a favourite venue. I would sometimes be invited
to lunch there. Madge Garland, who had worked on *Vogue* under
Condé Nast, was a frequent fellow-guest. She was a close friend of
Rebecca's and liked nothing better than just to listen while
Rebecca held forth. Madge had also been a close friend of the
painter Marie Laurencin. That long ago, pre-war Parisian world
when they were both beautiful young women would be evoked by
Rebecca in corruscating detail. As the epigrams detonated from
Rebecca's lips like a string of fire-crackers, Madge would laugh-
ingly turn to me and say: 'I hope you are writing all this down.' I
wasn't, alas.

The one time a conversation I had with her was recorded was
on her 80th birthday in February 1973 for Radio 3. I asked her to
begin with if she minded being typecast as an expert on trials. 'I
do, intensely,' she replied. 'Some interviewer proceeds to question
me not about the case but about the law of treason and it's obvious
he doesn't know enough to ask the right questions and he wouldn't
understand the answers, possibly, whoever gave them. The number
of times that I've had to gape like a fish out of water when it wasn't
me that was the ignorant one.'

I then asked her about her career as a novelist:

> I wrote novels when I had time. I always had to make money, quite
> a bit of money. I've always written with my left hand. I've always had

an exacting domestic life and I've always had lots and lots of interruptions. I remember when I was writing a book about musicians called *The Fountain Overflows*, which made it necessary for me to listen again to Mozart's Concerto in C minor. It took me three days to get the space of time to listen to it entirely played through on the gramophone. People always came in and asked what biscuits there were to be for tea, who was coming to lunch, and that sort of thing. I just never got on with it. It's a terrible handicap to be a woman.

Of all the women in her generation, Rebecca stands as a shining example of how that handicap could be overcome.

5

From Greene to Snow

E ven with Dennis and Rebecca writing regularly, the search for
star-reviewers continued. A lit ed is always looking for an extra
trump to add to his hand with which to discomfit his rivals. Like
other lit eds, I wasted much time writing to Graham Greene on
the remote chance he might be willing to do a review. 'Why don't
you try Greene with it?' McLachlan would say at conference,
pointing to a likely book on my list. 'He writes well.'

He did indeed and there was nothing I should have liked more
than to have led my page with a review by him. He had at one
time been a regular reviewer (of books as well as films) as his
Collected Essays prove, but by now Greene's reviewing days were
over. The only hope was a book that strongly aroused Greene's
sense of being able to put right an injustice. One such injustice in
Greene's mind was the reputation of R. L. Stevenson, whom he
considered had never received his critical due and who happened
to be his cousin. When James Pope-Hennessy's biography of
Stevenson appeared in 1974, Terence Kilmartin, lit ed of the
Observer, succeeded in getting Greene to review it, one of the last
reviews he wrote.

So far as I and the *Sunday Telegraph* books page were concerned
it was always a polite refusal, typed by Elizabeth Denys, his sister
and amanuensis, on writing-paper of super-fine thinness headed
'C6 Albany London W1', Greene's London address:

21st August 1964:
Dear Mr Curtis,
I'm afraid it's simply impossible for me to review Evelyn Waugh's

autobiography as I'm working morning noon and night on my play.
I'm sorry.

Yours sincerely,
Graham Greene

The play was *Carving a Statue*, about the painter Benjamin Robert
Haydon, which had its première at the Haymarket Theatre a
month later, and was among the least well-received of Greene's
works. He might have been better off doing what surely would
have been a memorable review.

However on the *Sunday Telegraph* we did strike lucky with Greene
as a travel-writer. He had been twice to Haiti and he was keen to
go back there and explore it more thoroughly. He sensed that in
the notorious régime of Papa Doc he would discover promising
copy for a novel. It had all the right virid ingredients – ruthless
tyranny, clamping down on Roman Catholicism, with folk magic
bursting through the surface, and everywhere on that surface love
for sale. The idea that Greene might be persuaded to undertake
such a tour and report on it came originally from Hugh Massingham, a renegade from the *Observer* to the *Sunday Telegraph*,
where he was in charge of special projects.

After he had been signed up, Greene was given a briefing lunch
at the Savoy Grill by McLachlan. The other members of staff
present were myself, Colin Welch, then a leader-writer on the
Daily, and H. M. Stephen, the company manager, who McLachlan
told me had always wanted to meet Greene. Hadn't we all? Among
those around the table only Welch had been to Haiti and he had
Greene and the rest of us falling about, with his matter-of-fact
account of being taken into custody by armed police. 'I flicked
back the safety-catch on the rifle that was pointing at me just as a
precaution . . .' Otherwise the talk was nearly all practical stuff, the
timing and logistics of the trip, rather than literature; but over
coffee it did turn to popular songs. Greene said he always tried to
put in a parody of one whenever he wrote a novel. At this
McLachlan flashed a triumphant glance at me, pulling out his
notebook to write one of his many daily memos to himself. 'We
must follow this up,' he told me. 'That is just the kind of lead you
only get through personal contact!'

I never did follow it up; not because I did not consider it a
fruitful idea for a piece – one could almost write a whole book
about parody and allusion to popular forms in Greene's fiction –
but because I knew the notion, if it ever got remotely near

inclusion in an edition of the paper would have been rejected out
of hand by Thack as being 'too liter-*ary*'.

Greene flew to Haiti via Mexico and Cuba, a country that he
had known in the bad old night-club days of President Batista.
That was the theme of article number one – 'Return to Cuba' For
all Cuba's awfulness under Castro, it was, Greene said, 'impossible
not to love this country . . .' and from there he went on to Haiti.
That was the theme of article number two, which appeared as
'Nightmare Republic'.

> A reign of terror has often about it the atmosphere of farce . . . It
> is impossible to exaggerate the poverty of Haiti. One has the sense
> that even the machinery of tyranny is running down.

In *The Comedians*, the novel about Haiti that appeared in 1965,
Greene adopted the mask of a Dutch hotelier who tells his
manager that while he is away it is to be business as usual because
'who could tell whether a couple of journalists might not stop for
a few days to write a report on what they would undoubtedly call
The Nightmare Republic'.

As for getting a review out of Greene's friend Evelyn Waugh, that
was a different, a much more promising matter. But it had to be the
right book as well as the right fee. Waugh was another Firbankian –
or so I thought – but when I tried to interest him in reviewing a
rare Firbank item Duckworth had reissued, I received the following
post-card from Combe Florey House: 'I am sorry to say your kind
invitation to review *The New Rhythm* reaches me 30 years late. In
youth I was fascinated by Firbank. Now I can't abide him. E. W.'
However, he was prepared to review such books as a life of Rossetti
(an even earlier enthusiasm than Firbank), a study of Victorian
book-illustration, and the text of John Osborne's play, *Luther*.
Equally prompt in her replies to my reviewing requests was his
friend Nancy Mitford, then living in Paris. Here too the answer was
usually no. Her eyes were giving her great trouble in consequence
of which, she explained, she was doing very little reading. However
a book on Ada Leverson by Violet Wyndham caused her for once
to consent. It was not a very good book, unfortunately, and what we
got was in the nature of a hatchet-job. The review began:

> London society has never known a sillier period than the years
> when it was lionizing Oscar Wilde. Silliness spread like a patch of oil;
> it affected all but the greatest men of the day and did much to spoil
> the charming talent of Wilde himself.

And it ended:

> Rather suddenly the Sphinx dies. 'What was her secret?' asks Mrs
> Wyndham. Perhaps it was that although she was very much of her
> age she managed to avoid the worst of its silly superficiality. We
> cannot say the same of her daughter's book.

It is always sad when the Big Name, signed up with high hopes,
subsequently turns in a thoroughly negative review. If the book
really is as bad as all that, why not scrap the review altogether? Or
do you decide that, though negative, the review is readable and
should be printed? There had not been a book about Ada
Leverson for ages. I felt it would do no harm to re-awaken interest
in her, while letting her daughter know that she had not done her
mother's posthumous reputation much good and so we ran the
review.

C. S. Lewis was not in those days quite the saintly transatlantic
hero he is today but he was another Big Name I had my sights on,
and here I did have some success in persuading him to review. I
reckoned I knew what would tempt him. I scored with a book of
essays by Dorothy L. Sayers, *Tragedy* by John Jones, Sir John
Hawkins's *Life of Dr Johnson*, the new verse translation of the *Odyssey*
by Robert Fitzgerald; but Iris Origo's *The World of San Bernadino*
bounced smartly back. McLachlan asked me if I could get Lewis to
write about Faith for Easter Sunday 1963. The reply came poste-
haste from Kilns, Headington Quarry: 'Sorry, but I've written on
that before and, as I'm no wiser now than I was then, you'd only
get sheppards' [*sic*] pie.' Lewis was in poor health at this time, with
long spells in hospital. I went to see him at the Kilns and had
coffee with him one morning and found him, though suffering,
still perfectly alert mentally and most willing to discuss literature.
He said he thought Henry James's style terribly affected. I said not,
surely, in the early books like *Portrait of a Lady*. Lewis then quoted
by heart most of the first page of the novel and I felt the ground
slipping away from me. Shortly after my visit, Lewis was back in
hospital. When his friend Hugo Dyson, the English don at Merton,
who had been my tutor, went to see him, he asked, 'How are you,
Jack?' Lewis smiled. 'Oh not too bad, you know. Managed to get
through the whole of Ariosto again.'

An approach to T. S. Eliot, enclosing the reissue of a collection
of articles that had originally appeared in the Cambridge critical
journal *Scrutiny*, met with a firm refusal and the caveat: 'While I

appreciate your interest I must point out that it is never desirable to send me books without having previously found out from me whether I am prepared to review them.' A fair point; but sometimes the sight of the book just tips the balance and, if you are prepared to risk losing the book, it *is* worth sending it. Eliot, after a lengthy negotiation, did agree to write a review for us of the *New Testament* volume of the *New English Bible*. He felt so strongly about its impoverishment of the language of the Authorised Version that it was an invitation he could not resist.

Which only goes to show that with a Big Name it is always worth trying. But the lit ed who takes this view must steel himself for plenty of rebuffs. It softens the blow if the refusal is wittily phrased, as when I offered Sybil Marshall's *Fenland Chronicle* to Kathleen Raine, who told me I had miscast her.

William Empson was just as forthright when turning down Nabokov's *Pale Fire*. 'Thanks very much, but what I thought from Mary McCarthy's review was it must be a horrible book, grindingly simpering all through; thank God I don't have to read it. Yours with apology . . .' (I thought Empson did not believe in God.)

Usually refusals are courteously phrased. Occasionally they contain revealing insights, as did one from F. R. Leavis in 1964:

> Thank you for your letter but I mustn't let myself undertake to review the Lawrence poems [*The Complete Poems of D. H. Lawrence*, in two volumes, London 1964]. I'm supposed to be retired but I'm heavily engaged on the battle-front. Suffer badly from distraction and find it hard to get on with the work I most want to do. At the moment I'm desperate to get something finished before the new academic year.

Equally courteous and confessional, but dictated and typed, was a reply from Harold Wilson when invited to review *The Political Economy of Communism* – one of those time-wasting ideas that crop up from time to time in conference :

> Dear Mr Curtis,
> I am afraid it would not be possible for me to do so as I am simply overwhelmed with work at the moment, particularly reading matter. Of course, I am also off to the United States at the end of the week.
> I am only just beginning to surface from the gigantic mail I received after the election, which added to the considerable amount of work to be done.

I am sure you will understand my difficulties. But, thank you again for inviting me to do this.

Yours sincerely,
Harold Wilson

The election Wilson refers to there was not a general election, but his election to the leadership of the Labour Party. That had been earlier, in February 1963 after the death of Hugh Gaitskell. It was the following year that Wilson became prime minister, a job he did uninterruptedly for the next six years. Meanwhile his political rival Harold Macmillan, relieved of the premiership in 1963, was free to cast a patrician eye over the family publishing house of which he had been an active member since the period before the war, when he had been responsible for marketing *Gone With the Wind* in Britain.

Macmillan's offices were at that time in St Martin's Street, where on my appointment as lit ed I had been bidden to lunch. My host had not been any of the eponymous directors but Rache Lovat Dickson who – many moons ago – had been a significant literary editor. He was Canadian and as a young man taught English literature at the University of Alberta. Then he had come to England and worked in literary journalism on the *Fortnightly Review* and the *Review of Reviews*. He represented an example of that comparatively rare species, the lit ed who metamorphoses into a publisher. One of the disadvantages of being a lit ed is that it does tend to be rather a full-stop as far as your next career move is concerned – should you wish to make one; the job rarely leads to higher things in journalism. Publisher or literary agent are sideways moves that have occasionally been made with some success. I was never tempted to try either.

In 1965 Macmillan and Co. moved to premises in Little Essex Street, opposite the Law Courts in the Strand. I wrote to Harold Macmillan to ask if I could come and talk to him about the move and draw on his memories of the old building in St Martin's Street where they had been since Victorian times.

From the Right Hon. Harold Macmillan
1st June 1965
Dear Mr Curtis,
I was very interested in your letter of May 27th.
I would be very glad to help you in any way I can to write a piece about Macmillans based upon our moving to new premises.

Perhaps the easiest way would be for you to ring up Mr Whitehead, our Managing Director, and arrange to call and see him together with Mr Alan Maclean whom I think you know. I feel sure you would then be able to work out a good story.

I, myself, am very heavily engaged during the next few weeks but after you have had this preliminary talk we might have a short meeting ourselves.

Yours sincerely,

Harold Macmillan

Alan Maclean, the firm's senior fiction editor whose authors included Rebecca West, Muriel Spark, C. P. Snow, Pamela Hansford Johnson, had been at the Lovat Dickson lunch. Thanks to him, an interview with the great man was now arranged. I pondered his literary ancestry. When Macmillan was at Number 10 he used to read a chapter of Trollope before a meeting of the Cabinet. These readings must have reminded him of the world of his parents and grandparents who had founded the company.

Trollope had died only twelve years before Macmillan was born; and when Macmillan was a child at least one of the great Victorian novelists, Hardy, was still alive. In old age Hardy rarely stirred from his house near Dorchester; but he did make an exception to attend gatherings at his London publishers – as which self-rusticated author, however grand, does not? There in St Martin's Street, the boy Harold would be brought along by his mother to be shown to the literary giants. Macmillan remembered Hardy on these occasions 'as a real countryman. He was just like a russet apple', he told me. Another Macmillan novelist of the period was Henry James, whom Macmillan described as 'a dear'. But the writer at these gatherings whom Macmillan remembered with the greatest affection was the diminutive Irishman James Stephens, the author of *The Crock of Gold*, who would take the child on his knee and chuck him under the chin while enchanting him with fantastic stories. As the recollections began to flow, Macmillan's formal manner evaporated and our talk became more and more intimate. Clearly I had tapped a vein of cherished memories.

Perhaps this is the place to reflect for a moment on politicians as book-reviewers, as seen through a lit ed's eyes. A former minister or prominent MP is often suggested to the lit ed in conference as the ideal reviewer for some hot potato of a book. 'Cast a fly over him,' McLachlan would say. I would nod assent, groaning silently, knowing that I was in for a highly tedious time. In such cases the proposal is made via the politician's secretary with full details of the book, the deadline and the fee (oh yes, they need to know the fee). Then there is normally a pause of several days. If the answer, finally, is yes, the lit ed would be wise to wait until he sees the script before starting to celebrate. It might be a great review but frequently it is a disappointing one. A politician tends to read the book for review while travelling from one public engagement to another late at night when he or she is tired. A first draft of the review is eventually dictated, typed by a personal secretary and given back to the writer who makes several changes. It is then re-typed, approved and sent off to the lit ed.

The appearance of the copy – immaculately set out on thick crested Houses of Parliament writing-paper of which members have unlimited quantities – is impressive, the contents usually less so. The review reads exactly like what it is: a dictated speech in which the book has been used to mount a favourite hobby-horse for one more ride. Indeed, the actual book will probably be mentioned most perfunctorily. A review – especially in a newspaper – is a much more tightly constructed text than a speech. A review is the journalistic equivalent of a sprint-race where you have to leave the starting-blocks at maximum speed and reach the tape in record time without faltering. Occasionally the two skills – for orating and reviewing – may be combined in one individual. Among contemporary politicians Enoch Powell, with his trained academic mind, stands out as a good reviewer not just on contentious political books but also on those dealing with classical literature. And Michael Foot is an even better example. Foot harks back to the days of Addison and Steele, when the two activities of literary journalism and political campaigning had not bifurcated as they have today. Richard Crossman was a brilliant campaigning reviewer in his *New Statesman* period – not when he became editor of it in 1970, but during the war and immediately after when he was a staff contributor. I had an unfortunate experience with him on the *Sunday Telegraph* over a review he did for me on a book about 1945 that he tore to shreds for its omissions. The author pointed out, via his solicitor, that all Crossman's alleged omissions were fully dealt with in the book, as indeed they were. Composing the apology we had to print took up an inordinate amount of time. I had to construct it in such a way as to satisfy both aggrieved author and unrepentant reviewer. I began to see the point of Betjeman's quip, Dick Doublecrossman.

I once signed up George Brown for a review. He did not land

me in such hot water – it was my poor wife who was dragged out of the hot water. As soon as he delivered his review, Brown wanted an instant reaction. Unhappily I was not in the office that day and could not ring him to congratulate him on it. He then demanded my home number from my secretary and rang around six in the evening. My wife happened to be taking a bath. She picked up the phone, dripping wet, clad only in a towel.

'I wish to speak to Mr Anthony Curtis.'

'Er who is that?'

'George Brown.'

'He is not in. You'll have to ring later.'

'Madam, you are talking to George Brown.'

'George. . . .' (the penny drops) 'Oh, *George Brown!* I'm awfully sorry, my husband is not back yet, but I'll tell him you called and ask him to ring you as soon as he gets in.'

'He's more difficult to contact than the Pope!' (Rings off).

But if signing up an eminent politician as a book-reviewer is usually a frustrating business, this is even more true of people in show-business. Occasionally, though, it seems worth trying. Alec Guinness politely turned down the autobiography of Michael Balcon ('I appreciate you having asked me and am delighted to hold on to the book') but I did get an interesting review out of Michael Redgrave on a book about method acting. Redgrave, once a schoolmaster, could write well, but he used a sentence-structure of Jamesian ornateness that needed a considerable amount of work before it was ready for the printer. One of his favourite roles, one that he strongly identified with, was the brooding, learned, pipe-smoking lighthouse-keeper in Robert Ardrey's play *Thunder Rock*. The play was reissued by Collins in a Collected Edition in 1968, and I hoped that this might be an excuse for Redgrave to make some statement about his experiences in performing in it both on stage and in the movie. But no, alas. 'Bob Ardrey's plays', he said, '. . . I have skipped through the interesting preface and think I have not the time to give the book adequate review.'

A leading actor who did have the time to review was Donald Wolfit. I happened to sit next to him one lunchtime in the Garrick Club and mentioned that a new life of Macready was being published soon, and I sensed a distinct quickening of interest from Wolfit. Would he, by any chance, be willing to review it? I then asked, thereby violating the rule that you are not supposed to discuss business in the Club. Yes, he said. Most certainly. There was nothing he would enjoy more.

The review he eventually sent me, penned without a blot, was fascinatingly personal. He described how he had grown up in a house almost entirely devoid of books. The one exception was a book that had a supreme influence over his life, Macready's Illustrated Edition of Shakespeare and it was the illustrations – magnificent colour plates of Macready in all the great roles – that had riveted him. The boy Wolfit stared at them for hours and dreamed of the time when he would play those roles, dreams that eventually came true. After the review had appeared I presented the manuscript to the Garrick Club library in silent atonement for my violation.

In 1970, after ten busy years, I left the *Sunday Telegraph* for the *Financial Times* where I was for two years both Arts and Literary Editor; after that I was, until retirement in 1991, solely Literary Editor. A year or so before I joined it, the paper had started a books column in addition to the regular reviews it printed of business books. This general books coverage had been begun by David Pryce-Jones and developed by John Higgins, the Arts Editor whom I succeeded. The book reviews were intended as a comple- ment to the paper's widely esteemed daily arts coverage. Higgins had found some general reviewers among his own gifted contem- poraries – people such as Julian Jebb and Philip French – as well as among the contributors to his arts page. These included T. C. Worsley, then the television critic; B. A Young, the theatre critic; and Denys Sutton, the art historian, and editor of *Apollo* magazine (at that time owned by the *FT*); and he had a hot-line to two distinguished men of letters of the old school, Alan Hodge and Peter Quennell, the joint editors of *History Today* (also then owned by the *FT*). *Apollo* had premises of its own but *History Today* operated from an office within Bracken House.

Alan and Peter Q. soon acquired the habit of dropping in on me on their way out to lunch to see if I had a book for one or both of them. Alan appeared at first to be rather morose and taciturn but on further acquaintance he became someone whose dry humour and quiet professionalism I much enjoyed. He was a marvellous proof-reader. He had worked as an assistant to the paper's great architect of modern times, Brendan Bracken, and had also assisted Winston Churchill when he was compiling *The History of the English Speaking Peoples*, parts of which were written by Alan. Though Bracken was long since dead, Alan still seemed to

be concerned about what 'B B' might think of his reviews. Any
reference to Bracken in the book he was reviewing, however slight,
would be taken up in his piece. Another of Alan's collaborations
had been with Robert Graves, whose circle in Majorca he had
joined as a young poet before the Second World War. They had
worked on books together, one of which was called *The Reader Over
Your Shoulder*, a salutary study of style, in which they quoted many
examples of sloppy writing from leading writers and reviewers.
Unfortunately, during their collaboration on this and other projects, Graves had looked over Alan's shoulder at his wife and run
off with her. When I became a colleague of his, Alan was re-
married to Jane Aiken, the novelist and daughter of the American
poet, Conrad Aiken. Alan had a shell-shocked look that may have
been attributable to the betrayal in his past life.

If Peter Q's many marriages – the tally was five, I think, at this
period – had left any traumas they were not in the least apparent
on meeting him. His classical good looks, beautifully cut blue suit,
wide-brimmed black hat, and his way of looking over rather than
at you, made me think of Beau Brummell and of Byron, Peter's
especial hero. Peter had been a poet of promise in his youth in
the 1920s. His slim volumes had gained him *entrée* to the London
literary world when he was still an undergraduate at Oxford.
Poetry had been abandoned thereafter and biography, with a
penchant for the eighteenth century, had replaced it. Concur-
rently there had been an extensive career of book-reviewing. If
anyone knew the business inside out it was Peter Q. Before his
then job as co-editor (and founder) of *History Today* he had been
a regular reviewer on the *Daily Mail*. Before that, he had been
editor of the *Cornhill* magazine until it finally expired. In his youth
he had reviewed regularly for the *New Statesman*.

Any literary book was safe in his hands; if it was no good he
would let you know and beg to return it unreviewed. For someone
so keen always to review, his rejection-rate was high. But if he did
take on a book, you knew you would get back a rich pen-portrait
of the subject, particularly if it was a biography. During the 1970s
volumes of Boswell's journal were still appearing at regular intervals from Yale University. They were ideal Quennell-fodder. On
Boswell: The Applause of the Jury 1782–1785, Peter opened his
account with some elegant stroke-play:

> Here is the twelfth but by no means the last volume of James
> Boswell's *Private Papers* – the great literary monument that began to

emerge over 30 years ago, and now forms one of the longest, boldest and most revelatory self-portraits in the history of European literature. It is more valuable than Rousseau's *Confessions;* for Boswell was completely innocent of Jean-Jacques' paranoiac bias, and sought determinedly to tell the truth, however injurious it might perhaps appear. He had 'a kind of strange feeling', he wrote in the 1770s, a particularly dissipated phase of his personal life, that he 'wished nothing to be secret that concerns myself'; and, throughout his whole adult existence, the habit of observing and analysing his own curious personality, and trying to discover – sometimes a difficult task – exactly who and what he was.

Peter's review was – as always – delivered hand-written in red ball-point on ruled A4 paper; calligraphic penmanship of a high order, but not the easiest of scripts for a secretary to convert into material for the printer to set. We were still in the hot metal era and the linotype operators insisted on typed copy. What added to the difficulty of deciphering Peter's copy was his unceasing quest for stylistic perfection that resulted in several words and phrases of the original being blacked out and new ones substituted in balloons in the left-hand margin; the string of each balloon led to where the new word was to be inserted. For example, in the paragraph quoted above 'dissipated phase' has been substituted for 'dissipated life' and 'personal life' for 'personal existence' and the earlier 'throughout his whole adult career, he kept up . . .' has been altered to 'throughout his whole adult existence, Boswell retained . . .'.

The revisionism did not just cease with the copy but would continue through to the galley proof-stage. In the present electronic era it is possible for a lit ed himself to accommodate second, third and fourth thoughts on the part of a reviewer; then it could lead to nasty altercations with the Head Printer – a terrifying presence on a newspaper – as well as bumping up production costs. Fortunately Peter – unlike Henry James, another inveterate revisionist – did not seem to mind if one ignored the more minor of these proof-marks.

Peter was in that line of descent of leading reviewers that started with Sir Edmund Gosse, whose weekly book reviews were essential reading for Edwardian book-lovers. When Ann Thwaite's *Edmund Gosse: A Literary Landscape 1849 – 1928* appeared in 1984, I should really have sent it to Peter to review but I could not resist taking it on myself. When my review appeared, I received an amusing letter from him that only served to increase my guilt at not having sent Peter the book in the first place:

> I was particularly interested [in the review, Peter wrote] because I met him twice in my youth – about 1925, I suppose – and have even published a description of our second meeting at his Regent's Park House, when he described Tolstoi, pointing to a lavishly signed photograph, as 'that old humbug!' He made me odd speeches and paid me surprising compliments – my *appearance*, of course, has changed a great deal since then; and there is no doubt, I think, that he shared his friend's John Addington Symons proclivities. You've no doubt seen Phyllis Grosskurth's biography of J A S, where she quotes from a letter that G. wrote to S. and he admits that he has had 'a fortunate life, but there has been this obstinate twist in it! I have reached a quieter time ... The wild beast is not dead, but tamer!' Is this passage quoted in the book you reviewed? Let's meet again one day and talk about it.

I was lucky to inherit such an able and lively panel of reviewers from Higgins, but I felt that the page needed some additional ingredient if it was really to make its mark. Could I discover the *FT*'s equivalent of Nigel Dennis among the London literati? He or she would need to have what McLachlan called *gravitas* and a very considerable range beyond the literary books and biographies. The typical reader whose image I had in mind was someone working in the City, in, say, a financial institution or a bank, who wanted information about *any* book published of general interest, not just those with a financial resonance. 'We don't want it *just* to be a City page,' the editor Gordon Newton had told me when I was interviewed for the job. One morning in my bath the idea come to me to ask C. P. Snow if he would consider having a go at being the *FT*'s Edmund Gosse.

In the 1950s Snow did a long spell of reviewing of new fiction in the *Sunday Times* on a fortnightly basis, in tandem with its literary editor J. W. Lambert. This was the period of the angry young men for whom Snow (who bitterly resented the Bloomsbury influence over the London reviewing scene) had been a path-finder and trail-blazer. My first and briefest job in journalism after leaving University was on an ill-fated travel magazine called *Go*, that was for a while in 1951 owned by the *Sunday Times* and edited from Gray's Inn Road by Leonard Russell, the paper's lit ed. This was in the days when the paper still belonged as a private fiefdom to Lord

Kemsley (Gomer Berry, Michael's uncle). *Go* only lasted two numbers before the Kemsley management, when they saw how much it was costing, disposed of it. But I was there long enough to gain an insight into how the book section of the *ST* in the next door office was run. Leonard Russell and J. W. Lambert, then his deputy, were kindly disposed towards me, throwing some reviews my way.

Russell sent me to take the proofs of an article Snow had written on Venice for him to correct while I waited. At that time he was working with his colleague Harry Hoff – the novelist William Cooper, author of *Scenes From Provincial Life*, another trail-blazing work – as one of the Civil Service Commissioners recruiting scientists into government jobs. Snow was also launched on his great work, the *Strangers and Brothers* novel-sequence; the first volume, *George Passant*, had appeared in 1940, followed by three more volumes featuring his hero Lewis Elliott: *The Light and the Dark* (1947), *Time of Hope* (1949) and *The Masters* (1951). It was the latter, with its account of the in-fighting leading up to the election of a new head of a Cambridge College, that had given Snow his greatest success. He seemed at this time to stand at the intersection of academic life, public affairs and literature, and was much in demand by editors on both sides of the Atlantic. He flew across it frequently to receive honorary degrees and give foundation lectures on campuses in many parts of the United States, accompanied by his wife the novelist Pamela Hansford Johnson, whom he married in 1950. It was her second marriage, his first. They had met through mutual admiration of each other's work.

A benign Humpty Dumpty beamed at me through pebble-lenses, sitting squarely behind a vast desk at the offices of the Commissioners. He looked up with a grunt and fixed his gig-lamps on me. 'Have you ever been to Venice?' he said in that gravelly, nasal voice I was to come to know so well. I had at that time never set foot in Venice, as I explained. 'Oh you should do! It's the most wonderful city.' Snow told me he went there once a year. As a novelist Snow's territory was confined to metropolitan and provincial Britain; his vision as a private individual was much wider. I had the sense (so strong in any encounter with him) that he was as much concerned to extend my capacity for fresh experience as he was to increase his own.

In 1966, when the first Harold Wilson Labour Government took office, Snow was co-opted into it. He was made the number two to Frank Cousins at the newly established Ministry of Technology. He was thrilled to be rewarded in this way by his old friend Harold; but very soon the whole Whitehall experience became an extremely unhappy one for him. Part of the trouble was that he and Cousins were such an ill-assorted pair. 'Frank really does believe that wogs begin at Calais,' he told me. Apart from that Snow soon found, as anyone could have told him before he took it on, the job totally monopolised his time.

> 14 January 1966
> I should have loved to review the Wells book [Norman and Jeanne Mackenzie's biography of H. G. Wells] but am completely preoccupied with governmental duties at the moment. I have got to make an official trip to Washington next week, and I don't expect to get back to writing until later in the year. I am so sorry.

Being a minister made Snow realise what he was really was: a writer. What brought his career in government to an abrupt end was an unfortunate remark he made in parliament, the result of his honesty combined with his naïvety. He was asked why as a socialist he was proposing to send his son to Eton. He said that he wanted him to be educated among the brightest boys of his generation and that if he succeeded in gaining a scholarship to Eton (which in the event he did, see Pamela Hansford Johnson's highly fictionalised account in her novel, *The Honours Board)* that is where he would go. His son's future career at Eton meant more to him than his own in government. The papers made a meal of it. Snow was soon relieved of office.

That defeat was all for the best: it meant Snow could get on and finish the novel sequence, brought to a close with the appearance of *Last Things* in 1970. With that behind him and no public office (apart from a seat on the board of English Electric and a consultative role at the Post Office, neither very exacting), Snow was perfectly placed to become a weekly reviewer for the *FT.* Before approaching him, I had a word with Sir Gordon Newton, the editor, to secure his approval of my plan. 'I'm not averse to it,' he said smiling, and I went ahead.

Snow responded with a certain amount of initial diffidence combined with conjugal modesty.

> 28th October 1969
> Dear Tony,
> May I brood over your suggestion for a little while? It would be

very agreeable working for you. I have an uncomfortable feeling
though that Pamela could do this job better than I should.

Yours ever,

Charles

Even for a writeaholic like Snow it was quite something to take
on. But I need not have worried. Snow responded to the weekly
stint like a duck to water, and (to muddy the metaphor) we were
soon getting along swimmingly. The reaction both from readers
and colleagues to his pieces was gratifyingly positive. Sir Gordon
told me he thought that the acquisition of Snow as a regular
contributor was 'an asset'. Lionel Robbins, the economist and
educationist, then a director of the *FT*, was ecstatic about Snow's
reviews, and made a particular point of saying so loud and clear
whenever he could. 'He's so much better as a reviewer than he is
as a novelist,' declared Robbins.

The only person at this level who was not completely over the
moon about Snow was the newspaper's chairman, Lord Drogheda.
He was always a great one for detail and he picked on a point in a
review Snow had done of Harold Acton's *More Memoirs of an
Aesthete*. Snow had said that the book, which he had enjoyed,
betrayed evidence of Acton's guilt at having come from such a
privileged background. 'Nonsense,' declared Drogheda shrilly,
'Harold never felt guilt about anything in his entire life and
certainly not about his *background*.' Drogheda, a friend of
Acton's, had a point there but what was more remarkable, I felt,
was Snow's capacity to respond so appreciatively to someone
from a milieu so different from and antipathetic to his own. Soon
after that episode, Snow and Drogheda came together when the
House of Lords debated the Arts and they became friends.
Drogheda was impressed by Snow's power of speaking most
cogently in debate without any notes. The culmination of their
friendship came in 1975 when Lord and Lady Drogheda held
a reception in their house in Lord North Street to celebrate
Snow's 70th birthday attended by many of the London publishing
establishment. 'How strange to see them all together amicably
under one roof,' said Alan Maclean to me of the leaders of his
profession.

When – in a letter quoted above – Dr F. R. Leavis told me that
he was 'still heavily engaged on the battle-front', what he meant
was that he was still conducting a long-running attack on Snow. In
1962 he had launched the *Two Cultures? The Significance of C. P.*

Snow, a lecture that caused surprise, havoc, outrage and, in many quarters of the London literary world, delight.

Leavis's Richmond Lecture, given in Cambridge, was designed to combat Snow's Rede Lecture also delivered in Cambridge, with the same two words for a title, but without the question-mark. The original lecture, *The Two Cultures*, had been delivered in 1959. Ten years later, when my close association with Snow as his lit ed began, the war had spread to the columns of the *TLS* with the publication of long pieces from the principals and many letters from other interested parties. It was one of the great literary rows of the century, comparable, in the amount of animus it generated, to the one between Kingsley and Newman more than a century earlier.

What was at stake here was not Christian doctrine culminating in apostasy to Rome, but the secular religion of literary appreciation and discrimination whose centre was Downing College, Cambridge. From there the excommunication and canonisation of novelists and poets emanated via the pages of *Scrutiny* edited by Leavis and his wife Queenie (Q. D. Leavis). In the eyes of Leavis, Snow was a 'portent of our civilisation', of everything that was wrong with the 'culture' of which he was a representative and which Leavis considered not to be a culture at all but a fraud, conferring reputation on people and works of little or no merit. The whole system of reviewing by the 'serious' London papers of which I had invited Snow to become a part was where the real damage to culture was being done. Someone once described Leavis as 'a rugged moralist'. 'I am proud to be known as a rugged moralist,' he replied, 'in a society where Mr Cyril Connolly is regarded as a distinguished writer.'

His views on Snow need to be seen in the light of earlier comments on the London literary world and its values that appeared in *Scrutiny* from its inception in the 1930s. Especially relevant are Leavis himself on 'The Literary Racket' (1932), on 'Mr [Alan] Pryce-Jones, the British Council and British Culture (1951–2)', and on 'Keynes, Spender and Currency-Values' (1951) (all of these articles are reprinted in that useful two-volume selection from *Scrutiny* of 1968 I failed to get Eliot to review). The 'Keynes etc.' article is a review-essay based upon two influential books of the early fifties that by the time it came out had been very widely reviewed: Stephen Spender's autobiography, *World Within World*, and R. F. Harrod's *The Life of John Maynard Keynes*. Leavis's article begins:

World Within World, the publisher's advertisement tells us, is in its
thirtieth thousand, and has been highly praised by Cyril Connolly,
Harold Nicolson, Christopher Isherwood, V. S. Pritchett, Walter
Allen, Edgar Anstey, Raymond Mortimer, T. C. Worsley, Phyllis
Bentley, Edmund Blunden, Richard Church, Leonard Woolf, John
Connell, and *The Times Literary Supplement.* Nothing, then, said about
it in *Scrutiny* can matter much to the author – a reflection that helps
one to say what has to be said; for this is peculiarly a case where one
wants it to be plain that all that one says, when constating the facts
(which seem to be very important) is necessary to one's concern for
general and impersonal significances.

Leavis manages in one fell swoop to mention all the regular
reviewers of the London reviewing establishment and one or two
others as well. He now turns to the object of their adulation.
Spender had confessed in the book reviewed that ever since
childhood he had wanted to be a poet:

> The desire to become famous as a poet (and, if possible, as a
> statesman – and a soldier too) is one that many are familiar with, or
> will recall if they look back far enough. The astonishing thing about
> Mr Spender's case is that he has achieved his desire – astonishing,
> because at no time has he given evidence of a more specific
> compulsion to poetry or to literary criticism.

This is the lethal rapier of the great nineteenth-century literary
periodical reviewers at the height of their power and influence –
wielded mercilessly as it had been in the *Edinburgh Review,* the
Quarterly Review, Blackwood's Magazine. Their reviewers regularly
lambasted Wordsworth, Byron, Keats, Leigh Hunt, and the other
members of the Lake School and what they called the Cockney
School of poets. Leavis in this vein is comparable to Francis Jeffrey,
Sydney Smith, J. W. Croker the Tory MP, John Wilson the Scot.
Scrutiny's admiration for the impulse behind this type of reviewing
was expressed in R. G. Cox's study of 'The Great Reviewers' in 1937.

Cox claimed that however 'impolite' (his word) they may have
been, these reviewers were defending values they held sacred – the
eighteenth-century values of Reason, Truth, Nature. In spite of
their scurrilous personal attacks, they were good judges with a
cultivated understanding of literature; they had a sense of responsibility and they had taste. 'They never doubted literature deserved
the serious concern of the adult intelligence', Cox concluded.

It was the application of the adult intelligence to literature to which Leavis devoted his life. He believed that the place where such an application should be best practised was not the commercially tainted hurly-burly of the metropolitan reviewing scene but a university, where people of taste, of discriminating sensibility might share their experiences of literature old and new, and through a continuous dialogue among themselves, arrive at critical judgements about texts, according some the supreme value of greatness and others the status of mere foils to that greatness. The bulk of new work could be safely consigned to outer darkness – though presumably someone had to read it at least once to do the consigning.

The number of people with the requisite taste and sensibility to make such judgements was limited. It certainly did not include every member of a university English faculty. Far from it. It was limited to people who had showed in published work their quality of judgement, never making any statement about a work that could not be supported by quotation from the text. Criticism rigorously based on the words of the text was a practice never to be lost sight of and woolly generalities wholly eschewed.

The place where this critical activity might be practised at its most rigorous was Cambridge or rather a particular enclave of Cambridge centred on Downing College. As we have seen, it found its published expression in the pages of *Scrutiny*. It was among such a clerisy that the real distinguished thing in literature might be identified and evaluated, the dross exposed; the rare genuine artist singled out from the hordes of literary careerists. It was Leavis's vision of this Cambridge-based élite – not all of its members might necessarily at any one time be resident in Cambridge – that fuelled his animus against those other Cambridges that in his view stood as 'portents' of the dilution and destruction of these aims of taste and discrimination.

There were three Cambridges in particular that aroused him to Jeffreys-like scorn: the Cambridge of genial bookish critics like Quiller-Couch, Dover Wilson, critics with an old-fashioned historical approach who were concerned as much with an author's sources as his text, whose academic descendants still ran the faculty. Number two was the Cambridge of Keynes, Strachey, Forster, Leonard Woolf, Thoby Stephen, centred on King's and Trinity, the charming, mainly gay, exquisite Cambridge of those people who went on to become the founder members of the Bloomsbury group, and whose descendants – Desmond Mac-

Carthy, the Oxonians Raymond Mortimer, Stephen Spender, Cyril
Connolly (though he was not a Bloomsberry) – dominated the
metropolitan literary world and ran the 'literary racket'. The
Harrod book is made the pretext for a full-frontal attack on them
and all they stood for.

Snow stood for something different. Snow was not born privi-
liged, like the Bloomsbury crowd. He had arrived at where he was
in public life by pulling himself up from near the bottom of the
system by his boot-straps. Snow was a boy from Leicester Grammar
School who found his spiritual home at Christ's College; someone
who, though he had always nourished dreams of becoming a
writer, was clever enough to take a top science degree. It led Snow
to research at Cambridge for a doctorate in the field of specto-
cropsy, until he published a paper claiming a sensational scientific
discovery in that field. Alas, the 'discovery' was soon proved to be
spurious.

What incensed Leavis was Snow's knowing air of authority in
both the fields of science and literature. After the research
débâcle, Snow never attempted any further original scientific work
and he was never to his chagrin made a Fellow of the Royal
Society. His detective novel *Death Under Sail* (1932), followed by
New Lives For Old (1933) and *The Search* (1934) drawing on his
attempt to become a scientist, pointed the way forward for him,
inaugurating his career as a writer of fiction. He used his experience of Cambridge for much of his material in the early books of
the *Strangers and Brothers* sequence. It was a Cambridge that Leavis
deemed a travesty of all he held sacred in the idea of Cambridge
as centre of civilised values. Leavis was especially contemptuous of
the much-praised volume on the intrigue behind the election of a
new college president, *The Masters*.

Leavis always denied that he and Snow had had any kind of
debate over the Two Cultures. This was true in the sense that they
never appeared together on the same platform and thrashed it
out; but then neither did Newman and Kingsley ever meet for a
live confrontation. It was all done by the printed word.

In his lecture Leavis had been guilty of one or two inaccuracies
and that gave Snow a useful plank on which to launch his
rejoinders. As late as 1970 Snow was still at it, publishing in the
TLS, an article 'The Case of Leavis: and the Serious Case'. A draft
of this landed on my desk one morning in May with a covering
letter:

My dear Tony,

I shall be most grateful if you will tell me precisely what you think. First, shall I go ahead with it? Second, if so, what alterations, major or minor, do you suggest? I am fairly clear that the piece about Zola on page 7 does not add much and should be eliminated, leaving three falsifications instead of four.

In the event the piece about Zola was eliminated but in retrospect this seems a pity. From a literary point of view, it is one permanently interesting aspect of the whole controversy. Leavis had categorised Snow's view of fiction thus: 'The truly significant novelists are significant in the way Zola, H. G. Wells and C. P. Snow are'. Snow jibbed at what one might have thought from his point of view was a rather flattering conjunction. By then well into his seventies, Snow continued to be a splendid weekly reviewer for the *FT* until his death in 1980, while the higher critical ground remained the province of Dr Leavis, who died in 1978.

6

Jim and Terry

When I began my job as literary editor in the early 1960s, the books pages of the *Observer* and the *Sunday Times* were the ones universally read by the literati. A lead review in either paper was highly important to morale and to sales. A lead review in both simultaneously on the Sunday before publication could make a lasting difference to an author's standing. The tradition of the Sunday Books Page that the *Sunday Telegraph* was challenging had evolved on these two newspapers over more than half a century.

The *Observer* had developed as the foremost Sunday paper for the cultivated middle-class at the end of the Edwardian period under its great editor, J. L. Garvin. He took over in 1908 and remained until 1942. The paper's readers were professional people, civil servants, politicians, doctors, academics, businessmen, their wives and families, comfortably off individuals who had servants to wait on them and whose houses often included one room known as the Library (a room that actually contained a much-loved, much-read collection of books); compared with their counterparts today their style of life offered them a great deal of leisure that was spent in reading books and reviews of books. Some of the books were bought, others borrowed from The Times Book Club, Boots or Mudies. These *Observer*-readers were also keen theatre-goers and music-lovers; and they cultivated such stay-at-home activities as gardening, playing bridge, solving crossword puzzles and chess problems.

Garvin was conscious as an editor of his readers' cultural and recreational needs as much as he was of his first priority, commentary on the political and financial news. Under Garvin the modern culture-conscious Sunday newspaper took shape. The main item

for which the paper was read was his leading article on a burning
issue of the day, signed with his name and set in an extra-wide
column measure to give it maximum prominence. What 'the
Garve' said about the way the country was being run mattered to
everyone but especially to the likes of Asquith, Balfour, Lloyd
George, Bonar Law and others at the centre of power. They
courted him as assiduously as they did the editors of the other
papers influential in forming opinion on such divisive matters as
Home Rule for Ireland and Tariff Reform.

As a poor boy at a Roman Catholic school in Birkenhead, Garvin
had read widely among the Victorian novelists and by the age of
sixteen he had read through the whole of Dickens, Scott, Thackeray, George Eliot, Wilkie Collins. Garvin's formal education
stopped at that point but continued informally as he made his way
in journalism with encouragement from bookish-minded London
editors like J. A. Spender and W. L. Courtney. When Garvin was
appointed editor of the *Observer* he developed strong book-review
and arts sections and he kept an astute eye on them. In 1920
Garvin signed up J. C. Squire at fifteen pounds a week as his lead
book-reviewer and in 1926 he made his daughter Viola assistant
literary editor and then lit ed. She remained in charge of the
Observer books pages until the early period of the Second World
War, resigning at the same time as her father was stood down as
editor. Garvin had an almost unbreakable contract of employment;
the only reason for which he could be fired was if he knowingly
opposed the policy agreed with the proprietor and this he did
over the question of Churchill's replacing Chamberlain as prime
minister. Garvin was a dedicated Neville Chamberlain man (he
had earlier supported the policies of Joseph Chamberlain, whose
biographer he became). On Churchill he was in open hostility to
Waldorf Astor, his proprietor. He therefore had to resign and
Viola as literary editor was asked to leave too. If Garvin's end on
the *Observer* was sad, he was made a Companion of Honour in
1942, an unprecedented distinction for a newspaper editor.

At the time of Garvin's departure, the man who would be his
successor, Astor's son, David, was doing his war sevice at Mountbat-
ten's headquarters, able to keep only half an eye on affairs at the
paper. An acting editor was appointed, the paper's theatre critic,
Ivor Brown, an able Scottish journalist who continued to write the
main theatre reviews. Brown was relieved of overseeing the political coverage. That was put in the capable hands of Donald
Tyerman and the books page was edited from the spring of 1942

until the summer of 1943 by Cyril Connolly, whose writing and editing of *Horizon* David Astor much admired. We identify Connolly now with the *Sunday Times* because of his long innings there and we ignore his brief but not insignificant period on the *Observer*, when he was both reviewing on its books page and getting his *Horizon*-friends such as Orwell, Logan Pearsall Smith, Evelyn Waugh and Peter Quennell to review for it too.

Connolly, not the kind of journalist to make concessions to a paper's overall policy, was soon in conflict with both Brown and Astor about who should review what. During a particularly fraught time Connolly invited Astor to lunch at White's to talk things over; at the coffee stage, when they got down to business, Connolly flew into a violent temper with Astor. Connolly then stormed out of the club leaving his guest, not a member, to fend for himself. That was the end of Connolly's association with the *Observer*.

For the remainder of 1943 the books and arts pages were edited by J. C. Trewin, a sub-editor and number two dramatic critic, an arrangement that remained in place until 1948. Cornishman John Trewin (author of *Up From the Lizard*, beside dozens of books on the theatre) kept the paper's books pages alive with pieces by reviewers of proven competence such as G. W. Stonier, Daniel George and Lionel Hale, topped by the occasional star-turn: Vita Sackville-West (on Rupert Brooke), Alan Pryce-Jones, Lord David Cecil, Christopher Sykes, A L. Rowse. Trewin was a stop-gap lit ed whose heart and mind were in the theatre not in the book-room. When Astor returned to civilian life to take up the reins in Tudor Street as the editor of the *Observer*, Brown, eager always to take on more work, hoped that he might now become literary editor in addition to his job as drama critic, but Astor wanted a completely new person for the post; someone who would be fully in tune with the plans he had for rejuvenating the paper.

E. J. B. ('Jim') Rose was a Rugbeian and Oxford undergraduate at Balliol in the 1930s, where he belonged to the circle of the famous don known as 'Sligger' Urquhart. He had been a wing-commander in the RAF during the war and had worked at the decoding centre at Bletchley. In 1948 Rose was looking for a job in journalism. His Bletchley colleague, Alan Pryce-Jones, newly appointed editor of the *Times Literary Supplement*, introduced him to David Astor.

Rose asked if he could be considered for the job of the foreign editor of Astor's paper. Astor said that he had already appointed a foreign editor; but he still needed to appoint a literary editor. 'I am afraid I don't know anything about books,' said Rose. 'Then you're just the man we're looking for,' countered Astor. 'You will have the advantage of not belonging to any particular coterie.' And Rose was given the job. Trewin went back to being the second-string drama critic and sub-editor.

Publishers had been able to sell almost anything they printed during the war, so great was the demand for reading-matter; now they had to work much harder and their habitual cautiousness returned. As an antidote to Crippsian austerity there was a vogue for elegant reprints of George Eliot, the Brontës, Jane Austen, Fielding, Defoe, Swift and there were also reissues of lesser English eighteenth- and nineteenth-century writers. The Oxford University Press had an ambitious project – never fulfilled – to bring out the whole of Trollope in separate volumes. He had been top of the bestseller list during the war; his work was perfect escapist reading in the blackout while the bombs were falling.

These reprints were marketed while more urgent books – the war-memoirs of statesmen such as Von Papen and generals such as Alexander and Alanbrooke, concentration-camp inmates such as Primo Levi – began to be written. The *Diary of Anne Frank* appeared in 1952. The era of the semi-fictional short-story, a form of war-reporting, was over and demand for the little magazines it had fuelled quickly faltered; but there was intense curiosity in Britain about contemporary continental writers now that the curtain on them had been lifted, inaugurating a healthy period for transla-tions from the French, German and Italian. The members of the established generation of British novelists – Waugh, Bowen, Powell, the two Green(e)s, Hartley – who had kept their fiction going while in wartime jobs were now in control of all their working time and ready to do some of their best work, soon to join them came the first post-war generation of British novelists led by Angus Wilson, Iris Murdoch and Kingsley Amis.

Contemporary poetry still had a wide middle-class readership. As a living, active survivor of modernism T. S. Eliot stood supreme; impressions of *Four Quartets* ran rapidly through the bookshops; the work was acclaimed as the outstanding poetic achievement of the war years. Eliot's more recent excursions into the West End theatre as a verse-playwright were widely noted but with much less acclamation. (It was not one of his plays but a *jeu d'esprit* in rhyming verse about cats that would give Eliot posthumously the theatrical success he strove for so earnestly in his latter years.)

Auden had continued to be read in Britain during the war, although disparaged by some for his residence in the United States. He became an American citizen in 1946 and he now became an intermittent visitor to the UK, where he was always much in demand to give readings. But there was a difficult problem in respect of Ezra Pound: could we just carry on absorbing his latest *Cantos* as if those outrageous wartime broadcasts from Italy whose virulent contents were now disclosed had never happened? Eliot and his Faber colleagues were determined we should; disciples like Peter Russell, editor and founder of *Nine*, and the actor-poet Denis Goacher were eloquent in Pound's defence. Others were not so sure.

In the area of book production the old-style books of pre-war days with wide margins and strong bindings were gone for good; but as paper became more plentiful there was a gradual improvement on the lean emergency format for books that had prevailed during the war years. The era of the eye-catching pictorial book-jacket now dawned; senior publishers like Victor Gollancz and Hamish Hamilton would take many years to become reconciled to the extra cost involved; and anyway it was part of their style to publish their authors in a uniform dustcover. The paperback for serious reading was coming into its own, with new imprints emerging to challenge Penguin's hegemony. Improved techniques of colour printing led to an effloresence of the illustrated book, both as a serious contribution to art history, and as an adornment of the purchaser's coffee table, a development orchestrated by formidable experts of pre-war art-publishing in Vienna who were now operating from London.

Astor and Rose thought hard about how this post-war publishing effort could be presented and assessed for the new kind of *Observer*-reader they wished to accommodate. They only had one page to play with, newsprint still being on the ration. They were conscious that the war had enormously widened the circle of those who would turn to the book-reviews. Their idea was not unlike the one outlined to me by McLachlan fifteen years later – to Fill The Gap. Let Rose explain:

> We had a somewhat difficult task in combining in one page the selection of books to be reviewed which reflected the best in contemporary publishing while at the same time catering for the 'new man' who had emerged from the Forces and from the Butler

Education Act. In other words we wanted to make the book page accessible and friendly to the new reader we were attracting, while maintaining standards.

One pointer to the widespread existence of the new man – and woman – came at the end of the war in 1945 when Allen Lane tentatively bought out a prose translation of Homer's *Iliad* by E. V. Rieu and had soon sold more than a million copies of it. A new series in paperback presenting the greatest works of literature in a form and at a price palatable to the ordinary reader was born, the Penguin Classics. Homer was followed by the *The Four Gospels*, by Virgil's *Aeneid*, and when *Don Quixote* appeared translated by J. M. Cohen, Rose decided to make it his, lead: 'a) it was better than any other book published that week and b) we could be sure that at least half our readers had never read it!'

Rose was soon confronted by The Great Fiction Problem – what to do about all those novels. It was a problem he could not afford to neglect. The *Observer*'s fiction reviews had carried a lot of weight before the war. Viola Garvin had employed Gerald Gould, poet and a friend of Squire, to review new fiction regularly. As we shall see, Gould had had experience of writing fiction reviews for Squire when he was lit ed of the *New Statesman* in its early days. Rose made the distinction between what I have called genre fiction and general fiction. The problem was how to deal with both. 'I tried to solve it by having one reviewer (Marghanita Laski) for "serious" novels and one for books written purely for entertainment. Of course Marghanita cheated by choosing to review a novel by Ruby M. Ayres! But on the whole, I think, it worked to separate chalk from cheese.'

In his quest for new reviewers, Rose was conscious of powerful opposition on the literary section of the *Sunday Times*, where star reviewers had also been signed up from the the books pages of the *New Statesman*, cultivated writers headed by Desmond MacCarthy whose judgment commanded respect in the literary world. By contrast the *Observer* had for its star turn Robert Lynd, a throwback to the Viola era. He also contributed to the *Statesman* over many years but at a middlebrow level in a weekly essay under the *nom de plume* Y. Y. His pieces were collected into volumes one of which has the title, *The Pleasures of Ignorance*.

Rose needed someone less anodyne than Lynd but who would not frighten away the new men and women. He had in Astor an editor who had his own views on the kind of reviewer they

required and who counted politically committed writers among
his friends. One was Arthur Koestler and another was George
Orwell, whose reviews Astor had much admired; Orwell had
already written several for the paper under Connolly and what
brighter star could they have wished for? Orwell had shown his
genius for the literary essay during the war in *Horizon*, where his
appraisals of Dickens, Kipling, Wodehouse had appeared as well
as his seminal pieces on boys' stories, *No Orchids For Miss Blandish*
and seaside postcard humour. He had also been a literary editor
himself on *Tribune*. He was now living on Jura, a small island in the
Outer Hebrides belonging to the Astor family, a mortally sick man,
desperately trying to finish *1984*. His state of health might, it
seemed, preclude him having much of an innings as a regular
reviewer; even if he was prepared to suffer the limitation of a
maximum of 800 words for a lead review. Nonetheless in the last
period of his life Orwell continued to contribute book-reviews to
the *Observer*.

On 2 January 1949, for example, Orwell reviewed a pictorial
volume, *The English Comic Album*, compiled by Leonard Russell and
Nicolas Bentley:

> The collection starts at about a century ago when the self-
> contained 'joke-picture' was just coming in to being. Unfortunately
> this was also the period at which English humour was being 'purified'
> for the benefit of a new largely feminine public. It is painful to
> compare, for instance, Tenniel and Charles Keene, or even Edward
> Lear, with 'Phiz' and Cruickshank.

The most important book Orwell reviewed for the *Observer* was
F. R. Leavis's provocative study of the novel, *The Great Tradition*.
When one thinks of the withering comments made by Leavis about
the literary racket and the Sunday reviewers, it is salutary to turn
to Orwell's fair-minded review of his book: masterly in its compres-
sion into the available space. Orwell singles out the part on Conrad
as the best: 'This does the thing that criticism can most usefully do
– that is, it draws attention to something that is in danger of being
neglected' (*Observer* 23 January 1947). But he cannot share all of
Leavis's enthusiasms. 'One would be a little more ready to accept
Dr Leavis's guidance if, for example, he were not an admirer of
T. F. Powys.'

Orwell's brief sketch 'Confessions of a Book Reviewer' gives us
his last thoughts on this activity:

The great majority of reviews give an inadequate or misleading account of the book that is dealt with. Since the war publishers have been less able than before to twist the tails of literary editors and evoke a paean of praise for every book they produce, but on the other hand the standard of reviewing has gone down owing to lack of space and other inconveniences. Seeing the results, people sometimes suggest that the solution lies in getting book reviewing out of the hands of hacks. Books on specialised subjects ought to be dealt with by experts, and on the other hand a good deal of reviewing, especially of novels, might well be done by amateurs. Nearly every book is capable of arousing passionate feeling, if it is only a passionate dislike, in some or other reader, whose ideas about it would surely be worth more than those of a bored professional. But, unfortunately, as every editor knows, that kind of thing is very difficult to organise. In practice the editor always finds himself reverting to his team of hacks – his 'regulars', as he calls them.

These are the observations of a writer who did not live to see the lifting of paper rationing and the expansion of reviewing that occurred after the war. Someone who did, and who played a significant part in it as part of the team Rose was assembling, was Harold Nicolson, one of the great ornaments of the book-reviewing profession. How did this one-time member of the diplomatic service come to spend so much of his working life reviewing books?

While on duty in Persia before the war Nicolson had a brush with his superiors that gravely wounded his pride. As a result he recklessly permitted himself to be tempted out of diplomacy by Lord Beaverbrook. In 1929 he resigned from the service and in January 1930 he joined the *Evening Standard* as part of the 'Londoner's Diary' team. That did not last long and in 1930–1 Nicolson was put under contract to write book reviews for both Beaverbrook papers, the *Standard* and the *Daily Express*. He soon acquired a reputation as being an effortlessly fluent book-reviewer of remarkable range and readability. After a time Nicolson abandoned Lord Beaverbrook for Lord Camrose, and was contracted to review five books a week for the *Daily Telegraph*. Tough going even for a reviewer of Nicolson's rapid turn-around rate for a lead-review; especially as he was also contributing a weekly column to the *Spectator*.

In 1949, without informing his father, Nicolson's son Nigel intimated to Jim Rose that he thought Harold Nicolson might be prepared to give up the *Telegraph* contract in exchange for the

luxury of only having to review one book a week. Rose jumped at
the hint and a deal between Harold and the *Observer* was soon
sealed. On 6 March 1949 the paper's weekly Profile – a widely read
regular feature, new to British journalism – was devoted to
Nicolson and on the following Sunday he began a series of weekly
reviews that would last for the next decade and a half, until
Nicolson was was well into his seventies. The book chosen for his
opening review was one of those reprints of a neglected minor
classic I mentioned as a feature of publishing in this period, *The
Autobiography of Leigh Hunt* edited by J. E. Morpurgo.

> As a book [declared Nicolson] it lacks the zest as it lacks the
> rancour of *Lord Byron and Some of His Contemporaries*. But it does
> reflect the literary excitements of three-quarters of a century and it
> does provide us with the most vivid portraits ever penned of Shelley,
> Keats, Campbell, Coleridge and Wordsworth.

When I read this I feel I am listening to someone, better read than
I am or ever will be, who makes me want to get hold of the book
and read it myself. The tone is that of a reviewer who if he did not
have to read the book for review would have read it anyway – or in
this instance clearly *has* read it anyway. One may disagree with the
judgement in the second sentence – what about Hazlitt's and De
Quincey's portraits of Coleridge and Wordsworth? – but it is
backed by the knowledge that would enable the writer to stick to
his point if you had the opportunity to dispute it with him. He is
engaging in a dialogue with the reader.

In the following weeks Nicolson reviewed *The Prince Consort* by
Roger Fulford, *Trial and Error: The Autobiography of Chaim Weizmann*
('his followers distrusted his Fabian methods and were tempted
to repudiate his leadership in favour of other more reckless
courses . . .'); *Studies in German History* by C. P. Gooch; *The Idol
and the Shrine: The Journal of Eugénie de Guérin*, translated by
Naomi Royde-Smith ('Her introduction has little to recommend it
being ill-written and confused' – Royde-Smith was the literary
editor of the *Westminster Gazette* and a powerful figure in literary
London in her day); *The Green Tree* by Alun Lewis (the Welsh
poet killed on active service); *Strange Defeat* by Marc Bloch (the
French Jewish historian of the medieval world who was murdered
by the Nazis); *Praeterita* by John Ruskin, introduced by Sir Kenneth
Clark.

Nigel Nicolson says that his father was 'at home in half-a-dozen

foreign languages and literatures, loved France but England
more . . .'. Nicolson's early books had revealed this double love:
one on Paul Verlaine in 1921 followed by volumes on Tennyson,
Byron and Swinburne, all of which were written while he was a
member of the diplomatic service. Nicolson also showed a mastery
of the broadcast talk; he was one of the first writers to discuss
literature on British radio. On one occasion he wished to discuss
the latest work of James Joyce; but Sir John Reith, the BBC's
Director General, forbade any mention of *Ulysses* to pollute the
United Kingdom's air-waves. His ban ultimately resulted in the
resignation from the BBC of Nicolson's producer, the courageous
Hilda Matheson. Matheson became secretary to Harold and Vita,
of whom she was greatly enamoured.

James Lees-Milne writes in his biography of Nicolson:

> He was a scrupulously fair critic. He read the book entrusted to
> him from cover to cover, making notes on the end-papers as he went
> along. He never used the book to air his own prejudices and
> affections. He was impartial and tolerant of opinions he could not
> share. He was only intolerant of vulgarity and obscenity, which he
> detested. Rather than hurt the feelings of an author who was a friend
> he would refuse to review a book he did not like. His reviews err, if
> anything, on the charitable side.

After Nicolson had been reviewing for the best part of a year he
took the opportunity in the blank week of 1 January 1950, to
reflect upon the kind of reader he was trying to address:

> I asked myself when I wrote those reviews whether I had any
> definite audience in mind. Did I visualise a given individual, or did I
> conceive of a corporate audience – those men and women of
> exquisite taste, wide erudition and profound ethical principles who
> on Sunday mornings read the literary pages of the Observer? I came
> to the conclusion that I did both. On the one hand, there was the
> ordinary reader, who was willing to receive suggestions as to which
> book he or she should purchase, borrow or otherwise acquire. On
> the other hand there was the individual author to whom I addressed
> myself secretly and in a tone of clandestine intimacy. The only
> person for whom I do not write is the person who seeks to obtain
> from a review sufficient information for him or her to talk about a
> book without having read it.

When she first met him in 1927, Nicolson struck Virginia Woolf as being 'an Englishman overlaid with culture; coming of sunburnt country stock; & not much fined even by diplomacy.' This was typically bitchy. Nicolson's culture was 'fined', as his reviews prove, but he did have his limitations. Reviewing sometimes came too easily to him. He deals always with the book in a gentlemanly not a critical manner and he is more interested in the literature of the past than the present, more interested in memoirs than novels. He was, as his biographer says, rarely willing to wound. These limitations would become apparent during the course of his long innings under Rose's successor.

Rose's aim in making up his one page was to get his readers to turn to the Nicolson review first. It was always in the same position across the two or three left-hand columns; there would usually be a six-inch 'independent' block (one not relevant to the reviews it faced) in the middle two columns – the only block on the page – and then a second lead-review occupying the remaining columns to the right with the fiction batch somewhere down-page. As the regular performer for the right-hand slot, Rose had signed up the poet and critic Edwin Muir.

Muir, son of a farmer on Wyre in the Orkneys, was one civilised Scottish intellectual who did not go to Balliol; from the age of sixteen to his early twenties, he had a variety of low-paid jobs in Glasgow. Eventually he became a clerk in a glue factory. In his late teens Muir was converted to socialism by reading Robert Blatchford's *Clarion* and joined the Glasgow branch of his *Clarion* scouts. He began to read the *New Age*, the Fabian weekly edited by the Yorkshireman A. R. Orage (more about this journal later).

The earnest young man envisaged a future where he would play a more significant part in life than that of a mere glue-factory clerk. He wrote some poetry and he wrote a letter to Orage confessing his ambition, asking for counsel. He received a long letter back in which Orage advised him to spend several years absorbing the work of one universal genius. When he was Muir's age, Orage had done this with Plato, reading everything of Plato he could get hold of. The author Muir chose for the same operation was Nietzsche.

Aside from the *Clarion* circle in Glasgow he met cultivated people like the stimulating French critic Denis Saurat, author of *Modernes*, then a lecturer at Glasgow University, people among whom Muir's musical and cultural education rapidly progressed.

He also met Willa Anderson, a graduate of St Andrew's University and lecturer at a woman's college, with whom he fell in love and married, 'the most fortunate event of my life' he later said.

The couple decided to leave Glasgow and try their luck in London, a bold move, and at first not a notably successful one. But then Orage offered to make Muir his assistant on the *New Age*, a part-time job of three days a week, leaving him the rest of his time for writing. Muir was on Orage's editorial staff for four years while also reviewing the London theatre for the *Scotsman* and writing book-reviews for the *Athenaeum* during Middleton Murry's editorship. Muir describes all this in his characteristically quiet modest manner; it was an incredible achievement for an obscure Orcadian in his early thirties who had no degree and no previous connections with the London literary world. It shows how at this time creative editors such as Orage and Murry, who had themselves come from equally humble backgrounds, empathised with young writers they thought had genuine talent.

The Muirs' struggles to earn enough to keep themselves continued, and in 1921 the wanderlust took hold of them and they moved to Prague. Now Muir's receptive mind was directly exposed to continental literature, an unusual and valuable process for someone who was to become a leading British reviewer and critic. He wrote a weekly article for the *New Age* and two articles a month for the *Freeman*, a short-lived American periodical of politics and the arts edited by Van Wyck Brooks. That kept Willa and Edwin going quite nicely but only for a while. By the time the *Freeman* folded they had moved to Dresden and had become fluent in German. At this time Edwin had his first volume of poems published, by Leonard and Virginia Woolf's home-based Hogarth Press. In 1926 the Woolfs took his critical book, *Transition*, with its chapters on contemporary poetry and fiction (a transition between the beast and the superman was how Nietzsche characterised human life). Muir was one of the first critics to examine modernist writing's penetration below the surface of appearance to an interior reality. The book found a sympathetic reader in the Paris-based American journalist Eugène Jolas, who copied its title for the literary magazine he was just about to start. Jolas thought the word would look more modernist if the initial T was put into lower case. Thus Jolas and his wife Maria started in Paris the journal *transition*, a major repository of work by Joyce, Beckett and other expatriates.

The Muirs' main source of income in the years before the

Second World War was translating from the German works by such writers as Hauptmann, Herman Broch and Kafka. They would have been surprised then to be told that their Kafka translations, *America, The Castle* and *The Trial* would have historic importance in the development of modern literature, comparable to those by Constance Garnett of the novels of Dostoevsky. Indeed, when Kafka-esque fantasies began to haunt Muir's dreams he was able to dismiss them because 'they had laws of their own, and this made them slightly unconvincing, not to be taken seriously'.

The Second World War saw Muir running the British Council office in Edinburgh and after the war he returned to Prague for the Council, where in 1948 he witnessed the Communist takeover at first-hand. Afrer that he returned to England to become involved in adult education and to review regularly for the *Observer*. Thus on 6 January 1952 Muir's right-hand lead-review was of Colette's *Creatures Great and Small*, translated by Enid McLeod.

Creatures was a book that could just as easily have been reviewed by Nicolson who would have articulated some generalities about the pantheistic outlook on life of Colette. By contrast, Muir applies the mind of a literary critic to it, comparing Colette's dogs with those in the books of Galsworthy that, Muir thinks, reveal a more truly canine reality. The dustcover (presumably written by Roger Senhouse of Secker & Warburg, Colette's great British promoter) claimed that Colette was never mawkish. 'Actually', said Muir, 'mawkishness is her chief fault.'

Two weeks later Muir was tackling Leavis's *The Common Pursuit* and here again it is difficult to see what cause that critic could have found for complaint in this review. 'It should be read by everyone concerned with literature' concluded Muir. Two weeks on Muir was writing about Gogol; and on 2 March warmly reviewing Rupert Hart-Davis's biography of Hugh Walpole; in late April he gets another translation from the French, Malraux this time, *The Walnut Trees of Altenbourg*. Next it is Angus Wilson's much awaited first novel, *Hemlock and After*. Wilson had already gained a reputation as a writer of ironic, exactly observed contemporary short stories with horrific climaxes but everyone wanted to know how he would make out in a full-length novel.

> The whole book has brilliance, wit, savagery and sometimes imaginative sympathy. But it is hard to discover where its moral centre lies. A recognition of the weakness of liberalism is not enough.

It was an uncomfortable book for Muir to review because the
paper had begun to employ Wilson as a reviewer, and by the time
this review was printed there had been a change of literary editor.
Rose had left the job at the end of 1951 to become director of the
International Press Institute in Zurich and his deputy, Terence
Kilmartin, whom Astor had met on active service in Germany
during the war had taken over. Astor, a major in the Marines, had
been wounded after a shoot-out with the Germans behind enemy
lines and Kilmartin working for SOE had been there and at risk
to his own safety tended to Astor's and others' wounds at the field
hospital.

Kilmartin, who was brought up in Ireland as the son of an Irish
forestry commissioner had been educated by Catholic lay-brothers
in Sussex; his father died when he was a boy and there was no
money for him to go to university, but as a young man before the
war he had held a tutoring job in France where he acquired his
lifelong devotion to French civilisation in general and to Proust in
particular. The paper's books pages throughout 1952 – the first
year when he was in sole charge of them – strongly reflected his
un-insular, catholic, European outlook as they would continue to
do thereafter. The regular performers Nicolson and Muir were
joined now by Philip Toynbee, with whom Kilmartin would sustain
one of the most fruitful literary editor book-reviewer partnerships
in British journalism.

But first let me recall some of the other reviewing talents that
adorned the page in the early period of Kilmartin's reign. Like all
literary editors he was at the start hungry for names. In that first
year Kilmartin printed reviews by Thomas Mann on Wagner's
letters, Louis MacNeice on E. M. Butler's *Fortunes of Faust*, Dylan
Thomas on Amos Tutoyala's *Palm Wine Drinkard*, Kathleen Raine
on Arthur Waley's translations from the Chinese, Auden on the
New Yorker's 25th Anniversary Album, Isherwood on Calder
Willingham's *End as a Man* (and Isherwood's historic travel-
piece,'Return to Berlin'), Graham Greene on Maugham's *A Choice
of Kipling's Prose*, Angus Wilson on Edmund Wilson's work of
fiction, *I Thought of a Daisy*.

Coverage from the regular trio included Nicolson on the poems
of Mallarmé translated by Roger Fry, the letters between Gide and
Claudel; Toynbee on Paul Valéry's *Monsieur Teste* and on *Freedom
and The Tragic Life: a Study in Dostoevsky* by V. Ivanov; Muir inter
alia on Thomas's Mann's *Holy Sinner*. Any of the new men needing
a briefing about the literary scene across the Channel could not

have done better than to have studied the *Observer's* books pages. They were distinctly educative while also being well-written. But not all new men appreciated the efforts made on their behalf, least of all John Osborne's Jimmy Porter:

> *Jimmy:* Why do I do this every Sunday? Even the book reviews seem to be the same as last week's. Different books – same reviews. Have you finished that one yet?
> *Cliff:* Not yet.
> *Jimmy:* I've just read three whole columns on the English Novel. Half of its in French. Do the Sunday papers make *you* feel ignorant?
> *Cliff:* Not 'arf.

I never saw Kilmartin at work in his office but I frequently met him at receptions. 'How are things?' he would ask and before long I was using him to sort out some problem connected with my page. He would in his unassertive way offer me advice based on his own vast experience of similar problems. He always appeared completely non-competitive, an exceedingly rare attribute in the literary-journalistic world. So far as I know he never once wrote a signed review for his own page. Despite constant urgings from his friends to write himself, it was an article of faith with him not to. Whatever the book, Terry felt he could get someone else to review it better than he could. His self-abnegation in this respect went with a flair for talent-spotting among the up-and-coming reviewers and an exceptionally high success-rate with his requests to the great and the good.

Muir and Toynbee alternated for a while; then Muir was dropped and Toynbee moved from the foreign department to become a salaried staff-member of the books page; his job consisted solely in having to write reviews and literary articles. This is a most unusual kind of appointment; most leading book-reviewers are, as we have seen, free-lancers under contract. Toynbee brilliantly justified the appointment over the next quarter of a century and I wish more editors would consider making an appointment of this kind in the context of today's books pages.

Kilmartin, Toynbee, and the foreign correspondent Patrick O'Donovan were among several crucial post-war appointments to the paper made by Astor. They became close friends and with other staffers and free-lance reviewers such as John Davenport, a regular fiction reviewer, formed the nucleus of an *Observer* clerisy. They would meet in the book-room, chatting to Kilmartin while choosing their review-books; then they would adjourn from the book-room to the nearby pub where more general discussions were held continuing until closing-time. Anthony Sampson, who used to attend these sessions, says his mind was exercised much more profoundly in the course of them than it ever was at Oxford.

Toynbee belonged to an intensely political generation, whose members had completed their university education in the 1930s just before the outbreak of the Second World War. They grew up during the great slump, the emergence of the British Union of Fascists, the Spanish Civil War in which some of them fought and were killed, Hitler, Munich, and then the war itself. In such a climate, Communism seemed to some to be the only real solution to the chronic ills of the period even as it did to their literary counterparts in the US. The Communist Party offered these Englishmen a way of combating fascism and revolting against their stiflingly charming country-house backgrounds. Toynbee joined the Communist Party under the influence of Esmond Romilly in between leaving school and going up to Oxford to read history. He and another great friend at this time, Jasper Ridley, helped to form Toynbee's intellectual cast of mind. Both Romilly and Ridley were killed in the war. Toynbee's literary memorial to them, *Friends Apart*, is a valuable recollection of the politico-literary cultural ambience of this period.

Toynbee worked in wartime in intelligence while at the same time writing critical articles in the little magazines in which he addressed himself to the problem posed for the novelist who tries to follow in the footsteps of Joyce and Virginia Woolf – to make the language come alive on the page in the way that it does in their books – and to avoid moribund linear narrative. Toynbee's own fictional experiments, *Tea With Mrs Goodman* and his *Pantaloon* sequence written in verse, require a fresh appraisal but they lie outside my scope in this book. Toynbee shed his youthful Communism and became in later life deeply religious without converting to any particular denomination. He worked out his own brand of religion incorporating those aspects of Christianity that appealed to his temperament – the gentle Franciscan strain – blended with transcendental meditation and ecological awareness. His 'Autobiographical Journals' 1977–1979, *Part of a Journey*, and *End of a Journey, 1979–81*, give a day-by-day account of his experiments in this direction.

Political activist, novelist, poet, mystic, polymath – these were all elements in his personality as a leading reviewer of the post-war era that gave his reviews their extraordinary richness. Through his combination of interests he took his readers into those difficult areas of philosophical and spiritual speculation that most lit eds tend to regard as beyond the reach of the average books page. I mentioned my failure to arrange a review of a work by Teilhard de Chardin. That is the kind of book I mean, one that causes a lit ed severe problems. If he sends it off to a specialist reviewer who has asked to do it, he fears he will get back a review of even greater obscurity than the book. On the other hand he is not especially anxious for it to be panned *à la* Nigel Dennis. Teilhard de Chardin, Simone Weil, Thomas Merton, the poetry of Saint-John Perse – the great no-go regions of reviewing – they were just the kind of bowling that Toynbee liked. Towards the end of Toynbee's career, Kilmartin said that his recurring problem was to keep Toynbee out of the pulpit.

The 1960s and 1970s were the last decades before commercial pressures made a devastating impact on civilised values in the publishing business. Terry, the most influential literary and arts editor in London, encouraged his reviewers to sustain those values by making challenging judgements that frequently went way beyond the scope of a straight review.

Let us recall some of these judgements for the first three months of 1960, by which time Kilmartin after eight years in the job had the luxury of two pages for the book-reviews. Harold Nicolson was still going strong. He began the year reviewing René Grousset's *Chinese Art and Culture* then he took an extended holiday and returned at the end of February to review Ellen Moers's book on *The Dandy*, a book that suited Nicolson to perfection ('Mrs Moers, I think, exaggerates the aristocratic element in dandyism: it was always a non-U excrescence'). Next Nicolson reviewed *New Light on Dr Johnson* edited by F. W. Hilles; after that the latest volume of Gide in English, *Pretexts*. Then Nicolson considered Gilbert Murray's *Unfinished Autobiography* ('Of all the men I have known he was the one to which the word "magnificent" in the Greek sense could be most rightly applied'); then *The Berenson Story* by Sylvia Sprigge and *The Truth About A Publisher* by Stanley Unwin. These last three books remain required reading for anyone interested in their subjects and so, I suggest, do Nicolson's reviews. As in many other instances he knew the subject of the book through belonging to the same social circle. This intimacy is both his strength and his weakness. It never seems to have occurred to him that he might have known someone just a little bit *too* well to be able to review his or her book. That does not matter perhaps when he is reviewing *Robert Ross: Friend of Friends*. Indeed it adds to the pleasure to have him lamenting wistfully: 'Those of us who knew Ross when we were young still "miss" him after all these years; how often do we sigh that it is no longer possible to drop into Half Moon Street and delight in that incomparable companionship!' But with the hindsight we now possess through the revelations of *Portrait of a Marriage*, was it right for Nicolson to review *Don't Look Round* – the memoirs of Violet Trefusis (his wife's lover) – for the *Observer* in 1952 without, as it were, declaring an interest? But he did so and there must have been some raised eyebrows. He said with infinite diplomatic tact that Mrs Trefusis 'has had many deep devotions in her life but perhaps the deepest is to France'.

Philip Toynbee began the New Year in 1960 having to write an obituary tribute to Albert Camus, who had been killed in a car accident at the age of forty-six: 'Since the death of George Orwell [ten years earlier] we have had no equivalent in England to this deeply thoughtful and honourable man.' Toynbee's next piece was on R. W. B. Lewis's critical work *The Picaresque Saint*, a creature located in the novels of Moravia, Camus, Silone and Faulkner. Then, under the heading 'Two Happy Events', Toynbee is signalling the appearance of the cultural periodicals, the *New Left Review* and *X*. This was generously contrary to normal Fleet Street practice. Newsapers tend only to give space to other periodicals if they have a financial interest in them or in order to rubbish them. I was once soundly ticked off by Brian Roberts, McLachlan's successor, for including a short paragraph on my page about an issue of Alan Ross's *London Magazine*. Roberts thought (erroneously) that it was still owned by the *Daily Mirror*. Toynbee's final review that month was of Elizabeth Hanson's study of Rimbaud, *My Poor Arthur* ; he considered it to be 'a bad and profoundly vulgar book'. These last two books reviewed were what was known in the trade as 'January books'; books that were deliberately published when the competition for review-space is reckoned to be at its slackest. Nowadays that principle no longer holds. January has become as busy a month for reviewable books as any other.

By the first week in February things were beginning to look up, with the publication of *Clea* – the last of the four volumes of Lawrence Durrell's *The Alexandria Quartet* – giving Toynbee the opportunity to evaluate the work as a whole. He was warmly appreciative of Durrell's achievement, partly one suspects because it represented the kind of novel he was trying to write himself. Any reader who might have felt it was a week when Toynbee could have eased up a little on comparisons with other writers was soon disabused: Proust, Pater, Conrad, Mann, Norman Douglas, Fitzgerald are all of Durrell's company, he says, and beyond them there stands the gigantic figure of Stendhal. Toynbee feels that the layered structure of the whole tetralogy likened by the author to a palimpsest 'doesn't work' but even so it is, at the final count, 'an astonishing success'. At the end of the month Durrell was the subject of the *Observer's* Profile feature. Here we can watch reputation-making in progress. Terry and Philip had decided with the approval of Astor that the moment had come for Durrell to receive the paper's supreme accolade, one rarely accorded to a novelist.

Unlike the other leading reviewers of that time, Toynbee was prepared to say what he thought of a new novel by a contemporary novelist. For instance, he put the boot hard into Henry Green for what turned out to be his last novel, *Doting*. Under the heading 'The Same Again' Toynbee wrote that the previous novel *Nothing*, 'was a sprightly *comédie de moeurs* – nothing more. The trouble with *Doting* is that it is an equally slight novel but not so funny in achievement or one assumes in intention.' After that dismissal we heard no more from Henry Green. It was not that Toynbee did not like comic writing in a novelist. Of Kingsley Amis's *That Uncertain Feeling* he wrote that Amis remained the only comic writer he knew who 'deserved to be compared with Evelyn Waugh and Anthony Powell'. Amis became an occasional contributor at this period. On the other hand, when reviewing *Molloy*, Toynbee felt that, 'Mr Beckett fails as a novelist because he has involved himself in false emotional simplifications'. It is of course unfair to pick out a few judgements in reviews by a hebdomadal critic about the work of his contemporaries some forty years on. All the great reviewers from Sainte-Beuve downwards have much to blush for. And no one was more aware of the dangers in the snap judgements of reviewing than Toynbee. He described some of its private absurdities in the Journal he kept:

10 October [1977]
Rereading yesterday's review has been a rather ludicrous experience. The book was a life of Elizabeth Bowen [by Victoria Glendinning], and the reviewer's tone of quiet authority and dignified self-

confidence suggests a very different provenance from the bedroom of a man sick with a hangover and groaning with remorse. The comic discordance between appearance and reality.

The book also reminded me of several different worlds I used to belong to in my earlier years; in this case the proud, respectable upper-class intelligentsia.

His reflections on re-reading his review of Bamber Gascoigne's *The Christians* raise once again the issue of the hatchet-job. (Reviewers often complain, as he does, about the headline to a review they've written which they do not normally see until they read their review in the paper. A carefully written review can easily be distorted by a headline, the work of a sub-editor, the one thing the reader remembers.)

23 August [1977]

Moral problems of a book reviewer. I have been brooding a little about my harsh, even snooty review of Bamber Gascoigne's *The Christians* which appeared on Sunday. In fact it was made all the snootier by the title – *Quizmaster's Christendom* – which was not my choice.

The general problem is that my near Christian beliefs don't accord very well with my profession. If all my reviews were written in a spirit of sweet charity and judge-not-that-ye-be not judged they would soon nauseate my readers. (They'd nauseate my editor even sooner.) But shouldn't it be possible to condemn a book without jeering at the author?

Yet weighty, Olympian disapproval without a touch of humour, falls into a moral pomposity which is even more insufferable than bitchiness.

In this case the problem was sharpened by the fact that Gascoigne wrote a very contemptuous and (of course!) shallow review of the first volume of *Pantaloon* when it appeared in 1961. I vowed in my early days as a reviewer that I would never write a hostile review of a book written either by a friend or by someone I might be thought to regard as an enemy. To do the first is surely an unnecessary laceration. To do the second offends against the principle that justice must not only be done but also be seen to be done. (On the other hand I have taken great pleasure in heaping coals of fire on certain heads – e.g. that of Hugh Trevor-Roper, the scourge of my father.) [See 'Arnold Toynbee's Millennium' by H. R. Trevor Roper in

Encounter, June 1957, a scathing attack on the 10-volume *Study of History*].

But unfortunately this principle sometimes comes up against professional obligations; even professional competence. I was the obvious person to review Gascoigne's book; and as the only salaried reviewer on the Observer's staff I haven't the freelance's right to refuse what my editor wants me to do.

Shouldn't I, then, have "declared an interest" at the beginning of my review? Should I have warned readers of possible prejudice? But this seems absurdly self-important.

In this case, as in all the (few) others of the same kind, I was on the look-out for personal spite from the very beginning, when I first started reading the book. I am as sure as I can be that my judgement of the book was right, and that I was right to say so. But a certain uneasiness remains. I wish I could review only books which I admire.

After Kilmartin had been in the job for a decade or more, his team had grown to include a group of regular reviewers on whom he could draw, relying on their loyalty without putting them under contract, something he was always reluctant to do. They came both from academic life and from the ranks of the free-lancers. As each fresh generation emerged in the literary world, he took his careful pick. Among the first batch was J. G. Weightman, the authority on French literature, stalwart of the *Observer* books section for more than twenty-five years. When Trevor-Roper was poached by the *Sunday Times*, Kilmartin acquired A J. P. Taylor in his stead. No bad bargain.

Taylor had been introduced to the *Observer* by its Russian expert, Edward Crankshaw. Born in Birkdale, Lancashire, to a prosperous cotton-manufacturer, and educated at Bootham, a North Country boarding public school, Taylor won a special exhibition to Oriel College, Oxford, where he was contemporary of Harold Hobson, the future dramatic critic, and J. I. M. Stewart. After a spell teaching in the University of Manchester under T. F. Tout, where he met Lewis Namier, Taylor returned to Oxford to become a Fellow in History of Magdalen College. Apart from his reputation as an academic historian whose lectures were invariably attended by capacity audiences, he had much experience of newspaper and periodical journalism, and especially of book-reviewing. Adam Sisman, his biographer, reveals that throughout the 1950s Taylor had averaged one review a week in either the *Manchester Guardian*, the *New Statesman,* the *TLS,* the *English Historical Review* or the American *New Republic.*

It was initially on the *Manchester Guardian,* under the editorship of A. P. Wadsworth, that Taylor's talent for reviewing began to blossom in the 1940s. Taylor's book *From Napoleon to Stalin,* the bulk of which consists of reprinted reviews, is dedicated to Wadsworth. With its lucid expositions of complicated issues of foreign policy and conflicts between the great powers, it contains many examples of Taylor's arresting and entertaining manner as a reviewer. What is notable is how briefly the actual books are treated, unless they were by ex-ministers or prime ministers. They were often dealt with in a few lines and cut out altogether when the reviews themselves were reissued in collected form. Taylor used his space to give his own lively summation of the matter in hand (as it might be the motives of the French Government, especially its foreign minister Delcassé, in arriving at an *Entente Cordiale* with Britain in 1904). Each reprinted and slightly truncated review is like a piece in a jig-saw puzzle; at the end the pieces do not all exactly fit but even so an overall picture outlining the genesis of modern Europe's balance of power has been sketched.

In Taylor's controversial book on *The Origins of the Second World War,* he argued that Hitler had no premeditated game-plan in his policy of German aggrandisement; in his summit meetings up to the outbreak of war he played it by ear and reacted opportunistically to events as they developed, grabbing whatever was given to him on a plate by the British and French prime ministers. Taylor's view of Hitler has been frequently disputed. What does now seem clear is that the approach he attributed to Hitler in the 1930s was Taylor's attitude to his work as a reviewer in the 1950s. Regular reviewing is a form of literary opportunism. The reviewer takes what comes. He can never be quite sure what will emerge from the parcel that lands with a thud on his doormat, but he tears off the wrapping gratefully and if he is A J. P. Taylor he takes most of what he is given. His reviews extend his own territorial claims over the books' subject-matter. In the end, Taylor's reviewing and public lecturing became an alternative profession that more or less destroyed his academic career. Just as Nicolson had been tempted out of diplomacy by Beaverbrook, Taylor was tempted out of academic history and serious scholarship.

In 1960 Taylor showed his versatility. He began the year with a review for Kilmartin of *Jolly Jack Tar: A Social History of the Navy* by Michael Lewis and then he reviewed *The Jameson Raid* by Elizabeth

Pakenham, both of which he praised, giving the impression he
knew more about the subjects than the authors. On 7 February
Kilmartin had an entire page away from the books pages where
Taylor could spread himself over the appearance of the latest
volume of the memoirs of De Gaulle, *Le Salut 1944–46*. To be able
to run a big, excellent piece of this kind by a writer who could
turn out at a week's notice was in itself ample justification for
having Taylor in the team. He was an exception to the no-contract
rule and securely bonded with one to the paper.

In March Taylor was back on the books page with *The Fall of
Parnell* and *The House Built on Sand: German Policy to Russia*, and the
rest of the spring showed him continuing to demonstrate his
command of diverse subjects, a new biography of *Lord Derby* and
then a fortnight later a book by the journalist R. J. Minney on *The
Private Papers of Hore Belisha*. This was the kind of journalistic book,
concerned with Whitehall skulduggery in which the entrenched
brass-hats ganged up against the Jewish ministerial new broom,
that gave Taylor the opportunity to do what he most enjoyed, to
make an ironic exposure of an episode that revealed the bad
behaviour of all concerned. 'That is the story,' says Taylor,
'discreditable to both Chamberlain and the generals, most of
whom were to be dismissed in their turn by Churchill.'

Apart from the *Observer* who had first call on his services to
review any book, Taylor had several more reviewing assignments
in weeklies such as the *TLS* , the *New Statesman*, the *New Republic*,
and there were in addition his television appearances. He had
made his mark early on as a panellist of formidable adversarial
skill in a free-ranging political discussion programme, *In the News*,
with Michael Foot, Robert Boothby and W. J. Brown. In the period
of the Attlee government it was compulsive monochrome viewing,
so much so that the party managers agitated by the non-party lines
adopted by the panellists ultimately killed it. But Taylor appeared
also as a solo television lecturer and these appearances confirmed
him as a national celebrity. His flawless, intimate and seemingly
spontaneous expositions of complex historical issues straight into
camera with no use of prompts or auto-cues made him the modern
equivalent of Goldsmith's village schoolmaster, 'the wonder grew/
That one small head could carry all he knew'. In 1957 Taylor had
begun his association with the *Sunday Express*; its editor John Junor
signed him up to write twenty leader-page articles a year with the
warm endorsement of Lord Beaverbrook.

'I don't read your *Sunday Express* articles,' Kilmartin told him with typical candour. It was a measure of Taylor's wide appeal that two rival Sunday papers were prepared to share him in this way, even though Astor disapproved of him as a journalist. One article of Taylor's that Kilmartin had to read was his review of Driberg's biography *Beaverbrook, A Study in Power and Frustration,* a hot potato for Kilmartin because Beaverbrook had a feud with the Astors. Reading the piece in typescript, Kilmartin thought it was far too favourable to Beaverbrook and was therefore unusable. He explained this to Taylor who said 'the editor is always right' (a favourite phrase of his) and then obligingly re-wrote it; in the second review he was still enthusiastic about the book but much less complimentary to the subject, ending with the jibe, 'Though Lord Beaverbrook has often made news, it has not been news of any significance.'

By contrast Taylor was full of admiration for Beaverbrook as an historian when later that year he came to review *Men and Power, 1977–1918,* the conclusion of Beaverbrook's trilogy about the leading British politicians of the First World War. That was the beginning of a close association between them that lasted until Beaverbrook's death. It resulted in Taylor becoming the head of the Beaverbrook Memorial Library and Beaverbrook's biographer after the press lord's death.

What brought these two men together in such, on the face of it, unlikely amity? To a literary editor the bond seems to be their faith in the short uncluttered sentence, in the art of hitting the nail squarely on the head. Beaverbrook's prose is an even more succinct, an even blunter instrument than Taylor's, but it is constructed on the same principles and is just as effective in hammering his polemical points firmly home. Words used like this have great power to mould majority opinion: a love of such moulding, the desire to be the Button-moulders of our society, was was what both men shared.

Important as the coverage of historical and political books is to a literary editor, it is on its reviews of the literary ones that his books page will ultimately be judged. If Kilmartin had keen awareness of contemporary literature in Europe, he was also mindful of the need to have strong regular coverage of home-bred fiction and poetry. One of Kilmartin's acquisitions in this respect was Al Alvarez, who took his degree in English at Oxford in 1952, and published his first book *The Shaping Spirit* four years later. It established him as an uncommonly perceptive writer about poetry. London literary editors competed for his services, Kilmartin to

make him the *Observer's* poetry critic in 1956 and Janet Adam
Smith, then running the back half of the *New Statesman* (see
below), to make him the paper's dramatic critic in succession to
T. C. Worsley. Alvarez did not take kindly to being a theatre critic
and only stayed in it two years; but he remained as the *Observer's*
poetry critic for the next decade. In the 1950s new poetry was
regarded by lit eds as something that required specialist critical
attention, with G. S. Fraser on Friday in the *Statesman* and Alvarez
on Sunday assessing the various 'movements' to which the most
important younger poets were alleged to belong.

One of the more controversial of these consisted of Scottish
poets who wrote in Lowland Scots dialect and who were known as
the Lallans Poets; Sydney Goodsir Smith and Tom Scott were prominent among them. At the beginning of 1960 a Lallans anthology,
Honour'd Shade appeared, edited by Norman McCaig, in which was
included a translation of a poem of Baudelaire's by Tom Scott
under the title, 'Gloaming frae Baudelaire'. In his review Alvarez
poured Sassenach scorn on the Lallans movement: 'Lallans, in
short, is an excuse for Scott to pad out a bad translation with a
kind of half-breed Scots Cockney and for Smith to write a brand
of romantic nonsense that is no longer possible in plain English.'

This was too much, not just for the poets concerned but also for
G. S. Fraser, a Scot and an occasional poet; he was moved to make
his protest in a letter published the following week: 'I think Mr
Alvarez the best reviewer of poetry in England, but I also think it
very dangerous for anyone to write about current poetry in
Lowland Scots as if Scots were a kind of poor relation of English –
a lower-class non-literary language what Mr Alvarez calls Scottish
Cockney.'

It was not only poets north of the border whom Alvarez attacked.
The reputation of Edith Sitwell as a poet had been under constant
attack by the scurrilous critic and editor of *New Verse*, Geoffrey
Grigson – one of Kilmartin's occasional reviewers – but had
survived Grigson's attacks. While her brother Osbert was publishing his memoirs of their extraordinary childhood and their
eccentric father, Edith was adding to her reputation as a poet
during the war with poems of universal lament like the 'Song of
the Rain' and the 'Song of the Cold' that expressed poignantly the
mood of the period. It was now the moment for someone to take
a look at her work as a whole with fresh young penetrating eyes
and Alvarez seized the opportunity.

Among established reputations there was also that of Ezra

Pound. A volume by Pound, *Thrones, Cantos 95–109* soon came his way. The review began disarmingly with an account of two visits made by Alvarez to Pound in hospital. During Alvarez's first visit the two of them had had a calm fruitful talk about poetry; the second time there were other visitors who admired Pound's politics as well as his verse and all the old strident slogans came out. The dichotomy in the man was, Alvarez showed, indicative of a fatal dichotomy in the work. 'The treason that will matter to Pound's ultimate reputation as a poet is his betrayal of his own strict artistic standards, the failure of his poetic intelligence and skill which makes these latest Cantos seem such a slap-dash, bitty, broken-backed achievment.'

Another young critic whom Kilmartin brought into his team was Karl Miller; after a brief spell as an assitant principal at the Treasury, he was now lit ed of the *Spectator*. He had to review C. P. Snow's Cambridge-based *The Affair*. It was not all that long ago that Miller had been up at Cambridge himself, reading English, and had become a member of that exclusive sodality, the Apostles. Miller's bi-weekly reviewing partner – one week on, one week off, was the form for fiction-reviewers in those days – was another Cambridge man, a contemporary there of William Empson and Malcolm Lowry, John Davenport. He was an individual much loved within his circle but whose frustrated genius could lead to him indulging in ugly, aggressive, drunken behaviour in public. In 1955 Davenport was among the first to acclaim Nigel Dennis's *Cards of Identity*. It was published in late January, when Davenport enthused about it, seeing Father Orfe as 'a pseudo-saint in the Greene-Mauriac mould'. By the following November it had become a cult-book among *Observer* readers, described by Philip Toynbee in his Books of the Year contribution as 'the most dazzling satire on the Human Condition since *Gulliver's Travels*'.

Marghanita Laski was no longer reviewing novels regularly as she had done under Rose, but she was still reviewing and was one of several women reviewers who appeared frequently; others were Naomi Lewis and Kathleen Nott. Laski tended to approach a book in a confessional manner and the books Kilmartin gave her such as *Women at Oxford* encouraged her in this ego-centred style of reviewing; another book she reviewed was Herman Wouk's credo, *This is My God*, where she presented herself as the representative of the lapsed Jew. Nott tackled the Christian apologetics that Toynbee avoided; she had recently made her name with *The Emperor's Clothes*, a devastating deconstruction of the work of the group later known as the Inklings headed by C. S. Lewis. Nott, Laski and Lewis were the forerunners of the many women writers who would write regularly for the page in the 1970s and 1980s. The fortunes of the paper had greatly changed since the days at the end of the war when Kilmartin had joined it. A watershed was the Suez crisis in 1956. Until then the circulation had been neck and neck with that of the *Sunday Times*, the *Observer's* marginally in the lead. But thanks to its outspoken condemnation of the whole adventure and the prime minister, Anthony Eden, it lost readers dramatically and fell behind its rival, never to regain the ascendancy in number of copies sold. By the 1960s this battle for circulation had become a question of survival. A direct appeal to the new men was essential to the paper's continuance. The fission of the quality Sunday initially into two sections, and then many more, including a colour magazine had begun. Kilmartin's Proustian aloofness from all this began to seem anachronistic to many of his colleagues and to Astor, even though his judgement on literary matters was still held in high regard. Astor told him one day that they ought to have an article about the Beatles. 'It would make us look very foolish,' replied Kilmartin. 'We already do look very foolish,' Astor countered.

After that Astor appointed Richard Findlater, an experienced arts journalist and theatre historian, to supervise the performing arts coverage along with George Sedden from the *Guardian*. Kilmartin, with from 1964 onwards Miriam Gross as his deputy on the books pages, became the elder statesman. But he had by then laid a firm foundation of the paper's post-war arts coverage; his team included Tynan, who continued to send back occasional pieces after he had left to join the *New Yorker*, and Philip French as film critic, and others who had been undergraduates during the Suez adventure. Kilmartin's flair for attracting a variety of talents among book-reviewers resulted in D. J. Enright, Anthony Burgess, Philip Larkin, Angela Carter, both Amises, Lorna Sage, Paul Bailey, among many other names to conjure with, writing regularly for the page. People would sometimes say that he had been doing it for so long that his pages had become predictable. If so, it was a kind of predictability that in retrospect seems the hallmark of the highest standards.

His star of stars remained Angus Wilson, who brought a remarkable passion and intensity to his reviews, that same, at times overwhelming, eloquence that was always the feature of his conversation whether in a formal interview or in a chance meeting in the stacks at the London Library. Wilson, who lived in Suffolk with his companion Tony Garrett, had by this time become Professor of English Literature at the University of East Anglia, a post he held from 1966 to 1978 when he became a Professor Emeritus. At the end of that period he became desperately anxious about his financial future. He felt that his fiction, in spite of his international reputation, was not going to bring him a sufficient income. He therefore approached Kilmartin for a reviewing contract as opposed to a gentleman's agreement. The paper's response was disappointingly negative. Margaret Drabble in her biography of Wilson reveals the sad story of the deterioration in their relations and Wilson's ultimate break with the *Observer* books page. It stemmed from a paranoia that caused him to quarrel violently with many of his closest friends and admirers and resulted in Wilson and Garrett going to live in France.

Long before all that happend, in 1964 when Wilson's reputation was at a peak, he reviewed the novel *Le Chaos et la Nuit* by Henry de Montherlant that had been translated by Kilmartin as *Chaos and Night*. Wilson revered the misogynistic French writer. (He told me that I should have gone much more deeply into the comparison between Montherlant and Maugham when my book on the latter appeared.) Such was his admiration that Wilson arranged for a copy of his novel *Late Call* to be sent to Montherlant on publication. He received a letter back – quoted by Drabble – questioning Wilson's wisdom in entering into such idiotic lives.

It was memories of translating Montherlant that prompted Kilmartin to make a brief speech to a gathering of literary people, the only time I ever heard him speak in public. It was in the Abbey of Fontrevaud near Saumur, to which a group of us went from Britain under the auspices of the Franco-British Council to discuss literature with a similar delegation from France. This was in September 1981, by which time the great post-war flood of translations of books from French into English and English into French had dwindled to a trickle. The aim of the conference was to see if anything could be done to revive the literary *entente cordiale*. The old Abbey, containing the tombs of the Plantagenet kings, had been used during the war as a prison where Jean Genet was one of the inmates; it was now an airy, colonnaded and altogether delightful setting for such an event. There was immense goodwill and bonhomie on both sides and some lively sessions. The French delegation included publishers, agents and influential figures in the world of broadcasting and the media such as Jacques

Rigaud as well as distinguished authors such as Maurice Druon and the novelist Michel Huriet, then the cultural attaché in London. The British, under the chairmanship of historian Alistair Horne, included Lord Weidenfeld, John Calder, Matthew Evans, Marina Warner, Patricia Williams, Michael Sissons, David Pryce-Jones, Pamela Hartwell, John Sturrock of the *TLS*, Patricia Crampton and James Hardy of the Franco-British Society as well as two lit eds, Terry Kilmartin and myself. Calder made his interventions in French. Marina Warner was another eloquent French-speaker. The rest of us veered between English and French. On both sides we looked nostalgically back to the post-war days when a new novel by Simone de Beauvoir or Grum Grin (Graham Greene) would be immediately translated and published across the Channel. But nowadays things were different, for many reasons: chiefly, there were simply no authors of that stature in either England or France whose books demanded such speed of trandslation. Also there were many more centres and sources of literature of international importance – in Spain, Italy, Germany, the United States and Latin America – engulfing the pre-war Anglo-French relationship.

Could anything be done, the delegates at Fontrevaud wondered, to redress the balance and activate more direct Anglo-French literary links? A really good bookshop in London would help, where you could buy new French books as soon as they were published, suggested Lady Hartwell, and we all agreed with her. An Anglo-French Book Week, someone else volunteered, when writers from both sides would cross the Channel, and interest would be aroused through meetings, interviews, signings and other types of publicity. Bigger subsidies for translations, said Ms Crampton of the Translators' section of the Society of Authors. The co-operation of the literary press would be especially important, said Lord Weidenfeld, with a look in Terry's and my direction; it was up to us lit eds to help initiate a new era of translation by promoting it in our newspapers.

Terry had not said a word at any of the sessions so far, though he had been a lively presence at the socialising in between; but this somehow prompted him to get to his feet. He spoke in English, more in sorrow than in anger, of an experience he had had as a translator. He had been signed up by a firm of English publishers, Weidenfeld & Nicolson as it happened, for the ambitious project of making an English version of all the novels of Montherlant. He had done one of them and when he was half way through the next one, the whole thing had been summarily cancelled and he had never understood why. Weidenfeld returned rapidly to the podium and explained that after they had published several of Montherlant's novels in English they found that the sales were so disappointing that unfortunately they could not continue with them.

We all signed a communiqué with plans for more translations from Montherlant and other neglected moderns, a French arts bookshop in central London and a simultaneous Anglo-French literary week. What we failed to see was that there was no possibility of a return to a golden age in cultural history. The pre-war and immediate post-war two-way fiction traffic across the Channel has now become a transatlantic shuttle, with many modern American novelists translated into French. The contemporary French cultural penetration of Britain has been largely in the area of non-fiction. The difficulty not just of translating but of understanding writers such as Barthes, Lacan, Kristeva, Foucault and Baudrillard has been faced. They now have the currency in Britain once enjoyed by Sartre and Camus. Also the French flair for historical synthesis, in the hands of a Braudel or a Le Roy Ladurie, has proved to be eminently exportable.

7

Leonard and Jack

When in 1952 I worked briefly for Leonard Russell of the *Sunday Times*, he was the most important lit ed in London; his power over the literary profession so far as reviews were concerned was comparable to that of his contemporary Binkie Beaumont over the London theatre. The reviews he ran, though packed tightly into one page, were eagerly read and carried enormous weight. Many of them were by eminent names in a variety of fields.

Any literary ambitions Leonard may have had himself (in his youth he had written short stories) had by now become channelled into making his pages as stunning a display of book-reviewing as he could; his was the impresario's gift for recognising fresh original talent and using it for the greater glory of his pages; it was a gift that revealed itself outside his newspaper work in *The Saturday Book*, a collection of essays on serendipitous items he edited annually with fine illustrations, a commercial success for many years as a Christmas gift book; and also in anthologies he compiled of parodies and specially written articles on English wits, essayists and eccentrics. Cyril Connolly's penchant for parody was nurtured by Leonard in one of these volumes where the hilarious 'Where Engels Fears to Tread' appeared. Leonard had soundly based editorial acumen combined with the instincts of a showman. He wanted his reviews to entertain as well as to enlighten.

He started life as an apprentice journalist on the *Daily Telegraph* in 1927, straight from school. The *Telegraph* and the *Sunday Times* were then under the control of the original Berry Bros – Lord Camrose (William Berry, Michael's father) and Lord Kemsley (Gomer Berry, his uncle) – and edited from Peterborough Court, the *Telegraph* offices in Fleet Street (now the headquarters in London of Crédit Agricole).

In his section of the centenary history of the *Sunday Times*, *The Pearl of Days* (a book with three authors, one of whom was Russell, revealing late in the day that he could have been a brilliant writer had he not been a lifelong lit ed), Russell refers to himself throughout in the third person. He describes how in the year 1927 a red-headed youth was sitting in a gallery on the second floor of the *Telegraph* building waiting for something to happen:

> He had no duties worth the name then. The review books came to him, and he entered the details of them in a ledger. Once a week the distinguished literary editor of *The Daily Telegraph* and editor of *The Fortnightly Review*, W. L. Courtney would pay him a visit. Dr Courtney was very old, like so many others about the place, and wore mittens, and was very frail, and very tall, and very bowed, and very charming. He would instruct Russell to send a book or two to Arthur Waugh, Evelyn Waugh's father and chairman of Chapman & Hall, publishers of *The Fortnightly Review*, who with Courtney himself wrote a weekly article for the book columns. There was nothing else for Russell to do. So he educated himself by reading the review books . . .

One day Russell was visited by one of Lord Camrose's entourage, a Welshman named Cyril Lakin, with a request with which all lit ed's are familiar. Lakin wanted to take home some detective stories for his own private reading:

> Russell explained the impossibility of the request. He was under strict instructions . . . that no one was to be lent any books, and that, anyway, they had all to be returned by the reviewers, including (in his time) Arthur Waugh. Lakin listened curiously. What happened to them then? They were all sold to Foyle's. Lakin looked amused, said something about it's all being rather different now, and disappeared to Camrose's offices on the fifth floor with half a dozen novels by J. S. Fletcher, Edgar Wallace, Sydney Horler and so on, promising nevertheless to return them in a fortnight. He never did. Regularly he came for more, and when Russell asked him what he was to do about the ledger he just smiled.

(Gordon Newton, when he was about to depart for a fishing holiday, would make similar representations to the lit ed of the *FT* in the 1970s. Fortunately his preferences among mystery stories did not often coincide with those of its crime fiction reviewer.)

In 1929 Lakin was made literary editor and an assistant editor of the *Telegraph*; by 1933 he was lit ed of both the *Telegraph* and the *Sunday Times* and Russell had become his assistant. As such Russell had his first encounters with Cyril Connolly, Rebecca West, Cecil Day Lewis, all of whom Lakin, who had a good eye for a critic, brought in as occasional reviewers.

The two papers occupied the same editorial premises in Fleet Street and the brothers signed an agreement whereby the *Daily* and the *Sunday* were printed on the same presses. Then in 1936 the two papers became separate entities, the *DT* becoming the exclusive property of Lord Camrose and the *ST* that of Lord Kemsley (but the printing arrangement remained in force until 1960, when Roy Thomson terminated it). The *Sunday Times* moved now to its own editorial headquarters in Gray's Inn Road. Lakin and Russell moved with it to work on the books pages.

These pages were abundant. The years between the wars in Britain were a prolific period for publishing, especially in the area of library fiction. The paper frequently ran five pages of book reviews replete with publishers' advertisements. Before Lakin and Russell took over the books pages, the review copies were all kept in the office of the editor where once a week they were farmed out for review, senior members of staff attending and taking away books they wished to notice. That was standard practice on newspapers in those days before the job of a lit ed with his own office had come into being. The editor then was Leonard Rees, an irascible little man who always sported an eyeglass, and whose favourite modern poet was Alfred Noyes, but he knew what he wanted when it came to books coverage. It was he who signed up Sir Edmund Gosse as the paper's main book-reviewer, a landmark in the history of British newspaper books pages:

> Rees [felt] rightly that Gosse was the man to establish the book page of *The Sunday Times* ... But it was not Rees who introduced Gosse to literary journalism. As long ago as 1904 he had been the director of a weekly literary supplement which Northcliffe, touched by *folie de grandeur*, gave away with *The Daily Mail*. It had lasted for eighteen months and had brought him in £400 a year until it was stopped abruptly without warning. [Then Gosse wrote book-reviews for *The Daily Chronicle* and after a while was also dismissed without a day's warning.]

This was early in March, 1919. A very eager Rees asked for an appointment with him. Gosse was always a temperamental man, and the benignness which he assumed in old age was easily cracked. Gleams of anger at often imaginary insults frequently flashed behind his gold-rimmed spectacles, when his thick crest of fair hair, hardly touched with grey even now, when he was 70, would fall distractedly across his forehead, his lips, half-hidden by a heavy moustache, would pout with incontrollable anger; and it wasn't unknown for him to glide across the floor at some high life party and hiss at an unwitting offender, "You have insulted me!" . . .

When it was all settled and in operation Rees became a worshipper of Gosse's; he counted the appointment as the biggest *coup* of his career and was stricken when the master died in 1928 still writing his weekly article.

Gosse had been active as a literary journalist even earlier than Russell indicates. His periodical journalism dates from the late nineteenth century when he contributed to such journals as the *Fortnightly Review*, the *Contemporary Review*, the *New Review* and the *Century Magazine*. He was a prolific exponent of the higher journalism beloved of cultivated Victorians with plenty of time to read long, learned disquisitions peppered with untranslated Latin and Greek tags. Gosse's career marks the transition between this essay-like reviewing and the kind we know in newspapers today. Gosse modelled himself on the great Sainte-Beuve. He aimed at doing what Beuve did so magisterially, the literary portrait, but in briefer compass.

A final volume of Gosse's journalism – *Books on the Table* (1921) – contained what he described as 'The ten-minute sermons which, for some time past, I have been delivering each week to the congregation of the *Sunday Times*'. Here we can sample Gosse on such publications as the final volume of Monypenny and Buckle's biography of Disraeli, books on Clough, on Zoffany, the Letters of Tchekhov (as it was spelt then), on Gorki's account of the last days of Tolstoy, on Pascal's *Provincial Letters*, on the young Paul Claudel and on Gosse's fellow man of letters, George Saintsbury: 'If there be any person ignorant of the fact that he is the prince of living gourmets, his *Notes on a Cellar-Book* would be sufficient to silence the infidel.'

Gosse's work was aimed at readers unafraid of erudition, at least in the form in which it was served to them by Gosse. He devotes a whole article to the late Latin poet Ausonius, whose works had

appeared in translation in the Loeb Library. 'To stop at Tacitus
and Statius is like stopping at Gibbon and Goldsmith ...' Gosse
tells his readers in encouraging them to tackle this writer. The
fifteenth-century Spanish Franciscan monk Don Antonio de Gue-
vara's *The Diall of Princes* also gets the full treatment in the
translation by Sir Thomas North. He devoted his entire space on
another occasion to Thomas Heywood's *The Hierarchie of Angels*.

> Apart from his dramas, [it] is Heywood's most valuable contribu-
> tion to literature ... We get into the habit of regarding *Paradise Lost*
> as a solitary monster, as the only religious epic in the language. But
> it is merely the best – by far and beyond approach the best. *The
> Hierarchie of Angels* is a poem on the same scale as Milton's, written
> more or less with the same purpose – that is to say to give an artistic
> rendering to Biblical theology.

Even if some of this is bluff, the range is impressive, also the
assumptions. Gosse writes as someone who is completely confident
his readers share his wide-ranging enthusiasm for literature and
for rare books. A taste for a weekly literary *causerie* linked to the
appearance of a new book was created in the national consciousness through Gosse's articles and a tribe of reviewer-critics arose
in England to carry on the good work. The *Sunday Times* was read
primarily for his contributions and those of its critics in the other
arts; news, sport, city matters were all secondary items. As Russell
puts it:

> For a good many years – from the 1920s to the early 1940s – the
> critics of the paper *were The Sunday Times*, just as Garvin in his heyday
> was *The Observer* ... When Gosse was appointed chief literary critic in
> 1919 he set a tone for the literary pages which was afterwards
> sustained by Desmond MacCarthy, Raymond Mortimer and Cyril
> Connolly.

After devilling for Lakin for a few months, Russell's editorial
fortunes rose; he was left by Lakin to run the literary pages on his
own. When Lakin suggested he should leave them and move on as
an assitant editor to even higher things, he was reluctant to be
promoted.

> Russell didn't particularly want to pass them [the books pages] on
> to someone else. He found the publishing world of the mid-1930s an

exciting place. There were cocktail parties for authors every night, and huge advertisements on Sundays from Gollancz and Walter Hutchinson, and everyone was fighting it out in a gentlemanly way, including of course *The Observer* and *The Sunday Times*.

An obituary tribute to Gosse appeared in the *Sunday Times* of 20 May 1928 by the Anglo-Irishman Desmond MacCarthy. '"How beautifully [MacCarthy began] *he* would do this" must be the first reflection of one who sits down to write a commemorative article in these columns'. By the mid-August of that year, MacCarthy had been appointed as Gosse's successor. By then over fifty, he too was highly experienced as a literary journalist. Dramatic critic and lit ed of the *New Statesman & Nation*, he had also been the editor of the literary periodical *Life and Letters*. Among the Bloomsbury set Desmond was notorious for his failure to write anything for publication except his reviews. His close friends expected a major novel from him which never came. Apart from reviewing the other activity at which he excelled – by its nature ephemeral – was conversation. His friendships with Asquith, James, Hardy, Meredith, Maugham, testify to the beguiling charm of his table-talk. His knowledgeable, pointful, easy style can be sampled in his reprinted reviews in *Portraits* (1931), *Criticism* (1932), *Experience* (1935), and in the anthology *Desmond MacCarthy: the Man and His Writings* (1984) edited by his son-in-law, the author and Oxford don Lord David Cecil.

As a reviewer MacCarthy was a terrible procrastinator, one of those maddening lead-reviewers who keep their lit ed waiting interminably while they put the finishing touches to their copy. Here he is seen by Russell when he was reviewing in the *Sunday Times* at the height of the guided-missile raids on London in the Second World War:

> On Friday afternoons Desmond MacCarthy would be found tightly wedged into Russell's cubby-hole, desperately trying to finish the article the printers had already begun to set up in type; if the V1 raids were on he would have with him a squiffy little attaché-case in which was a bottle of port. On this particular Friday Desmond collapsed spectacularly with what he and everyone else thought was a heart-attack. But the doctor who appeared with magical speed prononuced it merely severe indigestion.

The false alarm over Desmond's collapse had made Russell, who was formally appointed lit ed in 1944, think that it was better to

have two lead-reviewers than one. The natural choice was again a
New Statesman writer from the back end, Raymond Mortimer,
eighteen years MacCarthy's junior.

Mortimer and MacCarthy jointly adorned Russell's pages until
1952 when MacCarthy died, having received a knighthood for his
services to literature the year before, and still contributing his
weekly article. 'How terrible about Desmond', wrote Cyril Connolly to Russell's No. 2, J. W. Lambert, now running the books
pages. 'I only heard yesterday and thought how gay and distinguished he looked in the pictures in Atticus.' And it was Cyril
Connolly, another Balliol Etonian, who was MacCarthy's natural
successor. I deal in the next chapter with the books pages of the
New Statesman where these critics learnt their trade and I shall
postpone until then a fuller account of their work

By the early 1950s Leonard Russell had signed up an impressive
team of regular reviewers by putting several distinguished writers
and university dons on an annual retaining fee for which they
agreed to review exclusively for the *Sunday Times*. The historian
Hugh Trevor-Roper was, as we have seen, recruited from the
Observer. These writers were available to review for the *ST* whenever
Russell wanted them, and when he didn't want them, they were
not free to review for the *Observer*, or later, the *Sunday Telegraph*.
By the time the latter started in 1960, Russell had so many people
on retainers that it became quite impossible for him to use them
adequately. He was in large part paying them them not to review
for the opposition rather than to review for the *Sunday Times*.

In 1943 Leonard married his colleague, Dilys Powell, the *Sunday
Times* film critic. Her first husband Humfry Payne, Director of the
British School of Archaeology in Athens, had died in 1936. With
no children from either marriage Leonard and Dilys devoted all
their energies to their journalism and the entertaining that
stemmed from it in their house in Albion Street near Hyde Park.
Leonard had the ambition to edit 'an English *New Yorker*' and he
acquired, or rather Kemsley acquired for him, a glossy called *Go*
which he ran in addition to his other duties from Kemsley House.
It was sold separately from the *Sunday Times*; in its format and
content it anticipated the paper's colour supplements of ten years
later. In 1952 I was to my delight asked by Leonard if I would assist
him in its production. Its brief Kemsley life-span was sufficient for
me to make the acquaintance of Jack Lambert, who was working
in the next office assisting Russell edit the *Sunday Times* books
pages and to meet again an RAF and Oxford contemporary

Godfrey Smith, who had just been made personal assistant to Lord
Kemsley. 'He's taken on a very tough job,' Russell told me. I also
gathered from Russell that his lordship was not quite as
enamoured of Connolly's reviews as Russell was.

Russell was one of those journalists who like to start late and
work late. He would turn up at around 5 p.m. to begin his day and
go through his mail; at around six he would start to dictate to his
secretary, Stella Frank. Much of his latterday work was concerned
with acquiring the serial rights of books for the paper to run
extracts from in advance of publication. The *Sunday Times* aimed
to provide its customers every Sunday with a compelling 'big read'
and it was usually an extract from a forthcoming major book.
Notable big reads were Field-Marshal Lord Montgomery's *Memoirs*,
Joy Adamson's lion-cub saga *Born Free*, Somerset Maugham's *Ten
Novels and their Authors* and William Manchester's *Death of a
President*. Russell liked always to work on the presentation of this
material himself and was a stickler for detail. He taught me the
trick of sliding a ruler slowly down each line of a proof as one read
it so that the impatient sense-comprehending part of one's mind
does not run on ahead and miss the typos and literals.

With his capacious *Sunday Times* chequebook at the ready,
Russell was the first port of call for any agent or publisher with a
hot serialisable property to sell. He had the reputation of driving
a hard bargain but he was prepared to make the sky the limit for a
book he was determined to serialise. Hitherto unprecedented
sums paid for serial rights marked the beginning of a casino-like
element that was introduced into quality journalism at this time.
Russell eventually reached the point where he bought the book
before it was even written, as in the case of John Pearson's *Life of
Ian Fleming*. In this instance Russell set up the whole package:
author, publisher, serial rights. And he appropriated fifty per cent
of the author's royalty for himself. The potential of the Bond
books was something Russell spotted before the boom, as he had
those of Dashiell Hammett and Raymond Chandler. Although the
distinction of first publishing Raymond Chandler in Britain
belongs to Hamish Hamilton, Russell helped significantly to make
his work known. He commissioned an interesting article on the
origins of the *Black Mask* magazine school of mystery writers to
which both Hammett and Chandler belonged for *Go*, by that
mysterious figure Ernest Borneman, which I subbed. I felt that
Russell saw himself as a kind of Philip Marlowe of the literary
world. During Chandler's visit to London in 1952 with his wife

Cissie, the Chandlers were entertained to dinner by Russell and Dilys in Albion Street:

> My wife and I [Chandler wrote to Russell on 29 October 1952] both feel that the evening we spent at your house, alcoholic as it was, was one of the high spots of our visit to London. And nothing would give us greater pleasure or joy than to repeat it at least twice a week for the rest of our lives.

But I must not let Russell up-stage Jack, who succeeded him. Interestingly, neither of them went to university yet both reached the pinnacle of the profession. Jack Lambert joined the Sunday Times in 1948 as assistant to Russell. He was the only child of a marine surveyor. His mother Ethel ran a village store at Looe in Cornwall where he was brought up. His father possessed a gramophone, along with many other gadgets, and nourished a passion for Gilbert and Sullivan that he communicated to his son. As a boy Jack would go for walks by himself along the shore, humming their songs, and stop to chat with the local fishermen.

He was educated at Tonbridge School in the 1930s after which he went straight into journalism, working for different trade magazines. Why the gifted Lambert did not go to university remains something of a mystery. Perhaps he did not want to be a financial burden to his parents. At any rate in 1924 he took a job on the *Electrician* and in 1937 he joined the *Newspaper World*. He then managed to persuade the editors of the Penguin Guides that he was a suitable person to write the one on Cornwall. It was published in 1939, by which time he was a mature twenty-two-year-old, and had been appointed editor of *The Fruit-Grower, Florist and Market Gardener.*

Then the war broke out and he joined the Navy as an ordinary seaman. He had fallen in love with Catherine Read, the daughter of a professional baritone, and in 1940 they were married with his Tonbridge school-contemporary Owen Chadwick, a future Regius Professor of Modern History and Vice-Chancellor of Cambridge University, as their best man. After he was married Lambert, who himself had a pleasant light baritone voice, took singing lessons from his father-in-law. The Gilbert and Sullivan renditions continued; he enlivened the monotony of naval lookout duty with D'Oyly Carte songs. These impromptu performances were not appreciated by his superiors and may have delayed his promotion. By 1941, however, he was in line for a commission as a cadet-rating on HMS *King Alfred*. Here his musical leanings proved to be an asset. He wrote the libretto of a G & S parody 'The Cadet-Rating's Farewell'. It was given at the end-of-training concert with C-R Lambert performing his own version of the Nightmare Song from *Iolanthe*. At this time Lambert made a friend of Peter Bull, also in naval uniform. Bull would create the role of Beckett's Pozzo on the London stage.

Lambert became a sub-lieutenant and was assigned to Motor Gunboat (MGB) duty in various waters, Atlantic, Arctic North Sea, Channel (Light Coastal Forces). By 1944 he had risen to the rank of Lieutenant-Commander in command of the larger coastal patrol vessel, the D-Boat. In one of the most memorable of Lambert's many encounters with enemy ships and aircraft for which he was awarded the DSC, he and his crew went on a rescue mission to pick up survivors from a passenger ship that had been abandoned. Lambert pulled the Greek actress, Katerina Paxinou, out of the water. They met again after the war, when she appeared in London in one of Peter Daubeney's World Theatre seasons.

When he was demobilised Lambert's prospects seemed bleak. His love of literature as well as music had grown immeasurably but jobs in literary journalism were very hard to find. He approached Ivor Brown, then still editing the *Observer*, for work on their literary section but was told that he had nothing for him. At this point a family friend drew Lambert's abilities and joblessness to the attention of Cyril Lakin, who was now in overall charge of the regional newspapers that belonged to the Kemsley Group. He found a job for Lambert in his part of the Kemsley organisation where Lambert's abilities as a journalist soon emerged. In 1948 Lakin was killed in a car accident while on holiday in the South of France, but by then he had introduced Lambert to Leonard Russell, whose assistant he became.

Lambert's career on the *Sunday Times* was thus exactly parallel to that of Kilmartin's on the *Observer*. Both men became closely identified with the papers for which they worked and both were to stay with their respective papers until retirement more than a quarter of a century later.

Jack and Terry – in retrospect one sees them as a double-act – were an awesomely fascinating pair for a new lit ed like me to observe at publishing functions such as those held by Sir William and Lady Collins, in the days when Collins was still owned and run at board level by members of the Collins family. The champagne would flow all too freely as lit eds and diarists mingled with a hand-picked selection of Collins authors in the elegant oak-panelled offices in St James's Place. Commissioning editors Philip Ziegler and Adrian House would weave their way gracefully around the great and the good, dividing their time most equitably; also present to put a discreet word in a lit ed's ear about a forthcoming Collins book, while a glass was re-filled by a tail-coated flunkey, were the members of a publicity team led at different times by Richard Simon, Eric Major, Michael Hyde, Rosemary Wurtzberg, Robert Ottaway, Gina Sussens. Billy Collins was one of the first publishers to appoint a publicity manager to drum up reviews. There was a legendary Collins director, a pioneer of the art of persuasion, called Ronald Pollitzer, often mentioned whenever the topic came up, who died before I arrived on the scene.

Both Jack and Terry would appear at these, and similar parties at Murray's or Jamie Hamilton's, in discreetly pin-striped or classic navy-blue suits. The casual, pony-tailed, tieless, Levi look affected nowadays was not then in fashion. Terry, who worked for the more liberal paper, would usually wear a matching blue tie, whereas the one neatly knotted around the neck of Jack, on the Tory sheet, would be a vivid shade of red or pink, to make quite unneccessarily the point that in spite of his suit he was not employed in banking or insurance.

By contrast to Terry, Lambert was an example of the lit ed as a public man always ready to take centre-stage. He was much in demand as an after-dinner speaker. He was, for example, invited to address that most exclusive body, the Detection Club, for which he was profusely thanked by Agatha Christie.

Apart from working extremely hard in the office he spent much of his time outside it in committee work for organisations to do with literature and the arts. He was on the Arts Council, where he fought many battles over funding; he was on the councils and committees of RADA, the Old Vic Trust, the Society of Authors, the Royal Literary Fund, the British Theatre Association, Opera 80 of which he was a director. He appeared on the original Third Programme *Critics* programme with his *Sunday Times* colleagues Dilys Powell, Harold Hobson, Eric Newton and re-appeared when the programme was revived on Radio Three as *Critics' Forum* produced by Philip French, for whom Lambert was one of the mainstays both as chairman and panellist. Kilmartin so far as I know never once made a broadcast.

Lambert was in addition a writing-editor who had no inhibitions about giving himself a lead-review. He wrote hundreds of reviews

for his own pages. If a lit ed is going to review regularly as well as edit conscientiously, he will need to have quite exceptional energy. That he certainly had. After a day's subbing reviewers' copy and sending out books, he would take home a batch of novels to read and would produce 1200 words on them by the following Tuesday. He also wrote a quarterly round-up of the main productions in the London theatre for *Drama*, the periodical of the British Theatre Association, as I did myself for a year or two when he at last gave it up in 1976. No better history of the post-war London theatre exists, charmingly written articles (in his case) now buried in the vaults with other defunct journals of the theatre.

But unlike some prolific writing-editors, Lambert's contributions were not made at the expense of abandoning the pastoral role as the sternly benevolent shepherd of his contributors, patiently scrutinising every word of the copy, steering the errant ones back to the straight and narrow path of clarity. In that he was Russell's disciple. Lambert's relations with Harold Hobson, the *Sunday Times*'s dramatic critic since the end of the Second World War would in themselves make a wonderful *novella*. Hobson was a man whose self-importance was only exceeded by his immense courage; there will never be a better example of the strength an upbringing in Christian Science affords in the overcoming of severe disability (he had polio as a child) than the career of Harold Hobson as critical arbiter of the London stage for some forty years. The trouble was that it went to his head. He really did think that playwrights like Beckett, Pinter and John Osborne owed their reputations largely to the pieces he wrote about them in the *Sunday Times*. He followed Agate's practice of keeping readers informed about the French theatre and the American. While he was away, Lambert would stand in for him.

If Hobson's absences from London were strictly on business to review plays in Paris or New York, Cyril Connolly's were quite the opposite; they were for the pursuit of pleasure. He was never fully reconciled to the harness of the weekly review. He lived in Sussex, coming in to London once a week to collect fresh review-books and correct his proof. But half the time he would be in Malaga or Provence or Haute-Savoie or Florence, or even further afield, and communication with the office would be conducted in hectic *Scoop*-like telegrams and post-cards.

ESTORIL
COPY EXPRESSED YESTERDAY TO ARRIVE AIRPORT 1035. TODAY

TUESDAY YOUR INFORMATION TOO LATE PLEASE CHECK COPY CARE-
FULLY. HORRIBLE WEATHER LOVE CYRIL. (Connolly to Lambert).

Here he is on a post-card at Annecy:

Weather good, children happy, lake too cold. Lunch *Père Bise* –
fabuleux.
Please check Christian name of Mrs Ford.

Only rarely would these wanderings render C. C. completely book-
less, but it did sometimes happen:

Greece is a kind of Mediterranean Scotland ... Reach London
Sunday evening Feb 29th [1964] – can you send a book to Bushey
[Lodge, West Firle, Sussex] that I can read Monday (not too long)
so as to get into March 8 paper?

Connolly had a deep concern for the sanctity of his copy. He
hated to be cut or for the word-order to be changed and especially
when it made him seem illiterate:

White's Monday
Dear Jack
Who was responsible for inserting that blood-curdling grammatical
howler into the 1st sentence of my review 'Two facts ... is' – as you
know I wrote it differently without a verb ... I can only think the
motive was SABOTAGE.

Such a letter is all part of the day's work in the life of a lit ed
and Lambert's deep affection for his star-reviewer was shown
ultimately in the moving piece he wrote in *Encounter* after Connolly's death.

The grand climax of their professional relationship came when
the *Sunday Times* gave a lunch hosted by Lambert to to celebrate
Connolly's seventieth birthday. It was held in the restaurant of the
Zoo in Regent's Park, a venue that echoed Connolly's passion for
books about wild-life, a category he seemed to prefer most of all to
review in his latter years. The guests assembled in the paved
garden and were regaled with champagne and then they moved
to the tables where a *placement* had been devised by the birthday
boy, Proustian in its subtlety. The guests consisted of his oldest and
dearest friends including John Betjeman, Anthony Powell, Cecil

Beaton, Alastair Forbes, Diana Cooper, Hamish Hamilton, Noel Blakiston, Harry d'Avigdor-Goldsmid, Robert Kee, Kenneth Clark. Connolly made by all accounts a brilliant speech; in thanking Lambert he only regretted the absence of Elizabeth Bowen, Maurice Bowra and Stephen Spender.

Terry, Jack and I were the last literary editors to use the star-system of reviewing where a regular chief reviewer takes on an important book each week and makes a general article or *causerie* out of reviewing it. The French word inevitably crops up when this topic is discussed because it is difficult to think of a precise English equivalent – chat, talk, chatty talk? A *causerie* is a cross between a formal appraisal and a personal reaction. It is written in such a way that the writer appears to be merely chatting to the reader, engaging his attention on a conversational level, but before the reader knows where he is the chat has developed into a challenging, omniscient judgement based on a reading of the author's entire work. There are manifest dangers in the *causerie*. The chatty tone may descend into flippancy and facetiousness. The air of omniscience may be more apparent than real, or if real, it may crowd out a fair appraisal of the book. But at its best the *causerie* is something from which literature – the reception of the new in literature – has benefited.

Buried in the sub-text of the word is the name of critic with whom the idea of the *causerie* was first associated: Charles-Augustin Sainte-Beuve (1804–69). Sainte-Beuve had the good fortune to live during the rise of a great literary movement in France – Romanticism. He was a protégé of Victor Hugo's and he fell in love not only with Hugo's poetry, a passion tempered by discrimination, but also with Hugo's wife, about whom Sainte-Beuve went beserk. The triangular situation between the poet, critic and the wife resulted in one not unlike that in Henri Becque's *comédie rosse, La Parisienne*. Only unlike that play it all ended in tears. The two founding members of this admiration society – Hugo and Sainte-Beuve – never spoke to each other again.

Sainte-Beuve is the classic instance of someone who, in spite of possessing a fine creative talent, immense energy and driving ambition, settles (though not without a heroic struggle) for being a reviewer-in-chief. He wrote a novel in the romantic George Sand tradition entitled *Volupté*, part of it inspired by his passion for Madame Hugo, and he wrote quantities of poetry addressed to her. He attributed some of his verse to Joseph Delorme, an

imaginary friend, whose *Vie, Poésies et Pensées* Saint-Beuve published
with a memoir, a portrait of a melancholy romantic, in 1829.
As a young writer he was drawn into the orbit of the *Globe*, a new
journal much concerned with Romanticism and the appraisal of
Hugo. Sainte-Beuve's perceptive piece on the latter gained him
recognition. He was soon writing also for another new critical
journal the *Revue de Paris*, getting the job thanks to Hugo. On the
Globe Sainte-Beuve found an editor, François Buloz, ambitious to
extend the scope of his journal. Sainte-Beuve worked closely with
Buloz and with the owner Dr Véron, who had made a fortune out
of patent medicine. Both editor and proprietor helped the critic
decide what he was to review.

Sainte-Beuve perfected the *Portrait Littéraire* and in painting
these portraits he tended to look to the past of literature rather
more than the present. His scope was catholic: he was interested
in anything that appeared between the covers of a book; as much
concerned with theology, philosophy, history, memoirs, gossip, as
pure literature.

A small, odd-looking man with a large head, he suffered a long
mid-life crisis after the collapse of his affair with Adèle Hugo and
toyed with giving up reviewing. For a while he relied for his
livelihood on his job at the Mazarin Library. Then he went to
Lausanne to give a series of lectures on the seventeenth-century
Janesensist religious community of Port Royal; in spite of his
charmless presence on the podium, his weak voice, and his
reading, rather than spontaneously improvising, his text, the
lectures were a *succès d'estime* among the Swiss savants who
attended. Though not a believer, Sainte-Beuve spent many years
after this writing his *History of Port Royal* in several volumes – that
work, alongside the volumes of the *Literary Portraits* and *Causeries*,
is the work for which nowadays he is remembered.

In 1844 Dr Véron, who was by now running the Paris Opéra and
the lover of the actress Rachel, bought *Le Constitutionnel* (founded
originally in 1815 during the Hundred Days as *L'Independant*). He
adopted a 'big read' policy, serialising novels by George Sand and
Dumas père that made the journal a great success with the Second
Empire public. He also signed up Sainte-Beuve to write a literary
causerie every Monday on anything he pleased. The famous *Causeries du Lundi* were born and they continued without a break for the
next twenty years.

Sainte-Beuve's articles circulated throughout Europe, translated

into English and other languages. No literary critic, not even
Edmund Wilson, has ever had such a wide international following.
The great French writers of the day begged him to devote space to
their work. He would maintain friendly personal relations while
sometimes publicly slighting them – or in the case of Baudelaire,
who called him 'Uncle Beuve', ignoring his work in public
altogether. Sainte-Beuve was elected to the Academy and made a
Senator but for the last twenty years of his life it was as the writer
of a weekly *causerie* that he kept his name before an international
readership.

Sainte-Beuve was the role-model for many of the leading reviewers I have described. Harold Nicolson's admiration was such that
he devoted a whole book to him in 1957, in which he wrote:

> A man who has read and reread the *Causeries du Lundi* and the
> *Nouveaux Lundis* and who possesses an even averagely retentive
> memory finds himself equipped with a wide acquaintance of French
> literature and the French attitude towards life. Not only is he
> provided with accounts of and comments on the leading French
> writers and personalities, but he is introduced to their lesser known
> contemporaries and thus afforded some knowledge of the back-
> ground against which they wrote and of the general climate of ideas.

Who better to review Nicolson's book in the *Sunday Times* than
their Sainte-Beuve, Cyril Connolly? He had already paid his own
tribute to the French critic in *The Unquiet Grave*, one of whose
presiding deities is Sainte-Beuve. Cyril Connolly compared his
wisdom with that of Chamfort, another of his heroes:

> Chamfort detested humanity, but, unlike Sainte-Beuve, he could
> find no compensation in the love of nature. Chamfort was classical
> pagan, Sainte-Beuve a double-minded critic who had passed through
> the mystical experience and the Romantic Movement to a scepticsm
> infinitely enriched by both.

Connolly began his review by pointing out the heavy debt
Nicolson's book owed to the earlier biography in French in two
volumes by André Billy. These volumes are 'ruthlessly pillaged' by
Nicolson, he says, adding, 'with acknowledgment'. Connolly then
goes in detail into the famous triangle: 'Saint-Beuve's love-affair
with Madame Victor Hugo is a classic of adultery. It should be
printed as a case-history and given to every young couple as they

leave the Registrar.' Finally we get Connolly's view of Sainte-Beuve the writer: 'He was a classicist and in his studies of the seventeenth and eighteenth century he is unsurpassed. He was the inventor of modern criticism and one of the most agreeable essayists of all time.'

Sainte-Beuve also has his detractors, the most celebrated of whom is Proust. The novelist wrote what seems as if it was intended to be a short book, *Contre Sainte-Beuve,* discovered among his papers after his death and published for the first time in 1954. There was an English translation by Sylvia Townsend Warner four years later. Terence Kilmartin wrote the introduction to that version. For once Terry utters publicly! He described Proust's work as:

> a curious amalgam of autobiographical fiction and literary theory centred on a critique of the great pundit and policeman of nineteenth-century French criticism against whose magisterial middlebrow judgments the really original and creative writers of the time had to struggle for recognition.

It is easy, as I have said, for the lead-reviewer to get it wrong when he turns to his contemporaries. Connolly advised the novice not to praise because 'praise dates you'. But so, alas, does dispraise or failure to praise and of this Sainte-Beuve was guilty in the case of Stendhal, Musset, Balzac, Flaubert, Gautier and Baudelaire. Quite a list. Even so, it does not invalidate his method or his achievement.

The Sainte-Beuve tradition dominated the practice of book-reviewing in Britain from 1900 onwards. It is time to take a look at some of its ramifications, starting with the *Literary Supplement* of *The Times,* a unique repository in Britain of the book review. That was where I gained my first experience of literary journalism as a member of staff.

8

Printing House Square

One afternoon in September 1959 I appeared at the office of the Manager of the *Times* newspaper in Printing House Square, Blackfriars, to be interviewed for the job of an assistant editor of the *Times Literary Supplement*. In those days we still called it the *Lit Supp*, as it had been from the beginning. It was not until the 1970s that it became the *TLS* and in what follows I will alternate between these two titles according to the period. Alan Pryce-Jones had recently retired as editor and had been succeeded by his deputy Arthur Crook, who had indicated that he wanted me on board. Before it was all signed on the dotted line I had to go through the formality – I hoped it would be a formality – of an interview with the newspaper's Manager, Francis Mathew, to fix my salary and with the Editor, Sir William Haley, for him to make sure he did not hate the sight of me.

I had recently returned to England after a year in the United States where I had (officially) been observing how books pages and book-reviewing worked and where I had accumulated a lot of material about George Gissing from various manuscript collections throughout the country. I had conceived, perhaps I should say misconceived, the idea of writing a life of this singular figure. Printing House Square was familiar territory. I had worked there as a sub-editor on the *Lit Supp* before I was awarded my Harkness fellowship; before that I had been on the staff of the *Times Educational Supplement*.

The *Times*'s attitude to my award had been – 'Go by all means but we don't promise there will be a job here when you get back'. The idea of offering a journalist in his late twenties or early thirties a year off to go to America to work and study, to re-charge his batteries so to speak, and then for him to return to his newspaper was a fine one; but in practice the kind of applicant they wanted was most reluctant to take up the offer. Many young journalists are unwilling to take a two-week holiday let alone a whole year off. But in my case, single as I was then, and bored by subbing, I thought it was too good an opportunity to let go; and now, as luck would have it, not merely was I going to work among former colleagues, I was getting promotion into the bargain.

I gave my name to a secretary who frowningly consulted a diary, and told me that Mr Mathew had not yet returned from lunch. She pointed to a brown leather club armchair in his office and returned to her typewriter next door. As I sat down I took in Mathew's handsomely furnished room. Was this the office, I wondered, that had been occupied by the newspaper's Manager from time immemorial? Had, for example, the legendary Moberly Bell sat at that desk when he had returned wounded in the leg from Egypt? Authority on the *Times* had ever since been divided between the Manager who controlled the money-bags and the Editor who controlled the editorial content. The Proprietor, at this period Colonel Astor (Lord Astor of Hever), was to most employees a shadowy presence, owning the majority of the shares of the company but not directly involved in its day-to-day running.

The clock on the mantelpiece over the fireplace indicated the hour was now three-fifteen and there was still no sign of Mathew. Had he forgotten all about me? Yes, probably. There was nothing to read, not even that morning's edition. Instead I reviewed my own life up to that point like the proverbial drowning man. In my case the literary virus had struck early, it attacked me while I was at school, and by the time of my sixth form year I had become totally infected with no hope of a cure. I hoped that somehow my working life would involve literature. In 1940 I was fourteen and a pupil at Midhurst Grammar School in Sussex. Such a school might seem an odd place for a Jewish boy from London, a natural for Highgate or Mill Hill; but we were on a family holiday near there when war broke out and my father decided that Midhurst was where I should go as a boarder. It was considered a safe place to be if and when London was blitzed – and so it proved; though I did not escape completely; I can still remember the deafening noise made by the ack-ack guns on Primrose Hill on bombing nights when I returned home for the holidays.

There were several boys from Nazi Germany who were boarders at Midhurst reconstructing their lives, preparing themselves for

Oxbridge and distinguished post-war adult careers. They all became my friends. And there were also Sussex-bred boys who under the influence of our remarkable Headmaster, N. B. C. Lucas and his wife Vera, were working to sit examination awards to Oxbridge. The most outstanding of these was our Head Boy, T. H. Aston.

Trevor Aston has had such a bad press since his death by his own hand that I should like put on record record how splendidly charismatic he was as a schoolboy. I can see him still in in his white flannels, blazer and bright orange cap (the first XI's colours), a born leader, tall, good-looking, mouth slightly open. The backdrop is Cowdray Park, what is now the polo-ground and was then our playing-field. Trevor, captain of the first XI, capable of knocking up an easy fifty most Saturdays, was our role-model both as a cricketer, a music-lover (he introduced us to jazz) and as an unremitting worker. Perhaps he worked too hard, harder than he need have done, and that iron-effort of will as a boy took its revenge after he had achieved his goal and become a distinguished historian, fellow of Corpus and the University's archivist. When I got to Oxford Trevor, already there, tempered my rawness and gaucheness by introducing me to the literary set at St John's, people like Ian Davie, Noel Hughes and John Wain. They all loved him and so did I.

My college was Merton, to which I was awarded a Postmastership (Scholarship) in History in 1944. We all did History in the sixth form as our main subject at Midhurst in those days. There was no other option. Science teaching was practically non-existent. Classics for some reason I never understood, the Lukes despised. By contrast French, taught by Mrs Lucas with Somervillian rigour, was taken very seriously indeed. English was a sideshow but an important one. There was no specialist English teacher and no one would have dreamed of doing it for a university entrance but we were encouraged to read widely in contemporary literature. All the novels of Virginia Woolf were on offer in the library, even as original paintings by David Jones, Mark Gertler, Frances Hodgkin, Jean Dufy (Raoul's brother), Adrian Hill (who lived locally) and Ivon Hitchens hung on the dead-white walls of the Lucases' drawing-room, to which we were invited for play and poetry-readings. I planned to switch to English as soon as I reached Oxford.

I left Midhurst in 1944, by which time I had already joined the RAFVR. I had my medical at a hotel in King's Cross culminating in an interview with a very camp Flight Lieutenant in the accountancy branch who pretended he was an Old Etonian. He asked me what I intended to do after the war. I told him I already had a scholarship to go up to Oxford. 'Hathe you, bai Jove!' he cried, his eyebrows shooting up several inches. But that meant I could go there straight away for six months as an officer cadet.

The 'short course' as it was called was a strange existence: you went into residence at your own college – I had lovely big rooms in Mob Quad – and for half the week you put on your gown, went to lectures and tutorials and led so far as was possible under blackout rationing conditions the normal life of an undergraduate; for the rest of the week you put on your RAF uniform (standard battledress with a white flash inserted in the fore-and-aft cap) to do square-bashing, morse-code, aircraft recognition, basic maths (ugh!), meteorology and eventually some flying in Tiger Moths. I greatly preferred the undergraduate part of the week, though out at the squadron one met one's 'peer group', several of whom I still see for occasional reunions, among them Anthony Smith, Godfrey Smith, David Dixon, David Vaughan, Hilary Rubinstein, Ray Kidwell QC, John Morrison (Viscount Dunrossil). The late Ronald Utiger, who after the war had such a distinguished career in industry, always came top of every test.

For the academic course which no one, dons or cadets, took very seriously, I did English and if I had been there a term or two earlier I would at Merton have had Edmund Blunden as my tutor, but he had resigned his fellowship in 1943. He had then left Oxford, divorced Sylva Norman and married Claire Poynting. No one had been appointed to replace him at Merton while the war lasted. Instead I went to Keble to Leonard Rice-Oxley, an experience not to be missed; he was the quintessence of Oxford about which he wrote a book. Theresa Whistler in her life of Walter De la Mare describes him as lively young man who became a close friend of the poet. The liveliness had long since departed to be replaced by a dormouse-like sloth. Waiting for his comments on the essay was a training in the pregnant pause. The only thing that would trigger him to an instant response was any reference to the work of Eliot and Auden, which he loathed.

Apart from Rice-Oxley such English dons who were still up seemed glad of pupils; all the since famous ones – Tolkien, C. S. Lewis, Nevill Coghill, David Cecil – were there and most accessible. Anthony Sampson and I used to go to a class once a week on Middle English given by Tolkein. There were never more than three other people and he used the time just to chat about literature and life generally. If only we had written down everything he said, Boswell-like, what best-selling books we would have now. But if anyone had said to us then that Tolkien's fantasies would one day become international best-sellers we would have told them to pull the other one.

Lewis was at the height of his early fame, having published *The Screwtape Letters*. His background lectures on medieval and renaissance literature packed out the Divinity School, most of the audience being female. I also used to go to Lewis's rooms in Magdalen once a week with a couple of other cadets for a class on *Paradise Lost* Books One and Two. It was held at ten o' clock in the morning and on the way in one would see Major 'Warnie' Lewis, his brother, starting to sort the day's post-bag of letters requesting spiritual advice.

We went through Milton's text line-by-line, as if construing. Lewis asked each of us in turn to explain the classical, biblical and astronomical references, and followed our stumbling expositions with his own authoritative ones. They were fascinating but by the end of an hour one felt very ignorant and humiliated, which I suppose was the idea. We arrived at Milton's reference to Limbo, the place where people go (mainly children) who have died untimely; it is Christianity's soft-option, being neither heaven nor hell; a doctrine that many theologians are reluctant to expound in case it becomes too popular. Lewis began his exposition by telling us: 'You'd better listen to this. This is probably where you'll go.'

He spoke truer than he knew. To join the RAF proper in 1945 was to enter Limbo and to stay there for what seemed like eternity but in fact was four years. We began by receiving some flying training but that petered out when the war was over. However our war-service was not then over by any means. We languished at the end of a long queue of people waiting to be demobilised. In the end I got a job at the Air Ministry at Bush House . . .

'Sorry I'm late. I didn't notice the time.'

The speaker was Francis Mathew, interrupting my reminiscent thoughts. He was a heavily built, broad-shouldered man who smiled at me from behind thick-lensed horn-rimmed spectacles; and had the kind of complexion novelists call rubicond. By the pleasant vinous aroma coming from him he had had a very good lunch. As I rose to my feet he waved me down again into the armchair with the cigar he was smoking, while he settled into the chair behind his desk; we soon agreed the question of my appointment as 'an' assistant editor of the *Times Literary Supplement* at £1000 a year. He told me I would be required to join the Times Pension Scheme B and went into its investment structure at some length.

Mathew was a printer by trade; before he came to the *Times*, to which he had been recruited in 1949 by Stanley Morison at the age of 41, Mathew had been Manager of St Clement's Press. Morison, in recommending him to the company, had said that Mathew had 'all the abilities required for management without any temptation to meddle with the editorial part, great as his sympathy would be with it.' That was not entirely borne out by events but clearly the Pension Scheme was something Mathew was proud of; and rightly, because pension schemes were not the normal part of newspaper employment that they are today. (Old hands at Peterborough Court used to tell me that the word 'pension' was not permitted to be uttered in the presence of the first Lord Camrose.)

As Mathew spoke, my wandering mind went back ten years earlier when I had attended a course of lectures on Medieval England by another member of this family, Fr Gervase Mathew, as part of my English degree. Fr Gervase told us that medieval man was enjoined to regard his wife both as his servant and as, in some sense, his companion. The *Times* at that period was still run on similarly hierarchical male chauvinist principles. Francis Mathew believed with his mentor Morison that the *Times* should aim at being what nowadays we should call élitist, that it should be a paper with a comparatively small but influential readership supported by advertising revenue. This view led to the 'Top People Read The *Times*' campaign and that, alas, proved to be the wrong way forward for the post-war *Times*. The paper's losses escalated even though its circulation increased. It is a very clever management that can contrive to lose money by putting on more readers but that is precisely what happened; it was all to do with the very expensive paper on which the newspaper was printed, a deal that Mathew had pulled off to defeat the newsprint rationing restriction which stayed in force long after the end of the war.

Mathew died suddenly of a heart attack in 1965. Two years later the Proprietor, by now Gavin Astor, the colonel's son, sold the whole Times package, the newspaper, the Supplements and the building, to Roy Thomson. A new company was formed, Times Newspapers Limited, pairing for the first time in their history the *Sunday Times* (which Thomson had bought in 1959) and *The Times*.

'I gather,' said Mathew with what could just have been a conspiratorial smile, 'you've already had experience of the *Literary Supplement* when Pryce-Jones was editing it.' Yes, it was Alan who had got me onto its staff originally. I had had to fill in one of the standard *Times* journalist application forms that included questions like 'Where educated? State any degrees and/or other academic qualifications'. Alan P-J's eyebrows went up as he hit my academic record. I sensed it was not going down at all well. 'You were very grand. *Very* grand!' he said reproachfully. However he gave me the job.

Once I had settled the contractual side of my appointment I had to see the Editor, Sir William Haley, who took a keen interest in the *Lit Supp's* affairs. Unlike Mathew, Haley was a non-drinker, a non-smoker, almost it seemed as I sat in front of him, a non-talker. Finally he broke his silence and asked me why I wanted the job and what I thought the essential qualifications for it were.

I was waiting for that. 'Well,' I said, 'I suppose one would need to be curious not only about literature but other subjects too – history, philosophy and so on. The *Supplement* covers these areas just as fully as literature . . .'

'Oh yes,' he said dismissively, 'I'm sure that that's important. But what you've got to be able to do is to create an impetus where none exists. One week you find that nothing much is happening in, say, biography; so you turn your attention to drama instead, and find your lead in a collection of plays.'

It is a good point – the need to have a strong lead even if it means creating one out of an unpromising batch of books; but not one that ever applied, I found, to the *Lit Supp* where books flooded in continually from many different directions, and with many eminent reviewers willing to write about them. There was always an abundance of lead reviews on hand to choose from for Fronts and Middles (as the two big reads were called in those days).

Haley must have been thinking back to his time on the *Manchester Evening News*. He had joined it as a cub-reporter in 1922, having earlier still been a foreign telephonist on *The Times*. When he became Editor there were still one or two people around who claimed to remember him in his former capacity. He left Manchester as Managing Editor in 1932 to go to the BBC of which he became Director-General during the war. He became editor of *The Times* in 1952 but it was the Manchester period that he looked back upon with the greatest pride. It was then that he continued his education, begun at Victoria College, Jersey, by avid reading and reviewing. In addition to being a newspaper journalist who had reached the top job in the profession, he was also a dedicated Man of Letters. During the lunch-break Haley would go to the Athenaeum Club and after a quick abstemious meal spend an hour or two there reading minor literature and writing about it in that club's well-stocked library.

He was a dedicated Gissing-man. Gissing's belief in the educative process as something to be pursued outside of an institution and available to anyone capable of constant, disciplined reading was one of the chief articles of Haley's credo. Wearing his Man of Letters hat, Haley contributed a weekly article to the *Times* books page under the pseudonym of 'Oliver Edwards' on the model of Arnold Bennett as 'Jacob Tonson'. He would recall the work of Cecil Torr, George Darley, Henry Kingsley, or some such forgotten writer in whom he attempted to revive interest. It was my job to sub Oliver Edwards's copy: in those days the *Times* books page was edited and put together in the office of the *Lit Supp*. There was no separate lit ed of *The Times* as such. The books to be reviewed were chosen by Haley and his assistant editor A P. (Patrick) Ryan, formerly head of BBC News Services, who was the virtual lit ed. The actual production of the page was executed by Arthur Crook and his colleagues, all acting unpaid, counting it as part of their *Lit Supp* duties.

Oliver Edwards' pieces always arrived very promptly on my desk from the editor's secretary, sometimes in a batches of two or three at a time. They were typed in a large-sized font as if for the partially sighted to read, on a cream-laid paper so thick that it took quite an effort to fold the sheets to get them into an envelope. As the sub, I merely had to mark them up them for the printer. It was not for me to tamper with the Editor's peerless prose. There was one occasion, though, when I felt moved to re-write: when Oliver Edwards based his article on *A Small Part of Time*, a book of essays by Michael Swan about Henry James and some expatriate authors in Italy, one of whom was Norman Douglas. Oliver Edwards praised Swan's gift of eliciting confidences from the people he met. 'Even Norman Douglas unbuttoned to him', he wrote. Surely, I reckoned, even if it is Haley Writ I mustn't let that through. I showed it to Arthur Crook and suggested I found some less risible way of saying what the editor meant. 'No,' he said 'to the pure all things are pure. Leave it exactly as it is.' – which we did. Haley was unwise enough to reprint his pieces in book form and suffered a murderous attack in a review from Bernard Levin.

Printing House Square consisted then in the mid-1950s of several buildings in Queen Victoria Street that had been knocked together as the newspaper had expanded during its pre-war period when the top people really did read *The Times*. (The building had suffered a direct hit one night during the war but the paper appeared as usual the next morning.) On the hill by Ludgate Circus was a works entrance where the compositors and linotype operators clocked in. At the front opposite Blackfriars Station was the main entrance to the editorial offices. In the eighteenth century the Proprietor had a private house adjoining the office; all that remained of it was an editorial dining-room known as the Mess where the senior editors had lunch. Then there were corridors full of offices of diminishing grandeur where leader writers, who at one time in the mid-1950s included both Peregrine Worsthorne and Henry Fairlie, worked. Then the sub-editors' room with its coal-fire and tea-making facilities where in the 1930s Graham Greene and Claud Cockburn used to run their competiton to see who could get the dullest headline into the paper. Greene said that that room was the nearest thing on this earth to the Kingdom of Heaven. People who worked there longer than he did are less apocalyptic in their descriptions of it.

In 1959 the paper was still without any news stories on the front page; that revolution happened in 1966; the page below the masthead was exclusively filled with eight columns of small, lucrative 'classified' advertisements. Inside the pages were correspondingly chaste, with long chunky articles and by-lines that read 'From our Correspondent' (almost everything was still anonymous); there were very few illustrations on the main pages; there was always one superb black-and-white photograph on the back page showing (say) early crocuses in bloom in Hyde Park captioned 'A touch of Spring' taken by a *Times* photographer, or sometimes the picture used was submitted by a reader. The picture editor, known as the art editor, had his own office with his name in big letters on the door – BOGAERDE.

Mr U. V. Bogaerde was the first picture editor *The Times* ever appointed. He had joined the paper in 1912, having previously been a designer of stained glass-windows, returning after war service in 1919. When you went to consult him about a photograph he was always very chuffed if you told him you'd been to see his son Dirk's latest movie.

The two Supplements (there was no *THES* then) were located at the furthest point away from this heartland of the main paper, with the Baynard Castle public house conveniently next door, then the bombed-out church of St Andrew-without-the-Wardrobe, then the headquarters of the British and Foreign Bible Society, then the rich crumbling pile of the College of Arms. It was a very old, pious and venerable part of London. My office commanded a splendid view of the Thames at Puddle Dock where I was able to observe the various phases of the building of the Mermaid Theatre under the personal direction of Bernard Miles. The big airy room had bookshelves up to the ceiling crammed full of books but these were not the review copies. The books sent in for review, shoals of them, were kept, carefully guarded, in the main editorial room next door.

In there when I first joined were Arthur Crook, then the Deputy Editor, who had been on the staff since 1930, a great custodian of the Supplement's traditions and upholder of the anonymity rule; a tireless worker, and a brilliant deputiser for long periods on end for his Editor, whom he subsequently succeeded for a highly successful spell as editor himself. The special supplements on History, French Literature, Children's Books that were regularly included in the *Lit Supp* in the late 1950s and 1960s were overseen by him. The advertising manager, a key player in the whole operation, was Frank Derry, who sported a hacking-jacket in the office and had a studied air of olde-worlde courtesy as he roped in ads for both the *Ed* and the *Lit Supp*. 'May I, dear lady, sign you up for eight inches across two columns at our special rate?' he would ask a publisher's publicity manager at the end of a rich lunch, and the answer would invariably be yes. Altercations about the advertising lay-out he gave us were not infrequent. There were no page-designers in those days. Editorial make-up was always done by Crook aided by his assistants, Charis Ryder and Anthea Fairfax-Ross (later Secker).

The new fiction when it came in was separated from the other books and put in chronological order of publication on specially designated shelves to be vetted by a fiction-reviews editor, who appeared only once a week to decide which novels were to be reviewed and by whom. Before my time this was Anthony Powell but he had gone to be the literary editor of *Punch* and had been replaced by the critic David Tylden-Wright.

By contrast to the review copies, the books that graced the shelves in my room were old books – a complete run of Leigh Hunt's *Examiner*, the diaries of Henry Crabb Robinson, the *Dramatic Essays* of William Hazlitt and other works of that period.

They were part of the library of Edmund Blunden who as a *Lit Supp* staffer had left them there while he was in Japan. Many of them were annotated in pencil with Blunden's comments. Browsing through them, I became aware of his intimacy with the work of the English Romantic poets. Occasionally a bus-ticket or a piece of toast used as a marker would fall out from the pages. 'Edmund left in rather a hurry!' my office companion, R. H. Hills, explained.

Bob Hills, a gleaming pink-faced man in a baggy suit, was a former foreign sub-editor who had been seconded to the *Lit Supp* from the main paper. Difficult at first to get on terms with, once I had become accustomed to his abrupt dry manner he became great fun. Anything I know about subbing copy, I learnt from him. He was never to be seen in the office without several lead-pencils of superfine sharpness, an India rubber, a long pair of scissors and a pot of glue, the essential tools of the trade, and he had beautifully legible handwriting. He was one of those people to be found on *The Times* then who seemed to be utterly content with sub-editing as a way of life. He took no interest so far as I could see in the actual content of what he was subbing – I mean from the literary point of view or the judgements made by the writer. Provided it made sense, it was fine; he marked it up; indented anything quoted in the piece longer than three lines, clipped it all together, and sent it down to the composing-room for setting.

Pryce-Jones, who used to spend a lot of time promoting the paper abroad and on lecture assignments for the British Council, was always difficult to pin down to any kind of meeting in the office. On arriving around ten in the morning I would sometimes find the forlorn figure of Haley trying to gain admittance to Alan's room, which would be locked and desolate. 'Is Mr Pryce-Jones not in?' he would say. 'No, not yet,' I would reply. 'Tell him I'd like to have a word with him as soon as he arrives, will you?' 'Yes, indeed' – and off Haley would trot, back across the building to his own enclave.

Presumably he knew as well as I did that Alan at that precise moment was many miles away from Printing House Square in somewhere like Barcelona or Lima but the ritual had to be gone through. When Alan did appear he would seem suddenly to materialise; it was as if he had never been away. He would say with a smile, 'You know people are extraordinary...' and launch immediately into a hilarious anecdote about something that had happened to him on his travels.

Alan had served his apprenticeship as a literary journalist under J. C. Squire on the *London Mercury* in the late 1920s. Squire had been the first literary editor of the *New Statesman* and had established its Books in General page, writing it himself every week. But that did not satisfy his huge ambition and in 1918 he had left to found his own monthly journal the *London Mercury*. Squire never at any time suffered from false modesty, as may be seen from his editorial notes introducing the journal to its readers in November 1919:

we may reasonably say that there has never been in this country a paper with the scope of the LONDON MERCURY. We have had periodicals which have exercised a great critical influence, such as the *Edinburgh Review* of Jeffrey's and Macaulay's day. We have had periodicals which have published an unusual amount of fine 'creative work' such as Thackeray's *Cornhill*. We have at this day *The Times Literary Supplement*, which reviews, with the utmost possible approximation to completeness, the literary 'output' of the time; we have weekly papers which review the principal books and publish original verse and prose, and monthly papers with articles on Molière or Chateaubriand, Byron or Mr Alfred Noyes. But we have had no paper which has combined as the LONDON MERCURY will do all those various kinds of matter which are required by the lover of books and the practising writer. In our pages will be found original verse and prose in a volume not possible to the weekly paper; full-length literary essays such as have been found only in the politico-literary monthlies; a critical survey of books of all kinds recently published; and other 'features', analogues to some of which may be found, one by one, here and there, but which have never before been brought together within a single cover. THE LONDON MERCURY – save in so far as it will publish reasoned criticism of political (as of other books) – will avoid politics. It will concern itself with none of those issues which are the field of political controversy, save only such – the teaching of English, the fostering of the arts, the preservation of ancient monuments are examples – as impinge directly upon the main sphere of its interests.

The first number – which opened with a new poem by Hardy, 'Going and Staying', and one written in Canada in 1913 by Rupert Brooke, 'It's Not Going To Happen Again' – if it did not fulfil all these aims, certainly whetted the appetites of all those thousands

of poetry-lovers who had accorded such a best-selling welcome to
Brooke's posthumous volume *Poems*, edited by Marsh the year
before.

Someone who wished the new literary journal ill was T. S. Eliot.
He likened Squire to Moses as he enumerated Squire's various
territories in an impromtu poem:

> God from a cloud to Squire spoke
> And breathed command: take thou this Rod
> And smite therewith the living Rock;
> And Squire hearken'd unto God.
>
> And Squire smote the living Rock
> And Lo! the living Rock was wet –
> Whence issue, punctual as the clock
> > *Land and Water*
> > *The New Statesman*
> > *The Owl*
> > *The London Mercury*
> > And the *Westminster Gazette*.

Virginia Woolf also heartily disliked Squire, the aura of male
heartiness, beer-drinking and devotion to cricket. But Woolf and
Eliot never knew him at close range as Alan did, working as
Squire's assistant editor on the *London Mercury*. Here is Alan's
picture of him, in the setting of The Temple Bar, the pub in Fleet
Street, near to the office:

> He was amazingly fluent. Always late, he could write admirable
> prose sense at the printer's last minute, propped against a bar
> counter and despatching his copy page by page, he corrected proofs
> with lightening speed and total accuracy. And although to his own
> family he must have been intolerable – grubby, insolvent, spendthrift,
> unreliable, tipsy, absurd – he exercised spontaneous charm on a
> wide range of friends ... He took himself very seriously indeed. One
> evening he clutched my arm and suddenly said, 'You've no idea, my
> dear fellow, what it is to carry the whole weight of English poetry on
> one's shoulders ...'

One morning Alan Pryce-Jones put his head round the door of
my office and said 'Are you doing anything for lunch? ... I've got
the Ionescos coming. Come along and give me moral support.'

Alan had seen *The Chairs* when it was first produced in Paris and
had been greatly impressed by it. He wrote a leader on Ionesco in
the *Supplement*, the start of Ionesco's recognition and subsequent
vogue in London. When I arrived at Alan's chambers in Albany,
Piccadilly, the other guests were already assembled. Apart from
Ionesco, whose head seem to cry out for Epstein to sculpt it, and
Madame Ionesco, there were two ladies of title whose names I did
not catch, one of whom, I gathered, was a duchess. The party was
completed by Alan's son David, then still an undergraduate at
Oxford reading history. What I had not quite bargained for was
that the conversation would be entirely in French. Neither my
host, his son, nor the other guests seemed to find this the slightest
problem. They all jabbered away to Ionesco, who was himself a
passionate talker, speaking in great outbursts, full of *aperçus* about
politics, not at all absurdist. Had the conversation remained at the
philosophical or literary level I might have just about stammered
my way through it; so many of the words are the same. But over
the roast beef followed by treacle tart (the menu was deliberately
English-traditional) it began to take an alarming turn. One of the
ladies had just had a new central-heating system installed in her
castle in Scotland, and the teething troubles of this came under
scrutiny. Ionesco emerged as being a world-class authority on
central heating. And for the next half-hour we were into pipes,
valves, air-locks, ducts, pressures, water, gas, oil-firing, the ball
being batted merrily around the table until it got to my place
where it landed invariably in the net. I enjoyed meeting the great
man, and Alan thanked me for my moral support, but I arrived
back at Printing House Square in a chastened mood.

By negotiating a labyrinth of corridors you could eventually
reach any part of that huddle of buildings from any other. Teenage
boys, early school-leavers, were employed as messengers to thread
through them taking copy to the composing room. A leader-writer
would press a bell by his desk and a boy would appear to take his
copy to the subs room where, if it was close to the deadline, the
boy would be told to wait while the sub-editor worked on it and
then it would be handed back for further delivery to the Copy
Desk in the Composing Room where more marks would be
inscribed on it by the Man on the Desk (a job given always to a
senior member of the printing staff) who would chop it up into
little slips of paper each containing one or two paragraphs. These
would be farmed out to various linotype operators. They would
each transform the paragraphs into gleaming silver slugs of type

ready to be inked. The slugs would then be assembled to become
a galley-proof. This would then be 'pulled' (i.e. printed manually,
by using a large rolling-pin sticky with printers' ink, on a long
narrow strip of unperforated lavatory-paper) by another man
specially employed as a proof-puller. This first proof together with
the slips of paper containing the original copy would then be
given to a boy who would take the whole package to the Reading-
Room situated on the floor above the Composing Room.

Here in contrast to the clatter of the linotype machines in the
Composing-Room a sussurus of muttering would emanate from
the figures bowed over large desks illuminated by strong concen-
trated light. The boy would give the material to the Head Reader
who would then hand it over to two of his staff. The Readers always
worked in pairs: one to read aloud from the author's script and
the other to check the proof. Their proof-corrections would be
transmitted back to the Desk and a corrected proof would be given
to the sub-editor responsible for the page for which the article was
destined. That proof would still contain quite a number of
mistakes, and further corrections would then need to be made.
No wonder producing newspapers by those means was a costly
business; also a very tiresome one until word-processors, electronic
setting and Rupert Murdoch came along and swept all those
ancient job-creating production practices away overnight.

In those days we used the *Times*'s Composing Room to set and
print our Supplement and we had the complete run of the
building. It had a very narrow lift where you were always in close
proximity to whoever else travelled up with you. One day I found
myself pressed against a beautiful young woman, Sarah Myers,
then on the staff of the *Educational Supplement.* One year after that
first meeting we were married and happily remain so, with three
sons, a daughter-in-law and (at the time of writing) one grandson
and one granddaughter.

By taking what seemed like a half a mile ramble within the
building I could get from my office to hers on the *Ed Supp* where I
could not only advance my marital prospects but hob-nob with
former colleagues like its editor Walter James (a great journalistic
talent scout among new graduates) and with L. R. (Len) Buckley,
John Knight, Jane Bennett, Tyrrell Burgess, Thomas Pakenham,
Irving Wardle, David Cairns. Like others, including Simon Jenkins,
Rivers Scott, Christopher Johnson, Godfrey Hodgson, John Shakespeare, John Pearson, Carol Cattley, most of them had been
initiated into journalism on the *Ed Supp.*

I was also a frequent caller at the office of the *Times's* Arts Page Editor, W. J. Lawrence. He was a burly white-haired Scot with a back-problem and a most curious, much-mimicked diction. He liked to set his free-lance critics, of whom he always employed a considerable number, off against each other, and would dangle carrots of an eventual staff-appointment in front of their noses while putting them to the grindstone. His regular arts page staff at this time included as chief music critic Frank Howes with William (Bo) Mann and Joan Chissell as the musical back-up; the art critic was Alan Clutton-Brock, summarily sacked one day by Haley; the film critic was Evelyn Waugh's friend Dudley Carew, and the theatre critic was A V. Cookman, a rare example of a number two theatre critic (which he had been in the pre-war period to Charles Morgan, the novelist) becoming a number one.

They were all gifted writers, impeccable in their prose as in their dress (with the exception of Mann, who wore a boiler suit with a large CND badge on it as a protest against the sartorial correctness of PHS); Howes, with his round wide-brimmed black hat, looked the part of an old fashioned man-of-letters critic to perfection. Many of the journalists on the *Times* still wore a hat of some kind. Lawrence's assistant Jan Stephens, for instance, sported a neat piece of country headgear. He was a fastidiously efficient sub-editor who took much of the work of running the page off Lawrence's shoulders. He had written regularly for the arts and for the books page from well before the war. It took him about twenty years to be taken on the staff.

Lawrence employed me as one of his free-lance theatre-critics and this continued after I had joined the staff of the *Lit Supp.* It was agreeable work even though the fee was minute and the reviews appeared anonymously. Cookman was often away sick, which meant that I frequently had to stand in for him and to review the mainstream West End productions. The first performance of *Waiting for Godot* in London was at the Arts Theatre on 4 August 1955, directed by Peter Hall. *The Times* commented the following morning: 'His work in two acts holds the stage most wittily, but is it a play? Its significance . . . would seem to be that nothing finally is significant'. The anonymous ass who wrote that was me.

A V. Cookman – always known as Guy – was a small silvery-haired man with a most courteous manner. He was much-loved by his fellow-critics. He had learnt his trade on the *Manchester Guardian* with people like Neville Cardus for his earliest colleagues.

To write prose as smooth as silk was his aim: he had great
admiration for the writings of Logan Pearsall Smith. He had been
a parliamentary sketch-writer before being a theatre critic and said
that his time in the Gallery was good preparation for his present
job. 'Writing a notice all depends on getting off to a good start. If
you can think of a satisfactory first sentence, the rest tends to write
itself . . .' he said.

Cookman would hang his navy blue overcoat with its lovely nap
and his black trilby hat on the hatstand, shoot the cuffs of his pin-
stripe suit, dip a steel-nibbed pen in the inkwell, and start away. If
all went well he would then write non-stop until he pressed the
bell for the copy-boy to take the script. If it wasn't going well, the
page was ripped off the writing-pad, crunched up, and thrown into
the wastepaper basket with a tut-tut until he got a first sentence
that pleased him.

For a journalist he had the sweetest of tempers. I remember
marvelling at his forebearance when an intruder barged into the
office when Cookman was writing a late-night review under
pressure saying: 'Tell me Guy . . . this play at the Savoy by Noël
Coward . . . I was thinking of taking the wife . . . is it any good?
Couldn't really tell from your notice.'

Most journalists would have uttered two short sharp monosyl-
lables; but Guy looked up from his script and said with a gentle
smile: 'Yes, it is reasonably amusing. But I'm a little bit busy now,
old chap. Let's talk about it later.'

If Cookman had ceased to have any ambition beyond his day-to-
day work, he did take a pride in being a part of the *Times* tradition
of theatre-criticism, of writing long dissecting notices. The theatre
had been a prominent feature of the paper's coverage from the
time it began in the eighteenth century. The Bill Page (Leader
Page) was so-called because in the early days that is where the
theatre bills were put; full critical coverage of the London stage
output was a tradition that went back to the Victorian period. John
Oxenford, who also adapted plays from the French, was the
dramatic critic until 1875, followed by J. F. Nisbett and then A B.
Walkley in the 1890s, followed between the wars by Charles
Morgan, the novelist, to whom Cookman had been deputy.

There was a promotional film made about *The Times* before the
war which showed Morgan coming back to PHS after the show
in his Inverness cloak, white tie and tails, entering the lift of
my courtship on his way to write a notice. He was, Cookman told
me, in an agitated frame of mind on that night in 1929, the day

before the Great Crash, when both he and Guy returned from the theatre.

Morgan said: 'I sat next to the Governor of the Bank of England in the theatre tonight. My word, the Market is going to take a nose-dive tomorrow!' Then he sat down at his desk, pushed his programme and notes to one side and telephoned his stockbroker who had gone to bed. He gave him precise instructions about what to do with his portfolio of shares as soon as the market opened in the morning. Then – and only then – he started work on his notice. In those days deadlines were much more flexible than they are now.

After Guy and I had both finished work we would unwind over a drink in the bar on the premises that stayed open for the benefit of the printers. Sometimes the arts page sub, knowing we would be there, would look in with a query in the copy. 'Is that meant to be Ben Jonson?' he'd ask. 'No it's Bjornson – exactly as it is'. '*Who?*' A Norwegian playwright, contemporary of Ibsen's.' 'Never heard of him.' 'I can assure you it is right.'

We would usually be the only journalists there apart from the obituaries editor, one Filmer. He had to be on stand-by until midnight in case someone important should die in time for the last edition. I used to play a rather morbid guessing-game with him over our pints of draught bitter. I had to try to guess how much space he considered certain people were worth. 'Three columns?' I'd say to him, mentioning a well-known contemporary poet. Filmer would shake his head. 'Good heavens, no! Three-quarters of a column at the most – without an illustration.'

They were happy days and nights, though there were hairline cracks in the ice on which we were skating had we heeded them. The *Lit Supp* (in spite of Crook's and Derry's efforts) never did much more than break even, though it flourished editorially. I remember one day arranging for a young critic whom I had met when we were both in America to come in to meet Arthur Crook; his name was John Gross. He went away with some paperbacks to review, an assignment about which he was very excited. He would eventually succeed Arthur as editor in 1977. He abolished anonymity and inaugurated the modern *TLS*. Gross brought about changes worked through by his successors Jeremy Treglown and Ferdinand Mount, editor at the time of writing. Literary life seems inconceivable without the regular appearance of the *TLS*. How did it come to occupy this position in our cultural life?

9

Richmond's realm

During the early nineteen hundreds *The Times* was stretched to keep its readers up to date with notices of new books in what were expansive times for general publishing. In 1901, 262 columns of reviews appeared, 55 columns being devoted to novels. But the book reviews were an optional item of the daily agenda. If parliamentary or foreign coverage – the core of the paper's editorial content – were especially heavy, book-reviews would be held over. In the latter part of 1901, however, the reviews came into their own because that autumn there was no parliamentary session to report, leaving space free for a greatly extended book-review section.

This went down well with readers and in January 1902, when parliament resumed, the paper's editor and general manager decided they would henceforth publish an occasional *Supplement* filled entirely with book-reviews, to be included free of charge with the paper. Without any prior warning to readers, the first *Literary Supplement* appeared on Friday 17 January 1902. The reviews were supported by publishers' advertisements, and complemented by shorter notices and a list of books received. The *Supplement* continued like this every week until 1914, when it was sold separately as a '*Times* publication costing one penny'. In appearance the *Supplement* looked like a half-size edition of *The Times*: it carried a replica of the-then gothic-letter *Times* masthead on its front page with the words *Literary Supplement* in smaller type. All letters for publication were printed addressed to The Editor of *The Times*.

The *Lit Supp* was advertised by *The Times* in other journals with which it was, or had been, associated. An insertion in *Academy and Literature* read:

A special *Literary Supplement* is published with *The Times* on Friday. This *Supplement* is an impartial organ of literary criticism and a comprehensive medium of literary intelligence. It can be had with *The Times* of Friday alone. *The Times Literary Supplement* is also sold with the *Mail* and with the *Times Weekly Edition* upon payment of an additional one penny.

The *Mail* referred to there was not the down-market halfpenny newspaper started by Alfred Harmsworth in 1890, with a wide readership among working men, the new 'gutter press' element of British journalism. Harmsworth had not yet taken control of *The Times* even though he soon would. This *Mail* was one of a number of subsidiary publications issued by *The Times* containing a digest of news and comment; its readership was largely confined to India. The offer of the *Lit Supp* to its subscribers meant that the new journal would have a circulation among the sahibs and their memsahibs whose way of life had been revealed in the early work of Kipling, now back in England at home in Sussex and laying the foundations of his reputation as a storyteller and poet.

The *Lit Supp* was one of a number of enterprises initiated by the *Times*'s energetic Manager, C. F. Moberly Bell (1847–1911). He was desperate to increase revenue, the paper's finances being in a parlous state. It had suffered grievously from its sensational publication of documents gravely damaging to Parnell, later shown to be forgeries.

Moberly Bell was a remarkable character, who in his youth had worked in the cotton trade in Egypt. He had also been a 'stringer' and then a regular Egypt correspondent for *The Times*. He moved among the ruling caste both British and Egyptian in Cairo and Alexandria, a close friend of Lord Cromer. His assessments of Middle Eastern matters in *The Times* frequently contradicted official communiqués from foreign service spokesmen. He was in Egypt during Gordon's fatal adventure in Khartoum. He was recalled to London after an accident boarding a train in the desert when he severely damaged one leg; he had the bone removed from his leg made into a walking-stick.

Back home he was invited to run the *Times* office as assistant to Arthur Walter, the proprietor, descendent of the founding family, and alongside the editor, the learned G. E. Buckle who had come straight to the job from All Souls aged twenty-nine in 1888. It was Moberly Bell who secured the services for the paper of W. P. Monypenny (previously editor of the *Johannesburg Star* and later biographer of Disraeli), Bruce L. Richmond who would become the editor of the *Lit Supp*, Leo Amery, Edward Grigg, and many others.

To extend the general book-coverage Moberly Bell had had the idea of starting a *Literary Gazette* as a separate publication. This appeared as *Literature*, edited by H. D. Traill who died in 1900; in January 1902 the journal was sold to the *Academy*. It then became the *Academy and Literature* which, as we have seen, carried an ad for the newly started *Lit Supp*.

Always on the lookout for ventures that might boost revenue, Moberly Bell joined forces with two American printers (packagers, we should call them), Hooper and Jackson, who saw the possibility of making a nice profit by reprinting *Encyclopaedia Britannica*. They bought the rights to the ninth (1875–88) edition from A. & C. Black and the separate volumes were offered on the instalment plan at a cut price to *Times* readers. The Americans' hunch was correct, even if some purchasers said that much of the information required up-dating; at which a series of *Supplementary* volumes were set in train. At this point a publishing hubris seems to have gripped Moberly Bell and he conceived the idea that the *Times* should start its own Book Club.

In 1905 Moberly Bell wrote to a friend:

> Well the scheme – so far as the poor, unfledged thing can be called a scheme – is, briefly, to open a large West End office of *The Times* well stocked with books, some 25,000 volumes of that sort of quality likely to be asked for by readers of *The Times*. It will not be a complete library; we shall assume that a *Times* reader is not likely to ask for a copy of *Hamlet* or *Vanity Fair* or *Pickwick*. We *may*, for the mere sake of having such books in a catalogue, have one copy of such works, but I suppose (and all this detail is likely to change) that we shall have most of the books of the last five years that have survived. We calculate that out of about 6000 books published each year in England there are about 2000 which are new editions, reprints, pamphlets and expensive illustrated books (*de luxe*) which

no library lends. That makes 4000 *ordinary* books per year. If we take
five years, that is 20,000, and of those 20,000 how many have survived
the five years! I should say 15 per cent would be a large estimate.
Then you get 3000 books from which subscribers can choose. Of the
more recent books and of the more alive books there will be many
copies; of the older books and of dying books there will be less. This
will be the nucleus on which we will build.

This led to *The Times*, with an investment from the Americans,
opening its own Book Club. In 1905 it took premises in 93 New
Bond Street where it operated a circulating library, a direct
challenge to Mudies and others. It soon ran into difficulties when
it offered a free subscription to the Book Club to subscribers to
the newspaper. And there was an angry response from publishers
to the new venture when The Times Book Club began its practice
of offering for sale *ex libris* books (those for which the demand
from its library subscribers had begun to peter out) at a price well
below the published price. The Net Book Agreement between
publishers and booksellers had come into force in 1900. A Book
War – similar to that almost a hundred years later, when the NBA
finally collapsed – began. This time it was the publishers, determined the NBA should be upheld, who won. It is against this
background that the *Lit Supp* emerged.

The member of staff mainly responsible for the book-reviews in
the main paper was Richard Thursfield, also the paper's naval
correspondent. In 1901 Moberly Bell asked Thursfield to compile
an anthology of extracts from *The Times* over the previous decade;
they made a book that sold well. Thursfield (later Sir Richard) was
the first person to be put in charge of the new *Lit Supp* but was
soon replaced by his colleague Bruce Richmond who, educated at
Winchester and New College, a Greats (*literae humaniores*) graduate, had come to the paper from Oxford by invitation in 1899.

A Wykehamist–Oxford network regularly provided top members
of the editorial staff, especially men from New College and Balliol.
Humphry Ward, husband of the novelist, a leader-writer until
demoted to art critic, was such another. Richmond was assistant to
Buckle, and thus at the centre of the paper's inner counsels. He
attended the daily editorial conference and belonged to the group
who were privy to all important editorial decisions. When Rich-

mond took on his new work he did not at once relinquish his old; his job-description might have been formulated 'assistant to the editor with responsibility for the *Lit Supp*'.

Richmond possessed the ability to recognise and nurture reviewing and writing talent across a wide range of interests. Apart from his *Lit Supp* reviewers he was responsible for people such as A. B. Walkley, the dramatic critic, Bernard Darwin, the golf correspondent, and Arthur Clutton-Brock (father of Alan) who wrote about gardening as well as reviewing books, becoming established on the paper. Harold Child, a Brasenose, Oxford graduate who when he went down had been briefly and unhappily a lawyer's clerk, and then briefly and happily but unsuccessfully an actor, recalled how 'my old Winchester friend Bruce Richmond, had waved his magic wand and transformed me into a writer for his newly created *Literary Supplement* of *The Times*'.

When he edited the *Lit Supp* Richmond worked on the main editorial floor in Room Number Five. He sat at a big mahogany desk, the drawers of which he filled with reviewers' copy, much of it hand-written. In those days, and indeed until well into the 1950s, the printers were prepared to set from hand-written copy; they received extra pay if it was deemed especially difficult to read. A script of a review by, say, Bernard Darwin would be cut up into 'takes' for setting; after it was printed the ribbons of paper to which the script had been reduced would be stored for six months in the Reading Room and then destroyed; thousands of pounds-worth of literary manuscripts in current values must have gone like that into the incinerator. An even more astronomical sum would be raised today by the sale of Richmond's letters from his reviewers, all of which he destroyed. There was a tradition among *Times* editors that correspondence should be destroyed lest it fell into the wrong hands. Whereas most of Moberly Bell's memoranda survive, none of Richmond's have. Unlike Bell, Richmond was a man who instinctively kept everything very close to his chest. He produced his *Supplement* each week with one assistant, F. T. Dalton, and he was also helped by Harold Child, the number two dramatic critic. During his lifetime Richmond published no original literary work of any kind; the only manuscript he left behind was a commonplace book filled with quotations. He was one of those editors who did not write himself.

Louis Heren, who began his life on *The Times* as a copy boy, was sitting in his cubby-hole reading a book, waiting for some copy to deliver, when Richmond brushed by him on his way to the editor's office for the morning conference. 'Hello,' he said, 'what's that?' and took hold of the book, *Lord Jim*. Handing it back, he added: 'You'll find *Nostromo* is much better.' Heren, who ended his career as foreign editor and deputy editor of *The Times*, but known thereafter to Richmond as 'our literary copy boy', confessed before his death in 1995 to even then preferring *Lord Jim* to *Nostromo*. Other employees of the newspaper recall Richmond's urbanity; the disarming manner with which he could turn down a suggestion for a review (a great asset in a lit ed). Richmond's wife Elena (née Rathbone) was a famous beauty much involved in London musical life. When Richmond was not editing he would help Elena organise subscription concerts and recitals.

Richmond was not the sole occupant of Room Five. Others included Dr H. J. Colles, the *Times* music critic; Charles W. Brodribb, another classicist and a leader-writer, compiler of the Old & True column; and the invaluable Child, the newspaper's cultural odd-job man (obits, leaders especially light leaders, arts features in addition to his book and play reviews). Child's prose may be sampled in the old brown-and-gold Cambridge Shake-speare volumes edited by Quiller-Couch and Dover Wilson, where his accounts of the stage history of each play are given after the main introductions. Apart from that he is completely forgotten; yet he was a mainstay of the *Times* arts pages and the *Lit Supp* over a great many years, contributing hundreds of anonymous reviews. He was a godsend to Richmond, who knew that he always had Child for anything tricky that needed to be reviewed in-house.

Apart from his PHS colleagues Richmond had the whole literary world of London, Oxford and Cambridge to choose from for his reviewers. There was hardly anyone at that time who did not regard it as an honour to review anonymously for the *Supplement* for a minuscule fee. Richmond's flair for picking reviewers went with a willingness to try young, unknown writers. Middleton Murry's earliest regular reviewing job was covering new French writing from Paris for Richmond.

When, as we shall see, Murry became editor of the *Athenaeum* at the end of the First World War, it was Richard Aldington who took over the reviewing of French books in the *Lit Supp*. Regular foreign books coverage was a feature of the paper then. Richmond always

read the book-reviews in the *Athenaeum* under Murry; he was
particularly struck by some on poetry over the initials TSE; and he
asked Aldington if he knew the writer. Aldington told him he was
an American-born poet in his early thirties based in London who
had a job in the foreign department at the Head Office of Lloyd's
Bank. Richmond then requested Aldington to bring this writer,
T. S. Eliot, along to Room 5. It would seem the meeting occurred
in 1920.

There is still a picture of the scene in my mind [wrote Eliot]: the
chief figure a man with a kind of bird-like quality, a bird-like alertness
of eye, body and mind. I remember his quickness to put the
newcomer at ease; and the suggestion in his mien and movement of
an underlying strength of character and tenacity of purpose. But to
be summoned to the presence of the Editor of *The Times Literary
Supplement* and to be invited to write for it was to have reached the
top rung of the ladder of literary journalism: I was overawed, by *The
Times* offices themselves, by the importance of the occasion, and in
spite of the cordial warmth of the greeting by the great editor
himself.

It was at Richmond's behest that Eliot began to write a series of
reviews of books on Elizabethan and Jacobean literature. In them
Eliot made fresh judgements about Donne, Middleton, Ben
Jonson, that, it is hardly an exaggeration to say, changed the face
of literary criticism in the twentieth century. It was Richmond who
commissioned Eliot to writer a leader for the *Lit Supp* on Bishop
Lancelot Andrewes. At a lunch to which he had invited Eliot,
Richmond discovered (over perhaps the Double Gloucester cheese
of which Richmond was especially fond) that Eliot had some
urgent thoughts about the prose of the sixteenth century divine. A
leader on Andrews was commissioned and soon printed.

When he became an editor himself, of the *Criterion*, Eliot's role-
model was Bruce Richmond. He learnt from him the value of
having a clerisy of contributors known personally to the editor.
Many of the reviewers he used regularly on the *Criterion* were, Eliot
admitted, poached from the *Lit Supp*. Another lesson Eliot learnt
through writing for Richmond was how to write anonymously.

I am firmly convinced that every young literary critic should learn
to write for some periodical in which his contributions will be
anonymous. Richmond did not hesitate to object or delete, and I

had always to admit that he was right. I learnt to moderate my
dislikes and crotchets, to write in a temperate and impartial way; I
learnt that some things are permissible when they appear over one's
name, which become tasteless eccentricity or unseemly violence
when unsigned. The writer of the anonymous article or review must
subdue himself to his editor – but the editor must be a man to whom
the editor can subdue himself and preserve his self-respect. It is also
necessary that the editor should read every word of what he prints;
for he is much more deeply inculpated in what he prints anonymously, than in what he prints over the writer's name.

Some of Richmond's regular reviewers were from the new
generation of women writers such as Virginia Stephen, whose
association with the *Supplement* started in 1905, preceding her
marriage to Leonard Woolf in 1912. She was a *Lit Supp* reviewer
until her death in 1941, tailing off in the number of her reviews
per year towards the end but out-lasting Richmond.

Leslie Stephen's library in the London house at Hyde Park Gate,
Kensington – most of the contents of which his youngest daughter
Virginia had absorbed by the time she was 20 – was a foundation-
course for a career as a reviewer and literary critic. When in 1904
Stephen died, a new way of life, in which he was no longer the
epicentre, began for Virginia that soon included regular book-
reviewing. She had the kind of friends and contacts who could put
her in touch with biddable lit eds willing to try her out. In February
1905 she wrote to her cousin and confidante Emma Vaughan:

> I am realising the ambition of our youth, and actually making
> money – which, however, I spend long before I make. I am writing
> for – now for my boast –
> The Times Lit. Supplement
> The Academy
> The National Review
> The Guardian
> – Aint that respectable.

The *Guardian* was a newspaper for the clergy. It was in its weekly
review of the arts and books that the talent of VW (as I shall call
her from now on) first emerged, in a review of a novel by W. D.
Howells, himself a veteran literary journalist on the *Atlantic Monthly*
as well as being a celebrated American exponent of realism in the
novel and a friend of her father's. If he ever saw VW's piece he

could hardly have failed to be impressed by the judicious grasp of the novel shown by this reviewer in such a short review.

The *Guardian* may seem an incongruous platform for the future *doyenne* of Bloomsbury and she soon wearied of conforming to its pious Anglo-Catholic tone, but it hardly matters where the novice-reviewer first appears in print. What does matter is that she should receive a regular flow of books, establish an amicable working relation with a lit ed whom she respects, and that the reviews she writes should appear without inordinate delay.

While keeping her *Guardian* connection going, VW looked around for other reviewing opportunities in the periodical press. The *Cornhill* was then edited by Reginald Smith, a barrister, an Old Etonian and a director of the publishers, Smith, Elder and Co. His father-in-law, George Smith, Charlotte Brontë's publisher, had launched the journal. Wearing his publishing hat, Smith was one of the chief opponents of Moberly Bell's Times Book Club retail price-cutting wheeze, but as an editor he was kindly disposed to the notion of including a signed review of a recently published book to be written alternately by VW and her friend Lady Eleanor (Nelly) Cecil. Here VW would use her early by-line, Virginia Stephen.

Before she started Smith made suggestions for a heading for the new feature.

Dont you think "Our book box" is *not* the right name? R. Smith suggests it this morning. Personally I should like something simpler, and not jocular. I dont know what you feel [VW. writes to Nelly]. "A monthly review" "The book of the month" "Our review" "The Reviewers Choice" – "The Book on the Table" – Lord how bad they all are. "A book! The Monthly Book" and that suggests nurse – Only I think it should be something formal and not trivial and chatty.

One of the books Nelly (who later became a reader of manuscripts for John Murray) had to review for the *Cornhill* was May Sinclair's novel *The Helpmate* (1907). VW had her doubts about this review, as she explained to Violet Dickinson:

Well, going through it again, I think it is fairly clear, that the whole of Nelly's objection to Miss Sinclair is a moral one. She thinks that Miss S. holds a bad man up to our admiration . . . I think her position is quite tenable *if* she could explain her reason for thinking that morality is essential to art – But this she refuses to do.

It was a question that would greatly exercise the Bloomsbury Group in the years to come; a more urgent problem arose over the choice of what *kind* of books they should review for the *Cornhill*. VW plumped for the literary ones. Her editor whom she called 'a good grocer' wanted her to do the ones of more general interest, especially biographies. Thus when it was a choice between doing the life of John Delane, the former editor of *The Times*, and a new volume of poetry by the poet Lascelles Abercrombie, he wanted her to do the former and she wanted to do the latter. Delane, the paper's editor during the Crimean War, whose support was eagerly sought by prime ministers and others, was a massively fascinating subject; yet hardly one for a non-political young woman fairly new to reviewing to cope with. But Smith insisted: 'Nay, my dear Miss Stephen, there is no comparison, for real human interest, which the *Cornhill* seeks, between Delane and Mr Abercrombie.'

Smith had his way and her reviews were almost all of biographies: Delane, Sarah Bernhardt, Lady Dorothy Nevill, Elizabeth Lady Holland, Theodore Roosevelt. 'I really believe,' Smith told her, 'that if you put heart and head into it, you will make a mark in reviewing.' He was perfectly right but that mark was to be made – anonymously – in the columns of the *Lit Supp*.

The first parcel Bruce Richmond sent her contained a volume on the Medicis by Edith Sichel, an earnest blue-stocking who stood for everything that VW most disliked in a writer, and VW had the salutary experience of having the review she wrote of this book turned down. Richmond explained that reviews for the *Lit Supp* needed to be more 'academic' than the style in which hers was written – an example of his tact.

But after this hiccup, the flow of Woolf reviews in the paper was fairly constant. She soon discovered that as a regular book-reviewer one becomes an expert on all manner of topics hitherto only remotely within one's ken. 'You will be surprised to hear', she writes to Violet on 30 April 1905, 'that I am authority on Spain – but so it is.' This was when she was sent *Letters from Catalonia and Other Parts of Spain* by Rowland Thirlmere (the pen-name of John Walker) and *The Land of the Blessed Virgin: Sketches and Impressions in Andulasia* by W. S. Maugham (which she enjoyed).

Spain was something a reviewer could easily ad-lib about. But what was there for her to say concerning the early days of the Wesleyan revival on the coast of Sussex? That was the subject of *The Letter Killeth* by A C. Inchbold (Mrs Stanley Inchbold), more a

book for a cleric to review in the *Guardian*, one might have
thought. Nonetheless Richmond sent it along and VW. obliged.
Many of the novels she reviewed, such as W. E. Norris's *Lone Marie*,
Dorothea Gerard's *The Compromise*, Vincent Brown's *Mrs Grundy's
Crucifix*, have as their sole claim on the attention of posterity the
fact that she reviewed them; but occasionally among all the dross
there appears one that has stood the test of time, for example
Edith Wharton's *The House of Mirth*, which VW. reviewed for the
Guardian.

> She gives us, as we do not remember to have seen it given before,
> a picture of that "set" in New York society which contains not only
> all that is wealthiest, but also that, for whatever reason, is most
> exclusive . . . There is no doubt that Mrs Wharton has so illuminated
> *The House of Mirth* for us that we shall not soon forget it.

Although VW came to review on an almost weekly basis for
Richmond, she never had any kind of formal contract. And when
there was a temporary lull in the flow of books, as sometimes there
is bound to be however highly valued the reviewer, VW would
wonder whether she had been sacked. Then she would console
herself by declaring she was glad of the opportunity to get on with
the current novel. In the midst of these sour grape-like reflections
the next parcel of review books would arrive and there would be
an opposite reaction.

> My dismissal is revoked. A large book on Pepys arrived which I
> spent the evening reading, & now another on Swinburne awaits me
> at the Railway station. I'm divided whether one likes to have books,
> or to write fiction without interruption.

In the end reviewing became, she said, the romance of her life.

Up to now I have aimed to follow the fortunes in each chapter of
one selected newspaper or journal's books section; but it is
necessary at this point to consider some other metropolitan
journals with which Richmond had reviewers in common in order
to give an impression of the nature of book-reviewing in the first
half of the present century and the comparatively small number of
individuals who dominated it. Most of the regular reviewers knew
each other well and frequently met socially. Some were related

through family or closely linked in other ways, professionally and amorously. When from time to time they ceased to be reviewers and became authors, they would put pressure on each other to get their own books reviewed.

Lytton Strachey was a regular reviewer for the *Spectator*, having made his début as a reviewer at about the same time VW made hers. The editor John St Loe Strachey employed his two cousins, James as his secretary-assistant, and Lytton, James's brother, to write a substantial review every week. The arrangement with Lytton lasted from the autumn of 1907 until April 1909; afterwards Lytton continued as a frequent *Spectator* reviewer until 1914.

St Loe combined being the journal's editor with being its lit ed and its every other ed. He was always mindful of the outlook of his army of subscribers who, like those of the *Guardian*, were mainly clergy. It was said that his journal was on the breakfast table of every vicarage in the country. We get an impression of St Loe Strachey at work from James Strachey, who later in life became a psychoanalyst and translator of Freud:

> St Loe was a tremendously fluent talker, producing floods of remarkable ideas and amusing anecdotes – many of which would have startled the vicarages. These he poured over the heads of his visitors at top speed, interlaced with with detailed instructions about what was to be written in the leader, the sermon or the review concerned. The visitors had hardly a moment for breathing before they were whirled out of the room. But this was not all. On Thursday afternoons, silent, perhaps for the first time in the week, St Loe sat back comfortably in a chintz-covered armchair with a pencil in his hand, and read through the galley proofs of the whole of the forthcoming issue. He altered a word here and there, he scribbled a fresh sentence in the margin, he struck out a whole paragraph and replaced it by one of his own. The final outcome was that each number of *The Spectator*, from the opening paragraphs of "News of the Week" to the final series of notes on "Current Literature", represented St Loe's opinions, expressed St Loe's policies and, most striking of all, was written in St Loe's literary style, with his unmistakable editorial first person plural. Needless to say, nothing that appeared in the paper was signed, except in the voluminous correspondence columns.

Thanks to James Strachey's preservation of his brother's copy, we can actually watch St Loe altering the sense of a passage by

Lytton. In a piece on Bacon, for example, marking the tercentenary of his election as Treasurer of Gray's Inn, Lytton had admiringly pointed to Bacon's Essay 'On Simulation and Dissimulation'.

> Bacon [he wrote] discusses with wonderful subtlety and judgment
> the various shades of concealment and deceit, the precise circum
> stances in which they are permissible and the rules which should
> guide a good man in his use of them.

In the article as printed, St Loe inserted before 'they are permissible' the words 'in his opinion'; and he changed 'the rules which
should guide a good man' to 'the rules which he holds should
guide a good man'. Bacon's apothegm is then quoted:

> The best composition and temperature is, to have openness in
> fame and opinion; secrecy in habit; dissimulation in seasonable use;
> and a power to feign if there be no remedy.

In case there should be any doubt in the reader's mind as to the
paper's line on the above precepts, St Loe added:

> We may not like his conclusion – for ourselves, we repudiate it as
> immoral and ignoble – but who can deny that is an epitome of the
> worldly wisdom on the matter under consideration?

Clive Bell had similar problems on the *Athenaeum* as he revealed
when his reviews were reprinted in book form under the title *Pot-
Boilers* in 1918. The *Athenaeum* was a weekly journal read by
academics and clubmen that prided itself on its high standards in
respect of its reviews of books and arts. It had been started to
strike a blow for freedom from all pressures both political and
commercial in reviewing. Ever since the eighteenth century,
periodical journalism had in its reviews of books been bedevilled
by 'puffery'. A new era of reviewing dawned when Charles Wentworth Dilke (grandfather of the celebrated radical MP) took
control of the *Athenaeum* in 1830 and established it as a forum for
fair-minded, impartial discussion of books while offering news of
what was happening abroad in publishing as well as at home.
When Bell joined it, at the start of the twentieth century, in
addition to reviews and general articles such as those by J. Dover
Wilson on Shakespeare, it printed regular columns of diverse
paragraphs headed 'Literary Gossip' and 'Art Gossip'.

Bell prefaced his collection with an open letter to Geoffrey
Whitworth, his publishing editor at Chatto. Reviewing anonymously for the *Athenaeum*, Bell explained, gave one a strong sense
of corporate identity:

> Not one of us, I am sure, would have expressed anything but what
> he thought and felt, but we all hoped that our thoughts and feelings
> would not be too dissimilar from those of our presiding genius,
> Athene the wise, our eponymous goddess; because if they were, her
> high priest, albeit one of the most charming and accomplished
> people in Fleet Street [Vernon Rendall] or thereabouts [Adelphi
> Terrace] stood ready with the inexorable blue pencil to smite once
> and smite no more.

Bell then added this caveat to the reader of the collection:

> Re-reading these articles – some of which were written nine or ten
> years ago – I come on such phrases as 'this is a notable achievement',
> 'his equipment is not really strong,' and I wonder, of course, what
> the devil I did say. No doubt it was something definite and particular,
> for in those days I was a most conscientious writer; but what subtle
> limitation, what delicately suggested reference, what finely qualifying
> phrase, what treasure of my critical nonage lies buried beneath this
> 'getting out' formula I cannot now remember.

When *Pot-Boilers* was published Bell, at the age of thirty-seven,
frequented places like the Friday Club in London where he would
meet his fellow reviewers. He was high on the visitors' list at
Garsington Manor, where he would meet them all again during a
long weekend as a guest of that generous, long-suffering hostess,
Ottoline Morrell; and when he was in town in the evening with
nothing better to do he would sit at one of the marble-top tables
of the Café Royal:

> He gives, or wishes to give [wrote VW] the impression that he sits
> drinking in the Café Royal with Mary [Hutchinson, his mistress] &
> the young poets & painters drift up, & he knows them all, & between
> them they settle the business. His book is stout morality & not very
> good criticism. He seems to have little natural insight into literature.
> Roger [Fry] declares that he doesn't know about pictures. On the
> other hand he has a strong English sense of morality.

But this (from someone who had nervously shown him her first novel in typescript for his comments) is to do him less than justice. Bell was an admirably eclectic and provocative journalist. Apart from reviews of exhibitions of work by Persian miniaturists, Chinese print-makers, French post-impressionists and modern British painters (in which he had no hesitation in naming his wife, Vanessa Bell, as among the most important), he reviews with authority books on Boswell, Peacock, Trelawny, Carlyle, Ibsen. His piece on 'Sophocles in London' is one of several on the drama of Ancient Greece in which he takes the likes of Gilbert Murray to task with extended quotations in the original Greek. Among masters of significant form he names Aeschylus, an insight worth a moment or two's consideration. The doctrine had already come under withering attack in rival journals long before Leavis dealt it the final body-blow. Bell spiritedly defended it.

Bell's volume also contains an attack on the critical standards of Arnold Bennett, challenging his judgment on contemporary novelists. 'In my judgment,' said Bell, 'Mr Wells, Mr George Moore and the late Sir John Galsworthy [a joke? – Galsworthy always refused a knighthood; nor was there anything 'late' about him at that time, he remained alive and active until 1933] are not artists at all.' Then Bell puts forward his own nominees for 'our three best living novelists ... Hardy, Conrad, and Virginia Woolf'.

Nineteen-eighteen saw the publication in book-form of further collections of reviews: Desmond MacCarthy's earliest collection, *Remnants,* and *Books in General* by 'Solomon Eagle', the *nom de plume* J. C. Squire used in the *New Statesman.* As its literary editor Squire had contributed a weekly article under the title of 'Books in General' since the paper began in 1913. The *Lit Supp* commented on Squire's collection:

> Perhaps it is unnecessary to feel a slight pang of consideration for Solomon Eagle when he talks of papers 'contributed weekly, without interruption, to the *New Statesman* since April 1913'. But it is difficult when a writer hopes that he has produced a book to read 'without tedium for ten minutes before one goes to sleep' not to feel slightly ashamed of oneself, as a single head of the many-headed beast, for not having gone to sleep hours ago.

Was that from the nimble pen of Harold Child? Strachey was equally sarcastic when commenting on MacCarthy's *Remnants* privately in a letter to Clive Bell:

> a book in the best of taste. But it's not difficult to think that the milk has been standing a very long time, and that though the cream is excellent, there's not much of it. However, nowadays, it would be absurd to complain of anything that is genuinely charming.

VW, in an unguarded moment, had promised to review *Remnants:*

> His book comes out on Monday; he, though forgetting everything, yet remembers a vague joking promise of mine, uttered at least a year ago, to review it in the *Times*. He is sending me a copy. He wants to stay here. I'm now debating how to deal with these damned authors –

Strachey was another of those 'damned authors' who tried to get VW to review his forthcoming book, *Eminent Victorians*. She had heard parts of it read by Strachey and had already begun to form an opinion. She felt on the strength of what she had heard that she could review it, in spite of her closeness to the author, and she told him she would. She then had the delicate task of approaching Richmond with a request to review two books by people he knew were among her closest friends. Richmond had, it seems, no objection to her proposal. 'Certainly,' he said, 'if you can keep it a secret'. But, as she confided to her Diary:

> I couldn't promise to do this, & therefore wrote to tell him not to send them. And now I must inform Desmond and Strachey. They won't suffer really I believe but they will be anxious instead of safe, & I'm in two minds as to whether I'm glad or sorry. I think I could have said some very clever things, & a few true things, but undoubtedly one cant avoid a certain uneasiness in writing formally of people one knows so well.

When she explained the situation to Strachey, she put the responsibility for the decision onto Richmond:

> I wrote to ask Richmond to let me do your book. He answers that though willing and anxious that I should, he has to make it a rule

that reviewers don't review their friends – not that he's afraid I
should be partial, but that people would guess, and *say* I was partial,
which he admits to be base on his part, but he's afraid he must stick
to it. I'm very sorry.

(An example of what Bacon in the above quotation described as
'dissimulation in seasonable use; and a power to feign if there be
no remedy'.)

In the event *Eminent Victorians* was from the moment of publication greeted by a chorus of praise from reviewers; with one notable
exception – the *Lit Supp*, where it does not appear to have been
reviewed at all. After VW had withdrawn, Richmond was either
unable or unwilling to find a reviewer for it; or it might even be
that he commissioned a review which he then he decided not to
use.

Edmund Gosse's anger had been aroused by Strachey's vignette
of his friend Lord Cromer (Evelyn Baring) in the essay on General
Gordon and wrote to the *Lit Supp* on the matter. Under the
heading 'The Character of Lord Cromer', Gosse quoted Strachey
where he says of Baring, 'he found it easy to despise those with
whom he came into contact'. Gosse commented:

> I do not know what intimacy Mr Strachey enjoyed with Lord
> Cromer but he has painted a picture of him which is a caricature
> and not a good-natured one. In his description our friend is hardly
> to be recognised. The conversation of Lord Cromer was copious; it
> was generally stimulating and often delicious. It combined warmth
> of feeling with vivacity of expression. Lord Cromer was accessible
> and responsive.

Strachey responded the following week with a letter to the editor
in which he said:

> All this may have been perfectly true in the drawing-room and at
> the dinner-table; but the question whether the temper of Lord
> Cromer's mind was not essentially cautious secretive and diplomatic
> cannot be determined by a test of that superficial kind.

That defence was knocked down in the *Lit Supp* of 18 July by Lord
Sanderson, who had been Permanent Under Secretary of State for
Foreign Affairs during the crucial period 1894–1906:

I doubt if Mr Strachey quite realises the nature and extent of the dissent which his description has excited. As far as my own experience goes, there is no one possessed of even a superficial knowledge of Lord Cromer who has not received it with a certain amount of ridicule. Mr Strachey explains that when he wrote that 'the East meant very little to Sir Evelyn Baring' who 'took no interest in it', he meant that Sir Evelyn Baring was only interested in the work of Eastern administration. But Lord Cromer's whole life, apart from family ties and private friendships, was in his work; and one of the mainsprings of his activity was a feeling of strong practical sympathy for the toiling inarticulate millions whose interests were under his care, and of eager inquiry into their habits of life and models of thought. Mr Strachey may put a low value on this kind of interest – he may prefer something more poetical, more sentimental, less controlled by plain common sense, but it would be absurd to deny it . . .

Meanwhile Mrs Humphry Ward, granddaughter of Arnold of Rugby, weighed in. She was distinctly unamused by Strachey's account of her forbear:

Sir –

I wonder if you will allow me, as an old literary worker and reviewer, to write a few words of protest against the praise – for the most part unqualified – which has been lavished on Lytton Strachey's book *Eminent Victorians*. Surely Mr Strachey has done one of the easiest things in the world, if only a man had, not the mind but the *heart* – to do it. I recall Sainte-Beuve's phrase: 'De toutes les dispositions de l'esprit, celle qui est le moins intelligente c'est l'ironie.' [Of all attitudes of mind, the least intelligent is irony.] Why? Because it is the least human; and the critic who uses it as his main instrument, in the judgment of men and women, is therefore doomed to failure. The coarse caricature of my grandfather, Arnold of Rugby, which the book contains, does not trouble me much. He will, I think, survive it. But the concluding pages of the article on Miss Nightingale, and – to take a minor point – the handling of that soldier of freedom, Arthur Clough, are to my mind unforgivable. Is this a moment when the same spirit of sheer brutality which we are fighting in the military field should be allowed, without resistance, because it is clever or immediately effective – the Prussian plea! – to penetrate the field of English letters? It has already, as we know, affected German literature and German thought with disastrous results. Mr Lytton Strachey's book seems to me a portent that may well make us all think.

Yours obediently,

Mary A. Ward

Stocks, Tring.

These letters were in effect the *Lit Supp's* review of *Eminent Victorians*. Hoisting Strachey with the petard of Sainte-Beuve was a clever adversarial tactic, as was the identification of his strategies with Prussian military might. Lytton and James Strachey were both pacifists.

Occasionally Richmond relaxed the anonymity rule to the extent of having a signed article or essay of wider scope than a mere review by someone of the eminence of Max Beerbohm on the front page. The author's by-line would appear, slightly apologetically, in brackets.

Richmond approached Henry James to see whether he would agree to write one of these front-page articles on the work of the younger generation of English novelists. Over seventy and in poor health, but still industrious, James, to Richmond's surprise and delight, acceded to the request. His one proviso was he wished to be selective about the novelists discussed. The result was an assassination, with consequences almost as dire as those in Sarajevo six months later.

Henry James's appraisal 'The Younger Generation' took the form originally of two 'fronts' in the *Supplement*, the first on 19 March 1914 and the second on 2 April 1914. They were later merged and expanded as the essay 'Notes on Novelists'.

Unlike George Eliot, who had returned the two volumes of *The Europeans* he had once sent her, unread, James kept abreast of the work of his juniors. Some of them anyway. He applied himself to the task of an assessment of them with considerable relish, and began by deploring the marked absence in England of serious criticism of the contemporary novel. He felt that such an absence was symptomatic of the contempt in which the novel was held in England. Or, in James-speak:

> We feel it not to be the paradox it may at the first blush seem that the state of the novel in England at the present time is virtually very

much the state of criticism itself; and this moreover, at the risk
perhaps of some added appearance of perverse remark, by the very
reason that we see criticism so much in abeyance.

By 'criticism' in that tortuous opening James does not mean the
reviewing of fiction in periodicals. There was plenty of that going
on, as we have seen. Nor does he mean discussions about the novel
in contemporary society, its optimum length and so on. The novel
was often discussed in these terms; the *Westminster Gazette,* for
instance, had run a correspondence over several issues on the
vexed question of how long a novel ought to be. H. G. Wells had
given a lecture on 'The Scope of the Novel' in 1911 in the Times
Book Club to some of its customers, printed in 1914 as 'The
Contemporary Novel'. Wells attacked what he called the Weary
Giant view of the novel, the novel as a means of relaxation for
tired businessmen. James had no quarrel with Wells's forthright
attempt to up-grade the standing of the form. It was the positive
aspect of Wells's claims for the novel that provoked his disagree-
ment: 'So far as I can see, [said Wells], it is the only medium
through which we can discuss the great majority of the problems
which are being raised in such bristling multitude by our contemporary social development' – the novel as an agent of social
change. Such a novel would not, in Wells's view, care about
incurring critical accusations of irrelevance in what it included
alongside the narrative, particularly in this 'Balfourian age' of
doubt over Victorian certainties. It would permit the author to
come forward from time to time in his own person, if he so wished,
and directly address the reader. 'Nearly all the novels that have, by
the lapse of time, reached an assured position of recognised
greatness, are not only saturated in the personality of the author,
but have in addition quite unaffected personal outbreaks.'
Wells's lecture was an eloquent plea for a more serious kind of
novel. Among his audience on that hot May day in 1911 was his
friend Arnold Bennett:

> Driven by curiosity I went to hear Mr H. G. Wells's lecture last
> Thursday at the Times Book Club on 'The Scope of the Novel'.
> Despite the physical conditions of heat, and noise, and an open
> window exactly behind the lecturer (whose voice thus flowed just as
> much into a back street as into the ears of his auditors), the affair
> was a success, and it is to be hoped that the Times Book Club will
> pursue the enterprise further. It was indeed a remarkable phenom-

enon: a first-class artist speaking the truth about fiction to a crowd of library subscribers! Mr Wells was above all defiant; he contrived to put in some very plain speaking about Thackeray, and he finished by asserting that it was futile for the fashionable public to murmur against the intellectual demands of the best modern fiction – there was going to be no change unless it might be a change in the direction of the more severe, the more candid and the more exhaustively curious.

The kind of novel Wells was proposing was the kind of novel he himself was now writing, novels like *Ann Veronica*, which had been trounced in St Loe's *Spectator*. It was not a view that Henry James, who held a much more purist conception of what a novel should be could endorse. James was in the position of a theologian like (say) Edward Norman faced by the onset of Liberation Theology. It was precisely that authorial *saturation*, that waywardness and disregard for the formal aspect, the unity of the novel, that James made the focal-point of his survey in the *Lit Supp*.

The novelists whose work James discussed in addition to that of Wells were Hugh Walpole, Compton Mackenzie, Arnold Bennett, Gilbert Cannan, Joseph Conrad and D. H. Lawrence (only *Sons and Lovers* had appeared of Lawrence's major work and James dealt with him summarily compared to the others). As a kind of afterthought, he added his friend Edith Wharton. Most of them were known to James and not all were young (in the usual meaning of the word). Edith Wharton was 52, Wells was 48, Bennett was 47, Compton Mackenzie was 31, Walpole was 30. The significant omission is Galsworthy, who was 47 but who had only published one Forsyte novel, *A Man of Property*; the rest of the *Saga* belongs to the 1920s. Maugham at 40 was known primarily as a playwright but was soon to publish *Of Human Bondage* to which the term 'saturation' would equally well apply. James uses it to describe novels such as *Clayhanger, Tono-Bungay, Kipps*, and even *Sons and Lovers*.

James judged them by the standards exemplified in his own work. With the exception of Wharton, and possibly Conrad, they fell woefully short of those rigorous standards. Here is a little taste of his flow at a point where James turns from Bennett to Wells:

what are we to say of Mr Wells who, a novelist very much as Lord Bacon was a philosopher, affects us as taking all knowledge for his province and as inspiring us to the very highest degree the confidence enjoyed by himself – enjoyed, we feel, with a breadth with which it has been given no one of his fellow craftsmen to enjoy anything. If confidence alone could lead [us?] utterly captive we should all be huddled in a bunch at Mr Wells's heels – which is indeed where we *are* abjectly gathered as far as that force does operate.

Some novelists might have been pleased by that but Wells, discerning derision beneath the surface, was very cross. We have seen how violently Wells reacted to what he considered to be hostile criticism of his work by one-time friends or lovers. He was angry now because he was perceptive enough to see just what James was getting at. As well as 'that force' (confidence) and 'all knowledge' (the detailed observation of external reality and the discursive play of mind in which the text of the novel is saturated) the novelist, James insisted, requires a penetration into the consciousness of his characters that he thought Bennett and Wells lacked.

While James's strictures were being absorbed by Wells and Bennett, war broke out in France and Belgium. Though everyone's life was changed in the most fundamental way, the discourse about the novel continued through the war and beyond it. The four years of war were indeed ones of intense literary activity in England. Conscription was not enforced until 1916 and those members of the Bloomsbury set who were writers or painters carried on with their writing, painting and reviewing. They were almost all pacifists, as were both Ottoline and Philip Morrell. Much of the pacifist effort, the No Conscription Fellowship (NCF) and the Union for Democratic Control (UDC) was orchestrated from Garsington – with Philip Morrell, a Liberal MP, as its spokesman in the House of Commons and Bertrand Russell and Clifford Allen as its main spokesmen elsewhere. By contrast, both Wells and James had the sense of participating in the war.

Living in Rye on the Channel coast, James was conscious of the war from the moment it was declared. He felt – in the phrase he used as the title of an article he wrote about it in 1915 – 'Within the Rim' of hostilities.

> The first sense of it all to me after the first shock and horror was that of a sudden leap back into the life of violence with which the American Civil War broke upon us, at the North, fifty-four years ago, when I had a consciousness of youth which perhaps equalled in vivacity my present consciousness of age.

James was appalled to see Belgian refugees flocking across the Channel and put himself at the disposal of the committee to aid and entertain them. He applied to be naturalised as a British subject; Asquith was one of his sponsors. He even questioned the validity of the sacred citadel of Art in the present circumstances.

Wells saw the war as a direct result of the ivory-towerism typical of the kind novel admired and written by James. He put his thoughts about Edwardian literary England in an odd rag-bag of a book, purporting to contain the literary remains of one George Boon edited by Boon's friend Reginald Bliss, to which he (Wells) had been inveigled by the publisher T. Fisher Unwin, to write an Introduction. The strategy was one that Wells deployed with confusing elaboration. *Boon* came out in 1915 with the following statement by Wells, writing in his own person:

> I do hope the reader – and by that I mean the reviewer – will be able to see the reasonableness and the necessity of distinguishing between me and Mr Reginald Bliss. I do not wish to escape the penalties of thus participating in, and endorsing, his manifest breaches of good taste, literary decorum, and friendly obligation, but as a writer whose reputation is already too crowded and confused and who is for the ordinary purposes of every day known mainly as a novelist, I should be glad if I could escape the public identification I am now repudiating.

Writing as Bliss, Wells cogitates about the future of literary work in contemporary England: 'Boon died with his age. After the war there will be a new sort of book trade and a crop of new writers and a fresh tone, and everything will be different. This is an obituary of more than George Boon ... I regard the outlook with profound dismay.' Boon had seen the whole of literature as a unity. Now it was disintegrating. Bliss describes a conference on Boon's great project, the Mind of the Race, that throws into sharp relief the world of the literary power-brokers of the Edwardian establishment.

> 'A sort of literary stock-taking' was to be Mr [William] Archer's phrase. Repeated. Unhappily its commercialism was to upset Mr Gosse extremely; he was to say something passionately bitter about its 'utter lack of dignity'. Then relenting a little, he was to urge as an alternative 'some controlling influence, some standard and restraint, a new and better Academic influence'. Dr Keyhole was to offer his

journalistic services in organising an American plebiscite, a suggestion which was to have exasperated Mr Gosse to the pitch of a gleaming silence.

In the midst of this conversation the party is joined by Hallery and an American friend, a quiet Harvard sort of man speaking meticulously accurate English, and still later by emissaries of Lord Northcliffe and Mr Hearst, by Mr Henry James, rather led into it by a distinguished hostess, by Mr W. B. Yeats, late but keen, and by that Sir Henry Lunn who organises the Swiss winter sports hotels. All these people drift in with an all too manifestly simulated accidentalness that at last arouses the distrust of the elderly custodian, so that Mr Orage, the gifted editor of the *New Age*, arriving last, is refused admission.

This 'gifted editor' is someone we must turn from the *Lit Supp* for a moment to consider. As John Carswell has revealed, A. R. Orage was born in 1873 in the village of Fenstanton, Huntingdonshire. His surname was there pronounced 'Orridge' which was how Shaw pronounced it when he wanted to tease Orage. Brought up by his mother, a penniless widow, Orage left Fenstanton for good in his twenties. He took a job teaching at a primary school in Leeds and married, a union that was short-lived. He had become a socialist and, as we have seen, he had spent a year reading the works of Plato.

Orage's surname now took on its stormy gallic resonance appropriate, surely, for such a human whirlwind. He formed a Plato Group in Leeds, one of whose members was Holbrook Jackson, a Yorkshireman in the lace business but with literary ambitions. He met Orage in a second-hand bookshop. Jackson introduced Orage to Nietzsche, lending him *Thus Spake Zarathustra*. Another Yorkshire platonist was A. J. Penty, an architect much influenced by the ideas of William Morris. After presiding over meetings of the Plato Group, Orage, Jackson and Penty went on to found something more ambitious, the Leeds Art Club, whose object was 'to affirm the mutual dependence of art and ideas'. Latterday members would include Henry Moore and Herbert Read.

Having got that off the ground, the trio came to London to seek their fortunes, eager to ventilate their ideas and determined to maintain their independence. What they desired was to have their own weekly journal where their ideas could be developed, a journal that would tackle political and social issues but within a broad cultural context that included literature and the arts. They found a radical periodical on its last legs called the *New Age* and took it over in April 1907 to make it the organ of a 'new Social Ideal'.

Jackson and Orage were joint editors. The initial capital was £1000. Orage approached Shaw, whom he knew through the meetings of the Fabian Society. Shaw said he would give them half if Orage could find someone else to match the remainder. Orage, who must have been very persuasive, soon succeeded in discovering another angel to back the venture. Not only did Shaw put up half the money, he was also one of the earliest contributors.

Orage encouraged Shaw and Wells to lay into a monster they dubbed 'Chesterbelloc' and then asked Hilaire Belloc and G. K. Chesterton, both brilliant polemicists to reply. This knockabout weekly entertainment continued well into 1908, by which time the *New Age's* circulation had risen to a phenomenal 20,000 (equal to that of St Loe's *Spectator*). At this point Holbrook Jackson (who later became an authority on fine printing, edited the literary magazine *Today* and wrote a definitive cultural history, *The 1890s*) dropped out, leaving Orage in sole command of the *New Age*. Under him alone it continued to flourish.

We saw how Orage was prepared to back his hunches in respect of an obscure young man like Muir. An earlier assistant was Clifford Sharp, whom we shall meet fully in the next chapter on the *New Statesman*. Orage manifested no gender bias. His closest colleague at this time was a young woman of twenty-seven whom he met at the Theosophical Society, Beatrice Hastings. She had been born in Hackney in 1879 as Emily Alice Haigh. Her adopted surname probably came from the girls' school in Hastings where she had been educated and her new first one from Dante. She certainly assumed the Beatrician role in Orage's journey through the inferno and purgatorio of Edwardian literary London. Between them Orage and Hastings contributed much of the editorial content of the paper under various *noms de plume*. He published his first book, *Nietzsche: the Dionysian Spirit of the Age*, in 1906.

The work of a much more celebrated woman writer, also using a reconstructed name, that of Katherine Mansfield, first saw the light of day under Orage. Almost every issue in the first six months of 1908 contained one of her stories, those that later appeared in her first collection, *In a German Pension*. She was ten years younger than Beatrice and they became firm friends until they quarrelled, when they became sworn enemies. Another writer who made his début in Orage's pages was the young American poet Ezra Pound. Orage saw nothing incongruous in printing a contribution from Pound alongside one by Arnold Bennett. Orage discovered an aspect of Bennett hitherto unrealised; as a popular books *causerie*-ist. Bennett wrote a regular piece under the heading 'Books and Persons' on everything in literature from Balzac to Baring-Gould under the name 'Jacob Tonson'. Bennett's period as the regular book-reviewer of the *Evening Standard* was a revival of his triumphs in this regard on the *New Age*.

The periodical was from the outset divided into two halves with politics – in which Sharp assisted – in the front and literature at the back; but there was a discernible consistency between the two, and, initially, a distinctly Fabian tone. Orage was always open to new ideas and he eventually abandoned Fabianism to become an advocate of Social Credit, and a disciple of the Russian therapist Gurdjieff.

The early years of Orage's editorship while Edward VII reigned over Great Britain with the Liberal Campbell-Bannerman as Prime Minister were a golden age for the paper, nurturing many brilliant talents. Orage's dingy office in Cursitor Street off Chancery Lane was next to an ABC where a cup of tea and a cake or a round of toast could be bought for a few pence. The Orage clerisy of *New Age* staff and contributors, whose remuneration was commensurate with the ABC's price levels, would assemble at a table there after their work to engage in dialogue.

In the steamy restaurant otherwise inhabited by lawyers' clerks and runners, one might find Bennett stammering out his observations, Beatrice earnestly arguing her corner as Orage or Pound laid down the law. Bennett would deplore the hidden censorship exercised over contemporary fiction by the circulating-libraries, a long-running complaint by novelists. In the assessment of new work he revealed a zealous partisanship. When he reviewed *The New Machiavelli* by Wells, 'Tonson' opened with a reference to 'the ignoble tittle-tattle' that had greeted the serialisation of the novel in the *English Review* edited by Ford Madox Ford. Of the novel's merits, now that it was published in full, 'Tonson' was in no doubt whatsoever:

> Astounding width of observation; a marvellously true perspective; an extraordinary grasp of the real significance of innumerable phenomena utterly diverse; profound emotional power; dazzling

verbal skill: these are the qualities which Mr Wells indubitably has. But the qualities which consecrate these other qualities are his priceless and total sincerity, and the splendid human generosity which colours that sincerity. What above all we want in this island of intellectual dishonesty is someone who will tell us the truth 'and chance it'. H. G. Wells is pre-eminently the man.

After such praise, James's dismissiveness in the columns of the *Lit Supp* was especially galling to Wells. It prompted him in the midst of writing *Boon* to include a new chapter entitled 'Of Art, of Literature, of Mr Henry James' in which, along with a cruel caricature of James and his involuted mature style, a clear distinction was made between the Jamesian view of the novel as a chaste work of art and the crusading novel strong on social awareness as practised by Wells. When *Boon* was published, Wells had the nerve to leave a copy for James at his club. That led to an angry exchange of letters between the two men, including this from James:

> It is art that *makes* life, makes interest, makes importance, for our consideration and application of these things, and I know of no substitute whatsoever for the force and beauty of its process. If I were Boon I should say that any pretence of such a substitute is helpless and hopeless humbug; but I wouldn't be Boon for the world, and am only yours faithfully,
> Henry James.

Their friendship was at an end.

In the era of the First World War the *Athenaeum*, edited by the socialist politician Arthur Greenwood, was mainly concerned with the problems of post-war reconstruction and the proposed League of Nations. As a cultural forum it seemed to be in terminal decline. Then Arnold Rowntree, Liberal MP for York from 1910 to 1918, stepped in with a rescue package. Chairman of the Westminster Press, which owned many newspapers in the north, Rowntree believed that a modern newspaper should be 'what the public square was to the Greeks'. His uncle Joseph's Social Service Trust had already invested heavily in the *Nation*, started in 1907. The *Nation's* editor was H.W. Massingham, whose regular Diary column signed Wayfarer (to be emulated a decade and a half later by Kingsley Martin) often included items on literature and music as well as politics. Massingham held court at the National Liberal Club, where he held a weekly lunch attended by Rowntree and other prominent Liberals. One can imagine a lively discussion there over who should edit the revived *Athenaeum*. In the event Rowntree offered the job to the thirty-year-old writer Middleton Murry. It proved to be an inspired choice.

The son of a clerk at the War Office, Murry was educated at Christ's Hospital from where he won a scholarship to Brasenose, Oxford. When he went up in 1909, Murry discovered that the college belied its reputation for heartiness. It not only had a civilised Vice-President but also a number of cultivated undergraduates. Murry soon acquired large circle of intellectual friends and led a full social life but that did not prevent him getting a first in Honour Mods. Everything seemed set fair for him to do the same in Greats and, possibly, to try to become a fellow of All Souls.

Murry observed the violent reaction in London by the philistine public to the painterly innovations of the first Post-Impressionist exhibition organised by Roger Fry, and he conceived the idea of starting a literary journal that would make a comparable stir. As the idea grew, he felt he could not wait until he had completed his degree to put it into effect. The first number of *Rhythm*, a quarterly journal of literature and the arts, edited by John Middleton Murry and Michael Sadleir, a fellow-undergraduate, appeared in June 1911. Murry spent the long vacations gathering material for it in Paris. He underwent a youthful life crisis there rather like that described by Maugham in *Of Human Bondage* and enjoyed an ambience similar to the one depicted by Clive Bell in *Old Friends*. Maugham and Bell had both been habitués of the bars and left bank cafés slightly earlier than Murry, who had his first love-affair in Paris, an Anglo-French one that left him him with a chronic sense of guilt.

Back in Oxford, academic work seemed irrelevant to his now burning life's ambition to become a writer. He decided to leave in mid-term and carry on editing *Rhythm* from London. Exciting events happening there on the literary front included the publication of the first volume of what was to become an annual anthology of new poetry, *Georgian Poetry 1911–12*, containing poems by Rupert Brooke, W. H. Davies, John Masefield, D. H. Lawrence, Walter de la Mare, Lascelles Abercrombie, Gordon Bottomley and John Drinkwater. It was edited by the civil servant and literary patron Edward Marsh, and published by Harold Monro, whose *Poetry Review* and later Poetry Bookshop promoted the work of these poets (not to be confused with Harriet Monroe, who was doing a similar job in America). Publication of the Marsh book coincided with the appearance of *The Oxford Book of Victorian Verse* edited by the genial 'Q', Quiller-Couch, Professor of English at Cambridge, and many journals reviewed them together, welcoming in the new while ushering out the old. Murry decided that D. H. Lawrence's inclusion in Marsh's anthology was no bar to his reviewing it in *Rhythm*:

> This collection [Lawrence wrote] is like a big breath when we are waking up after a night of oppressive dreams ... What are the Georgian poets, nearly all, but just bursting into a thick blaze of being? They are not poets of passion, perhaps, but they are essentially passionate poets. The time to be impersonal has gone. We start from the joy we have in being ourselves, and everything must take colour from that joy.

Murry returned to Oxford to take his Schools and, in spite of the interruption, managed to obtain second class honours. But that was the end of his academic career and the beginning of his controversial career as an editor of literary journals.

An introduction from his former tutor at Brasenose to J. A. Spender, the editor of the *Westminster Gazette* whose literary pages were some of the best in London, led to the one source of regular work that would be Murry's standby in the appallingly difficult years to come – book-reviewing. The *Gazette's* lit ed was the striking-looking Naomi Royde-Smith, with whom at least one Georgian poet (Walter de la Mare) had fallen in love. Spender arranged with her that Murry should write write a regular review at £5 a week, a good wage in those days. Murry also found a sympathetic editor in Massingham.

Among the contributions that came in unsolicited for *Rhythm* was a short story from Katherine Mansfield who, after she had quarrelled with Orage and Beatrice Hastings, turned to Murry. He was soon in love with her. The passionate emotional see-saw worked by Katherine and Murry from the time they met until her death is well beyond the scope of this book. One of the great scenarios of modern literary biography, it has been told several times both from her point of view and from his. My concern is with Murry and Katherine as reviewers of their contemporaries, as literary journalists. As such they interact with all the people mentioned so far in this chapter; also with D. H. and Frieda

Lawrence, to whose marriage at the Kensington Register Office on
13 July 1914 they were witnesses, and from whom afterwards they
became alienated.

These writers were members of a literary clerisy reading and
reviewing each other's books while writing their own. It was while
writing reviews that Lawrence and VW were re-inventing the novel
and KM re-inventing the short story. All four couples – the
Lawrences, the Woolfs, the Middleton Murrys, Orage and Hastings
(five if we add Ford Madox Ford and Violet Hunt) – had to
combine reviewing with other work because of financial pressure.
Murry's financial position was especially bad because he was left
with a heavy backlog of printers' bills after the collapse of *Rhythm*.
Re-named *The Blue Review* and jointly edited by Murry and Mansfield, it now petered out. In the end in spite of a generous subsidy
from Eddie Marsh, Murry had to file a petition for bankruptcy.
KM did have an allowance from her father (like Beatrice) but her
resources were drained by her illness. She was consumptive and
constantly moving house in search of an environment that would
suit her; biographers find it hard to chart in full her peregrinations
at this time around London, Cornwall, the French and Italian
Rivieras, involving many trips back and forth across the Channel
despite the war.

In 1916 Murry became a translator in the War Office attached
to MI7. He added a working knowledge of German to his other
linguistic accomplishments and settled down to the life of a desk-
bound civil servant as conscientiously as his father had before him.
His colleagues included the Cambridge Greek scholar J. T. Sheppard (the Garsingtonian who had with Keynes and others recommended him for the work), Adrian Boult and D. L. Murray, a
Balliol prizeman and scholar who soon showed he had novel-
writing talent too. Murry rose to the post of chief censor and after
he left government service was awarded the OBE.

Murry and KM were formally married in May 1918 . A few days
later they had lunch with Leonard and VW:

> She looks ghastly ill [wrote VW]. As usual we came to an oddly
> complete understanding. My theory is I get down to what is true rock
> in her, through numerous vapours & pores which sicken or bewilder
> most of our friends. Its her love of writing I think.

An uneasy but intimate friendship between the two women developed. When the Murrys lived in Hampstead, VW became for a

time an almost weekly visitor to their house to see KM. The Woolfs
chose *Prelude*, KM's story about a New Zealand family moving
house seen from a child's viewpoint, for one of the Hogarth Press's
earliest titles. In July 1918 VW recorded that she had spent much
of the day glueing the bindings of 50 copies of it, but doubted
whether they would sell more than 100.

If the London reviewing clerisy had a venue, a location where
everyone went to gossip about each other, it was Garsington. In
the Summer of 1918, during the dreadful last phase of the war
before the Armistice, the movements of Bertrand Russell, the
clerisy's most formidable intellect, whose love-affair with Ottoline
was still intermittently in play, were temporarily restricted. He was
in prison on account of his pacifism. Garsington Manor, in the
Oxford countryside, was as we have seen a haven of pacifism.

Among the visitors was the poet Siegfried Sassoon, recuperating
from a wound suffered at the Front where he had been awarded
the Military Cross (his brother had been killed at Gallipoli). On
the eve of the Somme offensive, 'Mad Jack', as Siegfried was known
in his battalion, had made a solo hand-grenade attack in broad
daylight on a German outpost and when it was vacated by the
enemy, stayed there reading a book of poetry. Sassoon had become
reluctantly converted to pacifism by his disgust with the high
command. In 1917 he wrote an open letter he called 'A Soldier's
Declaration', in which he said: 'I have seen and endured the
sufferings of the troops, and I can no longer be party to prolong
these sufferings for ends which I believe to be evil and unjust.' He
sent one copy to his Commanding Officer and another to the
Bradford Pioneer.

Before the inevitable Court Martial was convened and disci-
plinary action taken, his friend and brother-officer, the poet
Robert Graves (another Garsingtonian) and anthologist Edward
Marsh intervened. Through Marsh's influence as secretary to
Winston Churchill, they contrived to get Sassoon certified as a
shell-shock victim and sent to a convalescent home at Craiglock-
hart, near Edinburgh. It was while he was there that he met
Wilfred Owen. Both men wrote some of their finest poetry in
'Dottyville', as Sassoon called it. Sassoon's poems were collected
under the title *The Counter-Attack* and published in the summer of
1918. The volume contained his most famous and most frequently
anthologised poems, acidulous accounts of the way the war was

being run by the top brass at the Front under orders from
Whitehall.

An early copy went to Ottoline at Garsington, who set about the
task of making sure it got some favourable reviews. She had
temporarily transferred her affections from Russell to Sassoon and
was especially keen to get it reviewed by Murry. She had also
helped Murry obtain his War Office job. Provided he wrote
anonymously, such a review would not compromise his position at
MI7.

Murry was heavily involved in the war, not just because of the
responsible position he held in Whitehall but also intellectually.
Of all of these writers, he was the one who was trying hard to make
some sort of sense of the war, working out what it was going to
mean for the future of literature.

He wrote in an article called 'The Sign-Seekers', published in
October 1916:

> Among the many as yet uncomprehended things that the war is
> doing to our souls, we can hold fast to one that is certain. Those who
> instinctively turned to literature and art in the years before it, as
> something permanent and real and true, have been confirmed in
> their devotion. More than this, what was a preference has become a
> conviction, and almost an idolatry. The faith in literature that could
> be lightly disturbed and easily intermitted is now unshakable. Per-
> haps the reality is higher and more remote than it was; it is the more
> fixed and unquestionable.

Murry's sense of literature as possessing intrinsic value needed
further definition: what kind of literature? What was the way
forward? 'We are conscious', Murry says, 'that this is an interreg-
num, and we allow for it.' What was now clear to him was that the
future of fiction did not lie with the kind of novel of which *The
New Machiavelli* was an example, nor with the kind of novel
outlined by Arnold Bennett in such articles as 'On Writing Novels'
in 1912. Murry felt that Bennett was wrong in suggesting there
that all novels belonged to the same kind of literary art. 'I
mumbled the names of Tolstoi and Dostoevsky to myself and
wagged my head', says Murry. The war had crystallised Murry's
hitherto undefined dissatisfaction with the Edwardian novel. He
now felt certain the the future of fiction lay in the work of the two
Russians mentioned above (currently being translated into English
by Constance Garnett) and not in that of the two Englishmen.

So far as discovering work in which the true meaning of the war might be directly discerned, Murry found something approximating to that in books by yet another foreign writer, the Frenchman Georges Duhamel. In June 1917 and in March 1918 Murry reviewed this writer's *Vie des Martyrs* and *Civilisation, 1914–1917*. Duhamel had qualified as a doctor while pursuing a career as a writer. He served as a French army surgeon during the war. Both books are set in emergency hospitals and describe scenes of terrible suffering and endurance. Duhamel belonged to the so-called *unanimiste* school of French writers, headed by Jules Romains. They showed the individual human soul merged into that of the group. What Murry found so admirable was Duhamel's compassionate observation of the suffering he depicts at first-hand and his revelation of its power to ennoble. From the suffering of the men at the Front came the the blessed spirit of *cameraderie*.

Such were the thoughts that were passing through Murry's mind when he took up Ottoline's suggestion and arranged with H. M. Tomlinson, the lit ed of the *Nation*, to review Sassoon's *The Counter-attack and other poems*. Tomlinson, a former war correspondent at the Front, had been sent home because his outspoken dispatches had displeased Northcliffe. He must have thought that Murry would be just as sympathetic towards Sassoon's poetry as he was to Duhamel's prose. But one of the delights of being a lit ed is the unpredictability of a reviewer's reactions. Murry's review 'Mr Sassoon's War Verses' is a fine example of that unpredictability. All that Murry had found so uplifting in Duhamel was, he thought, conspicuous by its absence in Sassoon:

> Mr Sassoon's verses – they are not poetry ... touch not our imagination, but our sense. Reading them we feel, not as we do with true art, which is the evidence of man's triumph over his experience, that something has after all been saved from disaster, but that everything is irremediably and intolerably wrong. And, God knows, something is wrong – wrong with Mr Sassoon, wrong with the world that has made him the instrument of a discord so jangling. Why should one of the finest creatures of the earth be made to suffer a pain so brutal that he can give it no expression, that even this most human and mighty relief is denied him?

Murry's review must have taken considerable courage to write and to publish. Even though it appeared anonymously, everyone at Garsington knew who had written it and never was there a greater flutter in that particular dovecote. Philip Morrell wrote a furious letter to the *Nation* protesting against its treatment of 'a gallant and distinguished author'. Bertrand Russell managed from his prison-cell to insert a letter in the uncut pages of a book for Ottoline to send to the *Nation* where it appeared under a pseudonym, 'Philalethes', expressing great admiration for the poems. Sassoon wrote to Ottoline enquiring who had written the review and when she told him, he wrote back saying, 'I wish I could do something to make Murry happier.' Virginia Woolf, staying at Garsington while all this was going on, was accused by Philip of being on Murry's side. He read the review and his letter out loud several times, raising his finger to make them all attend. It was the end of Garsington for the Murrys. Even if Ottoline had been prepared to forgive (as she was for other betrayals in print), KM was not; as she wrote to VW: 'after the great San Philip's a-running down of the little Revenge in this week's *Nation* I don't think I *can* break a crumb in their house again . . .'

When Murry's Whitehall job ended he had his freedom again combined with the habitual precarious financial outlook. Then came Arnold Rowntree's proposal that Murry should edit the *Athenaeum* at £800 a year and he was saved. 'It should give English kultur a leg up,' Lytton Strachey told Ottoline. Murry, installed in April in the office at No. 10 Adelphi Terrace, had six weeks to get out his first number.

VW saw him during this period, when he had already signed up Paul Valéry and George Santayana.

> Success has already begun to do for Murry what I always said it would do. He is more freshly coloured, even in the cheeks than when we last met; & his mind has its high lights. Why, he chuckled like a schoolboy; his eyes shone; his silences were occupied by pleasant thoughts . . .'What will you write VW?' he asked. Am I too modest in thinking that there was a shade of the perfunctory in the question? Anyhow I didn't persecute him with any degree of pressure. I offered to look in on Thursdays sometimes & get a book, sometimes to suggest an article; he ageed quite cordially . . . Katherine will do 4 novels every week – pray to God she don't do mine.

It was not only VW whom Murry approached but the rest of the Bloomsbury clerisy, plus his old friends from MI7, D. L. Murray

and J. W. N. Sullivan. Aldous Huxley, who had given up a career
as a schoolmaster at Eton, became Murry's assistant editor. James
Strachey, who had resigned his job on the *Spectator* in 1916 because
of his pacifism, unacceptable to St Loe, became the dramatic critic.
Music was covered by Edward J. Dent. Both Roger Fry and Clive
Bell reviewed art exhibitions in London and there were regular
reviews of art in France by André Lhote. Letters from abroad were
another regular feature, including those of Ezra Pound from
America, Richard Aldington and Guido de Ruggiero from Italy,
Paul Valéry from Paris, the Dutch novelist Louis Couperus from
Holland.

Some of the main pieces, such as Strachey's pen-portrait of Lady
Hester Stanhope, E. M. Forster's 'Pharos' serialised in several
parts, and philosophical essays by Bertrand Russell, were signed.
Dent's musical criticism was also signed, but many of the reviews
appeared over initials. It was the best of both worlds: the reviewers
spoke with the voice of Athene but were all identified in the
annual index. Thus C. A. was the American poet Conrad Aiken,
the Harvard friend of T. S. Eliot who was himself a frequent
reviewer as T. S. E.; E. B., Edmund Blunden; J. D. B., the novelist
J. D. Beresford; E. M. F., E. M. Forster; K. was not Maynard Keynes
but his medical brother Geoffrey; F. R. was the Northern Ireland
novelist Forrest Reid; F. M. P. was the historian F. M. Powicke and
R. H. W. was the art historian R. H. Wilenski.

Murry used the lordly M. by itself and J. M. M. for his general
editorial pronouncements and for his reviews. He was a frequent
contributor in both capacities – the very opposite of a Richmond.
J. H. was Julian Huxley and A. L. H. Aldous Huxley, who also
wrote a series of Marginalia as 'Autolycus'. These were improvisa-
tions on whatever topical thought came into his head. The mantle
of Oscar Wilde as a purveyor of paradoxes had descended upon
Huxley and he wore it with a difference. On 9 July 1920 he
confesses that he finds himself taking less and less interest in
politics. He still reads the papers but it is the reports from the
police or divorce courts that he studies most closely:

> doesn't one, after all, get a very much rosier view of human nature
> from the police and divorce court news than from the political
> columns of the daily paper? When the judge is set and the books are
> reckoned, I fancy that Crippen will cut a better figure than some of
> the folk at present engaged in making Europe what it is.... Our

civilisation does not look as if it would long outlast the run of *Chu Chin Chow*...

Katherine Mansfield's translations of Chekhov's Letters done jointly with S. S. Koteliansky were another regular feature of the journal and she was the fiction reviewer whose reviews, signed K. M., she mailed to Murry from the south of France.

It was an oddly miscellaneous collection of books that came her way. They included Conrad's *The Rescue*, about which she was fairly enthusiastic; a late Mrs Humphry Ward, *Cousin Philip*; *Legend* by Clemence Dane; and Maugham's *The Moon and Sixpence*, which she hated. KM had never met Maugham and could therefore say what she liked about his novel without any fear of an irreparably damaged friendship. It was different when, six months later, Murry sent her *Night and Day*. VW's prayer for her not to review it went unanswered. The review that appeared in the *Athenaeum*, 'A Ship Comes into Harbour', was the turning-point in their relations. KM regards the reviewer of novels as one of those who

> love to linger down at the harbour, as it were, watching the new ships being builded, the old ones returning, and the many putting out to sea ... [To such an observer comes the strange sight of *Night and Day*] sailing into port serene and resolute on a deliberate wind. The strangeness lies in her aloofness, her air of quiet perfection, her lack of any sign that she has made a perilous voyage – the absence of any scars. There she lies among the strange shipping – a tribute to civilisation for our admiration and wonder.

KM sees the novel as up-dated Jane Austen, with the important difference that whereas the Austen magic lasts after a novel has been read, VW's does not. In considering the minor characters KM says:

> it is true that these characters are not in any high degree important – but how much life have they? We have the queer sensation that once the author's pen is removed from them they have neither speech nor motion, and are not to be revived again until she adds another stroke or two or writes another sentence underneath.

The review gave VW great displeasure:

A decorous elderly dullard she describes me; Jane Austen up to
date. Leonard supposes that she let her wish for my failure have its
way with her pen. He could see her looking about for a loophole of
escape. 'I'm not going to call this a success – or if I must, I'll call it
the wrong kind of success.'

At this distance of time the review does seem perfectly fair. And it
taught VW a lesson: Do not review your rival's book, even if she did
not always heed it. When Richmond sent VW Dorothy Richardson's
Interim, part five of her novel-sequence *Pilgrimage*. VW reflected:

> The truth is that when I looked at it I found myself looking for
> faults; hoping for them. And they would have bent my pen, I know.
> There must be an instinct of self-preservation at work. If she's good
> then I'm not.

VW was always in a terrible state when any of her own books was
about to be published, even when she was a well-established
author. She minded dreadfully about reviews long after KM had
ceased to write them; and was never more apprehensive than when
towards the end of the Richmond era on the *Lit Supp*, in 1937, *The
Years* was about to be noticed.

She tried to immerse herself in the writing of her next book,
Three Guineas, and to banish all thoughts of the forthcoming
critical onslaught; but as publication day approached the panic
rose ever higher: 'Today the reviewers (oh d—n this silly thought)
have their teeth fixed in me ... I'm going to be beaten, I'm going
to be laughed at, I'm going to be held up to scorn & ridicule ...'.
Finally the moment comes and the *Supplement* lands on the mat,
containing its review of her book:

> Oh the relief! L. brought the Lit Sup to me in bed & said It's quite
> good. And so it is; & T. & Tide says I'm a firstrate novelist and a
> great lyrical poet [the reviewer was Theodora Bosanquet]. And I can
> hardly read through the reviews: but feel a little dazed, to think then
> that its *not* nonsense; it does make an effect.

That was on Friday 12 March. Sunday was the next hurdle. She
cleared it triumphantly: 'I am in such a twitter owing to two
columns in the *Observer* praising *The Years* that I cant, as I foretold,
go on with *3 Guineas*. Why I even sat back just now & thought with
pleasure of people reading that review.' The reviewer was Basil de

Selincourt (one of the Viola Garvin people) whose high praise mitigated the comments in the *Lit Supp* that, on further consideration, had seemed to her to miss the more profound aspects of the book. It 'spoke as if it were merely the death song of the middle classes: a series of exquisite impressions; but he sees that it is a creative, a constructive book.'

Encouraged by that, she was able to ride the punch in the *Daily Telegraph* where John Brophy, a much-loved pre-war library novelist, put her novel in the batch and lashed out at it as a tired, anaemic middle-class book. 'That sneer is already rubbed out', she told herself but even so, work on *Three Guineas* was halted. The sneer certainly was erased for good when the rest of the reviews began to come through.

> *Friday March 19* [a week after publication day]. Now this is one of the strangest of my experiences – "they" say almost universally that *The Years* is a Masterpiece. The Times says so. Bunny. &c: Howard Spring: If somebody had told me I shd. write this, even a week ago, let alone six months ago, I shd. have given a jump like a shot hare. How entirely & absolutely incredible it would have been! The praise chorus began yesterday . . . bought the *E. Standard* & found myself glorified as I read it in the Tube. A calm quiet feeling, glory: & I'm so steeled now I dont think the flutter will much worry me. Now I must begin again on 3Gs.

'Bunny' was David Garnett, writing in the *New Statesman*, an old chum who had been to tea with her the week before; others who had murmured the word masterpiece in her ears were Maynard Keynes and Stephen Spender. They were chums too but Howard Spring, the *Evening Standard's* reviewer, was at that time an industrious writer of working-class background about to score his own first great popular success as a novelist with *O Absalom!* (later called *My Son, My Son!*) in 1938. His plaudits meant that she really had reached a new and less in-group readership. *The Times* – it continued to publish book reviews in the main paper every week, in addition to the *Supplement* – had led with her novel in a 'Books of the Week' column signed J.S., who said that it was 'a book that might be called, in more exacting times, a masterpiece . . .' – the words are those of my one-time colleague, Jan Stephens.

Far from being the author's masterpiece, *The Years* seems to posterity to be a regression to a way of novel-writing VW put behind her when she wrote her truly modernist masterpieces, *To the Lighthouse* and *The Waves*. It is a classic instance of the undiscriminating nature of the reviewers' 'praise chorus'. There is a reviewing tide in the affairs of major authors that flows over many years of misunderstood work. Taken at the flood it overflows in a chorus of universal acclamation for a work no better or in this case rather less distinguished than others.

As her reputation as a novelist continued to grow, Virginia Woolf became less and less happy with the system of book-reviewing as practised in the daily and weekly press. In 1939, two years before her death she set down her thoughts on the subject in a pamphlet, 'Reviewing'. She sees the arrival of a time when the reviewer, as we know him, will be elminated altogether and his role taken over by the Gutter who will simply write out a short statement of the novel's plot and then put either an asterisk or a dagger against it to signify approval or disapproval. Her fantasy anticipated the modern listings page; but that service to readers has not eliminated the reviewer, whose reviews are still published quite separately on the books page.

She confessed that the reviewer did have one indispensable function – to tell the author whether or not he had liked her book and to give reasons; but this she felt could be done privately, on payment of a consultation fee. Here again she anticipated events: the relationship she envisaged is essentially one that many authors have nowadays with their editors and their agents. The Woolfs did not have either agent or editor because they were the publishers of all their own books. For them, reviews were the first outside reactions to their books.

Leonard Woolf reckoned that Virginia's paper raised 'questions of considerable importance to literature, journalism, and the reading public'. But he demurred from its main conclusions and took the unprecedented step of publicly disagreeing with Virginia when *Reviewing* was re-printed in book-form. In a Note appended to the end of his wife's paper, Leonard began by pointing out that around the the middle of the eighteenth century an author's livelihood shifted from dependence upon a patron to that of the public. Oliver Goldsmith, who described the process, had no regrets over the disappearance of the patron. And it is at this point of altered dependency that the reviewer emerges – as the representative of the public. He or she is not concerned with the morale of the author. His or her role is solely to monitor and articulate the interests of the public; a function that remains as valid today as it ever was.

As the war-clouds gathered and the *Times* championed the policy of appeasement, the *Lit Supp* continued to print anonymous reviews in the same way that it had done for a quarter of a century. By now the editor had his team of regular reviewers upon whom · he relied heavily. His desire to experiment with new reviewers had diminished, as it usually does when a lit ed reigns for more than two decades. Richmond had become the grand old man of the profession, presiding over what was essentially the mixture as before, even if it was a somewhat different paper in appearance from the sheet of unalloyed reviews in 1902. Stanley Morison's typographical face-lift for the main paper in 1935 had extended to the *Lit Supp*. Richmond had to submit to the power of the designer and agree to use some illustrations to break up the reviews. As war began to seem more and more of a certainty, Richmond was ready to retire. He wrote to some of his regulars like Virginia Woolf, thanking them for the reviews they had written over the past thirty years.

He was succeeded in 1938 by Hamish Miles from Jonathan Cape, whose abilities as a literary editor had emerged when Cape took over the monthly *Life and Letters* and Miles became its editor in succession to Desmond MacCarthy. Miles was 'a short, slim, elegant man full of intelligence and wit' in the recollection of his colleague Rupert Hart-Davis. He was now in his forties and he seemed as if he might possess the power to effect the quiet, painless transformation the *Lit Supp* needed at that point in its history. But after he had been in the job for six months Miles died of a brain tumor and the *Times* journalist D. L. Murray became, somewhat reluctantly, the new editor.

Murray was a man of varied talents. Up at Balliol before the First World War he had been an able student of philosophy, and had written a book on pragmatism after he had graduated. Then, as we saw, he went to the War Office and worked with Middleton Murry who introduced him to Richmond. In 1920 Murray joined *The Times*. He combined his journalism with writing popular fiction. His reluctance to take on the *Lit Supp* editorship was partly because he lived in Sussex and partly because he was already making a decent living as a library novelist. Murray had supervised all the *Lit Supp* fiction reviews. Familiar with the office and its ways, after some hesitation he agreed to fill the vacuum created by the untimely demise of Hamish Miles.

Murray had an assistant, Philip Tomlinson, who had worked on *Adelphi*. He was the brother of the novelist H. M. Tomlinson and he was an able reviewer, but of deeply conservative taste when confronted by modernism. Philip Tomlinson's most infamous review was of *East Coker* under the heading 'Mr T. S. Eliot's Confession'. It began:

> 'East Coker' is not a pastoral in the Somerset dialect, nor in the dialect of 'pure poetry', which Mr Eliot, not for the first time, scorns as a device outworn, the pretty plaything of times when poets had nice manners but only trivial themes – such as *Hamlet* and *Lear* and *Paradise Lost*, poems basically misconceived because the motives were insufficient.

After that the review conceded that Eliot occasionally in the poem 'excites the reader with sudden felicities', but it concluded: 'This is the confession of a lost art and a lost heart. These are sad times but we are not without hope that Mr Eliot will recover both, finding even that hearts are trumps and that Keats was not far out about the ore in the rift.'

The review provoked a letter by return from Downing College, Cambridge.

> Sir, – Mr Eliot needs no defending, nor do I flatter myself I am the defender he would choose if he needed one. But as a matter of decency there ought to be some protest against the review of 'East Coker' that appeared in your issue of yesterday, and I am writing in case no one whose protest would carry more weight has written and made my protest unnecessary.
>
> If your reviewer had pronounced the technique of 'East Coker' not altogether successful, or made limiting judgements of value in respect of the mood expressed in the poem, there would have been no call to do more than agree or disagree. What is not permissible in a serious critical journal is to write in contempuous condescension of the greatest living English poet (what other poet have we now Yeats is gone?) and exhibit a complacent ignorance of the nature of his genius and of the nature of the technique in which that genius is manifested . . .
>
> F. R. Leavis

A regular feature of the *Lit Supp* during the Second World War was the long rumination written by the novelist Charles Morgan, who had given up dramatic criticism to work in naval intelligence. In 'Menander's Mirror' philosophy, religion, manners, morals,

national characteristics and above all the future of Europe after
the war were discussed by turns in his easy, thoughtful manner.
His consistent theme was the necessity of sustaining the traditional
values of European civilisation in the years to come. Sometimes
Morgan's essay would be anchored to a recent book – C. M.
Bowra's *The Heritage of Symbolism* or David Cecil's *Hardy the Novelist*
– but more frequently he would evoke the spirit of Montaigne or
Pascal without any pretext other than his own random thoughts as
he walked through St James's Park on his way to the Admiralty.
The pieces when read now seem to belong to another era
altogether, when Britain had an imperial role to play in cultural
affairs.

Morgan was a friend of Murray. They met by chance one
evening at the theatre. 'Why David, I hear you're standing down
as editor!' said Morgan. 'Where did you hear that?' said Murray,
alarmed. 'From Barrington-Ward. As a matter of fact I've been
offered the job myself,' said Morgan.

Murray, whose first knowledge of his impending dismissal this
was, immediately tendered his resignation. Barrington-Ward had
been displeased by the *Lit Supp's* attitude to the Beveridge Report
but now he told Murray that there had been a misunderstanding
and persuaded him to stay on for a little longer. But the episode
had exacerbated Murray's discontent and in 1944 Murray's resignation was accepted. Set free, he wrote *Folly Bridge*, a novel set in
eighteenth-century Oxford with Thomas Warton, Professor of
Poetry, as the hero. His successor as editor was someone who had
for some time been regarded as the *éminence grise* of Printing
House Square.

Officially Stanley Morison was the paper's typographical adviser,
historian and archivist; unofficially he was the power behind the
throne. He had one base in PHS, another at the Monotype
Corporation and another at the Cambridge University Press.
Morison managed his career with assistance from his American-
born companion, Beatrice Warde, herself no mean typographical
authority. Morison's editorship of *Fleuron*, a publication concerned
with typography and the history of printing, regarded as a bible
among designers and printers, had with its seventh number
recently come to an end. Now Morison was asked by Barrington-
Ward if he would take over the editorship of the *Lit Supp*.

He agreed to take it over but on his own terms, set out in a six-
point memorandum. It stated that the *Supplement* should be made
much more of a serious organ of criticism and scholarship, less

discursive in its approach to reviewing; it needed more articles on
philosophy and religion, a fuller books-received feature; and
regular space devoted to bibiliography and library matters, and it
should be seen to have a consistent policy when it came to the
reviewing of political books.

The Morison memo represented a complete reversal of the
move towards giving the *Lit Supp* less solemnity and more accessi-
bility, something that Morison had begun to initiate, visually at
least, in the 1930s. It was a policy aimed at a discriminating,
educated readership that Morison, through Mathew, would wish
on *The Times* itself. In the event Morison was in the chair at the *Lit
Supp* for less than two years but his influence was profound. He
left a legacy from which the paper took a long time to free itself,
especially in the the treatment of books about the Russian
Revolution.

This important area was under the jurisdiction of E. H. Carr, a
former member of the Foreign Office and early wartime Ministry
of Information. Carr joined *The Times* as an assistant editor and
leader-writer in 1941, an appointment he owed to Morison who,
though a Catholic, had been when younger sympathetic to Marxism. In pre-war days Carr was an appeaser; during the war he had
become an admirer of Stalin and a Marxist. He was a prolific
author of books about Russia, beginning with studies of Dostoevsky, Bakunin and Marx, and culminating in his fourteen-volume
History of the Soviet Union, published between 1950 and 1978.

Carr became the *Lit Supp's* Commissar. All books about Russia
were either reviewed by him personally or by a reviewer of his
choice. Thus when Isaac Deutscher's biography of *Stalin* appeared,
it received a 4,000-word anonymous 'front' in the *Lit Supp* from
the pen of Carr. He explained that Deutscher's book was not so
much a straight biography as 'an analysis of his hero's political
achievement' and as such it 'has been brilliantly executed'. The
remainder of the review was devoted to an analysis by Carr of the
dictator's political achievement. Carr sees Stalin as the proponent
of 'socialism in one country' – a post-Leninist concept that both
explains Stalin's policies and justifies them. Because of the isolation of that 'one country' in a capitalist world and because of its
own economic backwardness, drastic methods were required if
progress towards the socialist goal was to be made

> it is clear that Stalin had to contend with far more apathy and
> disillusionment in the masses, far more opposition and intrigue in

the party élite than Lenin had ever known and was driven to apply correspondingly harsher and more ruthless measures of discipline. It is also significant that most of the appeals by which Stalin justified his revolution were to instincts normally the reverse of revolutionary – to law and order, to the sanctity of the family, to the defence of the fatherland and to the virtue of cultivating one's own garden: it was as a restless international adventurer, a man who cared nothing for his country, a champion of 'permanent revolution,' that Trotsky was pilloried.

When Carr's own book on *Socialism in One Country* appeared, it was hailed by many – including A. J. P. Taylor – as a masterpiece. It was only in 1983, after Carr's death, in a review by Leopold Labedz of Carr's posthumous book, *The Twilight of the Comintern, 1930–1935* (even longer than Carr's review of Deutscher) that readers were given a full exposure of Carr and his flawed scholarship.

Carr was still a *persona grata* on the *Lit Supp* and still writing frequent Fronts and Middles when I was copy-editing on the paper in the mid-1950s. I have encountered many facile reviewers in my time, but none more so than Carr. His reviews, often delivered personally, were written like Cookman's with one of the steel-nibbed pens provided by the management but on the back of a spare set of galley-proofs of his own monumental *History*. If one forgot to delete the printed matter it led to confusion in the composing room; the bewildered printer was not sure which side he was supposed to set. Nicolas Barker once commented on this thrifty eccentricity of Carr's to Morison. 'But you know what is most extraordinary about it, don't you?' said Morison pointing to the copy. Barker shook his head. 'There's not a single word crossed out,' Morison said. Carr's first drafts were his unaltered final versions.

In his two years Morison imposed his stamp on the *Supplement's* back page, avidly read by the library and bibiliographical community. That was where his own interests lay. Morison was the first to concede that he really did not have the knowledge to edit the paper satisfactorily in the new period of literary experiment and explosion that occurred after the end of the Second World War. He was happy, with much else to absorb his energies, to make way for Alan Pryce-Jones in 1946 under whom I had, as I have said, the great good fortune to serve.

Pryce-Jones's accession meant an enormous broadening of the

reviewing panel; the paper became a parliament of all the talents, during which many fresh reviewers of distinction were bonded to the paper. This bonding had one drawback, to my mind. Regular reviewers were encouraged to request books they wished to review; these requests would all be carefully filed; and when the editor supervised a sending-out session, the accumulated requests would be produced with the books. People did not *always* get the books they requested by any means, but frequently they did.

Such a system led to the development of 'corners', entrenchments, where books in certain categories went as of right, it seemed, to certain reviewers (as in the case of Carr). There would be several hundred possible reviewers on the files, yet in any given week the paper seemed to be largely written by the same small group of trusties: Peter Green on anything to do with Greek or Roman literature; D. W. Brogan on anything to do with modern French or American history; A. J. P. Taylor and Elizabeth Wiskemann on Germany and the rest of Europe; 'the Pope' (John Pope-Hennessy) on Italian Renaissance art, Douglas Cooper on twentieth-century painting and sculpture, and so on.

A reviewer who had a violent prejudice against a certain author would give rein to it not just once but again and again, as in the case of Cooper on books by Herbert Read or Geoffrey Grigson on the poetry of Day-Lewis, or John Sparrow on anything to do with A. E. Housman. If that is what Morison meant by having a consistent policy, it was certainly carried through; but it fell short of the notion of 'an impartial organ of literary criticism' announced when the *Supplement* first started.

In the field of literary biography and literary criticism the range of often-used reviewers was wider, including nearly everyone who was anyone in the literary world and several who were quite unknown, such as Sylva Norman, one of Blunden's ex-wives and a prolific reviewer. G. S. Fraser wrote many of the major Fronts. There were reviewers from the clubs of Pall Mall and from the pubs of Fitzrovia such as J. Maclaren-Ross and the young poet James Burns Singer, and there were the surviving stars of a bygone era such as Murry, Clive Bell, H. M. Tomlinson, Alfred Duggan. On the occasions when he felt moved to write there was A. P.-J. himself. And there was, too, a wealth of an in-house talent from Lawrence's Arts page for music and theatrical books, while from the main paper foreign correspondents or ex-correspondents such as James Morris (as she then was) and T. E. Uttley who wrote *Lit Supp* leaders in the form of short, sharp, right-wing shocks. And

from outside Graham Hutton would turn a clutch of *FT*-type books
into a polemic on the economy.

I was often handling copy of magisterial power that was a joy to
sub and send to the printer. The paper was – still, happily, is –
central in the position it occupies in the literary culture on both
sides of the Atlantic; the only journal that aimed to give some kind of
space to every worthwhile book. It was still what that first announcement described it as being: 'A medium of literary intelligence'.

There was always the Letters column in which redress could be
sought by those who felt they had been misinterpreted or
maligned, in itself a literary history of the twentieth century. I
recall one sequence in particular, apropos of a long review of a
critical book on the poetry of MacDiarmid published in 1950. The
review concluded by quoting one of his shorter poems that began:

> I found a pigeon's skull on the machair
> All the bones pure white and dry and chalky,
> But perfect
> Without a crack or a flaw anywhere.

The review suggested that the English reader put off by the
Scottish dialect of much of this poet's work 'can at least appreciate
this small imagist masterpiece'.

This prompted a letter from Glyn Jones of Cardiff, who pointed
out that except for the first line the words of the poem came
verbatim from a short story of his published in 1937: 'This is not a
question of similarity or echoes; the words are identical – apart I
repeat from the first line – and describe in my story the skull of a
seagull found on the shore.' The resulting correspondence continued enthrallingly for several weeks, turning on two fundamental
points: 1) can plagiarism be unconscious as well as conscious?; and
2) can prose be turned into poetry by setting it as verse?

If I am to complete my picture of twentieth-century reviewing in
London from the perspective of places where I have worked or
contributed, this latterday anonymous *Lit Supp* needs to be seen in
the perspective of a weekly journal where a strong literary section
at the back co-existed with a crusading political section at the
front, each section gaining strength from the other, as in Orage's
New Age. I mean the *New Statesman and Nation*, where many of the
great literary journalists of the twentieth century first emerged. It
is to 'The Staggers', to its back half, especially its book-reviewers
and literary editors, that I turn next.

10

Cuthbert, Janet and John

The *New Statesman* was started by the Webbs in 1913 with the aim of giving currency to their views on social and political issues and those of their fellow-members of the Fabian Society. In particular, they were concerned to sustain the impetus of their National Campaign for the Break-up of the Poor Law. It had a membership of 20,000 from which they reckoned they would acquire a nucleus of readers. From the start Bernard Shaw was part of the journal, both financially and ideologically, but he proved to be a capricious editorial bedfellow. As a radical weekly the journal would be in direct competition for readers with the Liberal *Nation*, edited by H. W. Massingham, funded by the Rowntrees, and Orage's *New Age*, now diverging more and more from its earlier Fabian sympathies. Beatrice Webb aimed at recruiting 2,000 postal subscribers who were offered a cut rate, hoping to match that figure with the same number of casual readers each week. In the event the subscription figure for the first year was 2,400 and the circulation more than 4,000, enough readers for the paper's initial survival.

The editor the Webbs appointed was Clifford Sharp, whom they knew as a member of their young Fabian group, the Nursery. Sharp had taken a course in engineering but left university without a degree. After a spell in his family's law firm, his career in journalism began under Orage on the *New Age*. He went on to edit *Crusade*, a monthly Fabian sheet devoted to the Webbs' attempts to reform the Poor Law. Beatrice was one of the members of the Royal Commission on this matter set up by Balfour. She and Sidney had dissented from its conclusions and put their views into a Minority Report. *Crusade* ceased publication in 1913, leaving

Sharp free at thirty to take on the much more challenging task of becoming the editor of the *New Statesman*. It was Balfour, a Tory friend of the Webbs, who had suggested the word 'Statesman' as a title for their proposed journal.

Two other writers, both friends of Sharp's and appointed by him to join the editorial staff, were the poet J. C. (Jack) Squire, another former *New Age* regular, who became the journal's literary editor, and Desmond MacCarthy, who became its drama critic. Thus from the start there was a distinct core of men of letters on the paper from which its cultural back-half developed. Early on Robert Lynd, an Irish-born journalist on the *Daily News* of which he was lit ed, and who could write readably on anything, was co-opted as a contributor. His discursive essays over the initials 'YY' provided a halfway house between the Fabian front pages and the Georgian back-half.

Squire and MacCarthy had previously been colleagues on the *New Witness* alongside Hilaire Belloc, Maurice Baring, G. K. Chesterton and his brother Cecil: that journal was a successor to the *Witness*, notable for its anti-Semitism; it had collapsed after it had lost a libel action arising from articles about the Marconi scandal. Before that MacCarthy had been a colleague of Belloc and Chesterton on the *Speaker*, founded by a group of Liberals during the Boer War. As its dramatic critic MacCarthy had from 1904 onwards covered the the Court Theatre during the Vedrenne-Barker management and had reviewed many of Shaw's plays. In 1906 the *Speaker* ceased: it metamorphosed into the *Nation* with a new editor, H. W. Massingham, who had no use for MacCarthy and dropped him. He confessed later that he had made a mistake.

MacCarthy attended a pre-launch weekend for the new periodical at the Webbs' place at Beachy Head. Sharp and J. C. Squire were among the other guests. It was a time of serious discussion spiced with light-hearted moments, as when Sidney and Beatrice joked about the caricatures of themselves that Wells had put into *The New Machiavelli*. In joining a Fabian paper MacCarthy, married and with a young family, desperate for a regular income, had crossed from one end of the political spectrum to the other, but that did not worry him: 'Of course to some extent I was a fish out of water in such company – or rather not out of water, for I was always easy and interested, but a fish in a strange tank.'

Sharp would have given an air of strangeness to any tank in

which he swam; a large, ungainly, shambling man, with a slow
speaking manner, the result perhaps of his fondness for the bottle;
but his unprepossessing appearance concealed a tough uncompromising journalist of formidable ability. His measured expository
prose seems the essence of sobriety. His strengths are described by
MacCarthy: 'Clifford Sharp possessed in an extraordinary degree
two of the rarest qualities in an editor: Creativeness (the power of
blending a whole paper into a publication with a homogeneous
character) and Decision. He never waited for the cat to jump, but
sprang to conclusions.' This was a time when journalists like
Massingham and Sharp (who heartily loathed each other), Garvin
and Leo Maxse of the monthly *National Review*, really mattered.
They could break ministers, through their pugnacious leaders;
even prime ministers, as Asquith discovered.

Every Tuesday Sharp, Squire, Lynd and MacCarthy would attend
an editorial lunch at the Webbs' London house to form policy.
However, it was not long before Sharp cut loose from the Webbs'
monitoring. 'You know', wrote Shaw to Beatrice, 'I have said from
the beginning the first thing Sharp would have to do would be to
get rid of us. I was quite serious.' Unfortunately the harder Sharp
worked, and the more autonomous he became, the more he relied
on alcohol to sustain him through his editorial labours.

To turn to the back half of the journal in its earliest days: in the
first number, on 12 April 1913, MacCarthy dealt at some length
with Arnold Bennett's play *The Great Adventure*, adapted from
Bennett's novel *Buried Alive*. It was a tactful review, praising
Bennett's artistic instincts. Although Bennett clashed with Mac-
Carthy's Bloomsbury friends over the nature of the novel, he was
a well-wisher of the *New Statesman* from the start. Indeed, as Shaw
withdrew Bennett took his place, becoming a principal share-
holder of the journal and a pseudonymous contributor.

MacCarthy's review was followed by the first 'Books in General'
article, signed 'Solomon Eagle', the pen-name, as we have seen, of
J. C. Squire. The Eagle swooped knowingly across the page in
paragraphs broken by lines of asterisks. 'I hear', his article began,
'that there is a scheme afoot for a translation of Meredith's works
into French . . .' He went on to discuss the popularity of various
English writers abroad, noting the vogue in Germany for Shaw
and Wells, Sherlock Holmes and Raffles. His was a chatty approach
rather than a structured *causerie*, lively and often provocative party
talk rather than penetrating criticism.

The book reviews as such opened with a notice of new fiction by

Hubert Bland. At fifty-eight, Bland was the writer of an opinion column in the *Sunday Chronicle* and a founding member of the Fabian Society. Married to the author E. Nesbit, Bland was by now almost blind. His assistant, Alice Hoatson, read the novels to him and acted as his amanuensis. Julia Briggs, Nesbit's biographer, has shown how the trio formed a *ménage à trois*, and that it was Alice, and not the author of *The Railway Children*, who was the natural mother of Rosamund Bland, Edith becoming her adoptive mother. Rosamund had had an affair with H. G. Wells, an affair ended by the efforts of Hubert and Edith. Then Rosamund made another conquest within the ranks of the Fabian Society, Clifford Sharp, whom she married in 1909.

The fiction reviewing was therefore in the hands of the editor's father-in-law. An example of the kind of fiction he had to review was that represented by the industrious Benson brothers. When A. C. Benson's *Watersprings* came out, Bland wrote: '[It] is Mr A. C. Benson's first novel and I fain to wish it were not, for the temptation to me to say I hope it will be his last is almost irresistible.' Bland's reviews continued non-stop every week for a year, a killing rate of production – as indeed it proved. For the paper of 14 April 1914 – exactly twelve months after the first issue – Bland dictated a review to Alice of a novel by Arthur Benson's younger brother Fred, E. F. Benson – the one Benson brother whose fiction has survived. 'It will be mildly interesting,' Bland mused, 'to see whether the great popularity achieved by Mr Benson's *Dodo the First* [whose heroine was based on Margot Asquith] will be accorded to his *Dodo the Second*.' Unfortunately, Bland did not live to see the answer to his speculation, because he died after dictating this review.

With Bland's demise the new fiction was for several weeks reviewed anonymously. Anonymity was the rule on the pre-First-World-War *Statesman* for all the reviews except the fiction, as it was on the *Nation* and elsewhere. Then Gerald Gould, a Fabian friend of Sharp's, a poet often present at E. Nesbit's salon, took over on the same regular weekly basis. From time to time a novel that is still read today – *Jacob's Room*, *Of Human Bondage*, *The Shadow Line* – came Gould's way. He honestly confessed he could 'get no excitement whatever' out of the Conrad but at the same time he gives an accurate account of it. In the issue of 27 June 1914 he had to review *Dubliners*. Joyce's volume went into a batch of three, sandwiched between Maxim Gorky's *Tales of Two Countries* and *The New Road* by Neil Munro: 'It is easy to say of Gorky that he is a man of genius. To say the same of Mr James Joyce requires more courage, since his name is little known; but a man of genius is precisely what he is. He has an original outlook, a special method, a complete reliance on his powers of delineation.' Gould singled out 'Grace', 'Araby' and 'The Dead' for special mention. He had one quibble in an otherwise favourable review: 'Frankly we think it is a pity (perhaps we betray a narrow puritanism in so thinking) that a man who can write like this should insist as constantly as Mr Joyce upon aspects of life which are ordinarily not mentioned.'

Apart from the book-reviews, Squire gave space regularly to original poems and sketches from writers such as Rupert Brooke, Charlotte Mew, W. H. Hudson, W. H. Davies. With the benefit of hindsight one has a feeling of a caretaker government in literature, hanging on doggedly while waiting for the election that will usher in a new revolutionary regime. Occasionally we have a sense of things to come, as when Squire publishes poetry by Yeats or reviews Ezra Pound's *Lustra* in a batch that included William Watson's *Retrogression*. The review was anonymous but the authorship is unmistakable, especially as Squire cannot resist his impulse for parody also seen in a series of contemporary parodies he published; they were so apt that some readers took them to be by the authors parodied.

> Mr Pound announces on his first page: 'I mate with my free kind upon the crags'. If the present volume is the first of these Alpine exploits, the sooner an avalanche interrupts his dallyings the better. Here is one of them, called Papyrus.
>
> > Spring
> > Too long
> > Gongula
>
> It is evident that as good a poem might be made by the first three names that should strike the eye on a casual perusal of the telephone books. As for instance,
>
> > Smith
> > Jacobs
> > Guggenheimer, Spitz and Co.

Amends for such levity came a few years later when, before he stood down from the *Statesman* to edit his own literary monthly, Squire ran an article by T. S. Eliot, 'Reflections on *Vers Libre*', written while Eliot was still working at Lloyd's Bank. It is a statement that anyone who wishes to study Eliot's poetic development still needs to consult.

The *New Statesman* was aimed at a reader who was conscious of living in a society in which there was much social injustice. The first numbers contained a re-definition of the Fabian position by Beatrice Webb, a paper titled 'What Is Socialism?' printed as a supplement. Supplements analysing Government White Papers and other topical issues were a regular feature of the early numbers. But they also contained literary supplements in the spring and autumn consisting of extra pages of reviews, essays, *contes*, gossip and lists of forthcoming books. From the start, readers' interest in politics and social affairs was seen as co-existing with an interest in music, art, theatre, history, literature, philosophy (T. E. Hulme's translation of Bergson was reviewed in the first issue); the reader was also viewed as someone who, while sympathetic to the Fabian notion of 'corporateness', might well own a small portfolio of equity shares. There was a City section always after the book reviews.

Shaw's 'intelligent woman' represented an important element in the readership, even if women were non-existent among the journal's regular writers. In November a Supplement included special articles on The Awakening of Women, The Arrested Development of Women, The Remedy of Political Emancipation, Militancy, Motherhood and the State, The Capitalist versus the Home, The Position of Women in Medicine and Surgery, New Types of Subordinate Women Brainworkers, Women in Public Administration. The following February there was another one with the emphasis on Women in Industry, Womens' Wages and Women in Trade Unionism.

To the fury of the Webbs, Shaw insisted that his contributions were anonymous while at the same time publishing letters signed with his name in rival journals like the *Nation*. Though he did relent to write at least one signed article, in the form of a reply to all the reviews of the revival in 1913 of his play *Caesar and Cleopatra*. It resulted in a prolonged discussion in the letters column about the place of historical truth in historical drama. And when his old friend Sir Almroth Wright – the pathologist whose discovery of 'phagocytes' he had satirised in *The Doctor's Dilemma* – published a book demonstrating with biological evidence why women should not be given the vote, *The Unexpurgated Case Against Women's Suffrage*, Shaw

slammed into it joyously above his initials G. B. S. – a much livelier
rebuttal of Wright than the corresponding one by Sir Robert
Ross in the *Nation*. The notion of the supposed intellectual inferiority of women returned in the pages of the *New Statesman* in the
1920s, when Virginia Woolf may be seen taking Arnold Bennett
and Desmond MacCarthy to task in some indignant correspondence.

As Sharp grew in stature he became more and more of an
Asquithian Liberal. The paper's orthodox Fabian line was upheld
by two academics, the young economist G. D. H. (Douglas) Cole
and Mostyn Lloyd who combined his work for the paper with a job
at LSE. In 1916, after two years of catastrophic conduct of the war,
Asquith came under heavy pressure to make way for Lloyd George
as Prime Minister. The final movements in his overthrow came just
as Sharp was writing an article in the *Statesman* in his defence,
headed 'Had Zimri Peace?' – a reference to 2 Kings 9:31, 'Had
Zimri peace who slew his master?' On hearing the news that LG
had kissed hands with the king and become prime minister, Sharp
scrapped the final part of his article but printed what he had
written, leaving the rest of the space blank. The journal also
published, as a supplement, Shaw's lengthy, tortuous cogitation
'Common Sense About the War', that resulted in Shaw's ostracism
by much of London society. Eventually Sharp was called up and
went away to work in the intelligence service on a secret mission
in Sweden, while Squire stood in as editor in his absence. Squire
was one of those all-rounders who are capable of fulfilling any role
in journalism with reliable competence.

After the war Sharp returned for a second alcoholic period as
an ever more isolated editor, and Squire resigned to start the
London Mercury. MacCarthy became lit ed but remained dramatic
critic with help from younger men, one of whom was Francis
Birrell, son of Augustine Birrell, Asquith's Irish minister who had
resigned in the aftermath of the Easter Rebellion in Dublin.
Meanwhile, fundamental changes were happening to the rival
periodicals. In 1922 Orage gave up editing the *New Age* to move to
Fontainebleau in the service of Gurdjieff, and at about the same
time H. W. Massingham joined the Labour Party and gave up the
editorship of the *Nation*. Murry's two-year blaze of editorial glory
had not been enough to save the *Athenaeum*; the *Nation* had
absorbed it to become the *Nation and Athenaeum*. But if this double-
title were to survive in the harsh economic climate of post-First-
World-War Britain it would need an injection of fresh funds and

of fresh editorial talent. In the event both of these came by way of the Cambridge economist and Bloomsbury luminary, J. M. Keynes. With the assent of the Rowntrees, he became the chairman of the board of the *Nation and Athenaeum* and he appointed one of his Cambridge colleagues who had been his pupil, the Scottish economist Hubert Henderson, to be the editor. T. S. Eliot was offered the literary editorship but he was not quite ready to leave his job at the bank. In the end it was Leonard Woolf – he had written for the paper under Massingham – who took on this post. With Woolf sending out books on one paper and MacCarthy on its rival there was bound to be a considerable amount of overlap; it was the *Nation* that became the most thoroughly Bloomsbury-fied of the two using Russell, Strachey, Huxley, Bell, Garnett, Lowes Dickinson, Forster, George (Dadie) Rylands, Raymond Mortimer. The candour of the reviews by these young Bloomsberries soon began to distress Henderson who, having in mind the older type of *Nation* reader, wanted their exuberance curbed. He and Woolf had a harsh argument over an attack by Mortimer on a play by A. A. Milne. Woolf offered to resign but it did not quite come to that; for the moment editor and lit ed agreed to differ.

Back at Great Queen Street it was MacCarthy who wrote the weekly 'Books in General' article, now signed 'Affable Hawk' in playful riposte to Squire as the Eagle; the pseudonym seemed to suit not only MacCarthy's literary style but also his physical appearance. He often wrote about the work of friends: Max Beerbohm, for instance. The Hawk lauded his book of drawings, *Rossetti and his Circle*, or the Hawk would hover delightedly over the latest volume in the posthumous collected edition of Henry James. On 23 October 1920 we find him discussing the *Memoirs* of W. H. Mallock, a writer whose extreme right-wing views were opposed to everything the front part of the paper stood for but of whose reactionary politico-novels, *The Old Order Changeth* and *A Human Document*, MacCarthy was appreciative. He also devoted one article to the first number of Eliot's new journal, the *Criterion*. A beguiling miniature Beuveish essay, a sharing of enthusiasm for a particular writer different in outlook from the paper's prevailing political climate, became the norm.

MacCarthy was throughout the 1920s in close touch with Leonard and Virginia Woolf, who was reviewing regularly for the *Lit Supp* and for several other journals as well. These three powerful members of the reviewing clerisy were sometimes under one roof comparing notes about their plans for forthcoming reviews. There

was an evening in July 1923 when Virginia's former classics teacher
Janet Case looked in on the Woolfs while Desmond and Leonard
were mulling over who was going to review what. 'They steal each
other's reviewers,' Virginia explained to her old friend. 'Desmond
steals my reviewers,' contradicted Leonard.

Raymond Mortimer was an example of someone who was a
Nation reviewer for Leonard and who became a *Statesman* reviewer
for Desmond. When the latter asked Leonard who he had reviewing in the *Nation* that week, Leonard told him Bertrand Russell
and Robert Graves. 'Oh that's all right,' said Desmond, 'my Bertie
comes out next week.' The talk then turned to Middleton Murry
who, after the demise of the *Athenaeum* and the death of Katherine
was editing the *Adelphi*, just into its second number. Desmond gave
an imitation of Murry overcome with remorse about his treatment
of Katherine, adding to the effect by beating his breast. Murry was
printing extracts from her Journal in the *Adelphi*. To assess
Katherine as a writer was something that still exercised the
Bloomsbury clerisy. Desmond alluded to Raymond's recent review
of her posthumous collection, *The Dove's Nest*. Raymond had noted
the Chekhovian influence and also Katherine's 'elusiveness'. She
was (he said) so good at getting into other people's skins that you
could never be sure what she thought herself. He felt that she,
'had a beautiful *flair* for whatever is good in the worst of us, but so
much occupied was she with this that she never, I think, portrayed
a really agreeable person – the sort of person, I mean, with whom
one would like to stay or travel.' Desmond felt that Raymond had
not truly understood her. 'Nor did I,' he added. Then Virginia, to
get conversation away from the work of another contemporary
fiction-writer, a topic distasteful to her, paid Desmond a compli-
ment: 'I say Desmond, whatever the reason may be, the Hawk gets
daily better and better. Its never been so good. People talk about
the Hawk: about reading the paper for the Hawk.'

Fiction reviewing in the *New Statesman* during the 1920s and
1930s evolved from the competent pen of Gerald Gould to the
brilliant one of Rebecca West. We can observe Rebecca, always her
own woman and never part of any clique, further developing her
powers as a reviewer after her *New Freewoman* period was over.
Peter Quennell, another of MacCarthy's acquisitions, was used
frequently as a reviewer of both fiction and non-fiction.

In 1928 Quennell reviewed Evelyn Waugh's first book *Rossetti:
His Life and Works*:

a new biographer has undertaken Rossetti's defence. And herein, perhaps, lies the chief weakness of the monograph; we could have spared Mr Waugh's lengthy analysis of Rossetti's pictures, as against a detailed and elaborate representation of the entire group. Rossetti is exalted at the expense of his contemporaries. We need a collective, not a single portrait. The conduct of the pre-Raphaelite adventure, its enthusiasm and impetus, is, on the whole, more entertaining than its actual results.

Quennell had been a close friend of Waugh at Oxford. After the appearance of this review, Waugh became Quennell's implacable enemy, and from now on Quennell did not make the mistake of criticising a book under review for not being the one he might have himself written on the subject.

Another contributor, Edward Sackville-West, heir to the fourth baron Sackville and Knole, had been 'up to' Aldous Huxley at Eton, before going on to Christ Church to read modern languages and history. Apart from his catholic knowledge of literature, Eddy was a fine musician. All these interests converged in his novel *Piano Quintet* (1925). The year before it appeared he had begun to make his mark as a literary and music critic in the *Spectator* and the *NS* but it was not until 1935, when his great friend Raymond Mortimer was put in charge of the back, that he began his series of Gramophone Notes that continued for the next twenty years. When authors such as Rilke or Leopardi cropped up for review, it was Eddy who was consulted to decide what should be done.

Someone from a very different background who became a fixture as an editorial assistant on the back half as well as a frequent contributor was the Australian-born, Oxford-educated journalist G. W. (George) Stonier. He was the poetry reviewer covering early volumes by Dylan Thomas and he served as the *New Statesman's* film critic for several decades. But of all these writers MacCarthy's most brilliant catch as a reviewer during his period as lit ed was the old Etonian Cyril Vernon Connolly.

In August 1926 Connolly was staying at Big Chilling, Logan Pearsall Smith's country house in Hampshire, where he met MacCarthy. Connolly described the encounter to his school-friend Noel Blakiston:

Desmond MacCarthy, the [literary] editor of the *New Statesman* has been staying here – a very good man indeed – wise humorous and kindly with a complete inability to finish anything he sets out to do, and a pathetic belief he is going to; the same gift of casual definition as you – we used to talk late every night.

The friendship between Connolly and MacCarthy ('the wisest man in the world', said Cyril) ripened on the literary front and over the chess-board to which they and their host were addicted. Soon MacCarthy asked Connolly to review a book; it was one by Paul Morand, the French diplomat and chronicler of Parisian night-life. Connolly's youthful admiration for Morand dates from this assignment. He recommended Morand to Noel Blakiston and wrote further reviews of Morand's work for a one-off magazine the Blakiston brothers and Connolly were at that time planning to bring out, to be called *The Athansian*. Had it ever appeared, it would stand as the ancestor of *Horizon*.

Although MacCarthy seemed pleased with the Morand review Connolly wrote for him, he never printed it. However it proved to be the forerunner of a magnificent flow of reviews by Connolly in the back half of the paper, starting in the autumn of 1927 when he was twenty-four with a reappraisal of the works of Sterne, and continuing for the next nine years. The young Connolly's reviews set the literary world on fire. This was especially true in 1936 when he revalued A. E. Housman after the poet's death; and no regular fiction reviewer on the *NS* or any other paper has laid into the Library Novel (the Walpoles, the Priestleys, the Galsworthys, the Louis Goldings, and so on) with such entertaining and acute virulence. Connolly's reviews, ephemeral in intention, have passed into literary criticism. They prepared the ground for the general recognition of the novel as a serious literary form in Britain, alongside the prefatory utterances of Henry James and the creative and critical work of Virginia Woolf.

Cyril Connolly belonged the post-Virginia Woolf generation. VW was born in 1882, Connolly in 1903. He was a committed hedonist who had an entertaining irreverence not only like Strachey about Victorian pieties and pomposities but about *all* pieties and pomposities. He matured as a writer in the decade 1920–1930 when his style and outlook as a reviewer was formed:

What we meant by the Twenties [Connolly wrote] is a climate of dandyism and artistic creation which came to a head in 1922, year of *The Waste Land, Ulysses,* Valéry's *Charmes,* Rilke's *Elegies, Jacob's Room* and *The Forsyte Sag*a. Proust was at his zenith, Bloomsbury buzzed,

Huxley and the Sitwells scintillated; Lawrence was still respectable. Hardy, Conrad and Moore were all alive. France was cheap to live in, demobilised fugitives from prohibition or the family business reinforced Montparnasse. The Diaghilev ballet flourished. Paris went expatriate.

Reviewing Robert Allerton Parker's book about the Pearsall Smiths, *A Family of Friends* in the *Sunday Times* in 1960, Connolly had the advantage – one that not infrequently befell him in his later years – of being a personage in the book he was reviewing. He was able to correct some inaccuracies regarding his job with Logan that had crept into the text.

> Far from my 'turning up' at [Pearsall Smith's London house in] St Leonard's Terrace, elaborate negotiations took place between my Balliol sponsor, F. F. Urquhart and Logan, who even gave some assurances to my family as to my salary and expectations. Both were generous, once I had accomplished my first test, the dating of a large bundle of letters to the Berensons from 'Michael Field'.
>
> At that time (aged 22) I was a stern young man who liked climbing in the Alps, walking in Greece or Spain, exploring classical sites and romanesque churches. I hated Paris, which Logan afterwards taught me to appreciate.

But Connolly had in his early twenties a knowledge of classical, English and European literature that many fail to acquire after a lifetime of reading and reviewing. His outstanding gifts were at once recognised by MacCarthy, who tried to recruit Connolly as his assistant as well as using him for reviews. 'Desmond has offered me £20 a night to do with him the whole of the literary *New Statesman!*' he writes Noel Blakiston in April 1927. As the reviewing-work snowballed, the epic and novels Connolly was trying to write were set aside until they were more or less permanently shelved. Out of his failure to produce a sustained imaginative work he derived the standards by which he judged the work of others in his reviews. He was one of the first fiction reviewers to recognise the importance of the modern American novel, while at home he singled out Isherwood's *Mr Norris Changes Trains* and Orwell's *Burmese Days* as rare correctives to the national complacency. Such was the force of the Connolly's attack on the indigenous fictional product that David Garnett was moved to protest in print at his dismissals.

The *New Statesman's* books pages were used at this time as a
hunting-ground by arts and books editors of the Sunday newspapers in search of new reviewers. Connolly's potential did not
escape the discerning eyes of Cyril Lakin and Leonard Russell.
Long before his post-Second-World-War appointment as a lead-
reviewer on the *Sunday Times*, Connolly contributed to its books
pages, and at the same time continued to write regularly for the
NS. As Jeremy Lewis has shown in his splendid *Cyril Connolly: A
Life*, in 1935 Connolly was not only coping with a batch of six to
eight novels each fortnight in the *NS* but doing a similar batch in
the *Daily Telegraph*, as well as the occasional non-fiction review for
the *Sunday Times*. On top of that, Connolly became a regular
crime-fiction reviewer for the *Sunday Times* in November 1935,
alternating with Anthony Berkeley writing as Francis Iles. Such was
the early career of the man to whom a reputation for indolence
has stuck like mud.

In June 1936 Connolly published his unforgettable valedictory,
'Ninety Years of Novel-Reviewing':

> The reviewing of novels is the white man's grave of journalism; it
> corresponds, in letters, to building bridges in some impossible
> tropical climate. The work is gruelling, unhealthy and ill-paid, and
> for each scant clearing made wearily among the springing vegetation
> the jungle overnight encroaches twice as far.

Looking back on the experience of reviewing contemporary novels
in the 1920s, he pointed to the puppet Petrouchka in Stravinsky's
ballet as the model of the contemporary pre-war fictional hero as
he emerged in books by Norman Douglas, Aldous Huxley, Joyce,
Hemingway, and in Eliot's Prufrock. These writers' heroes:

> knew that they had been 'had' and they were in a hurry to tell the
> world about it. Those who had been fooled most were young men
> who had fought and survived the war; the literature of that time in
> consequence is predominantly masculine, revolving round a theme
> which may be called 'The Clever Young Man and the Dirty Deal'.

A comparable discernment about the work of his elders and
betters animated that combination of autobiography and criticism
Enemies of Promise (1938). Like his hero Sainte-Beuve, Connolly
tried his hand at a work of fiction at least once – in the drop-out

Mediterranean novel *The Rock Pool* (1947), a cult book among those who identified with its ineffectual hero. Connolly was a masterly parodist and a brilliant exponent of a peculiar form he invented – a collage of quotation, apophthegm and confession – in *The Unquiet Grave*, published under the Virgilian pseudonym Palinurus in 1944. Like *Horizon*, a monthly 'Review of Literature and Art' he edited, it penetrated beyond the wartime British blackout to those many illuminations continental and American culture still had to offer us. Connolly's post-war critical distillation *The Modern Movement* (1965), a hundred short paragraphs about a hundred major books, has its admirers; but his main lifetime's effort as a writer went into his weekly causerie and some longer travel articles. He published collections of his journalism at intervals: *The Condemned Playground* (1945), *Previous Convictions* (1963), and *The Evening Colonnade* (1973). Sadly and scandalously, there is no collected edition of Connolly's reviews.

These reviews, still brilliantly readable, reveal complete mastery of the author or period under discussion. Connolly makes connections that send you scurrying to the library for all the books he has mentioned in passing. The sequence of reviews of the *fin-de-siècle* English writers of the 1890s – Symons, Dowson, Wilde – in his last collection, *The Evening Colonnade*, amount to a minor history of the period. His clowning and his hedonism, his love of good living and travel, are part of the general liveliness and enthusiasm for literature as a way of life that makes his reviews so compelling. No critic has ever conveyed in his reviews so pervasive a feeling of sensuous delight – his signature tune was Baudelaire's *luxe, calme et volupté*. The people he writes about seem to inhabit his mind like living presences, whether they are ancient Romans, inhabitants of eighteenth-century London, or close contemporaries. If most writers review to live, Connolly lived to review and to travel.

Part of the reason for his neglect is his own fault. Never before has a critic denigrated the task to which he devoted his life more than Connolly. In *Enemies of Promise* he quoted those lines of George Crabbe's *The Village* describing flourishing weeds to identify the pressures that prevent a young writer from developing his gift. The flamboyant blue bugloss is journalism, 'deadliest of the weeds on Crabbe's Heath'. A writer,' he continues, 'who takes up journalism abandons the slow tempo of literature for a faster one and the change will do him harm'. True of many, yet there are exceptional instances, writers who seem to be able to modulate at

will between the two tempi, quick quick (for the reviewing), slow
for the novels. Anthony Burgess, for example, who had such a rich
period as a regular reviewer for Kilmartin on the *Observer*.

In 1928 MacCarthy started the monthly literary magazine *Life
and Letters*, with backing from Oliver Brett (brother of 'Brett', the
deaf woman painter who belonged to the D. H. Lawrence circle)
as Bloomsbury's rival to the *London Mercury*. Then in 1929, in the
first of what was to become a regular exodus of *Statesman* literary
journalists to the *Sunday Times*, MacCarthy was translated to
Gosse's vacant slot. After MacCarthy left, Stonier became acting lit
ed for a time until the appearance of an obscure figure, Clennel
Wilkinson, a friend of Sharp's, and author of a life of the
seventeenth-century navigator William Dampier. He did not last
long as lit ed but for a while 'Books in General' ceased, replaced
by articles from Hilaire Belloc.

Ellis Roberts, a Fabian, an Anglo-Catholic and a bibliophile,
whose previous career had been on the *Church Times* and the *Daily
Chronicle*, was next to occupy the lit ed chair. V. S. Pritchett
describes Roberts as resembling 'a fat soft cooing priest'. Roberts,
an occasional poet, had written many book-reviews in his time,
including an appreciative one of Edward Marsh's anthology,
Georgian Poetry 1911–12. His party piece was to read aloud choruses
from the work of Vachell Lindsay in the voice of a southern black.

Throughout the 1920s the eventual merger of two highbrow
weeklies with so many reviewers and attitudes in common and
insufficient readers to make either really viable, was often secretly
mooted, but it was not until 1931 when Hubert Henderson
resigned from the *Nation* for a job in Whitehall and Leonard
Woolf resigned as literary editor, that the moment of truth arrived.
The *Nation's* circulation of around 8000 was inadequate for the
journal's viability and Keynes decided that he had no alternative
but to negotiate with the *New Statesman* (circulation 10,000 but
also losing money). By now the *Statesman* had acquired a business
manager, John Roberts. Although Keynes emerged as chairman of
the reconstituted board, it was Roberts who triumphed by dictating
terms greatly to the advantage of the *Statesman*. The result was the
beginning of a new series of the journal that became – to give its
full title – 'the *New Statesman and Nation* incorporating the *Athenaeum*'. For a week or two after the merger the paper's circulation
jumped to 18,000, then settled down at 14,500, around the break-

even point. A medallion depicting the head of Athene came onto the *Statesman's* masthead, a circular woodcut that stood as an earnest of the journal's Hellenism, especially in its cultural pages.

After a long sabbatical Sharp's tendency to get involved in costly libel actions – to say nothing of his tendency to get stoned – did not diminish. After much hesitation, he was painfully fired. Kingsley Martin, aged thirty-four, son of a Unitarian clergyman, was appointed editor. Martin, a pacifist, had served in the Friends Ambulance Unit during the last part of the war and had then gone up to Magdalene Cambridge to read History. After Cambridge, where he was awarded a Bye (part-time) Fellowship, he spent a few years at the London School of Economics as an assistant lecturer in politics. He clashed with its director, William Beveridge, over a pamphlet Martin published on the General Strike; at the same time he made friends with colleagues such as Harold Laski and R. H. Tawney. Martin as a young historian had published scholarly books on the French Enlightenment and on Lord Palmerston. His future career was at this period delicately balanced between the academic life and journalism.

In 1927 an invitation from C. P. Scott, editor of the *Manchester Guardian*, to become a leader-writer on the staff of the paper tipped the balance. Martin's academic work came to an end. He proved to be a born journalist, developing the easy clarity and readability that were his hallmark, and were to be seen soon in the *New Statesman* when, borrowing the mantle of Massingham, he began to write a discursive weekly Diary as Critic. In this role Martin acquired a large following.

When Martin became editor of the *New Statesman* he inherited Ellis Roberts as his lit ed but soon disposed of him. Stonier temporarily took over the back half once again, while Martin looked around for a permanent incumbent as lit ed. Martin's first approach was to Harold Nicolson, who turned him down: Nicolson was already earning £600 a year as a free-lance; the job would have given him only another £400 and would have tied him to London four days a week. Besides he felt that the position, with its salary of £1000, should go to Raymond Mortimer who happened to be his lover. Nicolson did write a series of 'Books in General' throughout 1933. Mortimer would get the job eventually, but for the present it went to David Garnett.

Garnett had scored a great success when he was thirty with *Lady into Fox* – a fable about a man who retains a deep love for his

young wife after she has physically turned into a vixen and is
stalking the fields outside his house. It was published in 1922, a
slim volume illustrated by Garnett's wife Rae, had gone into several
editions and was for weeks the talk of literary London, praised by
Virginia Woolf among others. Charles Ryder finds it in Sebastian
Flyte's rooms in Christ Church and reads it while waiting for him
to return from Mass. Only D. H. Lawrence remained unapprecia-
tive; he thought it was 'playboy stuff'.

After the First World War in which he had worked for the Red
Cross in Normandy and on a fruit farm near Charleston, Garnett
and Francis (Frankie) Birrell ran their own bookshop in Soho.
They specialised in fine books and first editions. Frances Marshall,
Garnett's sister-in-law (who would marry Ralph Partridge after the
death of Carrington), worked as an assistant:

> There were sets from the libraries of the fathers of the two partners
> – Augustine Birrell and Edward Garnett; Constance Garnett's trans-
> lation from the Russian and all the publications of the Hogarth Press;
> modern French novels settling on their haunches as French books
> will; seventeenth and eighteenth-century books in warm brown
> contemporary bindings. We did a profitable trade in Henry James –
> having discovered that the first editions of several of his books were
> still in print at Macmillans, we issued a catalogue including for
> instance "*Spoils of Poynton*. First Edition; mint condition, as new" and
> as orders came pouring in, especially from America, one of us would
> hurry round to the publisher's trade door, buy copies and despatch
> them.

Garnett's wide circle of friends and lovers contained Bloomsberries such as Lytton Strachey and Duncan Grant, the open-air
literary loner T. H. White, the bibliophile Francis Meynell, with
whom he started the Nonesuch Press, the lesbian genius Sylvia
Townsend Warner, and people at the centre of power such as
Maynard Keynes, who at the end of 1932 invited him to become
literary editor of the *New Statesman and Nation*. At least that is how
Garnett remembered the sequence of events, but Adrian Smith in
his book on the *New Statesman* suggests that it was Garnett who
approached Keynes.

At any rate, Garnett got the job as lit ed. Entering his office for
the first time, Garnett was horrified by the amount of unused copy
it contained:

I found an enormous number of reviews, poems and stories which had been accepted by Ellis Roberts, many of them in proof. The majority were either without merit, or positively bad. They would have filled the literary columns until the following summer and their publication would have killed the paper. I decided to use nothing which I should not have chosen on its merits myself. But there were also drawers full of contributions which had been lying unread for several months. One night during my first week as literary editor, I was alone in the old building reading these arrears. Eleven o'clock (closing time) had just struck when I heard the bare wooden staircase creaking under a heavy uncertain step. Someone was coming up it, with difficulty. Whoever it was reached the landing outside and went into Kingsley Martin's room. I knew from the lurching step it was not Kingsley. Presently the light under my door must have attracted the visitor's attention, for he crossed the landing and threw open my door. A big heavy man with a heavy lined face stared at me.

'Who are you?' he demanded.

I might well have asked the same question but I replied gently: 'I'm the new literary editor. My name's Garnett.'

'Oh. Are you?'

At that moment I recognised him as the ex-editor, Clifford Sharp, whose place had been filled some months previously by Kingsley Martin. In his day Clifford Sharp had been a great journalist and right up to the end of his tenure he was credited with being able to sit down and write a two-page political leader in the early hours before the paper went to press. When the staff arrived his copy would be lying on the desk with scarcely an erasure and there would be an empty whisky bottle in the waste-paper basket. Sharp sometimes had no memory of even the subject which he had chosen, still less of the line he had taken, but when the proof came from the printers it seldom needed alteration. Such was the man's legend.

The bloated face stared in on me from the doorway in the most macabre fashion. Finally Sharp gave up the problem, and saying: 'Well – carry on', he turned and went back into Kingsley's room where he slumped into the editorial chair. But my presence had disturbed him, and a few minutes later I heard him stagger out and go creaking down the stairs. The explanation of his visit was simple. When he had been sacked, he had kept a key of the building and at a certain stage of the evening he was apt to forget that he was no longer the editor and go back to the office, to exercise ghostly supervision of the paper which had been his life for so many years. What a subject for Henry James!

One of the reviews awaiting publication was of a work by T. E. Lawrence, a close friend of the new lit ed's father. Under the name of John Hume Ross, Lawrence had recently been thrown out of the RAF by Trenchard. While he had been at Miranshah on the frontiers of Afghanistan, Lawrence had finished his prose translation of *The Odyssey*, which had come out in a limited edition designed by Bruce Rogers and then in a more general one from the Oxford University Press. It was credited to 'T. E. Shaw,' another Lawrence RAF cover-name. It had been sent in for review to the paper in the last days of the Roberts regime. Roberts had reviewed it himself and slammed it; his review was still in type.

Garnett's first decision as lit ed was to kill this review and request another copy of the book. He dispatched the fresh copy to J. T. Sheppard at King's, who promptly sent it back, explaining that he did not have time or inclination to review it. Garnett then tried C. M. Bowra at Oxford, suggesting he combined T. E. Shaw's *Odyssey* with a review of *The Odes of Pindar Rendered into English Verse* by Alexander Falconer Murison. Bowra soon obliged:

The order of [Mr Murison's] words gets distorted; adjectives follow their nouns; the verb waits disconsolately at the end of its sentence. Pindar's great clinching maxims, his pondered contributions to the art of life, sink below the copybook level when they appear as

A warning that man should not aspire
Loves not within his power e'er to desire.

The twenty-eighth English rendering of the *Odyssey* assails an easier task with far greater success. Aircraftman Shaw was right to chose prose as his medium, because it is the natural medium for English narrative and the *Odyssey* is first and foremost a story. All verse translations of it have failed, because they are too literary and lose its essential freshness, and only in the prose of Malory has English any kind of parallel to this epic art. Indeed this translation of Homer is by far the best translation of Homer into English. It conveys more of his qualities and is infinitely more readable than Pope or Mackail or Butcher and Lang. It is not a crib, and the plodding student may be led astray by it, but it stands on its own as literature and can be read for its own sake. It is as exciting, humorous and technical as the *Odyssey* is. The muscular rhythm of its sentences is no poor substitute for the Homeric hexameter, and its complete lack of trite phrases and exhausted words gives it the youth and gaiety of Greek.

On the strength of Bowra's review Sheppard went out and bought the book, read it, and sent a letter of apology to Garnett saying he was full of admiration for the freshness of Lawrence's version.

One reviewing system Garnett left unchanged when the journal moved to new premises at Great Turnstile off High Holborn was that of the shorter notice. Shorter notices are a useful device for a lit ed to increase the ratio of books reviewed in relation to those submitted for review (something that may trouble his conscience when he first takes on the job); but it is notoriously difficult to get satisfactory copy for this feature. Often the lit ed and his assistant are reduced to writing these notices themselves during those rare moments when they are not checking copy or on the phone. Garnett explained how the system operated in his day:

> 'Shorter Notices' was the one column which I did not attempt to change. It was run as a charity. Certain impoverished writers were, by custom, allowed to range round the shelves of books for review and pick out one or two on which they would write three or four sentences. For this they received about 7/6. Naturally they chose the most expensive books which they could sell for half-price. Thus if one of them got a book selling at a guinea it would bring his remuneration up to 18/-. It was a good system. The publisher got a review and was encouraged to send books to the *New Statesman*. And five or six meritorious down-and-outs in the literary world received a meagre pittance.

Garnett, a fluent confident writer, contributed regular Books in General under his own name; and now the other reviews were all signed too. His Books in General (never re-printed) are different in tone from the Hawk's and reveal a much more extroverted taste in literature. With reference to Quennell's *Byron The Years of Fame* – the book above all on which Quennell's reputation rests – appearing at the beginning of 1936, Garnett makes a comparison between Byron and Wilde saying that they both belonged to that category of writers 'most completely themselves when they abandoned themselves to a pose'; then, using the asterisks cross-head device, he switches to the second edition of Buxton Forman's *Letters of Keats* and points to 'the consumptive's love of the external

beauty of the world'. It was writers who revealed the external
beauty of the world – W. H. Hudson, Richard Jeffries, and more
obscure authors on English village life – as well as exotic characters
like Siamese White, on whom Garnett reflected in subsequent
pieces. A reference to Charles Laughton as Captain Bligh in the
smash-hit film *Mutiny on the Bounty* prefaces his consideration of
The Letters of Fletcher Christian. Chaplin's *Modern Times* was another
of Garnett's springboards used to introduce a discussion of Wells's
Things to Come. The *Memoires de Jacques Casanova* seemed a natural
for Garnett but it is Garnett the bibliophile not the Don Juan who
finds most to praise noting the good printing and good type therein.

Garnett deferred to Martin about who should review important
political and topical books: Harold Laski, Alexander Werth, Cyril
Joad, R. H. S. Crossman, and Hugh Gaitskell all now appear as
among the reviewers of such books. A book entitled *Why the Church
Has Failed* by the Revd Joseph McCulloch (of later BBC fame) was
reviewed by Basil Martin – Martin *père*. But the entire cultural
coverage – the cultural 'policy' – was the province of the lit ed. It
was Garnett who nurtured the considerable reviewing talents of
Wells's and Rebecca's son, Anthony West. He also brought in the
least literary (so it was said) of the Ham Spray folk, Ralph
Partridge, to write a regular round-up of detective stories. Partridge went into the merits of Agatha Christie and related matters
with aplomb. He became a reviewer of general books as well and
was a regular contributor until after the Second World War.

In 1935 Garnett's two-year innings as lit ed came to an end, but
he continued writing weekly 'Books in General' articles until the
outbreak of the Second World War, when (no longer a pacifist)
he joined the intelligence unit at Air Ministry. Looking back on
the whole experience of literary journalism, he said: 'I wrote only
one book – and a very short one – in the seven years which
followed. Journalism was destructive to me as a creative writer for
a long time.'

Garnett was replaced by Raymond Mortimer, who had often
stood in for him and was by now well-established on the paper as a
reviewer of books and of art. For the first time there was a
separation between the lit ed job and writing the weekly 'Books in
General'. After Garnett's departure in 1939, Mortimer asked
Virginia Woolf if she would like to write a regular 'Books in
General' article. She said she was greatly flattered by the invitation
but turned it down.

Raymond Mortimer, son of a West Country solicitor, retained, he once said, 'many characteristics of the Victorian professional class to which his family belonged'. He learnt to read when he was four and to speak French from the age of six. He chatted to his Swiss nannies in French and boasted that at the age of eight he used to play *petits chevaux* in the casinos of Northern France. His mother died when he was a boy and he was sent away to school at Malvern, where he was beaten and miserable. Happier times followed at Balliol, where he went as a commoner and where he had history tutorials from Sligger Urquhart, who became a friend. Before he went up to Oxford he lived with a French family in Paris for six months, attended lectures at the Sorbonne and began the love-affair with French literature that was to be lifelong.

His Oxford career was interrupted by the war. In 1915 he worked in the south of France in a hospital for French soldiers and then for a time at the Foreign Office. Afterwards he was awarded a BA degree without returning to Oxford. He then wrote an Oxford novel with Hamish Miles, *The Oxford Circus – A Novel of Oxford and Youth*, published by John Lane in 1922 and now a very rare book indeed. John Betjeman thought it was 'an at times delightful burlesque or parody of previous serious novels [about Oxford]'. That appears to have been Mortimer's sole excursion as a writer of fiction. Instead he visited America and became a critic and journalist in London as well as a friend of the Woolfs and the Nicolsons (they called him Tray); for a while the lover and travelling-companion of Harold, to whom he always remained devoted.

Mortimer paid tribute to the 'patient tutorials' he received from MacCarthy. It was MacCarthy's practice to go through a review with the writer of it, weeding out sloppiness and solecism. It was Connolly who said that MacCarthy had the catholic taste of a great editor but could not tolerate obscurity. He wished to print 'nothing that he could not talk about at a dinner party'. When he succeeded to the lit ed's throne, Mortimer followed MacCarthy in his criteria of standards in reviewing. He told verbose young men to remember that no one had the time to read anything twice. V. S. Pritchett and T. C. Worsley were colleagues whose writing benefited from his scrutiny and who in turn would take over the show as lit eds when he accepted the Kemsley shilling.

The *Statesman's* arts and book-review section now began to exert an influence on taste and sales of books as profound as the two quality Sundays and the *Lit Supp*. Its literary supplements every spring and autumn, with a comprehensive list of forthcoming books, were eagerly scanned and so were its reviews; they were an essential guide to what anyone who wanted to be in the swim should read. And although its profitability was slow to improve under Martin, the paper's circulation grew steadily.

In the literary pages modern French writing was given a generous amount of space, reflecting the francophilia of the clerisy. The French connection had begun with Murry in the *Lit Supp* and the *Athenaeum* before and after the First World War; it was strengthened by R. S. Flint and Richard Aldington in the *New Age*, and by Eliot and Montgomery Belgion in the *Criterion*. Desmond MacCarthy had become interested in the French novelists who took for a subject the social group and the collective consciousness, the *unanimiste* school. Mortimer promoted them in the *Statesman* and with Sydney Waterlow, a Bloomsbury friend, translated Jules Romains' novel *Mort de quelqu'un*, a key *unanimiste* work.

In January 1936 we find Mortimer writing a composite review of *Les Jeunes Filles* by Montherlant, *Beloukia* by Drieu la Rochelle, *Fils du Jour* by André Thérive and *Journal d'un Curé de Campagne* by Bernanos. These novelists were very right-wing and supported the Action française. Both Drieu la Rochelle (who edited the *Nouvelle Revue Francaise* during the Second World War) and Montherlant eventually committed suicide because of their political views. Bernanos, who denounced Hitler, emigrated to South America in 1938 and returned to France after the war. There was nothing remotely Fabian about any of them.

The gap in outlook between the two halves of the *Statesman* widened under Mortimer. It became a standing joke among readers who formed an affection for the 'pantomime horse', the front and back being frequently out of step with each other; the fore-part consisting of the Diary by Critic (Kingsley Martin, though other members of staff would sometimes contribute items), articles in support of the Soviet Union and of Chamberlain's appeasement policy; and the hind-legs where the arts, 'Books in General' and literary reviewers would dance to the gallic music from across the Channel orchestrated and conducted by Mortimer.

If Mortimer was at one with Lytton Strachey in love of France and things French (Strachey's *Landmarks in French Literature* was itself a landmark in English Francophilia), Mortimer did not share Strachey's animus against the Victorians. In Mortimer the pendulum swung the other way and we find him writing with a nostalgic longing about ninteenth-century clerics, headmasters, governesses as well as on more general issues. He would on average write a

'Books in General' every month as well as reviews of art exhibitions as Roger Marvell (a pen-name he abandoned when a real Roger Manvell began to write about films). In a knowledgeable review of Henry Romilly Fedden's *Suicide* in 1938, Mortimer revealed that he had once contemplated writing such a book himself. When he talked about it to his friends, he discovered suicide 'like the more eccentric manifestations of sex, to be an improper subject'.

The publication of poetry (for example Yeats's 'Easter 1916'), very short fiction and literary parody initiated by Squire continued to enliven the paper after his departure; there was a satirical poem always on a topical issue by 'Saggitarius' (Olga Katzin) and more lasting poetry included Auden's Song 'As I walked out one evening...' among much Georgianism. The weekly reflective essay by Robert Lynd writing as 'Y. Y' already mentioned was a feature that ran for years. The Literary Competition which appeared at the back of the back became an institution.

Naomi Royde-Smith had pioneered the idea of a competition giving readers the opportunity to show off their skills as poets and parodists when she was literary editor of the weekly edition of the *Westminster Gazette* before the First World War. She continued to run these competitions in the *Week-End Review*, started in 1930, at a time when the notion of 'the weekend' as a space for cultural pursuits was coming into its own. The *Review* was financed by Samuel Courtauld and edited by Gerald Barry, who had resigned from the editorship of the *Saturday Review*. As well as having a social conscience, publishing articles on malnutrition in the wake of the hunger marches, Barry introduced a note of high spirits and fun into weekly journalism that was much appreciated. He was unwise enough to print an article by Sharp (now a freelance and supposedly writing the life of Rhodes) attacking a member of the judiciary that resulted in a costly libel action and Courtauld pulled out. After barely four years of its existence, the *Weekend Review* merged with the *New Statesman and Nation* and Barry came onto the *New Statesman* board. The *Review* bequeathed its Literary Competiton – and 'This England' column – to its new owner. The Competitions continued uninterruptedly from the one paper to the other with Royde-Smith printing her report on the final one set in the *Review* (a translation of a German poem) in the *Statesman* on 13 January and Frank Sidgwick setting Competition 200 – a verse dialogue between two B.B.C. announcers – as the first one to appear in the *New Statesman*. The series has continued to the present time.

The Competition was set under various jokey names by Mortimer and his colleagues, Stonier, Pritchett, Worsley and others, who devised ways of appealing to the readers' love of composing light humorous verse, especially limericks and a new form of witty doggerel, the clerihew, invented by E. C. Bentley, and given his own middle name; competitors were also asked to write obituaries of fictional characters, famous last words and many other tests of literary ingenuity. Though they never set any more German poetry, Mortimer's requests for a verse translation of a French poem always elicited a strong response.

Sometimes a poet of repute such as Frances Cornford (as F. C. C.) or Henry Reed would enter. Reed's much-anthologised parody of T. S. Eliot, 'Chard Whitlow', was originally a competition prize-winner. Reed also a became a critic of distinction in the paper. Graham Greene on a famous occasion entered under a pseudonym and carried off second prize with a parody of his own style as a novelist. He revealed his identity in the letters column later. Regular winners such as Allan M. Laing, whose immortality is entirely due to winning these competitons, would sometimes be invited as poachers turned gamekeepers to set and judge a competition. Many of the entrants used pseudonyms. One frequent winner was Naomi Lewis. She also became a setter and under her own name appeared as a reviewer of literary biography and books for children. The competitions became themselves the subject of parody by J. Maclaren-Ross in *Punch*.

Some competiton winners during the war were schoolboys such as F. H. King – better known nowadays as Francis King the novelist – whose poem 'Bookshop Charing Cross Road' summed up the literary scene during the Second World War, ('A row of books where one may rest one's eyes on/ A New Apocalypse or Old Horizon . . .'), and the present writer, whose last words for Rousseau, '*Moi, je . . .*', pleased Mortimer. Recalling the names of people who cropped up week after week as winners or highly commended may give an insight into the kind of reader who subscribed to the paper for the back rather than the front. Such people included Sir Robert Witt, H. J. d'Avigdor Goldsmid, M. R. Ridley, Theodora Benson, Thomas Bodkin, Felix Aylmer, Lady Juliet Duff, Alec Clifton-Taylor, Edward Marsh.

Not everyone who read the paper was enchanted by these highbrow diversions and the prevailing aesthetic climate in the rear half. The discontent came to a head at Christmas time in 1937 when, in addition to the regular literary competition, a

General Knowledge Paper was set as a seasonal entertainment with
a first prize of two guineas (202p in today's money) An indication
of the kind of question aimed at testing readers *general* knowledge
may be seen from the following sample (there were lots more of
the same) :

> By whom is each of these quotations, and to whom does it refer:
>
> 1) He brays, the laureate of the long-eared kind.
>
> 2) Gentle and joyous, delicate and strong
>   From the far tomb his voice shall silence mine.
>
> 3) Say that thou pourest them wheat
>   And they will acorns eat,
>   'Twere simple fury still thyself to waste
>   On such that have no taste.
>
> (Answers: 1. Byron on Coleridge; 2. Landor on Shelley; 3.Ben Jonson
> on himself)

Lancelot Hogben, then professor of social biology at the London
School of Economics, author of the best-seller *Mathematics for the
Millions*, was incensed. 'In view of the challenge of dictatorship to
education in democratic countries,' he wrote, '[the General
Knowledge Paper may] throw light on how far the *NS & N* is
actually in touch with democratic educational machinery'. He
pointed out that of a total of 133 items, 95 were 'literary, pictorial,
architectural, virtuosity'; 15 involved 'classical knowledge'; 2 'natural science' and zero 'civics, modern history, archaeology'. He
used these statistics as an opportunity to launch an attack on the
aestheticism of the rear half, concluding with the confession:
'Though I am a lifelong socialist, perusal of Mr Raymond Mortimer's articles has sometimes almost tempted me to go out and buy
a copy of *Action* [the journal of Oswald Mosley's British Union of
Fascists]'.

The letter confirmed what some people inside the office and on
the board felt strongly too. (When in 1942 Mortimer's volume of
collected reviews, *Channel Packet*, appeared, a wag said it ought to
have been called *Chanel Packet*.) The initial impetus behind the
attack may even have come from the political half. But a show of
editorial solidarity was maintained: 'Tut, tut! Our correspondent

takes the fun too seriously, we cannot salvage democracy in every column of the paper – Ed. *N. S. & N.*'

In November there was an anonymous article in the front half revealing the brutalities of Dachau concentration camp that prompted one short letter to the editor. By contrast, this attack by Hogben started a storm of correspondence from both readers and writers, anticipating the post-war debate about the Two Cultures. It raged throughout the whole of January and even succeeded in drawing E. M. Forster into the fray; he said that the great strength of the *New Statesman* lay precisely in its double-mindedness:

> I trust that it will continue to have two minds, and that if there is a Christmas 1938, it will again give its readers (a) ruthless analysis and (b) cultural tradition. Both of these are, in my judgement, essentials of democracy, and it puzzles me that anyone who calls himself a democrat should try to make trouble between them.

If many of the regular literary reviewers had been recruited via Bloomsbury connections, one outstanding writer was an exception. V. S. Pritchett, whose name was to become closely identified with the literary pages, came onto the *Statesman* by a different route. When he left Alleyns College, Dulwich, he had a period in the parental leather business (described in his memoirs *A Cab at the Door*). Then he went off to Paris for two years, surviving as best he could through a number of *ad hoc* occupations, such as becoming a photographer's assistant, while he absorbed French literature from Rabelais onwards and started to write fiction. The religion in which he had been brought up was Christian Science, and it was thanks to the *Christian Science Monitor's* manager in London that Pritchett got his first job in journalism in his early twenties. He was sent to cover the troubles in Ireland. In Belfast he met his first book-reviewer, the novelist Forrest Reid, who gave him tea.

Little did Pritchett realise, when he saw the piles of novels sent for review from the *Manchester Guardian* in Reid's room, how many books he was going to review himself before he was finished. He then went to Spain and it was living in pre-Franco Spain, he says, that 'brought about a fundamental change in my life'. He became a humanist and a writer of short stories. One of these stories, 'Tragedy in a Greek Theatre', was published in the *Cornhill* magazine, then edited by Leonard Huxley, the father of Aldous and Julian, who had taken over from Reginald Smith. As a Hellenist Huxley had been attracted by the story's setting, the

ancient theatre at Taormina, and suggested that Pritchett should
call on him in the office. Pritchett went to see him and 'for an
hour or so he poured out charm, quotations and classical references very fast' in a mellifluous Huxley voice, but no reviewing
work resulted.

Edward O'Brien, an expatriate American living in London, who
had published one of Pritchett's short stories in *Best Short Stories of
the Year*, told the young man that if he wanted to get onto the *New
Statesman* it was essential for him to make contact with members of
the Bloomsbury group. Pritchett had little idea what the Group
was, or that it had anything to do with the *New Statesman*, or even
where to find Bloomsbury. He then discovered that his lodgings in
London were almost in Bloomsbury, but that brought him no
nearer his goal.

What turned the tide was the appearance of his book *Marching
Spain* in 1928. It got reviewed and his name started to become
known. He at last secured an interview with MacCarthy at the *New
Statesman* – or rather, he thought he had. When he arrived at the
office in Great Queen Street he discovered that MacCarthy had
not been there for some months. The writer S. K. Ratcliffe – a
Scottish Fabian and journalistic all-rounder who was deputising for
the lit ed – saw Pritchett instead. He asked him what he had read
at university. Pritchett confessed that he had not been to a
university. 'Totally uneducated,' said Ratcliffe laughing. 'Like me.
I didn't go to one either.' Ratcliffe had at one time edited the
Calcutta Statesman, the Indian daily; he was the only journalist to
work on both similarly titled periodicals which otherwise had no
connection with each other. He then told Pritchett to go through
to see Sharp, having carefully checked first with the secretary that
Sharp was in a fit state to conduct an interview. In went Pritchett
to meet the great man. Sharp glanced at Pritchett's cv and said
thickly: 'You've been in Spain? There's a book by a young man
called Pritchett. Will you review it?' Pritchett explained that he
was the author of it and was sent back to see Ratcliffe, who was
highly delighted by the encounter. 'I've got just the thing for you,'
he said pulling down a history of the Coptic Church and asking
Pritchett for 150 words on it. 'Do you know anything about it? No?
That's good. Look it up.'

The Coptic Church got Pritchett off the mark and he was
promoted next time to 600 words on Pérez Galdós and the Spanish
novel; after that there was a fat biography of Christopher Colum-
bus, an opportunity to expatiate on Spanish discoveries in the New

World, and with a high re-sale value. Inevitably he had been type-
cast as an expert on Spain (no bad thing to be pigeon-holed if you
are hungry for reviewing). But then, as sometimes maddeningly
happens to a reviewer just when he is getting on nicely, the lifeline
was severed. Ratcliffe left for America. The flow of review-books
from the 'Staggers' (as the reviewers called it) ceased and Pritchett
turned to the *Spectator*, for which he became novel reviewer. He
was warned by well-wishers to take heed of his creative aims: 'Once
you use book-reviewing as a crutch you'll be on crutches all your
life,' they told him. 'You'll never be able to throw them away.' It is
an admirable maxim for any young writer who can afford to take
it seriously. Pritchett was that rare exception, a creator *and* an
appraiser, as his tomes of more than 900 pages each, *The Complete
Short Stories* (1990) and *The Complete Essays* (1991) prove, along
with his many novels, travel books and memoirs.

It was during the reign of Raymond Mortimer as lit ed that
Pritchett's gifts as literary journalist-critic took firm root in the *New
Statesman* and flowered abundantly. He had got onto the editorial
staff before the Second World War broke out and during the war
he turned himself into a *causerie*-writer of enormous range. The
wartime cultural policy of Martin and Mortimer was that 'Books in
General' should be about the re-reading of a classic. That proved
to be the perfect assignment for Pritchett, who would turn his
mind week after week to an English, French, Spanish, Russian or
American author who deserved a reappraisal. It would often be
one he had been put onto by Mortimer, to whose breadth of
literary knowledge he acknowledged his indebtedness.

The war gave its own resonance to some of these pieces, as to
'Gibbon and The Home Guard' or one on Erckmann-Chatrian's
History of a Conscript during the Napoleonic period. More fre-
quently Pritchett would generalise about novelists as familar as
Thackeray, Mrs Gaskell, Peacock, Fielding, Richardson, Smollet,
Hardy, the Grossmiths, and usually find some wholly fresh perspective on them; or he would look abroad to a work not then well
known in Britain, Constant's *Adolphe*, Le Sage's *The Adventures of
Gil Blas*, Zola's *Germinal*, Svevo's *Zeno*, extending the range of
'Books in General' immeasurably. The wry, confidential, down-to-
earth critic that Pritchett became drew strength from Pritchett the
writer of fiction, the depicter of extraordinary ordinary people in
short stories appearing in *Penguin New Writing* and other little
magazines that flourished then. We can catch him mulling over
his own aims when he writes of Gogol:

Dead Souls belongs to that group of novels which most novelists dream of writing. I mean the picaresque novel of travel, in which the episodic adventures of a single character open up the world. Given the brilliant idea the task, it seems, should be easy. Yet has there been such a novel of any quality since, say, *David Copperfield*? I can think of none.

In 1947 Mortimer left the *New Statesman* to go to the *Sunday Times* and Pritchett – always known by his colleagues and friends as VSP – became the literary editor. He did not relish the job and left much of the administration to his colleague T. C. (Cuthbert) Worsley, who had started writing for the paper before the Second World War. The tall, owlish Worsley, whose grainy complexion reminded me of Auden's, was a striking contrast to VSP. After going down from Cambridge he had been a classics master at Wellington. He gave an entertaining account of his progress up to 1945 in his auotobiography, *Flannelled Fool*. As a public schoolboy he had been a fine cricketer. It was while he was at Cambridge that he came under the influence of Leavis and started to undergo a profound character-change; the cricket blue and hearty turned into a lover of literature and a poet. During the Spanish Civil War he went to Spain as an ambulance-driver and wrote a book about it, *Behind the Battle*, another appeared from him in 1940 summing up his views on education, *Barbarians and Philistines: Democracy and the Public Schools*, somewhat prematurely heralding their demise.

While he was working as a schoolmaster in the homoerotic ambience of the pre-war English public school, one of Worsley's pupils whom he loved was killed in a car crash. Worsley wrote a sonnet in his memory in the sardonic Siegfried Sassoon manner. He sent it to J. C. Squire at the *London Mercury* who wrote back accepting the poem for publication, with an invitation to Worsley to call at the office with any more there might be of the same.

When Worsley penetrated Squire's sanctum, he appeared to have forgotten all about the invitation:

'What did you say the name was?'
'Worsley.'
'And the initials?'
'T. C.'
He tried them over several times: T.C. Worsley: T.C. Worsley: T.C. Worsley: and then something clicked.
'Not *the* T.C. Worsley?'

Heavens! Was I so well known already? I had published nothing
but this one sonnet in his magazine. Did this make me *the* T.C.
Worsley? How amazing! Was it as good as that?

No it wasn't as his next question showed:

'Let me see. Let me see,' he rummaged through his memory. 'I've
got it! Marlborough v Rugby at Lord's three years running. Forty-
three in the second innings of the second year. Perambulators
against the Etceteras, eighty-two. Fenners 1929. University v Yorkshire
same year. Am I right?'

He was, within a run or two, and was delighted to be told so.

'There you are. Of course I'll publish your poems. Leave them
with us.'

But those weren't, of course, the conditions on which I wanted to
be published. I was turning rapidly against my excessively athletic
past. But better that I supposed than nothing: and two others were
printed. The rest disappeared into that general muddle which
seemed to be a permanent condition at the *London Mercury*.

It was Worsley who in 1947 succeeded MacCarthy as the *New
Statesman's* dramatic critic, becoming only the second person to be
given that title in the paper's history. He was apprehensive at the
prospect but he soon established himself as a critic in the Mac-
Carthy tradition. He gave a reasoned view of the current state of
the drama, concentrating more on the play than on individual
performances. It was a fruitful period for such a critic. The London
theatre was in process of reconstructing itself after the war. Peter
Brook and Tyrone Guthrie were turning Shakespeare production
inside out – Worsley pitched furiously into Guthrie's *Henry VIII*.
H. M. Tennent management, in the person of Hugh 'Binkie'
Beaumont with Kitty Black as his girl Friday, was busy bringing
playwrights from across the Atlantic and the Channel – Arthur
Miller, Tennessee Williams, Sartre, Anouilh, Cocteau – to Shaftes-
bury Avenue.

Looking at Worsley's notices in the light of the current rating of
some of these playwrights, he seems often to have 'got it wrong'.
He had the gravest reservations about plays like *A Streetcar Named
Desire* and *Death of a Salesman*, regarded now as classics of the
modern theatre, but his adverse view were expressed cogently and
they remain, with Mary McCarthy's reviews, the *locus classicus* of
the dissenting minority. As a former classics master at a public
school, Worsley was certainly the right critic to review Terence
Rattigan's *The Browning Version*: 'Schoolmasters seem to lend

themselves very easily to sentimentalism in the hands of popular writers, whether they are treated as success or failures; but Mr Rattigan has felt and thought his originally, imaginatively and truly.' It was Worsley who fought a rearguard action in the *Statesman* to save *Variation on a Theme*, the play (an update of *La Dame Aux Camélias*) that in 1958 terminated Rattigan's long run of success on the London stage and led to an eclipse from which his work has only now started to recover. By this time Worsley and Rattigan had become close friends and were occupying the same house in Brighton. The friendship derived from a similarity of background and temperament. They were both raffish and rather grand, with the charm and courtesy that goes with it; both lovers of cricket as well as of young men, and both in spite of their success, intensely lonely people. Worsley is reflected in the character of a leading book-reviewer, the protagonist of Rattigan's one-acter *In Praise of Love*.

I cannot continue in an impersonal vein when writing about Cuthbert Worsley because he was the editor who gave me my first regular book-reviews and was later my colleague on the *FT*, and I feel great personal affection for his memory. I met him when I was twenty-two, during my RAF Air Ministry period in London. I was by now desperate to return to my studies at university. But I simply had to wait my turn in the queue to be 'demobilised' and it took several years. The frustrating situation did have compensations: I could live at home, wear ordinary clothes, read widely and spend most evenings and some of my pay in the then bohemian world of the Fitzrovia taverns in long stimulating conversations with the poet John Heath-Stubbs, the radical Paul Potts, the novelist Peter Vansittart, indulge in games of spoof and Hitchcockian fantasies with the story-writer J. Maclaren-Ross at The Wheatsheaf in Rathbone Place. That was certainly preferable to getting shot down in flames over Germany, which might well have happened to me had I been a year or so older.

I was an assiduous member of the Arts Theatre Club in Great Newport Street, where they did some adventurous productions during and just after the war under the aegis of Alec Clunes, including Sartre's one-acter *Huis Clos* in 1946, directed by a very young Peter Brook with Alec Guinness – just out of the Fleet Air Arm and not yet a Catholic – as Garcin and John Lehmann's sister Beatrice as the lesbian Ines. It made a great impact on me.

Inspired by it I managed in one of my leaves to get over to Paris
and see more of the existentialist theatre. I met Anouilh and
arranged to translate his one-act play *Medée*. He was charming but,
alas, my version was not the one eventually used. I also met Simone
de Beauvoir for a drink at the Café Flore and arranged to translate
her play *Les Bouches Inutiles*. This play was never performed in
London, so far as I know, in my version or in any other, which
seems odd considering her immense fame later. I wrote to a small
publishing company in Goodwins Court, St Martin's Lane, called
The Curtain Press, who were issuing a series of elegantly illustrated
essays on the theatre by Ivor Brown, Sacheverell Sitwell and others
under the general title of 'The Masque', to see if they would like
one on the new French playwrights. The answer, from the man
who ran it, Lionel Carter, was yes; he offered me the princely sum
of £25 for the rights. It was published in 1948 while I was up at
Oxford.

In addition to this I began to do book-reviewing. My first ever
review was for Miron Grindea's international literary journal *Adam*
where, like many other unknowns, I was welcomed and encouraged. It was of Matthiesson's *Henry James: The Major Phase*. I wrote
one or two book reviews for *Tribune*, commissioned by T. R. Fyvel,
who had succeeded Orwell as its lit ed. I did once see Orwell plain
when I visited the Tribune office in the Strand opposite the Law
Courts. I can remember only a black corduroy jacket as he bent
over the typewriter banging out his diary column. He was a book-
reviewer of genius who hated reviewing. Fyvel was assisted by Bruce
Bain, better known later as the theatre critic, and journalist
Richard Findlater, who became one of my earliest editors.

On the strength of these appearances in print I wrote off to the
Statesman asking if there was any chance of writing some reviews
for them. I received a hand-written letter back from VSP saying
that unfortunately they were well-covered in the areas in which I
specialised (a standard response and one I would later often use
myself), but if I liked to ring his secretary he would be happy to
see me. I turned up at Great Turnstile and found that access to
the literary office was gained by an external iron straircase, the
fire exit. I mounted, my heart thumping with excitement. Both
VSP and Worsley were there that day; they interviewed me jointly,
Worsley doing most of the questioning, VSP smilingly benign.
Worsley mentioned that some plays by Camus had come in and
perhaps I might like to try my hand at reviewing them. The only
trouble was he had taken the book home to look at. 'Well,' said

VSP drily, 'when Mr Worsley recovers the book we'll send it to you and you can try writing 800 words on it.' Somehow I got down the fire escape and into the sobering air of Lincoln's Inn Fields. Would the book ever arrive, or was it all some mad daydream? Eventually the book – *Caligula; Cross Purpose: Two Plays* by Albert Camus translated by Stewart Gilbert – did arrive, accompanied by two other volumes – Cocteau's *The Eagle Has Two Heads*, adapted by Ronald Duncan and Ostrovsky's *Diary of a Scoundrel*, adapted by Rodney Ackland – with a request for a composite review.

I wrote it after a day at Air Ministry and it appeared in the paper of 4 September 1948. The 'Books in General' that week was by Edward Sackville-West on *The Journal of Eugène Delacroix* translated by Walter Pach. Then there followed – after me – the veteran journalist H. N. Brailsford on *Early Indian Civilisation* by Ernest Mackay; the *Story of the Arab Legion* by John Bagot Glubb reviewed by R. H. S. Crossman; *Russian Economic Policy* in Eastern Europe by T. E. M. McKitterick, a pamphlet published by the Fabian International Bureau, reviewed by Maurice Edelman; *A New View of the Plays of Racine* by Vera Orgel, reviewed by Martin Turnell (who said there was nothing new about it) and the fiction batch reviewed by Walter Allen in which the lead novel was *The Gallery* by the American writer John Horne Burns, one of the outstanding novels of the war, since then several times re-printed, 'certainly [Allen wrote] a most remarkable picture of Naples during the Allied occupation, but the book is a sandwich rather than a unity; first, a layer of personal recollection, than a sharp study of character seen in the gallery.'

This typical issue of the post-war *Statesman* shows how strong the paper's cultural commitment was to contemporary French literature; also to Crossman as a campaigner for the Zionist cause through the book-review columns. He was warm about Glubb personally: 'If Glubb Pasha's story cannot rival Doughty or Freya Stark in its beauty of style, it has a directness of narrative and an evocative charm that makes it vastly superior to the average soldier's reminscences.'

Then came the sting:

Reading the story of the Arab Legion, one sees clearly enough the danger of permitting our Middle Eastern policy to be made by Anglo-Arabs. It is rather as though our Swiss relations were in the hands of the Alpine Club and based on the assumption that the Matterhorn and the Zermatt guides were the focal point of Swiss life.

My Camus review led to a renewed invitation to look in at the office and I was given by Worsley *Imaginary Conversations* edited with an introduction by Rayner Heppenstall. This is the kind of book you give to a young man dead keen to review. Heppenstall was one of that group of literary men who were subsidising their careers as writers by working as features producers of the recently started BBC Third Programme, and was himself an occasional *Statesman* reviewer. He was also someone very easy to rub up the wrong way and with a most malicious tongue.

Heppenstall had conceived the promising idea of reviving on radio Landor's favourite genre. He had commissioned work from both Pritchett and Stonier as well as Rose Macaulay, J. I. M. Stewart, Sean O'Fáoláin. The Imaginary Conversation can in the right hands be an entertaining form. Peter Ackroyd used it to give some light relief between sections in his life of Dickens and many of his novels are extensions of it. My point was that

> while the novelist has to create an intimacy, the writer of an imaginary conversation can assume it, for at the very beginning, he is able to take so much for granted. Once he has established the character of Aristotle, Milton or Ophelia, then he has at his command a series of literary or historical associations capable of being set in motion by the slightest phrase.

As we corrected the proof, Worsley gave me a MacCarthy-style tutorial. He warned me against my tendency to write over-loaded sentences. He also invited me to lunch. On the way there we talked about Sartre and Camus, who were much discussed in London in bookish circles at this time. Sartre's 1946 lecture *Existentialism and Humanism* had recently appeared in an English translation by Philip Mairet and had been reviewed in the paper by Joad, who wrote:

> in the course of a fairly long experience of philosophical and pseudo-philosophical writing a more pretentious farrago of metaphysical abracadabra has rarely, if ever, come my way. Take a little pessimism, a little atheism, a little nihilism, mix with a little mastery of their fate by heads that are bloody but unbowed, thicken with sibyllic utterances like 'Man is the future of man,' or choice is 'a crisis of subjectivity,' stiffen with assertions of man's freedom and mastery of his destiny, sweeten with the assurance that everything is permitted, but sharpen with the reminder that man is nevertheless not excused,

add 'anxiety', 'abandonment' and 'despair' from stock to give weight,
stir and allow to simmer and the existential dish is ready for serving.

Worsley had read the lecture before sending it off to Joad and he
queried with me that part of the argument where Sartre says 'that
since, when I choose . . .' – as Joad paraphrased it – 'I always
choose the better, I am by implication committing the rest of
humanity to my choice.' Worsley complained this did not make
sense. 'For example,' he said, 'I am homosexual. But I don't want
the rest of humanity to be homosexual, otherwise I should never get
a boy to go to bed with.'

I said I thought Sartre meant that by his choice Worsley would
be committing the rest of humanity *in a similar situation*, i.e. other
people of the same sexual orientation. The discussion stayed at a
hypothetical level, luckily; and then switched to a different tack
when we arrived at the restaurant where we were joined by Giles
Romilly, a man of letters who had been a pupil of Worsley's at
Wellington and was now his literary protégé on the *Statesman* from
which he had a retainer. He wrote articles for the front, reviewed
for the back and assisted Worsley to edit. Giles, the younger
brother of Esmond, Philip Toynbee's great friend, and related to
Churchill, had been re-reading D. H. Lawrence for a forthcoming
radio talk on his poetry and while he admired the poetry was
disappointed by the novels. 'The prose is like wood-ash,' he said.
'It proliferates uncontrollably.'

The time for me to return to university approached. The RAF
let me go at last but would not accelerate my release-date by only
two weeks (after four years service) so that I could arrive on time
for my first term; they were adamant about this in spite of letters
of protest on my behalf to the Air Minister (Geoffrey De Freitas)
from the MP for Oxford University and the Dean of Merton.

My *New Statesman* experience had given me some knowledge of
the difficulties involved in writing reviews and some exposure in a
journal read by my contemporaries; it had also given me a silly,
misplaced sense of superiority towards participating in undergraduate journalism when I got up to Oxford. Who wants to write for
Isis when he has already appeared in the *New Statesman*? What I
failed to see was that at that age it does not matter where you write
so long as you continue to develop. I was confirmed in my lack of
interest in undergraduate journalism by the attitude of friends like
Francis King and Maurice Cranston, who were already possessed
of literary reputations in London but had returned as students to

post-war Oxford. King had published his first novel at eighteen and had had several poems published in the *Listener*. Cranston had published detective stories and was a frequent contributor to the *New Statesman* as a book-reviewer. Worsley had a high regard for his skill. They did not wish to write for *Isis*, so why should I?

I thus gave up the chance of writing alongside contemporaries like Kenneth Tynan and Alan Brien, who were the stars of the undergraduate press at this period. Still, I was busy enough writing essays for a degree course crammed into seven terms (less two weeks) and the usual hectic undergraduate social life. I emerged in the summer of 1950 with a first in English but still hooked on the French theatre. I returned to Paris for an extended stay to study it and to lecture at the British Institute of the Sorbonne for the Agrégation Course in English. It was while I was in Paris that I was summoned by telegram back to Oxford for a prize fellowship viva at Magdalen College.

I had sat this fellowship examination before going off to Paris 'just for the hell of it', I told myself, and having done the written part, had not given it another thought. I now boarded an aircraft to London and spent one night at home chatting to my parents rather than preparing for what I stupidly did not realise would be a considerable ordeal. The vivas were held in front of the entire Magdalen senior common room which awarded two fellowships by examination each year. My inquisitors were C. S. Lewis and J. A. W. Bennett. It did not go too badly to begin with (Chaucer ... poetic diction, etc.) but then we got on to Sidney's *Arcadia* and with my head currently full of Montherlant, Salacrou, Giraudoux I had just not done my Arcadian homework. In the glazed silent presence of A. J. P. Taylor and those other formidable minds, Lewis made mincemeat of me.

After that *débacle* I re-activated my *Statesman* connection. Worsley, who had become the lit ed in 1951, gave me me some more books. I became a *Statesman* novel reviewer and the paper's first tv critic. By now VSP had moved to a seat on the board of directors, while continuing to write his regular 'Books in General' pieces. Romilly had disappeared from the office; and a new assistant literary editor had been appointed, Janet Adam Smith, who had graduated from from Somerville in 1928. She had then joined the BBC just as it was about to launch the *Listener;* she was made assistant editor and shortly after that became its lit ed.

Let me turn for a little while to the *Listener*. It was from the start in competition as a source of reviews with the *Statesman* as well as with the *Nation*, the *Spectator* and *Time and Tide* (founded in 1920 by Lady Rhondda, with the support of Rebecca West and others of feminist outlook), and so far as its arts and books section was concerned it soon represented a most serious challenge. The other weeklies had tried hard to prevent it coming into existence on the grounds that the BBC as a state monopoly had no right to meddle in this particular area of a weekly publication of comment and reviews. They failed, and the *Listener's* subsequent importance for literary and arts journalism in Britain during the half century of its existence was great. Janet Adam Smith, working with her editor R. S. Lambert (no relation of J. W.), helped to lay the foundations of its review section. The BBC had agreed that only ten per cent of the *Listener's* editorial space would be devoted to topics not related to broadcasting. It was a cunningly negotiated compromise on the part of the BBC, because there was precious little that was not in one way or another related to broadcasting; as an editorial in the first number on 16 January 1929 explained: 'It follows from this concept of the *Listener* as an auxiliary to the microphone that its scope can be hardly, if at all, narrower than that of the programmes themselves.'

Thus in the first issue there were two articles on music; one on William Boyce – 'A Half-Forgotten Composer' – by Constant Lambert, apropos of his 8th Symphony to be broadcast in a BBC Symphony Concert two days later, and one on 'Team-work in Music' by Sir Walford Davies, apropos of the BBC's and other choruses. There was a piece on theatre 'From Pantomime to Peter Pan' by Geoffrey Whitworth, extracted from a broadcast talk, and another similarly extracted on 'The Artist and the Lithograph' by Ernest Jackson. These articles put down markers for the outstanding musical and art coverage that was to continue throughout the paper's existence. The first issue also contained the *Listener's* 'Book Chronicle', a rather dense anonymous round-up feature of recent publications covering many books not remotely related to broadcasting. That was the forerunner of an anonymous book-review section that would soon develop and occupy several pages at the back, with regular quarterly literary supplements to rival those in the *Statesman*.

A specially written literary feature (not a reprinted radio talk) was included in the form of a signed article by John Buchan on what in his view was 'The Most Difficult Form of Fiction', the historical novel. This was a response to 'Books in General'. A footnote explained: 'Mr Buchan contributes as the representative of literature on the Central Council for Broadcast Adult Education.'

To promote the cause of Adult Education, closely allied to radio broadcasting at this time, was the paper's secret weapon. The seeds of the future Open University were sown here. Unlike its rivals, the paper did not have a political front half as such; instead it reprinted dispatches from the BBC's foreign correspondents and other topical broadcasts. Several of these before the war were by Donald McLachlan in his role as a foreign correspondent in Germany. Belonging to the impartial BBC, the paper could not have any views of its own, which made its anonymous leading articles curiously anodyne.

At 3d – half the price of the *Statesman* – the *Listener* soon caught on and acquired a loyal body of readers. The initial circulation was just under 28,000 copies, almost twice as many as the *Statesman* at that time. Many of the readers were schoolteachers. They were keen to be informed about current developments in all the arts and books but found the *Spectator* reviews a trifle dull and the *Statesman*, with its reviews from people like Brian Howard (Waugh's Anthony Blanche), somewhat flashy. The *Listener* acquired the reputation of being knowledgeable about avant-garde activities while rooted in traditional values; in the swim but eminently sound. The new journal had another attraction at this period that its competitors lacked: it was illustrated with excellent half-tone blocks made from photographic prints from the *Radio Times* Picture Library.

Janet Adam Smith left the *Listener* in 1935 when she married Michael Roberts, the schoolmaster, poet and mountaineer. Her farewell gesture was the editing and publication of an anthology of poetry that had appeared in the *Listener, Poets of Tomorrow*. Her successor, J. R. (Joe) Ackerley, came from within the Corporation where he was working as a talks producer. Ackerley was to remain as lit ed of the *Listener* for the next quarter of a century; he retired in 1959. He had started his writing-life as a poet. One of his poems printed in the *London Mercury* by Squire had attracted the attention of E. M. Forster, who had written a letter to him about it. It was thanks to Forster that he had gone to India to take up the post he described in *Hindoo Holiday*, his account of his experiences as private secretary to a Maharajah. Its publication gave Ackerley renown as a prose-stylist, a reputation greatly enhanced by his later books, including his autobiography *My Father and Myself* (1968), revealing his extraordinary up-bringing and his homosexual pre-deliction for rough trade. Had Sir John Reith been able to read these later books it seems most unlikely that Ackerley would have been given the *Listener* job. As it was, Ackerley was the perfect counter to Reithian pressure; the irremovable object that time and again met his chief's irresistible force without yielding a milli-metre. In his biography of Ackerley, Peter Parker gives several instances of Ackerley's spirited resistance to censorious diktats from the Director-General, such as one attempting to ban the publication of poems by Auden.

Ackerley's circle included Leonard Woolf as well as Forster; and in the next generation Christopher Isherwood and William Plomer, both like Ackerley fastidious writers and resolutely gay. Under his editing, the cultural section of the *Listener* became yet another outlet for the clerisy; a clerisy widened by recruiting writers of the younger generation, the Auden generation, and later still the generation after that, the Francis King generation. The standards were high, the style always urbane. The reviews remained anonymous except for the re-printing of a broadcast book-review and for the monthly fiction review. There were several pages of signed reviews in the extended spring and autumn book numbers, where Ackerley would draw on people outside his usual circle – Herbert Read, Shane Leslie, B. H. Liddell Hart.

In March 1936 we find Christopher Isherwood, then still a British subject, reviewing *Abinger Harvest* (a collection of pieces by E. M. Forster written between 1902 and 1936) under the heading 'Mr Forster Tidies Up'. It is one of Isherwood's rare book-reviews. He comes to the conclusion that *Abinger*, despite its miscellaneous contents, 'is a book not a mess . . . it is his involuntary autobiogra-phy.' He makes no mention of the fact that in a prefatory note to the collection Forster wrote:

> As for dedication. A miscellany can have no value as an offering. All the same I should like to offer this one to some of the friends in a younger generation who have encouraged me to compile it; most particularly to William Plomer and also to J. R. Ackerley, R. J. Buckingham and Christopher Isherwood. [Bob Buckingham was the policeman who was a life-long gay companion yet married friend of Forster.]

Ackerley must be considered a non-writing lit ed in the sense that he did not do any signed reviewing himself. He was, however, highly articulate in his responses to reviewers' copy, frequently sending them detailed criticisms of their articles, requesting certain parts be re-written; and always dispatching an annotated proof to correct before the review appeared. And Ackerley continued the tradition of publishing original poetry in the *Listener*. Under him and his successors the magazine chalked up a fine record of first publications of poems by Auden, Day Lewis, Vernon Watkins, Roy Fuller, Laurie Lee, Richard Church, Robert Conquest, W. R. Rodgers, Alan Ross, Philip Larkin and many more.

The 'Fiction Chronicle' appeared once a month. A fiction reviewer would remain for a strictly limited term. No one was permitted to become jaded. Edwin Muir, Sean O'Fáoláin. Stephen Spender, John Lehmann, George D. Painter, P. H. Newby, Geoffrey Grigson, Simon Raven were among the regular team. O'Fáoláin was an exceptionally lively critic of new novels. Here he is in 1949 on Sartre as a novelist; further evidence of the defensive reaction to Sartre after the war by our cultural mediators:

The amount of cleverness in modern fiction is simply appalling: the knowingness, the brightness, the intelligence and the heartlessness. It is a form of blackmail. One is so intimidated that one fears to say that it is boring. One sees the eybrows of the highbrows rise in slow contempt, the interchange of supercilious glances, the almost imperceptible shrugs, On my word, I am exhausted from stimulating intelligence when Sartre is mentioned. But if they would only let me look stupid, how happy I should be to read him. I could smile as foolishly as when a clever conjuror starts to saw a lady in half, or at the music-hall, a man in tights keeps four balls, a plate, two oranges and a mousetrap all twinkling in the air together. Sartre is such a good music-hall turn as a novelist. Last week it was Vico. The week before we all clapped Spengler. I have forgotten the name of the clever man who, it must be twenty years ago, enchanted Bloomsbury by dividing everybody into schizoid and cycloid, but always, alas, one had to be serious and look intelligent and never admit that one would give the whole boiling lot of them for one little story – wan weeshy little warm-hearted story by Alphonse Daudet or A. E. Coppard.

La Nausée, now translated as *The Diary of Antoine Roquentin*, is about

as much a novel as the heel of my boot, which is not to say that it
does not as fictionalised philosophy contain brilliant observation and
piercing criticism and wit. Briefly and – with an apologetic bow to
the black hats – crudely, it is, as a novel, a study in neurosis. M.
Roquentin is a man who is fast losing self-definition. He wishes to
live, but in such utter freedom that he will be free even of himself.
He goes pretty well off his chump trying to work this out.

This kind of scepticism about fiction from abroad was typical of
the period in the London literary world. It was a time of re-
adjustment. In 1940 the suicide of Virginia Woolf had signalled
the end of the aesthetic Bloomsbury dream. On the day she died,
Leonard Woolf happened to be standing in as editor of the *New
Statesman* for Kingsley Martin. After Woolf had received the tragic
news he came up from Sussex to London, saw the paper away, and
then returned home without mentioning the fact of his wife's
death to any of his colleagues.

And Bloomsbury attitudes now came under attack by the new
generation. Angus Wilson made a broadcast about the work of
Virginia Woolf in August 1950, 'Sense and Sensibility in Recent
Writing', in which, writes his biographer Margaret Drabble, 'he
mocked her stream-of-consciousness technique and its content in
a parody which bought her into the deadly company of Mrs
Miniver – he traced her influence through Elizabeth Bowen,
Nancy Mitford and Angela Thirkell, and he deplored it.' In later
years Wilson went back on this to voice his new-found admiration
for Virginia Woolf's fiction.

Graham Greene felt that after the death of James a disaster had
overtaken the English novel. The hopes that James had uttered in
his *Lit Supp* articles for such young novelists as Compton Mackenzie, Gilbert Cannan and Hugh Walpole had proved to be futile.
The world of fiction had lost a dimension, the religious dimension;
'the characters of such distinguished writers as Mrs Virginia Woolf
and Mr E. M. Forster, wandered like cardboard symbols through a
world that was paper-thin', said Greene and he contrasted Mr
Ramsay in *To the Lighthouse* with one of Trollope's clergymen and
concluded that the Trollopian figure exists in a way that the latter
does not, 'because we are aware that he exists not only to the
woman he is addressing but also in God's eye'. Greene was making
that judgement in a world still torn by war, but even as he wrote
the religious dimension was making a popular fictional comeback

in such best-selling novels as Huxley's *Time Must Have a Stop*, Maugham's *The Razor's Edge*, Waugh's *Brideshead Revisited* and a few years later in Greene's own *The End of the Affair*.

After the death of Michael Roberts in 1948, Janet Adam Smith resumed her career in literary journalism; as we have seen, she joined the staff of the *Statesman* as Worsley's assistant. Up to then Worsley had been assisted part-time by one of the regular fiction-reviewers, Walter Allen. He was a graduate of Birmingham University who had begun his career as an author by writing several novels and, as he explains in his autobiography, had ended by becoming a full-time critic and literary historian. After he finished his fifth novel, *Dead Man Over All*, in 1950, drawing on his experience of an aircraft factory near Bristol where he had worked in the early part of the war, Allen began to write his best known-work of literary history, *The English Novel*. He had been a regular contributor to the 'Books and War' articles in *Penguin New Writing* and in 1937 he appeared in the short-lived periodical *Night and Day*, edited by John Marks and Graham Greene, whom he had first met in its office. He and Greene shared an interest in the novel of the underworld.

It was thanks to Allen that Graham Greene became a *New Statesman* reviewer. Greene's pre-war lit ed on the *Spectator*, Derek Verschoyle, had become a publisher and Greene was happy now to write occasional reviews for the *Statesman*. He had read Henry James during the war and set out his considered view of James in a number of review-articles. And it was not only literary books Greene reviewed. He wrote about the memoirs of a prostitute, *To Beg I Am Ashamed* by Sheila Cousins, a book banned before the war but now in the new permissive era published. 'Honesty produces its own odd poetry and perception', Greene commented.

Worsley began to find scrambling out the paper every week (as he put it) an intolerable burden. Like many dramatic critics, he had an urge to write plays of his own. One was tried out at Bristol but never reached London. Then he went through a personal crisis with one of his male lovers that involved his prolonged absence from the office. In 1952 Janet Adam Smith became the *Statesman's* lit ed and Worsley – the crisis over – returned to work simply as dramatic critic and as a fiction reviewer on the *Evening Standard* under the name of Richard Lister, doing one novel a week. John Raymond became assistant to Janet. The flow of review copies became a torrent as paper restrictions on British publishers eased; but the centre of gravity in the literary world was shifting

from Europe to America and it took some time for the London
intelligentsia to realise what was happening. The serious study of
American literature in Britain awaited the founding of universities
at Sussex, Warwick and East Anglia. Dylan Thomas, whose poetic
rhetoric had seemed such a powerful antidote to the terrors of the
bombing, began to shuttle back and forth across the Atlantic to
American venues, until the strain of it all killed him in November
1953. 'A poet takes his lasting place among those whose work lives
after them', wrote Kathleen Raine in an obituary tribute in the
New Statesman.

Raine, a close friend of Janet Adam Smith, was one of a gifted
group of writers who had been up at Cambridge together in the
1930s: Muriel Bradbrook, J. Bronowski, Malcolm Lowry, John
Davenport and William Empson were among them. Empson's
Seven Types of Ambiguity was now succeeded by *The Structure of
Complex Words* and it was Empson who replaced Auden as the
poetic master of the new generation. Raine's idea of a poet was
someone like Robert Graves or Blake, Saint-John Perse or David
Jones, painter and poet, who now published his long-gestated *The
Anathemata* in 1952.

> So to the question: What is this writing about? I answer [Jones wrote]
> that it is about one's own 'thing', which *res* is unavoidably part and
> parcel of the Western Christian *res*, as inherited by a person whose
> perceptions are totally conditioned and limited by and dependent
> upon his being indigenous to this island. In this it is necessarily
> insular; within which insularity there are the further conditionings
> upon his being a Londoner, of Welsh and English parentage, of
> Protestant upbringing, of Catholic subscription.

In spite of appreciative reviews from Raine and others, and
dramatised broadcasts on the radio produced by his friend and
publisher Douglas Cleverdon, Jones has never occupied the mainstream position as a writer and poet that his admirers (who
included T. S. Eliot) claimed for him. But the proud insularity of
which he speaks there was one shared by many outside his own
clerisy of Roman Catholic writers, artists, engravers and thinkers.

John Raymond, Janet's assistant, was a literary journalist of my
own generation. To us, his contemporaries, Raymond was to book-
reviewing what Tynan was to dramatic criticism, an ace-performer;
someone whose writing came off the page with a consistently
brilliant readability we all envied. He was the son of the actors

Cyril Raymond and Iris Hoey. He was educated at Westminster School in the late 1930s, where he was an outstanding pupil especially in history and classics. Then his parents split up and Raymond was abruptly removed from Westminster. It was a blow comparable to the one Dickens suffered as a child when he was removed from the educational system and sent to work in a blacking factory. Raymond turned to literature to pull himself out of the emotional trough. He read ceaselessly, acquiring on his own a much wider and deeper knowledge than the average university student who studies English.

But he had to earn a living and went as a trainee to the Kemsley group of newspapers and became an apprentice-reporter on the *Daily Graphic*. He joined the army when he was eighteen and served with Field Security Personnel in Ceylon; after he was demobilised he had a job on *The Times* and began to write reviews in literary journals. One of his pieces was read by Desmond MacCarthy, who alerted the *Statesman* to his existence. It soon became clear to Worsley that Raymond's reviews had the arresting readability the back pages had lacked since the departure of Connolly. He became a brilliant addition to the staff of the cultural pages and as a Books-in-Generalist Raymond was the in-house substitute whenever Pritchett had a week off.

Raymond's perceptiveness and range of literary-historical allusion may be sampled in this extract from his piece on Evelyn Waugh's novel *Helena* in the *New Statesman* on 21 October 1950:

His new novel is a quasi-historical sortie in the style of Maugham's *Catalina* (though a good deal wittier) on the subject of Helena, saint and dowager, whose discovery of the true cross became one of the great medieval legends of the Christian Church. The author eschews history in favour of the tradition ("invented", wrote Gibbon, "in the darkness of monasteries"), that Constantine's mother was an Essex princess. This gives him the opportunity to surrender to one of his favourite vices in the way of characterisation – the clear-eyed, clean-limbed daughter of Diana, with a niche in Debrett and an ultimate refuge in the Great Good Place. Waugh's heroines, even when, as in the case of Brenda in *A Handful of Dust*, they have betrayed the County, remain like Miss Mitford's 'Hons', sheathed in a strange primary virtue engendered by prayers in the gaslit nursery and long, golden afternoons spent in the paddock. While Graham Greene's characters make the frontal approach to Catholicsm – undergoing the betrayal on the pier or the Pascalian agony in the shrubbery –

Waugh's converts generally get to Heaven the back way, through having had the right kind of Nanny. In a non-Catholic writer such a scheme of salvation would look dangerously like predestination.

The reader who feels that Waugh's Roman Empress is only an atavistic manifestation of Lady Seal, is bound to find Helena disappointing. Waugh has done nothing in this book that he has not done as well or better elsewhere. It goes without saying that *Helena* is amusing, shapely and well-written, and it also contains some extremely witty incidents: the Empress Fausta's description of the Council of Nicea, for example, is Anatole France of the best *Isle des Pingouins* vintage. Nevertheless, one cannot help feeling that Waugh has been pulling his punches in this book. A Christian saint and empress is not perhaps the most suitable theme for a satirist who is irrevocably on the side of the angels.

Raymond contributed a series of 'Books in General' on Newman, Belloc, Chesterton, Ronald Knox, Thomas Merton that indicated the spiritual direction in which he was moving, even if he by no means restricted himself to writing about Catholic apologists. Knowledgeable appraisals of Winston Churchill the writer, Rabelais, Pope, Dr Johnson, Sidney Smith, Kipling, flowed from his pen. He joined in the attack on Bloomsbury in articles on Strachey, Forster and VW, to which Leonard Woolf responded by inviting Raymond out to lunch. Raymond always gave the reader an exciting sense of re-discovery when writing about figures from the distant and recent past, the true art of literary journalism. Churchill was not just a literary admiration. He identified with Churchill the politician at a time when the writers on the front half of the paper were doing their best to discredit him. 'I'll put you in my cabinet' was one of Raymond's favourite sayings to his chums when drunk. But in 1959, when his alcohol-intake increased to the point where he was in danger of becoming another Clifford Sharp, Kingsley Martin decided that Raymond for all his talent would have to go.

Raymond, who always preferred writing to editing, left without any great regrets and Walter Allen was asked by Martin to replace him. Luckily Raymond had a contract from the *Sunday Times* to fall back on. His reviews would appear there underneath those by Connolly or Mortimer. He had converted to the Roman Catholic faith and become a much less abrasive companion, but as his drinking became ever heavier his work lost its cutting-edge; he never made anything like the impact writing for the *Sunday Times* that he had on the *Statesman*. His most sustained flights of enthusiasm now came in conversation, especially with his great friend Judge W. H. 'Billy' Hughes, a distinguished member of the legal profession. He and Raymond were two of the best-read, most convivial companions I ever encountered. Kingsley Martin summed up John's decline cruelly in my hearing when he saw him at Janet Adam Smith's wedding reception at Westminster School in 1965. Her second husband was John Carleton, the headmaster, who had been Raymond's housemaster before the war. Kingsley said in a hoarse voice to Raymond: 'You know you got God and gin at the same time. A fatal combination.'

Walter Allen succeeded Janet as literary editor in 1960 but only for a few months. Later that same year, when Kingsley Martin ceased to be editor, Allen resigned. He was never happy as a lit ed, as he was the first to admit, and he had other sources of literary work as one of the regular reviewing panel on the *Daily Telegraph* and in visiting professorships at various colleges in the United States; afterwards he became for some years a full-time academic as the first professor of English at the University of Ulster.

The next two decades were to witness the appointment of five new *New Statesman* editors, none of whom could prevent the circulation which had peaked around 100,000 during the war years steadily declining. Martin's successor was his deputy, the former Labour MP John Freeman. He was there until 1965; then the editors were Paul Johnson (1965–70); Richard Crossman (1970–2); Anthony Howard (1972–8) and Bruce Page (1978–82).

By 1960 the angry young men had arrived; the London culture of pre-war England had begun to be displaced by a more widely diffused regional one. *Such Darling Dodos* – one of Angus Wilson's stories used as the title of a collection – was the epitaph on the clerisy (who even then had more life in them than it implied). The journal needed an arts and books supremo in tune with this cultural change who would introduce a new generation of reviewers. The appointment was one of Freeman's first tasks when he took over from Martin. His choice fell in 1961 on Karl Miller, a twenty-nine-year-old Scot whose education had been at the Royal High School, Edinburgh, and then at Downing College, Cambridge where he had read English. He was one of the New Men of literature, representative of the post-war generation who had come through all the way on merit and not through belonging to any kind of charmed circle. He was drafted from the *Spectator*, where he had been the lit ed.

Miller tells us in his memoirs, *Rebecca's Vest*, that at the age of
fifteen 'I was a Bloomsbury man in my preference for books and
personal relationships'. After two years post-war National Service
spent with the British Forces radio network in Germany, he went
to Cambridge where he edited *Granta* (then an undergraduate
magazine). Mark Boxer was a colleague until he was sent down for
printing a poem considered to be blasphemous. Ted Hughes and
Thom Gunn were among Miller's Cambridge contemporaries and
contributors; so were Nicholas and Claire Tomalin (as they
became). Although Miller was a pupil of Leavis he never, he says,
became a Leavisite.

Miller was a rather different kind of *Statesman* literary editor
than Squire, MacCarthy, Mortimer or Worsley and not just because
he was devoted to football rather than cricket. He shared with
Janet the severity, the moral stance, that runs through the whole
of Scottish literature from Henryson to Alan Massie. In Stevenson's
Kidnapped the pleasure- and adventure-seeking self is in a perpetual
quarrelsome dialogue with the salvation-seeking self. In Hogg's
Justified Sinner, these two selves are split between two separate
characters one of whom is the other's *doppelgänger*, a phenomen
investigated by Miller in his critical work *Doubles*. When Janet was
in charge, her Scottish severity would be leavened by John Raymond's wit and panache. With Miller as lit ed, an era of unremitting seriousness dawned on the review pages. The reviewer as
entertainer vanished. A cap-and-bells act like that of Arthur
Marshall, good for a laugh on a clutch of theatrical or royal
memoirs, ceased altogether. In scrupulously respecting the highest
critical standards, Miller was a courageous lit ed to be sure, but
one who did not seem always to heed MacCarthy's great precept
that a reviewer must capture the reader with his first sentence and
hold him until his last.

It was part of a change that came over books and arts pages
generally. The old-style reviewer was a free-lance. Reviewing was
his livelihood. He had to sing for his supper. If the other diners
yawned at his performance or went on talking, he did not get
much supper. He could not afford to be boring. Philip Hope-
Wallace, reviewer of theatre and opera in *Time and Tide* and the
Guardian, was supremely the reviewer as an entertainer while
remaining a formidably intelligent critic. The new-style reviewer
had in addition to his literary journalism a job of some kind;
reviewing was a sideline even though he hoped it might expand
into a lucrative one. His or her reviewing was done in combination

with full-time work for 'the media' or as an academic with a university career to be pursued. The voice of the old-style reviewer, even if he was (like F. L. Lucas) a Cambridge don, was conversational; it was pitched to be heeded in the wide world outside the groves of academe; the voice of the new-style reviewer seemed to emanate from the SCR and sometimes from the lecture room.

Sir Frank Kermode, who was to be one of the most prolific reviewers of the period, was a lecturer in the University of Reading 1949–58; John Edward Taylor professor in the University of Manchester 1958–65; Lord Northcliffe Professor of Modern English at University College London 1956–67; King Edward VII Professor of English Literature at Cambridge 1974–82, and Charles Eliot Norton Professor of Poetry at Harvard 1977–8. This ascent of the Eng lit academic ladder to its highest rungs was combined by Kermode with regular reviewing for Miller and other lit eds on both sides of the Atlantic.

To his surprise, Kermode was invited to succeed Stephen Spender as co-editor of the monthly journal *Encounter* in 1965. He has given his own account of his period there in his memoirs, *Not Entitled*. It coincided with the furore, started through a lecture given in New York by Conor Cruise O'Brien and reported in the American press, alleging that the journal was the instrument of its paymaster, the CIA. Spender seemed genuinely surprised at the revelation but others, including several contributors to the journal, could be heard saying that Spender and Kermode must have been the only people working for it who did not know of the CIA's involvement. Kermode resigned his co-editorship in spite of pressure from Cecil King of the *Daily Mirror* group, at that time taking a paternalistic interest in *Encounter*, to make him stay on.

Whoever the ultimate paymaster, Melvin Lasky's cultural editors always had difficulty in getting enough literary material into the paper to justify their names on the masthead. Current affairs, economic issues, sociology, indeed anything that might serve as ammunition in the cold war against the Soviet Union, formed the top priority. Even so Lasky, a dominant, politically *engagé* editor whose anti-communist stance had been taken up originally in Berlin after the war as editor of the US Army's *Der Monat*, was not a philistine. He picked his British co-editors carefully to represent the best in the prevailing literary culture. Under Spender, Kermode and the co-editors who succeeded him, distinguished men of letters who included Nigel Dennis, there was an impressive tradition of book-criticism, much of it by authors who were also academics. They included Lionel Trilling from America and nearer home, John Wain, George Steiner, Laurence Lerner, George Watson, Bernard Bergonzi, Malcolm Bradbury, David Lodge, A. S. Byatt – in addition to people not in university life like Gillian Tindall, Ronald Hayman, Jan Morris, Colin Wilson. The strength of *Encounter*'s criticism and book-reviewing was such that at the height of the crisis, Kermode was moved to try to start a *Counter Encounter*, with the support of Stuart Hampshire, John Wain and Isaiah Berlin. That never happened but there remained afterwards in the mind of Kermode the notion of a *London Review of Books*, eventually launched in 1979 with Karl Miller, long since departed from the *Statesman*, as its editor.

The importance of the *Statesman* as a source of book-reviews began to decline at this period, though it was bravely kept alive until well into the 1970s under Miller's successors as lit eds, the poet Anthony Thwaite (1968–72), and the critic and literary historian John Gross (1973). With the appointment of Gross there was a perceptible widening of the ranks of reviewers and it seemed as if the review section might be going to be in for a period of significant renewal; but before the end of the year he had left the paper to edit the *TLS*. Claire Tomalin succeeded him for four years, until in 1977 she became the literary editor of the *Sunday Times* in succession to Jack Lambert.

Miller disproves my observation that lit eds never get promotion. He left the *Statesman* to become the editor of the *Listener*, from 1967 to 1973. He succeeded the historian Maurice Ashley, a staunch Cromwellian, who had been editor since 1958. He found in Mary-Kay Wilmers colleague who had a similar role to that of Janet Adam Smith in the early days. She moved with him to the *London Review of Books* and ultimately succeeded him as its editor. As editor of the *Listener* Miller was succeeded by George Scott (who had had such a blaze of glory as a nurturer of critics when editor of *Truth*, from 1954 until it ceased publication in 1957). Scott was succeeded by the political biographer and writer Anthony Howard (1979–81), after whom came the *Radio Times* journalist Russell Twisk (1981–7).

From 1965 until 1986, under all these editors, the lit ed of *The Listener* was Derwent May. (K. W. Gransden had intervened as lit ed between the retirement of Ackerley and the appointment of May.) After completing his English degree at Oxford, May had been a professor of English in Indonesia and in Poland. His own writings include several novels and regular newspaper columns on wild life and birds. During the Miller period, when the *Listener* had a former lit ed as the editor of the whole paper, and an exceptionally versatile editor in May to run the cultural section, the journal remained as good a forum for criticism and poetry as it had ever been; its problem was the contents of its front half at a time when the period of the Spoken Word, the radio talk or feature, to be reprinted in full or extracted, was clearly coming to an end. The old readers of the *Listener* stayed loyal; new ones were hard to recruit. There were too many other cultural pages on offer and the culture had itself changed to something more diffuse and less exclusively verbal.

More and more it was to the heavy Sundays rather than the serious weeklies that readers turned for their books coverage. As we have seen, the two existing Sundays that ran quality books pages were joined by a third, the *Sunday Telegraph*. Meanwhile the dailies expanded their book reviewing sections, *The Times* under Michael Ratcliffe and then Philip Howard, and the *Guardian* under William Webb. The end seemed to be nigh for the old-style cultural weekly for so long an essential part of English life, but in spite of the change in cultural habits, it has stubbornly refused to die.

The literary outlook now, as I have indicated, became a transatlantic one. In an average week half of the new fiction that landed on the lit ed's desk would be by American authors. Enterprising publishers developed the co-edition, a book initiated in Britain, sold to publishers around the world at the Frankfurt Book Fair, whose UK printing costs would be heavily subsidised by using the same sheets, but not the same binding or jacket, on both sides of the Atlantic. Words like *honor* and *flavor* began to appear under British imprints to the horror of purists of the English tongue.

When this American penetration first became apparent in the late 1950s, I asked myself: what was the state of book-reviewing and literary journalism on the other side of the the Atlantic? In 1958–9, as I have said, I was fortunate in being able to take a year off work in London to try to find out.

11

Open doors

A lit ed who goes among strangers will from time to time have to face the question:'Do you write at all yourself?' To which he replies: 'Why yes! I *review.* I write for my own pages, you know.' The interrogation does not stop there but normally continues: 'I meant do you write *books* yourself?'

At this point the lit ed meets the enemy within whose affray wrecks his peace of mind. He may seek shelter in the thought of the books he wrote before he became a lit ed, combined with the thought of those that he intends to write when the pressures of the job relax to give him more time (a morrow he will never see); in neither thought will he find aught for comfort. He may then say, as Jack Lambert always used to do: 'If you see as many newly published books as I do every day you become most reluctant to add to them.' That is the official line, as it were, and usually serves to shut your tormentor up; but it is not really true. In Lambert's case he wrote what amounted to a concise biography of Saki for the Bodley Head collected edition and on retirement a history of the Bodley Head, almost finished when he died, completed by Michael Ratcliffe, as well as the youthful book on Cornwall and detailed wartime diaries not so far published. The Kilmartin solution – to translate – is an excellent one, but not every lit ed has the talent or the temperament for it.

For a lit ed there usually hovers somewhere in the clouds above the production of pages, the project of a book, *his* book which the job prevents him from completing.

In my case it was for many years a book about George Gissing. I had been given two of his novels, *The Whirlpool* and *In The Year of Jubilee,* for my twenty-fourth birthday when they were reprinted after the war in the Watergate Classics and I became fascinated by the mind behind them. The series had been edited by John Betjeman and the introductions by William Plomer and Myfanwy Evans (later Piper) stimulated me to investigate Gissing. I began to peel away some of the protective layers surrounding his life put there by his family. His career as a precociously brilliant student at Owens College, the forerunner of Manchester University, was abruptly terminated. He had befriended a young Manchester prostitute and had stolen money on her behalf. Like a young Gladstone he had seen himself as a redeemer of fallen women.

In 1956 I compiled a BBC. a radio feature-programme about him to mark his centenary. I went lugging a Uher tape-recorder, on loan from from Broadcasting House, to the Swiss mountain village of Les Marécottes in the Rhône Valley where lived Alfred Gissing, the novelist's surviving son. He ran a small skiing hotel that housed parties of boys from British prep schools during the winter sports season. He and his wife put me up for a few days during a gloriously hot summer; they could not have been kinder or more hospitable.

Alfred, proud of his father's achievement, was more than willing to discuss his work and career with me. On the first day he showed me the vast biography he had written of his father that had never been published. On the next he took me for a walk up the mountain to see the peak of Mont Blanc in the distance. When we reached the viewpoint I was the one who was out of breath, despite the gap of years in my favour. It all went splendidly except that Alfred had precious little in the way of personal memories for me to record. His father had deserted him when he was a small child and had gone to live in France with Gabrielle Fleury, the French woman with whom he had fallen in love, and who thereafter adopted the style, Madame Gissing. The only direct memory Alfred had was of being picked up by his father and put into the carriage of a railway train. Presumably that was the last time he saw him. At least I was able to get that memory on tape in Alfred's fine cultivated voice and hoped that it would justify to my producer the expenses of the trip.

Luckily she (Sasha Moorsom, who later married Michael Young, the sociologist, now Lord Young of Dartington – Sasha died of cancer in 1993) said it would make a good lead in to the programme and we put the rest of it together from other sources that were then available. As I write, a scholarly edition of Gissing's letters in nine volumes is on the way to completion. It adds much to the sombre picture whose outline I tried to trace. After the programme went out publishers began to inquire, was it the pilot for a full-scale life? But it is one thing to write a Third Programme radio feature about Gissing; quite another to write a cradle-to-grave biography. While I was pondering this possibility, a whole year off in the form of a Harkness Fellowship in Journalism for the purpose of study in America fell into my lap. It came like manna from heaven.

The bulk of Gissing's letters, diaries, notebooks and manuscripts were in the United States. I proposed to the Harkness selection committee that I would divide my time between studying American literary and arts journalism in newspapers and magazines while also investigating the life of Gissing. They agreed to this programme and in September 1958 I arrived in New York as one of a fresh batch of fellows who included Bamber Gascoigne, John Gross and Douglas Wass (on leave from the Treasury on a Harkness Fellowship for members of the civil service). Wass and I shared a cabin on the QE2.

I began by researching the daily press. The leading paper in New York for book reviews, then as now, was the *New York Times* with quality opposition from the *Herald Tribune*, the *Post* and other afternoon and evening papers that all reviewed books. The *Journal American* ran a column by the publisher and humorist Bennett Cerf, chairman of Random House. Both the *Herald Tribune* and the *New York Times* offered their readers two separate kinds of books coverage: the weekend book-review supplement, and reviews of selected books on publication as part of the daily coverage. The appearance of a new book was on certain mornings each week treated just like a news story. Staff journalists were – are still – employed to write reviews as their only occupation, something unknown in the UK then or now. Alfred Kazin recalled in his *Starting Out in the Thirties* the impact made on him by the journalist John Chamberlain's daily book column in the *New York Times*. Chamberlain became a fierce upholder of entrepreneurial capitalism in his old age but he was then a disciple of Marx and his reviews, Kazin says, examined radical solutions to the Depression. Twenty-five years and a world war later no one looked to the book column for radical solutions but daily book reviewers like Orville

Prescott of the *Times* or John K. Hutchens of the *Tribune* were
powers in the land of publishing; Prescott especially could cause
demand for a new book to rocket:

> Only in the case of his reviews could the publisher watch the
> 'ticker-tape' and measure the impact on orders of an exuberant or
> bristling Prescott review. The phone would ring and the jobbers
> would re-order: fifty copies, one hundred, even five hundred. He was
> the only book reviewer with a power comparable to that of the *Times*
> theater critic.

To turn to the weekend book coverage: there was the *New York
Times* Sunday Book Review, part of the New York Sunday newspaper package (something we were soon to have in the UK); it was
excessively bland at this time, a halfway house between our
newspaper books coverage and the *Lit Supp*. Historically its first
number preceded the *Lit Supp's* by a decade and a half. On 6
October 1996 an extended centenary number, *100*, reprinted the
original reviews of *The Brothers Karamazov, The Interpretation of
Dreams, An American Tragedy, The Castle, For Whom The Bell Tolls, The
Four Quartets* among other seminal works. If many of these reviews
lacked bite, they revealed a consistent record of recognising what
was new and important at home and abroad; books by authors
such as Proust and Pound ignored by middlebrow British papers.

I wrote to the editor, Francis Brown, who invited me to call on
him at his office in the building on 43rd Street where I was greeted
by Lewis Nicholls, a staff-member who wrote a regular weekly
literary gossip column in the Review. He showed me into a board
room where Brown, his deputy, Nicholls and I sat round the table
for an exchange of views. It was an impressive contrast to the
accommodation at the *Times Lit Supp* and to the kind of reception
a visiting American journalist of my status would have been
accorded there. I was encouraged to hold forth and I began by
asking why they had never had a star critic, someone like Connolly
on the London *Sunday Times*, whom everyone wanted to read,
instead of farming the front page lead review out to all and sundry
with inevitably no consistent viewpoint in the critical outlook.
Brown replied that the Sunday issue of the *New York Times*
circulated across the whole of the United States. In addition, the
Book Review had readers who subscribed for it on its own and
received it through the mail. This readership precluded the

appointment of a mandarin like Connolly. Here again we would
follow suit.

Brown was eager to talk shop. He asked me who wrote and
edited the shorter notices at the end of the *Lit Supp*, a feature that
had continued since the paper's origin. I forbore to reveal what a
precariously run feature it was; that Crook, ever fearful that it
would break down, was always having to pressurise the junior staff
to keep it alive. I said that most of it was written in-house by people
like me. He replied they liked it very much and were thinking of
doing something similar. Then Brown asked me about the préva-
lence of 'log-rolling' by British reviewers who were also authors.
He said that C. P. Snow had referred to this in an article he had
written in the *New Statesman*. He had asked Snow to expand on the
matter in an article for the *New York Times Book Review*. Snow had
refused. I said I was not familar enough with the American
situation to make a comparison, but I thought that more log-
rolling probably went on in our cosy little island, especially at
Christmas time with the Books of the Year pages, than in the
United States; but that the practice was probably not wholly
unknown in the US. He agreed and we both felt it would be
difficult to get someone to write about it authoritatively and name
names. I had not then come across the survey of American book-
reviewing published in the *Nation* in the 1930s.

While at the *Times* I also met the paper's drama critic, Brooks
Atkinson, the counterpart of the London *Times's* A. V. Cookman,
whom Atkinson knew and greatly liked. For one of the fabled
butchers of Broadway, in the tradition of Alexander Woollcott
capable of making or breaking a show with a stroke of his pen,
Atkinson made a remarkably mild impression. He might have
surfaced from some academic backwater rather than a New York
newspaper office. We talked about the current offerings on
Broadway such as Speed Lamkin's play *Comes A Day*, whose plot
turned on a woman from beyond the pale and her frigid reception
by American society. It was drawing capacity audiences, not
through any particular merit of its own but because of the presence
of Judith Anderson. The 'star system' was still much in evidence
then on Broadway. Actors like the Lunts, Helen Hayes, Maureen
Stapleton, Ina Claire and Geraldine Fitzgerald had loyal follow-
ings. Atkinson said that he visited London every year to catch up
on the British theatre, and complained of not being able to hear
the words properly in Shakespeare productions at the Old Vic (the

National Theatre had not yet opened). His visit was the subject of one of his Sunday articles, think-pieces about some aspect of the current theatre, another American newspaper tradition. Live drama was in those days a more central part of the culture then it is now and critics contributed to a dialogue about it in which everyone joined; certainly everyone in New York I met.

Atkinson was coming to the end of his innings and had only a few more months as a night watchman. His colleague on the *Trib*, Walter Kerr, would eventually take over the *Times* job, in 1966. This was after an explosive element had been introduced into drama criticism in New York. Against all precedent an Englishman, Kenneth Tynan, one of my Oxford contemporaries, was to be appointed to the *New Yorker*.

My talk with Atkinson ended at twenty to three, leaving me just enough time to get across town to Columbia University for a meeting with Lionel Trilling timed for three o' clock. I arrived breathless and was directed to his office only to discover he was not there. In the hiatus of waiting for him, I studied the serried ranks of back numbers of the *Hudson Review* and *Partisan Review* on his bookshelves, consecutive runs from way back. Trilling had been on the editorial board of the latter.

I knew that in any consideration of literary journalism in America the importance of such monthly cultural journals was crucial. They were descended from the nineteenth-century tradition in Britain and America of the learned literary and political periodical, in which different clerisies made appraisals of contemporary culture and campaigned for the causes in which they believed. In some of these periodicals much of the highest quality that was new in literary criticism, poetry and imaginative prose could be read. Some, like those on Trilling's shelves, had great longevity; others such as *The Dial*, with contributions from Eliot, Ford, Yeats, Aldington, Proust, Aragon, Benda, and many other magical names of modern literature – brought to its columns by Ezra Pound in the early 1920s – blazed gloriously and then were extinguished.

There had been at least four *Dials*. One in Boston edited by Margaret Fuller and Emerson, a vehicle of Transcendentalism, lasting from 1840 to 1844; the second in 1860 was edited from Cincinnati by Moncure Conway, a Unitarian clergyman concerned with the division between North and South. His *Dial* did not survive the Civil War, which began the year it came out. Then the *Dial* was re-started in Chicago in 1918 and was moved to New York in 1920, taken over by two young men who had been contemporaries at Harvard and editors of the *Harvard Monthly*, Scofield Thayer and James Sibley Watson Jr. They developed the *Dial* as the monthly periodical of literature and the arts that has such an honoured place in the history of modernism.

The presence among the editors of individuals like these, whose family wealth enables the journal to survive, is often a part of the pattern. That was true too of *Hound and Horn*, also of Harvard origin, founded in 1927 by Lincoln Kirstein and Varian Fry. It then moved to New York, with Kirstein as its editor-proprietor. From it came attitudes that veered from Marxism and Freudianism to regionalism and neoclassicsm, stemming from the different editors Kirstein co-opted, such as R. P. Blackmur and Yvor Winters. Eventually Kirstein became bored with it, and having published distinguished work by Eliot, Pound, Kenneth Burke, Allen Tate, Katherine Anne Porter, Gertrude Stein and Edmund Wilson, turned his attention to creating an American ballet. It folded in 1934.

'I am sorry. I didn't see you. I was next door' – the softly-pitched voice was that of Trilling, small and dapper, with whitish grey hair. I guiltily put back the journal I was holding muttering something about the periodical as a feature of cultural life. 'An obtrusive one,' said Trilling. I felt as if we were resuming a conversation between old friends or close colleagues rather than engaging in one between two people meeting for the first time. I mentioned my Gissing quest. He confessed he had not read Gissing, which surprised me, but said he felt that the neglected figure of that period in English culture was Gissing's early patron Frederic Harrison and that one of his students was researching into Harrison's career. He compared Gissing's disastrous love life to that of Mark Rutherford, whom he said was an example of 'free passion' breaking through Victorian constraints.

Then we turned to book-reviewing in New York. Like all literary people in their fifties he felt there had been a falling-off, a lowering of standards. In the old days the reviews in the *Nation* and the *New Republic* were 'really something'; now they were both in decline. Not only they but New York City was in decline; fifteen years ago it was a gracious place in which to live, even though he had been chronically hard-up. It was not so any more, he said.

I had not then, as I have recently, had the benefit of reading

Diana Trilling's account of Trilling's early years and their marriage, *The Beginning of the Journey* (1993). If I had I would, I feel,
have noted that Trilling's quiet air of aplomb and serenity betrayed
no hint of the difficulties he had had to face in his youth; no
external traces had been left by such traumas as the bankruptcy of
his father, a Jewish tailor, and the in-fighting with his faculty
colleagues at Columbia when he was first appointed. When his job
came up for renewal the old guard tried to get him sacked because
of his independence of mind. It was only an unexpectedly tough
reaction to the *putsch* by the hitherto compliant Trilling that foiled
them.

As a student at at Columbia, Trilling had been a pupil of Mark
Van Doren, Columbia's professor of English from 1920 to 1959,
also for a time literary editor of the *Nation*. The Van Dorens as a
family had a patrician hold over the the mainstream New York
book-reviewing clerisy of this period comparable to the Bruce
Richmond-Bloomsbury axis in London. There were four of them
in one generation who played a significant role in American
literary journalism: Mark Van Doren, Dorothy his wife, Carl his
brother, also a professor at Columbia, and his sister-in-law Irita, all
of them at one time or another influential lit eds. The Van Dorens
epitomised 'the good life', rooted like that of their English
counterparts in an easy familiarity with European and classical
literature, an ambience emanating from a family mansion in
Cornwall Hollow, Connecticut, that was recreated in the movie
Quiz Show. Mark Van Doren called one of his books expounding
his attitude to literature *The Happy Critic*.

> I make haste to agree once more with Mr Eliot that for the normal
> critic, the purpose of literature is to amuse. If that word feels too
> light, then substitute another: entertain. And if this word still feels
> light, then remember that it is only in the mind in which human
> beings are ever entertained. Entertainment is a tremendous as well
> as a delightful thing, and there are plenty of writers, God knows,
> who do not succeed at it.

This sense of amusement, entertainment, pleasure in literature
was effortlessly communicated by Van Doren to his students, as
Alfred Kazin recalled:

> Van Doren was unforgettably the poet in the classroom, direct full
> of the most concrete feeling about Virgil's lines which he would read

with a shy, straight, Midwestern pleasantness. As the early winter twilight crept over the Columbia campus, Van Doren's craggy face looked as if he expected the sun to come out because he was teaching Virgil. He was in such pleasant relation to his text, his teaching, his students, – after the lecture several of them regularly joined him in the Seventh Avenue local in order to hear more – he spoke in such accord with the fall of the lines and the fall of the winter outside, that he embodied all the harmony and smiling charm and love of beauty which I associated with the writers of every generation and place but my own. All Van Dorens had this particular, 'American' and rhythmical charm, but no one more than Mark at his teaching. Everything smiled. America was a sweet revolution in itself. Even in these informal lectures beauty came out of beauty, and poetry gave birth to poetry; the voice of the poet's eloquence and of the poet's nobility was calm, easy, undismayed by any terror outside Philosophy Hall.

Van Doren, ten years Trilling's senior, was an English don who published not only poetry but also fiction, as did Trilling. In addition to his celebrated and only novel, *The Middle of the Journey* (1947), Trilling is the author of several short stories that like his early book-reviews were written for the journal of the Menorah Society, a publication that circulated widely among Jewish college students. Its charismatic editor, Elliot Cohen, turned it into a significant periodical centred on Jewish culture in the broadest sense. When it folded, Cohen started the magazine *Commentary*, to be edited when he retired by Norman Podhoretz and still going strong.

The young Trilling became a part-time editor of the *Menorah Journal* at a salary of $45 a week, which he supplemented by lecturing, teaching and reviewing. In 1929 Trilling began his reviewing career by writing notices of up to a thousand words of novels by Jewish writers, taking a very independent and frequently hostile line. 'No-one', he wrote, 'who has followed the Jewish novel can miss the mean qualities that almost inevitably characterise even the best of the genre . . .'. He was also employed as a reviewer on the *New York Evening Post*, where he reviewed a wide spectrum of books, for example on the Gothic novel, the journals of Amiel and the latest volumes of Scott Moncrieff's translation of Proust, *The Cities of the Plain*. 'I must have written hundreds of reviews for the *Post*,' he said (a slight exaggeration). Simultaneously he became a part-time teacher of literature at Hunter College and in

1931 he had a research fellowship at Columbia to complete his
doctoral dissertation on Matthew Arnold. In 1932 he became an
instructor in the English department at Columbia at $2400 a year,
the first Jew ever to be appointed to such a post. But his need to
turn out literary journalism continued without let; he was by now
supporting his parents financially. His completed thesis became
the first of his books, *Matthew Arnold*, in 1939 to be followed by
E. M. Forster in 1943.

By then Trilling had graduated to writing reviews regularly for
the book section of the *Herald Tribune*. In those days, he told me,
it was 'a critical thing', now it was 'moribund'. Trilling began to
spread himself as a writer of the Arnoldian review-essay, in which
a book or an author is viewed in some depth as an aspect of a
culture. His mature essays appeared across the board in such
prestigious journals as the *American Quarterly, Horizon, Kenyon
Review*, the *Nation*, the *New Leader, Partisan Review*. A selection of
these essays was published as *The Liberal Imagination: Essays on
Literature and Society* (1950), a book that had a crucial influence
over a younger generation of New York intellectuals, among them
Steven Marcus, Robert Gottlieb, Jason Epstein, Norman Podhoretz
(all pupils of Trilling's at Columbia).

Trilling said that he was sometimes asked to write a review for
the Book Review Supplement of the *New York Times* but was
reluctant to accept on the grounds that the editor had suppressed
reviews he had written because they were considered too nasty. At
that time he had reached a plateau of reviewing, where he was
exceptionally well paid for writing only three or four long pieces
in a year, for a journal called the *Griffin*, the monthly magazine of
the Readers' Subscription Book Club of which Trilling was one of
the editors, the other two being his Columbia colleague Jacques
Barzun, and W. H. Auden.

Trilling may have had his reservations about the current state of
the book-reviews in the *Nation* and the *New Republic*, but I could
not afford to neglect them. Indeed Mrs Trilling has said that both
journals were read avidly by everyone she knew in New York
during the 1940s. She was herself a regular fiction reviewer for the
Nation for many years during that period. Diana Trilling's work as
a literary journalist and writer tended to lie unappreciated in the
shadow of her husband's high profile until quite late in her life.
At any rate for me the *Nation* and the *New Republic* were the

counterparts of the *New Stateman* and *Spectator* back home. I
needed to take a close look at their cultural sections now as well as
at earlier times during the century.

The *Nation*, begun in 1865, was the older of the two by far and
among American weekly publications the pioneer of serious book-
reviews. Its founding-editor, E. L. Godkin, is a comparable figure
to Garvin. Godkin, who had emigrated to America from Ireland at
the age of twenty-five, was a Benthamite who believed that democracy meant the greatest happiness for the greatest number. He
invited Longfellow, Lowell, Henry and William James, Henry
Adams and W. D. Howells to contribute to a magazine which
would be free from all political pressures and outside interference
in its discussion of 'the topics of the day' and one that also pledged
itself to giving 'sound and impartial criticisms of books and works
of art'.

In the turbulent period after the end of the Civil War, the
magazine addressed itself to the problems of reconstruction and
especially to the rights of the freedmen, the former slaves. Its
financial backers included such notable Abolitionists as George
Luther Stearns, a lead-pipe manufacturer who had supplied John
Brown with weapons, and James Miller McKim, one of the foun-
ders of the American Anti-Slavery Society. McKim saw the *Nation*
as the successor to the *Liberator*, the magazine edited by the great
Abolitionist William Lloyd Garrison (who, incidentally, helped
George Gissing to go to America and start life afresh after his
prison sentence). McKim's daughter married Garrison's son, Wendell Phillips Garrison. He became the first literary editor of the
Nation and started the system of sending out books for review to
specialist reviewers; their reviews were published anonymously, the
common practice at that time. From the beginning book-reviews
were of comparable importance to the topical discussions in the
front.

The magazine was to be closely linked with the Garrisons.
Wendell Phillips Garrison's sister married Henry Villard. Of Ger-
manic Bavarian origin, he had studied law in Illinois and was a
close friend of Lincoln. Villard went on to become one of the
railroad kings in Oregon and California and made a vast fortune.
In 1881 he bought the the *New York Evening Post* and offered
Godkin a job on its staff. Godkin accepted and became the editor
of the *Post* from 1883 to 1900; at the same time Godkin arranged
for the *Nation* to be published under the aegis of the *Post*. He now
left the editing of it to his brother-in-law. It appeared as a weekly

supplement of the *Post* and was generous in the amount of space devoted to books.

When Garrison retired in 1909 the editor was Paul Elmer More. He had taught Sanskrit at Harvard and Bryn Mawr. In 1914 he returned to academic life at Princeton after he had ceased to be in charge of the *Nation*. An erudite Platonist, More was a leader of a movement that became known as the New Humanism; other names associated with the movement in America are those of Irving Babbitt and Stuart Pratt Sherman.

Humanism, which reduced Jesus to the status of a mere prophet, was like Positivism and Rationalism, fashionable among intellectuals before Freudian theory and Marxism became the orthodox religions of the non-believer. T. S. Eliot regarded it as a sufficient danger to attack it in a review of Babbitt's *Democracy and Leadership* in the *Forum* (1927) and to return to the subject two years later in the *Criterion* in an essay, 'Second Thoughts About Humanism'.

A distinctly Humanist flavour emerges from the pages of the *Nation* in the First World War years. Thus we find Babbitt being given space in the front to write a long appraisal of Arnold in the light of Sherman's *Matthew Arnold How To Know Him.* Babbitt discerns in Arnold the emergence of 'the modern spirit synonymous with the critical spirit, the refusal to take things on authority'. In November Sherman contributes to the front half apropos of a book by Mencken, an article called 'Beautifying American Literature'. Sherman has an ironic dig at Mencken's style ('To prove the beauty of his phrasing, one has but to open the book and dip in anywhere'). He also jibbed at Mencken's description of Philadelphia as 'that depressing intellectual slum' and other red rags that Mencken liked to brandish inflammatorily in front of the middleclass American reader.

Rescue for the *Nation* from Humanism came after the death of Villard when Oswald Garrison Villard, his son, became the editor-proprietor of the magazine from 1918 to 1932. He continued the tradition of political independence with an anti-imperialist line on foreign policy, while campaigning for the extension of civil rights at home. We find Garrison Villard turning his attention to Britain in 1935 and lamenting the resignation of George Lansbury as leader of the Labour Party and the succession of Major Clement Attlee who, he felt, was not up to the job, a view shared by the paper's London correspondent, Harold Laski.

The next editor was a woman, Freda Kirchwey, who had joined the paper soon after she had graduated from Barnard College,

and had been literary editor, before she took over the top job. In
the periods of the Depression and the New Deal under the
Kirchwey regime the paper was required reading among intellectuals, as was its rival, the *New Republic.* The editorial board in the
mid-1930s consisted of Kirchwey, Joseph Wood Krutch (another
member of the literature faculty at Columbia and the magazine's
dramatic critic) and Raymond Gram Swing, its Washington correspondent. The associate editors were Margaret Marshall, Maxwell
S. Stewart and Dorothy Van Doren. It was Marshall who ran the
Book Reviews including regular reviews from Mark Van Doren
(also the movie critic), Lionel Trilling, William Troy, Louis Kronenberger and other members of the East Coast academic clerisy.
Margaret Marshall became literary editor in 1937 and remained as
such until 1953.

   In 1935, before fully taking over the job, she and Mary McCarthy
made a study of the state of book-reviewing in the American press.
The result was five articles under both their names and the general
heading 'Our Critics, Right Or Wrong' starting in the Fall Books
Number in October.

   The investigators made a close study of the book sections of the
daily and the weekly press, the *New York Times*, the *Herald Tribune*,
the *Chicago Daily Post* and other newspapers, as well as of journals
exclusively devoted to books such as the *Saturday Review of Literature*, the American *Bookman*, and of political weeklies and monthlies including the Marxist *New Masses*. They found them afflicted
by a galloping disease of puffery and of incestuous back-scratching
among their little exclusive coteries of author-reviewers, and they
uncovered links between the Book Clubs and the journals to which
they were attached, with reviewers puffing books chosen by selection committees of which they were members.

   The reviewers they singled out as given to hype(rbole) over
minor talents like (say) Thornton Wilder included Burton Rascoe
(Literary Editor of the *Herald Tribune's* weekly supplement *Books*
and a writer for the *Bookman)*, Arnold Bennett (who thought that
Wilder's *Woman of Andros* was 'unsurpassed'), William Rose Benét
(who considered it had 'stuff of genius'), Clifton Fadiman (who
compared Wilder to La Fontaine), Fanny Butcher, the literary
editor of the *Chicago Tribune* who thought it as 'as classically
beautiful . . . as any exquisite fragment of Greek culture . . .' and
Dr H. S. Canby in his *Saturday Review of Literature.* He had an
enormous influence over an author's reputation but, though well-
meaning, the critical faculty was not Canby's strong suit. Here he

is on Dorothy Parker's slim volume, *Death and Taxes:* 'If I compare
her to Horace and Martial, I do so largely since I am no Latinist,
and can better describe the perfection of her admirable lyrics by
comparison with the almost forgotten humorist Thomas Hood
who had a gift of beauty second only to his contemporary Keats.'
'A good writer will always elicit from Dr Canby a respectful if
uncomprehending tribute', said Marshall and McCarthy, 'just as
soon as a less publicized but more intellectual critic has brought
him to his attention.'

The fourth article on 4 December 1935 was headed 'The
Proletarians', and pinpointed the peculiar dilemma facing the
Marxist book-critics in the *New Masses.* Such reviewing absurdities
are quoted, as one by Henry Flury on Proust: 'We never see how
the aristocracy is linked to French industry and financed by
marriages and investments', and the slighting of Malraux's *Man's
Fate* because it took Trotzky's [sic] line on the Chinese Revolution.
The difficulty that these Marxist reviewers face is that though they
are committed to a concern with an author's attitude to society,
artistic considerations will keep breaking in. Thus though the
hated Wilder gets nought out of ten in this magazine for his
content, he gets surprisingly high marks for form and expression:
'Dismissing Wilder's ideology as utterly reactionary, we nevertheless cannot help admiring his superb structure, his economy of
means, his chrystaline [*sic*] style.'

The *Masses* has its Book Club, the Book Union, towards which
its writers are just as partisan as the selectors of the Book of the
Month Club and the Literary Guild. Charles Van Doren, they
continue, who last year was described as 'a fascist' is today an
adviser to their Book Guild. Kyle Cricton reviews for the *New
Masses* under the pen-name Robert Briffault and also reviews for
Henry Luce's *Time* under his own name, where he showers praise
on his colleague Robert Forsythe's book of essays *Redder Than the
Rose* that he had previously reviewed pseudonymously in the *New
Masses.* The Marxist book-reviewer may have cut himself off from
the bourgeois critics but traces of bourgeois intellectual life still
cling to him.

The final article, headed 'Literary Salesmen', dealt with the
fraternity that reviewed a new book *every day* in a newspaper. The
main members were John Chamberlain of the *New York Times*,
Lewis Gannett of the *Herald Tribune*, Harry Hansen of the *New York
World* and William Soskin of the *Evening Post.* Marshall and

McCarthy pointed out that these men – with the exception of Chamberlain – came to reviewing from reporting and leader-writing not criticism. These reviewers aimed to 'promote' books not to review them objectively. Marshall and McCarthy suggested the underlying economic reasons for this approach:

> It is not to be imagined that Gannett, Brickell, Soskin, *et al.* are the only literary salesmen disguised as critics who function in the book world of today. The reviewers on the *Herald Tribune Books*, the *Saturday Review of Literature*, and the *New York Times Book Review* are performing precisely the same service for the publishing houses. Among the literary weeklies *Books* [the *Herald Tribune* one] is the most conscious of its role as a book-selling medium. There was a time, in the middle and late twenties, when *Books* was a moderately respectable literary journal. Its back pages were filled with reviews of trivial pieces of fiction and non-fiction, but its cover and front sections were often devoted to articles by important men and women of letters. Virginia Woolf, Rebecca West, Paul Valéry and Lytton Strachey were making in *Books* stimulating contributions to critical thought. Today any Sunday's *Books* looks like a trade journal. No distinguished critical name adorns its cover; an entire page in the back section is devoted to a tabulated account of the best-sellers as reported by book-stores all over the country; a downright unfavorable review, particularly of a work of fiction, is a rare and distinguishing phenomenon, though some harassed reviewers have learnt how to insert a hint of their real feelings between the favorable or equivocal lines.
>
> The causes of this change of policy are readily perceived. Book publishers were among the first to feel the pinch of the depression. Lowered sales meant a lowered budget for newspaper advertising. What was more natural than that *Books*, recognizing the publishers' plight, should do what it could to get a larger slice of the reduced advertising budget. Before the realities of depression literary pretensions faded. The effort to make the date of its review coincide with the date of publication of the book reviewed was intensified until at present *Books* frequently appears with its consistently favorable review, several days before the book is actually on sale. It began to feature lists solicited from well-known persons of 'Books I Have Liked', 'Good Reading', 'Books I Have Read Recently', 'Books I Expect To Like This Season', 'Books I Wish I'd Read'. Later it introduced a Popular Fiction Number and a Mystery Story Number.

During her long reign as its literary editor, Margaret Marshall saw that the book reviews in the *Nation* maintained unimpeachable critical standards.

Trilling had said that one of the key people in American cultural journalism was William Phillips, editor of *Partisan Review*, and that I should certainly try to see him before I left New York. I needed no prompting and went to see Phillips in his apartment one evening. He had told me on the phone that he had a regular contributor to the journal coming and it might be interesting for me to talk to him too. The man in question turned out to be Steven Marcus, a professor in the English department at Columbia University. He was sitting on a time-bomb: his book on Victorian pornographic writing, *The Other Victorians*. When it came out with a very loud bang on both sides of the Atlantic in 1966, it made his reputation. His writings on English literature ranged from Dickens to Orwell and extended to V. S. Pritchett, whom he described in an appreciative article as 'the Ideal Reviewer', pointing to 'the general, unorganised intelligence, and the disciplined powers of perception that illuminate with a kind of random regularity every one of [Pritchett's] essays.'

The conversation that evening sprayed haphazardly over various targets from Tolstoy to Angus Wilson, all soundly riddled by the time we had finished. Phillips talked more or less non-stop and would often immediately qualify what he had just said. He was a thinker aloud, trying out ideas, then discarding them. From time to time Marcus took over, speaking deliberately and authoritatively from his academic point of vantage. I would try to intervene but it was quite hard going. They seemed more interested in the theories they were propounding themselves than in listening to anyone else. The wives, Edna Phillips and blonde Mrs Marcus, were mainly silent observers. It was all too easy, I discovered, to find yourself in the doghouse. I stupidly launched into a story about Ezra Pound during which I felt the atmosphere freeze to well below zero. Everyone looked anxious as I ploughed on. When I got to the innocuous punch-line, it thawed again.

The talk turned to Kenneth Tynan, who had begun appearing in the *New Yorker*. Under the influence of Eric Bentley, another English exile in America, Tynan was currently abandoning his championship of individual heroism in the theatre, the cult of 'He that plays the king. . . .' that had dominated his outlook at Oxford;

it had been exchanged for a newly-found crusading belief in a drama of social awareness. He had, in other words, discovered Brecht and he had found sustenance not only in Bentley's writings but in a work that applied Marxist theory to the contemporary scene as a whole, *Studies & Further Studies in a Dying Culture* by 'Christopher Caudwell' (Christopher St John Sprigg), a member of the International Brigade, killed in Spain in 1937. Phillips told us that Tynan had taken a Caudwellian line in a conversation he had with him at which Phillips had cut him short with a *mot* that has since become famous: 'I'm sorry but I have forgotten the arguments.'

Phillips had the satisfaction of putting Tynan down on that occasion, but in the 1930s Phillips and his fellow writers on the *Review* had known the 'arguments' all too well. *Partisan Review* started in February–March 1934 as the journal of the New York John Reed Club. John Reed Clubs had sprung up throughout the United States as meeting places for writers famous and obscure who believed with varying degrees of commitment in a Marxist solution to the country's current ills. Reed was a radical, Harvard-educated poet much involved in literary journalism. In 1912 he had assisted the poet and critic Max Eastman edit the recently founded journal *Masses*, a publication with considerable literary as well as political content. He became a well-known presence in New York's bohemian circles, a regular attender at the salon in Greenwich Village of Mabel Dodge, whose financially supportive and amorous role in the American radical life of her times was the equivalent of Ottoline Morrell's in England. She came from a wealthy banking family and later uprooted herself to New Mexico. Reed was one of her lovers.

He contributed some of his most graphic dispatches of industrial unrest to *Masses* and later filed copy from Russia during the siege of Petrograd, where he met the American woman journalist Louise Bryant who became his wife. His first-hand account of the Revolution, *Ten Days That Shook the World*, was published in 1919 after *Masses* had been suppressed. The same group then started the *Liberator*, a journal that in 1922 became affiliated to the American Communist Party. It was suspended in 1924 and in 1926 it was revived as the *New Masses*, with the usual mixture of a political front and a literary-artistic back, both sections being aggressively Marxist.

Reed died and was buried Russia in 1920; his legend became the inspiration for the next generation of radical writers. The First

National Conference of John Reed Clubs was held at the Lincoln Center, Chicago, in May 1932. The delegate from San Francisco was the young poet Kenneth Rexroth. Between 1934 and 1936 *Partisan Review* existed alongside the *New Masses*, as an outlet for radically minded contemporary writing. Whether it was a rival to, or a companion of, the earlier journal is a moot point. They certainly had several contributors in common, but there was from the start in *PR* a fastidious concern for good writing. It soon acquired readers who were not necessarily sworn Communists or fellow-travellers.

In 1935 the Communist Party staged a take-over of the John Reed Clubs. A Writers' Congress was called and held in May 1935 at which it was announced that all the John Reed Clubs would be dissolved and replaced by a League of American Writers to be affiliated to the Communist-controlled International Union of Revolutionary Writers (IURW). At this point *PR* declared its independence, and after the Fall Number in 1936 temporarily suspended publication. The journal was then 'stolen' by its editors, Philip Rahv and William Phillips, and re-launched at the end of 1937 when, though still anti-capitalist and Marxist-oriented, it acquired its reputation as a journal of ideas across the whole spectrum of political and cultural activity. Its way with literature and its way with politics were not always in harmony with each other but that only made it all the more interesting to read:

> these two radical impulses came together in an uneasy but fruitful union; and it was in those years [1936–41] that the magazine seemed most exciting and vital as a link between art and experience, between the critical consciousness and the political conscience, between the avant garde of letters and the independent left of politics [wrote Irving Howe].

Its strength lay in finding contributors in all fields of the highest quality and seriousness; and from the dynamic presence of Rahv. Like Sharp, like Orage, like Harold Ross, Rahv for all his maddening qualities was a great editor whose journal conditioned attitudes.

If Van Doren was the self-styled Happy Critic, Rahv was precisely the opposite. "Oos 'appy?' he would inquire mournfully of his friends. Born in the Ukraine, son of a Jewish shopkeeper, Rahv was in Russia during the civil war until the whole family moved to Palestine where his parents, early Zionists, started a small furniture factory. Rahv and his older brother emigrated to America. A relentless self-educator and speaker of several European languages, Rahv migrated to New York during the Depression where he became a Marxist and met William Phillips.

Rahv's Marxism was combined with a literary critical gift of originality and elegance. He rapidly became an expert on American, as well as Russian, literature; and it is to Rahv that literary criticism is indebted for the often-used division of American writers into the two main categories of Redskins and Palefaces. He was the magazine's 'alter Iago', a 'manic impressive' – to quote a couple of the quips his presence inspired. There is an affectionate portrait of him in Mary McCarthy's novella *The Oasis*, where he appears as Will Taub; first seen 'pounding his fist on his coffee-table, upsetting a highball over a rather proprietory article on Tocqueville he was preparing for the press'.

The group around him included Dwight MacDonald who, as an American isolationist in the late 1930s, left to edit his own journal, *Politics*. Mary McCarthy, whose lover Rahv became, was given the task of writing theatre reviews which she did with devastating brilliance. She agreed with Worsley about the dramas of Williams and Miller. Saul Bellow's friend Delmore Schwartz – another legend, the original of Bellow's Humboldt – was a colleague on the magazine and so was F. W. (Fred) Dupee, on the faculty at Columbia. He had an admiration for Henry James that did not inhibit him from becoming literary editor of the *New Masses* in the 1920s. Trilling was never of the inner core but was a frequent contributor and adviser. Delmore Schwartz introduced William Barrett, a philosophy teacher, knowledgeable about existentialism, and a fluent *causerie*-ist, who for a time in the 1940s became the level-headed *goy* on an editorial board otherwise dominated by volatile Jews. Schwartz and Barrett were associate editors, with Rahv and Phillips as joint-editors.

The Moscow Show Trials faced them with some agonising choices, as they did their colleagues on the *Nation* in New York and the *New Statesman* in London. It was a long divisive struggle before the journal completely repudiated the Soviet Union. *Partisan Review* was one of a number of journals where the debate about Marxism and cultural values was heatedly argued. Another with whom it shared some significant writers was the *Modern Monthly*, edited by George Goetz, a Baltimorean of German background who adopted the name V. F. Calverton. He saw through Stalin after the first of the Moscow Trials in 1936 but gave

space in his journal (though not remuneration) to anyone –
famous or obscure – who wished to develop an interesting Marxist
line. He opened his columns to powerful intellectual antagonists
like Eastman and Sidney Hook. Alfred Kazin, while writing his first
book-reviews for the *New Republic* in the 1930s, found a mood of
engagement chez Calverton that was a corrective to the high
Athenian culture of the Van Doren Happy Critic ambience.

> Calverton's house, like Calverton's magazine, was a natural gath-
> ering place for all sorts of radicals not in the Communist fold – old
> Russian Mensheviks and social Revolutionaries, German Marxists
> who had known Engels and Bernstein, American Socialists and
> libertarian anarchists, ex-Communists who had fallen off the train of
> history or had been pushed off it, somewhere up the line possibly in
> 1921 at the time of Kronstadt, or in 1927 at the time of Trotsky's
> downfall, or in 1935 with the increasing savagery of Stalin to all
> former opponents and thus presumably present critics. The *New
> Masses* could not mention Calverton, Norman Thomas, Max East-
> man, Sidney Hook, Eugene Lyons without accusing them of literary
> plagiarism, sabotage against the Soviet state, poisoning little children,
> and any and all other crimes necessary and logical to miscreants
> opposed to Stalin. But there they all were busily arguing with each
> other at Calverton's many parties, looking rumpled and all too
> human against the solid walls of bookshelves, the walls and walls of
> books whose severe intellectual front engloomed those long and
> violet dark rooms put in shadow by the tree outside.

In the years immediately after the Second World War *Partisan
Review* was at a peak of influence, with copies on sale in the UK.
under the aegis of *Horizon*. The 'Letter from London' was contributed by Orwell and after he died by Koestler, and at least on one
occasion by Connolly, the 'Letter from Berlin' by Melvin J. Lasky,
from Paris by Raymond Aron, from Italy by Nicola Chiaromonte.
   At the beginning of 1947 in the January–February issue, while
Barrett was discussing 'Writers and Madness' in the wake of
Trilling's earlier piece 'Art and Neurosis', the magazine ran a
symposium on the question 'What Is Socialism?' with answers in
the form of articles throughout the year from Sidney Hook, James
Burnham, Granville Hicks, Orwell, Koestler, Arthur Schlesinger
Jr, and Victor Serge.

The editors of *Partisan Review* had now come to the conclusion that, 'The Russian Revolution has not only failed to realise the hopes invested in it, but has actually produced a totalitarian system with a dynamism of its own that throttles the development of socialist thought and democratic socialist movements.' Where did that leave the likes of Sidney Hook?

> I am a democrat [he wrote]. I am a socialist. And I am still a Marxist in the sense in which one may speak of a modern biologist as still a Darwinian. I am a democrat because I believe that the guiding principle of social life should be an *equality* of concern for all individuals to develop their personalities *freely*. I am a socialist because I believe that the conditions upon which the moral and political ideals of democracy depend require a large measure of planning in production, and that to be effective this planning must carry with it in basic sectors of industry those powers of control which define social ownership. I am willing to call myself a Marxist because I believe that Marx's leading ideas, as I interpret them, and revised in the light of the scientific method which he himself professed to follow, are better guides to achieving socialism – *if* it can be achieved – than any other alternative set of ideas known to me.

The book reviews reflected the magazine's political commitment. One of the books reviewed in this issue was *The Wild Flag* by E. B. White, a collection of his wartime editorials in the *New Yorker*. White's punning whimsy is the pretext for a frontal attack on the magazine itself.

> The *New Yorker* [wrote Robert Warshow, an associate editor of *Commentary* and one of *PR's* regular reviewers] at its best provides the intelligent and cultured college graduate with the most comfortable and least compromising attitude he can assume toward capitalist society without being forced into actual conflict.

The poetry reviewer of *PR* was John Berryman and there was no political correctness here; just one major poet's reactions to the work of his peers. Of *Lord Weary's Castle* he said:

> Robert Lowell seems to me not only the most powerful poet who has appeared in England or America for some years, master of a freedom in the Catholic subject without peer since Hopkins, but also

in terms of this distinction, a thematic poet. His work displays in high degree, passion, vista, burden.

Another book in Berryman's batch was a selection from New Directions of recent work by Dylan Thomas.

> Instead of comparing [Dylan Thomas] to Shakespeare and cooing over his development, his English admirers should thank heaven and his character that he has continued to write *extremely well* without undue self-imitation, and with a mildly expanding range of subject.

To publish new poetry and the appraisal of new poetry were among the primary concerns of *Partisan Review*. Eliot chose the journal for the first publication of *The Dry Salvages*; and it was apropos of Eliot, Eliot as the champion of Pound, that it became involved in one of its bitterest and most interesting controversies. In 1948 Paul Mellon donated funds for an annual poetry award for 'the highest achievement in American poetry'; it was called the Bollingen Prize because he wanted to associate it with Jung's home in Switzerland. In the first year it was worth $1000 to the winner. The panel of judges consisted of the Fellows in Letters of the Library of Congress who in 1948 included Eliot, Auden, Robert Penn Warren, Katherine Anne Porter and Robert Lowell. Another member was the poet Allen Tate, who had been editor of the *Sewanee Review* from 1944 to 1946. He, Robert Penn Warren, John Crow Ransom, Stark Young, and others had long campaigned for the recognition of 'regionalism' in literature, by which they meant a literature that drew its strength from its roots in the American South. As far back as 1922 Tate had edited the bi-monthly journal the *Fugitive* dedicated to this cause; in 1930 after the paper had folded he had edited a symposium *I'll Take My Stand*, with contributions from the all above-mentioned, further defining their separatist position linking it to the Agrarian movement that demanded that the South should have its own self-contained rural economy. Regionalism was examined by T. S. Eliot in the parallel context of post-war Europe in an essay, 'The Man of Letters and the Future of Europe' originally published in Norway in the *Norseman* and re-printed by Tate in the *Sewanee Review* in the summer of 1945:

> The man of letters should see also, that within any cultural unit, a proper balance of urban and rural life is essential. Without great

cities – great not necessarily in the modern material sense, but great
by being the meeting-place of a society of superior mind and more
polished manners – the culture of a nation will never rise above
rustic level; without the life of the soil from which to draw its
strength, the urban culture must lose its source of strength and
rejuvenescence. *Fortunatus est ille qui deos novit agrestes.* [Blessed is he
who knows country gods].

In Eliot's case this attitude was part of his anxiety that the City,
with its cosmopolitan mixture of rootless individuals including a
large quantity of 'free-thinking Jews', would dilute – if not pollute
– the purity of the culture; it was an attitude stated publicly in
lectures at the University of Virginia that stemmed from his
admiration for the writings of Charles Maurras, author of such
anti-Romantic and anti-feminine books as *L'Avenir de l'Intelligence*
and *Barbarie et poésie* as well as his notorious political writings, his
monarchism and anti-Semitic journalism, his membership of L'Action française and editorship of its journal. All of this was no doubt
going through the minds of the editors and readers of *Partisan
Review* – who included many 'free-thinking Jews' – when by a
majority vote the Fellows of the Library awarded the first Bollingen
Prize to Ezra Pound for the *Pisan Cantos*.

The award was announced in *Partisan Review* of April 1949 along
with the announcement of the *Partisan Review* Award, also for
$1000, 'to give vigorous affirmation to the importance of literary
standards in the present cultural situation'. The journal then
published an appraisal of Pound as a poet by Berryman, along
with an editorial by Barrett, 'A Prize for Ezra Pound' in which he
cited the Bollingen judges' explanatory statement accompanying
the announcement of the winner: 'To permit other considerations
than that of poetic achievment to sway the decision would destroy
the significance of the award and would in principle deny the
validity of that objective perception of value on which any civilised
society must rest.' It was a statement that raised many more
questions than it answered. These were skilfully opened up by
Barrett, who adopted the tactic of re-writing in plain English the
judges' gnomic utterance, referring to what it had avoided and
evaded, the actual content of the poem, and asking whether form
can be dissociated from content in the way the statement implied.

A heated debate ensued, not only in the columns of *PR* but
throughout the whole republic of American letters. In *Politics*
Dwight Macdonald declared the award to be 'the brightest political

act in a dark period'. The editors of *Partisan Review* invited the judges to comment on Barrett's article in its columns. The majority of them, including Eliot, declined but among those who did was Auden, who sent them a contribution in which he managed to compress the two opposite theories of the social function of art: (1) art as the purging of our bad feelings (Plato's and Tolstoy's view); and (2) art as 'a mirror . . .' (Auden had recently written his long poem about art, *The Sea and The Mirror*) – 'a mirror in which the spectator sees reflected himself and the world, and becomes conscious of his feelings good and bad, and of what their relations to each other are in fact.' Does it therefore follow from (2) that *anything*, however noxious, is permissible in a work provided it falls into the category 'art'? – a view nowadays more or less universally held by writers and artists. Yes, says Auden, but – an enormous 'but' – then we have to face the question of censorship because a work of art cannot compel the spectator to look at it with detachment and prevent him from using it as a stimulus and excuse for feelings which he should condemn and which 'we' as the representatives of society condemn:

> For instance, Baudelaire's poem *La Charogne* would not be healthy reading for a necrophilist. Antisemitism is, unfortunately, not only a feeling which all gentiles at times feel, but also, and this is what matters, a feeling of which the majority of them are not ashamed. Until they are, they must be regarded as children who have not yet reached the age of consent in this matter and from whom, therefore, all books, whether works of art or not, which reflect feeling about Jews – and it doesn't make the slightest difference whether they are pro or anti – the *New York Post* can be as dangerous as *Der Sturmer* – must be withheld.

If we take this paternalistic view of the mass of people's response to art, *The Pisan Cantos* must be withdrawn from circulation along with *The Merchant of Venice, Ivanhoe, Oliver Twist* and much else of greatness in literature. 'That', Auden added, 'would not however prevent me awarding the *Pisan Cantos* a prize before witholding it from the public.'

It was a very clever *reductio ad absurdum* of the argument for not giving Pound the Prize. Allen Tate, who also responded to Barrett's editorial angrily, interpreted it as implying that he, and his colleagues who had voted in favour of Pound's getting the prize, were anti-Semitic, and this provoked a furiously bellicose denial:

I consider antisemitism to be both cowardly and dishonorable; I consider it cowardly and dishonorable to insinuate, as Barrett does, without candor, a charge of antisemitism against the group of writers of which I am a member.

I hope that persons who wish to accuse me of cowardice and dishonor will do so henceforth personally, in my presence, so that I may dispose of the charge at some other level than that of public discussion. Courage and honor are not subjects of literary controversy, but occasions of action.

In the face of Tate's explosion Barrett said that it 'was a complete and unwarranted misconstruction of my editorial, which contained absolutely no allegation whatever of antisemitism on the part of the judges. The question was, and is, the public wisdom of an award to Pound and not the private psychology of the judges.'

The whole controversy grumbled on for many months. It revealed a huge fissure in the literary culture of the United States. One immediate result of the controversy was for the Library of Congress to dissociate itself from the Prize. It was awarded henceforth by the Yale University Library. Tate himself won it in 1957 and most of the major American poets have received it including Berryman, Frost, Wallace Stevens, Marianne Moore, Yvor Winters, Delmore Schwartz, W. S. Merwin and Auden.

Both *PR* and William Phillips, my generous host on that distant evening in 1958, have proved to be great survivors. At the time of writing Phillips is still contributing lively, often reminiscent, editorial commentaries and *PR* is still *engagé* while the enemy has taken new social forms; recently it has been concentrating attention on the notion of 'multi-culturalism' that has acquired such stranglehold on the constitution of university courses in the arts and humanities. It is significant that many of the most outspoken articles and opinions have come from the descendants of Jewish immigrants whose careers have shown the benefits of assimilating the traditonal Western culture rooted in the classics and works of the highest excellence in Matthew Arnold's sense. It was Trilling the Jew who after Sherman re-interpreted Arnold – the enemy of Hebraism – for American and British culture.

I had introductions not just to cultural magazine editors and reviewers but also to writers working in more popular forms. One was to S. N. Behrman, the Broadway playwright. His London publisher (Rupert Hart-Davis) had told him I was in New York and this resulted in an invitation to lunch. Sam Behrman was a small man physically but large in talent and vitality. I felt son-like in his genial twinkling presence when he greeted me in his apartment, where I noted the signed photographs of Maugham and Coward proudly displayed in stand-up frames on the piano. The grand room in which one instantly felt at home might have been the set for one of his comedies. We went to the Ritz for lunch, where the head-waiter greeted my host warmly and showed us to a quiet table by the window. Behrman ate little, his abundant energy seemed to be fuelled mainly by an insatiable curiosity. We talked about the film *Jacobowsky and the Colonel*, made from his play, which I had seen the day before. He had wanted Rex Harrison for the colonel but had been rail-roaded into having Curt Jurgens, who he said was not really right. He told me about the autobiographical play he was now trying to adapt from *The Worcester Account*, his memoirs of his Jewish boyhood in Massachussets published in England by Rupert; it was for production at the end of the current season and he was late with it. 'I shall shut myself up in a room for a week to write and see what happens,' he said.

After that we discussed the *New Yorker*. Behrman belonged to the magazine's inner circle of contributors. I gathered he had been consulted by Shawn on the question of whom he should appoint as theatre critic in succession to Wolcott Gibbs, an old New Yorker hand, who had died suddenly. The appointment of Tynan – a Briton unknown then in the States – was as bold a move as Tynan's previous appointment as the dramatic critic of the *Observer* by David Astor. 'Do you know this guy Kenneth Tynan?' Behrman shot at me over apple pie topped with vanilla ice cream. I replied that we had been Oxford contemporaries and I had had a small role, that of Rosencrantz, in his production of *Hamlet* that played in London.

'What do you think of him?'

'Well, he's a wonderful critic. But, personally, I feel rather ambivalent about him.'

'*Do you?* Why? Tell me.' The sharp little eyes had expanded into headlamps turned on me full-beam. I was dazzled like a rabbit at night, startled out of my wits by their sudden intensity.

The short answer was that I was dead envious of Tynan but I do not think that that was the one I gave, though I am sure Behrman deconstructed it accurately. Wherever I went Tynan had got there first and I was getting fed up with it. When I finally got to Oxford, he was already famous throughout the university and beyond as an undergraduate director and actor. Then in London in the early 1950s, when I was reviewing plays anonymously for *The Times*, often sitting in a seat adjacent to his, Tynan was the toast of the town on the *Evening Standard* and then on the *Observer*. And now, dammit, he was here again, or about to be, to make his conquest of New York. I hated the imposition of Tynan's tendentious opinions whenever we met. Two quick examples – '*L'Avare* . . . a great bore, it contains the dullest prose Molière ever wrote . . .' – 'Italy! Why go to Italy, for Heaven's sake! It's just a perfumed and pomaded version of . . . Ssspain!' I hated the invariable attempt to detonate several tons of Semtex under one's most cherished beliefs. But I loved the exhilarating sense that everything was possible that I always felt in his presence. When he was nice he could be very very nice.

Behrman inquired about my plans while I was in America and I explained about looking closely at traditions of American book-reviewing and also about Gissing. He had not read him either. I told him about Gissing's terrible life: how he had stolen money from fellow students at college in Manchester in order to buy a sewing-machine for a young street-walker; how he had been tried and convicted; how on his release from prison he went to the United States where he taught and survived living off 'pea-nuts in a town called Troy' and publishing short fiction in local news-papers. How he came back to England and married Nell the street-walker and tried to live by writing those long three-decker novels that were still for some writers, but not for him, a lucrative occupation in the England of the 1880s.

Behrman appeared genuinely fascinated by my recital. 'It's marvellous material,' he said. 'Marvellous! But why do you need to come to the States to work on it? I don't follow.'

I explained that in the edition of Gissing's letters that his brother and sister had made they had cut out all reference to Gissing's catastrophic marriages. The letters as published were so bowdlerised as to be worthless as biographical evidence. However at the same time they had sold parcels of the originals unmutilated to American collectors, whose dollars their impecuniousness made it impossible for them to resist. Among the keenest collectors had been two New York doctors, Henry and Albert Berg . . .

Behrman interrupted me to say that he had known the Bergs. In fact he had once consulted one of them professionally. 'Everyone who could afford it went to them. They made a fortune . . .'

Part of that fortune had been spent on acquiring unpublished manuscript material in the field of nineteenth and twentieth century English literature. Neither brother had married and when Albert died in 1950 he had left the New York Public Library, of which he had been a trustee, the whole collection as memorial to his brother. The Henry and Albert Berg Collection was now open to researchers and I planned to spend some time there. I explained that this was but one of sizeable caches of material that I wanted to see in various collections all over America. In the end the trail would take me to Yale, to Los Angeles and to San Francisco.

'California!' he said wistfully. 'You know there are some wonderful people there! Wonderful people!' He told me to let him know before I left for the Coast so that he could put me on to some of these wonderful people and that we must stay in touch. And he meant it, as events were to prove.

The curator of the Berg Collection in 1958 was Dr John D. Gordan, a fifty-year-old Virginian, an avid reader of the *Lit Supp*. Being on leave from the *Supplement's* editorial staff meant that I received a warm welcome at any rare book library or English department in the United States I wished to visit. Gordan always turned eagerly to the bibliographical back page of the paper, much of it then written by John Carter, who had made his name as one of the co-authors of the work that had unmasked the rare book villain and forger Thomas J. Wise. Jake (as Carter was known) was now one of the experts in the rare book department at Sotheby's. Married to the fashion journalist Ernestine Carter, an American, he was frequently back and forth across the Atlantic. It was a high-point of Gordan's week when Jake looked in on Berg. Work ceased while they chatted animatedly for an hour or so about what was on offer in terms of unpublished manuscript material. This was the time when American collections like Berg had seemingly unlimited resources to spend on buying the literary remains of those who were truly great and in some cases of those who were not so great.

Gordan, who controlled Berg's purse-strings, was a powerful figure in this world. Among his rivals and peers were Harry Ransom, who controlled the oil-based riches of the University of

Texas at Austin, William Jackson of the Houghton Library at
Harvard, Frederick B. Adams of the Pierpoint Morgan, Fritz
Liebert of the Beinecke Collection at Yale and Bradford A. Booth
at UCLA, to mention but a few of the scholar-tycoons whom I
would meet. When they were not at large in the market-place,
their contributions to bibliography were to be found in their
catalogues and articles, works of fastidious scholarship.

Gordan was related by marriage to the British MP Philip
Goodhart, who when he was a small boy had stayed in the US. 'I'm
the only *Amurrican* who has inspected behind the ears of a Member
of Parliament!' Gordan told me proudly. Gordan was at this time
negotiating with Leonard Woolf for the purchase of Virginia
Woolf's Diaries, and had also just pulled off his greatest coup,
heavily under wraps, of acquiring the draft manuscripts of *The
Waste Land*. In 1923 these came into the possession of John Quinn,
the Irish-American lawyer and collector. When Quinn died they
were inherited by his sister. After her death in 1934 and her
husband's, they came into the possession of her daughter, who put
the many boxes full of her uncle's papers into store. She was
unaware of the precise nature of the contents of these boxes but
Gordan had picked up the scent and he persuaded Mrs Conroy,
as she was, to open them.

After a prolonged search she found the original manuscript of
The Waste Land, completely intact and with Ezra Pound's deletions
and emendations, made before the version we all know was
published in 1922. No one – except Gordan – not even, it seems,
Eliot himself had any idea where these papers were. On 4 April
1958, six months before my arrival at Berg, Gordan had concluded
a deal with Mrs Conroy whereby Berg purchased the *Waste Land*
manuscripts for $18,000. He kept all this very much to himself.

He was, however, delighted to meet a fellow-Gissing enthusiast.
He had laid on an exhibition to celebrate the writer's centenary
the year before and showed me the catalogue he had compiled of
the material. He told me there was further Gissing material in the
Pforzheimer Library, another such millionaire's endowment, but
that the stuff in Berg would keep me going for some while.

As I read the letters in the Berg Collection that Gissing wrote
from London to his mother and sisters in Wakefield, I could not
help but contrast my present Harkness affluence and delightful
circumstances with Gissing's embittering struggle as a writer. The
prosperity of the modern literary biographical researcher is often
in stark contrast to the indigence of the dead writer on whom he

depends. I felt the time I spent meeting the staff and familiarising myself with some of the contents of these collections when I was not visiting newspapers and literary journals was time well spent. The two kinds of institution, literary journals and manuscript collections, complement each other as components of American literary culture.

I discovered that it was not only the theatre that was part of the living culture in New York but literature too. Writers appeared in public and drew sizeable audiences at places like the George Kauffman Hall of the Young Men's Hebrew Association. I attended a reading there given by e. e. cummings. Listening to this tall, spare man in a grey suit meticulously reading his work I felt that no poet ever actually looked and sounded more lower-case than cummings.

I began also to infiltrate New York University attending a discussion at the faculty club by the Corsican-born poet Joseph Ciardi on the problems of translating Dante and a lecture on poetics by the critic R. P. Blackmur who had become since *Hound and Horn* days an embodiment of the New Criticism. In a melodious monotone he made the distinction between linear logic in the structure of a work such as *Paradise Lost* and 'form by analogy' in a work like, say, *The Waste Land*. Form by analogy was, he said, the quintessence of modernism. I instinctively mistrust form by analogy because it is all too often a pretext for formlessness. Blackmur was courteously hostile to my view in the discussion afterwards.

Several of the scholars I met told me that I really ought to look in at the annual conference of the Modern Languages Association to get a true perspective on American academic life. It was being held that year at the end of December in New York at the Statler Hilton on 33rd Street. I attended the final day of what, for the profession of scholarship in many disciplines, serves the same function as the Frankfurt Book Fair for the publishing industry, that of a vast market-place. There are many specialised sessions over two or three days as well as general assemblies that every delegate attends. Pinning a name-badge on my lapel with 'Asst. Editor *Times Lit Suppt*' inscribed on it, I was soon absorbed into the crowd.

One face I knew was that of Arthur C. Young, a professor of English at Rutgers. He was a fellow Gissingite currently engaged in editing Gissing's correspondence with Eduard Bertz, a refugee to America from Bismark's Germany. 'What are you doing here? Looking for a job!' Art said with a huge grin. I told him that the terms of my fellowship precluded me from doing that. Fellows were pledged not to use their fellowships seek employment in America. 'Then you had better watch your step,' he said. 'The head-hunters are out in force today.' But there was no cause for concern in my case.

If Columbia University's English department had Trilling, F. W. Dupee, Jacques Barzun and Steven Marcus, New York University also had its stars of the English faculty, as I discovered when I attended the faculty club luncheon in the New Year. Chief among them was Leon Edel, who was then half way through his great biography of Henry James. Edel, who had been born in Pittsburgh in 1907, had taken his master's degree at McGill University, Montreal, before the Second World War and then became a docteur ès lettres at the Sorbonne. The topic he chose for his dissertation was Henry James and the theatre. A printed version of his thesis, *Henry James: Les Années Dramatiques*, published in Paris in 1931, was the acorn from which sprouted the many-branched biographical Jacobite tree. I had acquired a copy of the thesis in the 1940s in a job lot of books about James, knocked down to me for ten shillings (50p) in Hodgson's Rooms, Chancery Lane. My copy had been inscribed by Edel 'as from one Jacobite to another' to the historian 'Philip Guedella, Montreal 1933'. When Edel came to my house in London in 1976 I showed it to him and he re-inscribed it for me. He told me that he had given it to Guedella when he had lectured in Montreal after which they had a talk and that only 300 copies of this volume had been printed.

In New York in 1959 we ourselves had a talk over lunch, at which Edel spoke about the danger with Henry James of misinterpreting his way of addressing his male friends, where the ornate gallic manner James adopted may suggest much greater intimacy than was in fact the case. I asked him if it was really true that Henry James never had a sexual relationship with anyone. He said he thought this was probably so but that it was not proven. Such questions he said never could be proven, 'as a biographer you can never get right underneath the bed' – a truth by no means universally acknowledged by later biographers.

Edel was then working on James's letters, of which he had assembled many more than those published by Percy Lubbock. 'What do I do,' he said, 'about the 250 postcards there are telling people how to get to Lamb House, Rye ['You take the convenient

11.15 am and you will be met on arrival ...' etc.], all most
elegantly phrased and no two exactly alike?' The criterion of
completeness must, he felt, in that instance be abandoned.

Edel had a question for me that was less easy to answer. He was
most curious to know who had been the author of the review in
the *Lit Supp* of a controversial book by Quentin Anderson, *The
American Henry James*, published the year before. The review had
endorsed the book's thesis that the source of James's master-
images in the later novels lies in the writings of Swedenborg,
where symbols like that of the dove and the golden bowl are to be
found. The Swedenborgian doctrine was embraced by Henry
James Sr whose influence on his son's outlook had, Anderson
argued, been neglected. Edel had written in to complain about
the review as had other members of the orthodox James lobby. I
put on my best po-face and said that as a member of staff I was
obliged to respect the anonymity principle and could not divulge
to him who had written it. The author of the review was in fact
sitting opposite Edel sipping coffee; but I was not going to tell him
that. 'You needn't worry,' he said. 'I know who it was – Michael
Swan. Shortly afterwards the poor fellow attempted to commit
suicide, and no wonder!'

I felt it was time I met some publishers as well as scholars and
critics. I went to see Alfred Knopf in the office of the company
that bore his name. Rupert Hart-Davis had told me he was the
greatest living American publisher but the occasion did not yield
anything very memorable apart from his imposing physical presence, his colourful shirt and tie combination. He was friendly but
I became tongue-tied. He had been in publishing ever since 1914
when, a graduate of Columbia, he had gone to work for Mitchell
Kennerley, the first publisher of D. H. Lawrence in America.

Knopf was responsible for the sales of a list headed by *Sons and
Lovers*. He was already planning his own imprint, however, and
when Kennerley caught him trying to poach the best-selling fiction-
author Joseph Hergesheimer, their association ended abruptly. In
1915 Knopf started his own firm and also that year married
Blanche Wolf; thus began one of the great American marital
business partnerships, Alfred A. and Blanche W. Knopf, publishers.
The distinctive colophon of a Borzoi was chosen not only because
they were both dog-lovers but because it had associations as a
Russian breed. Russian literature was to become a house-speciality,
along with modern American literature and modern English
literature.

It was not only the young Knopf's book jackets and his own jackets that were eye-catching. He made a determined bid for review-space, bombarding newspaper offices with 'flyers' headed 'To the Literary Editor' pressing the claims of his major titles, the same direct forceful approach as our Victor Gollancz, of whom Knopf was an American equivalent. D. H. Lawrence went to Knopf for his American publisher, his fourth, in 1925 with *St Mawr* and Knopf published *Lady Chatterley* in 1928 after Lawrence's death.

Starting in January 1924, Knopf also published a seminal journal, the *American Mercury*, edited by H. L. Mencken and George Jean Nathan, the successor to their earlier magazine the *Smart Set*. After a few issues Mencken became the sole editor. Mencken, whose utterances still arouse controversy, raised American literary journalism to a popular influence that it had not previously known. I will postpone further comment on Mencken's contribution as a moulder of opinion until I describe a visit I made to Baltimore. His roots lay in that city's large community of German origin.

Ben Huebsch, head of the Viking Press, who took Lawrence on after the novelist had quarrelled with Kennerley, invited me to a dinner party at his apartment in Central Park West where the chief guest was the British author Rumer Godden, a soft-voiced lady in a black velvet dress, of quiet charm and genuine modesty about her own work, over for a promotional tour of *The Greengage Summer*. Rumer Godden always stayed with the Huebsches when she was in New York; 'beloved Ben' (she said) was her 'literary father'.

Two leading journalists at this period who fulfilled an ambassadorial role between Britain and America were Edward R. Murrow and Alistair Cooke. Cooke was an example of an Englishman who had originally gone to America on a Harkness Fellowship and returned to make his career in America and become an American. I had begun to see how tempting that scenario was. At this time he was writing for the *Manchester Guardian* (as it was then) and broadcasting his weekly 'Letter from America' for the BBC (continuing still – an astonishing innings of radio broadcasting). He also 'topped and tailed' television drama series and was busy with numerous public-speaking engagements. I went to hear him talk extempore for about an hour to an audience of more than a hundred students. He reeled off the anecdotes effortlessly, like a conjuror producing a stream of dazzling silks from his top-hat. During the questions I asked him about pressures (if any) on a

foreign correspondent in America. He told us a story about a
wartime restriction whereby all his copy had to be vetted and
cleared by someone in the State Department in Washington DC.
He had responded by deluging them with interminable articles on
such weighty matters as the history of ice-cream in America until
the restriction had been waived.

Ed Murrow was more directly approachable. He had fond
memories of his time in London during the war, when he had
broadcast radio dispatches to the States describing the blitz. He
was always happy to give a drink to any Harkness journalist-fellow.
His *See It Now* programme with Fred W. Friendly made an impact
nation-wide, as when he tackled the controversial school-integra-
tion bill introduced by Eisenhower. In October 1958 he had begun
a new series of three-cornered exchanges, *Small World*, of which
the opening trio was Aldous Huxley, Thomas E. Dewey and Nehru.
For the Christmas week edition Murrow's guests, all in the same
room this time, were Samuel Goldwyn, Vivien Leigh and Kenneth
Tynan. The conversation from this alluring trio never got very far
off the ground. 'Tynan', Murrow confessed to me, 'was not nearly
as abrasive as I had hoped.'

It was true. America seemed to mellow Tynan. He even appeared
glad to see a fellow-Briton when I bumped into him at the New
York opening of the Old Vic's tour of *Hamlet*. He introduced me
to Marlene Dietrich, slinkily resplendent in leopard-skin; defying,
if not belying, her years as she clung to his arm. The 1958/1959
Broadway season he was reviewing in the *New Yorker* included Sam
Behrman's play about his childhood in Providence, for which
Behrman gave me tickets. It was called *The Cold Wind and Warm*.
There was some pleasant nostalgic stuff in it but it was below his
best form. With new work from him, Lillian Hellmann, Tennessee
Williams, and a Eugene O'Neill play performed for the first time,
Tynan had plenty to write about. When he turned to Tennessee
Williams it was clear the venom had not left his pen:

> Apart from the performance of Geraldine Page, a display of knock-
> down flamboyance and drag-out authority that triumphantly quells
> all doubts about this actress's ability to transcend her mannerisms,
> almost everything connected with *Sweet Bird of Youth*, Tennessee
> Williams's new play at the Martin Beck, dismayed and alarmed me.

The review by Tynan that gave most offence during this time
was not of a play but of a book, Moss Hart's *Act One*, the first

volume of Hart's autobiography. Tynan's all-out attack on this Broadway legend was courageous and salutary. By contrast he raved about the great sustained hymn to Success, with Ethel Merman as the driving force behind it, which is the musical *Gypsy*.

At the end of 1958 most of the New York critics were silenced by the newspaper strike that began on 11 December and lasted until the end of the year. This was a foretaste of things to come, anticipating later strikes, that would kill the *Herald Tribune* as a New York daily newspaper, and severely damage the London *Times*. From my point of view as an observer of the reviewing scene in New York, the stoppage was instructive, allowing me to study how people behaved when they were deprived of almost all reviews. The effect was quite marked, even though the strike only lasted eighteen days. It was a calamity for any book published or show opening during the period. The effect on book-publishing was so dire that the concept of a book-review sheet with no newspaper ties began to be mooted, the first number of which appeared in 1963, the forerunner of the *New York Review of Books*.

The stoppage underlined how inadequate radio and television were as substitutes for newspapers. As Bob Williams wrote in the *New York Post* on 29 December: 'The dismal failure of the TV and radio industry to keep the public informed was one of the most disappointing developments of the New York newspaper blackout.' The *New Yorker*, not being a newspaper, was unaffected and did continue to appear. I read it not just for Tynan but also for the rest of its arts and books coverage. It has made such a significant contribution to American book-reviewing that it needs a separate chapter.

12

Ross and Wilson

'Is Moby Dick the man or the whale?' Harold Ross is alleged to have inquired while reading the proof of an article about Melville and we are assured that the rest of the cultural scene – music, ballet, painting, even movies – left him equally cold, with the exception of theatre and night-clubs. For Ross, the rebellious son of a mining prospector from Aspen, Colorado who had come to America from Ulster, the major contemporary art-form was playing poker. Yet when he started the *New Yorker* in 1925 he recognised the importance of having a strong cultural section. He might possibly have been kidding when he asked about Moby Dick, casting his doubt on the clarity of the article. 'Amusement and the arts will be thoroughly covered...' Ross announced in the magazine's prospectus. 'Judgment will be passed on new books of consequence. The *New Yorker* will carry a list of the season's books which it considers worth reading'. The example of *Punch*, which had always carried book-reviews, was present in Ross's mind as a model but he aimed at a sophisticated metropolitan American counterpart.

The first *New Yorker* on 21 February 1925 contained a couple of pages devoted to book reviews, flanked by a large advertisement from Boni and Liveright, one of New York's leading book-stores. The two Boni brothers, Albert and Charles, and Horace Liveright had been a radical force in New York publishing from 1912 and had founded the Modern Library, reprinting English and European classics. It was an ideal advert for the *New Yorker's* book columns to carry, with its apeal to a cultivated reader. Like the rest of the arts, leisure and sports coverage, the book reviews were pseudonymous. The aim was to establish the magazine at this stage, not individual writers. The book reviews appeared above the signature 'Touchstone':

> If you like your novels professionally clever and intellectual, the new one for you is Aldous Huxley's. [Touchstone was reviewing *Those Barren Leaves*] There are at least three of this much talked about young Englishman. No. 1 The literary cut-up. No. 2 The young man of learning who shows it off. No.3 The very promising writer, afflicted with a mocking distrust of his own gift.
> To us [this novel] is Huxley trying harder than before to get the trio into step and make it do something.

The spate of English authors who dominated the books page in the early days was in contrast to the Manhattan-based outlook of the rest of the magazine. The list of recommended books accompanying the main review in the first issue, under the heading 'Tell Me a Book To Read', included *The White Monkey* by John Galsworthy; *A Passage to India* by E. M. Forster ('A foaming up of India's race-hatred pictured with searching skill'); *The Green Hat* by 'Michael Arlen'; *Sard Harker* by John Masefield; *The Old Ladies* by Hugh Walpole; *The Cask* by Freeman Wills Crofts; *The House of the Arrow* by A. E. W. Mason.

Fillmore Hyde, the literary editor, a wit from Harvard with a talent for light verse and a friend of Ross, kept an eye on the fiction and verse contributions as well as the reviews. He was soon inundated with unsolicited stories and poems. The *New Yorker* did not have then, and has not had until fairly recently, a literary editor in the sense in which the term is used throughout this book, someone whose primary responsibility is to run the book section. Ross was a hands-on editor who monitored everything that went into the magazine himself and that included the reviews, and this was even more true of his successor, William Shawn. After a while Hyde suggested to Ross that they should get someone to help sift through the mounting pile of would-be contributions and he nominated a New England neighbour of his, Boston-born Katherine Angell (née Sergeant), educated at Bryn Mawr, contributor to the *New Republic* and the *Atlantic Monthly*, who had also been a social worker. She joined on a part-time basis but very soon was doing a full week.

After two years in job Fillmore Hyde 'got out early' as Thurber put it, and Mrs Angell took his place. Along with Ross, Thurber, Wolcott Gibbs and E. B. White (who became her second husband),

Katherine White had a major influence over the content of the magazine in its formative period. But it was Ross who made the appointment in 1928 that got the books coverage talked about. This was the signing of Mrs Dorothy Parker to write the main book column every week over the by-line 'Constant Reader'.

Parker and Ross had been colleagues before the magazine began. Their acquaintance dated from the early 1920s. Much of their verbal sparring occurred over lunch at exclusive venues like the Coffee House Club and the Algonquin Hotel – known by them as 'the Gonk' – where a round table had been set aside for a clutch of journalists, critics and editors who habitually lunched there. The *New Yorker* has become closely identified with the wise-cracking ethos of the Algonquin Round Table, but one should remember that historically the Table came first and the magazine second. Several of its founder-members' main jobs were on papers other than the *New Yorker*. Alexander Woollcott was, for instance, the dramatic critic of the *New York Times* and only when the *New Yorker* magazine was well established did he contribute his gossipy pieces under the heading 'Shouts and Murmurs'. F. P. Adams worked for the *Herald Tribune*, where he ran a much-read column called 'The Conning Tower', a ragbag of sketches, anecdotes and light verse to which readers contributed for no payment. Heywood Broun was on the *New York World*.

Before the *New Yorker* appeared chic weeklies included *Vogue* and *Vanity Fair*, both part of the Condé Nast group, and edited by Frank Crowninshield, a hirer and firer almost as volatile and discerning as Ross. It was Crownie – as he was known – who employed Robert Benchley and Dorothy Parker, among contributors who later became famous beyond the pages of Ross's magazine. It was Crownie who first gave Dottie – we seem to have slipped unwittingly into nicknames – her first job on *Vogue* in 1917 aged twenty-three, when she was about to marry Edwin Pond Parker II, a young New York stockbroker, of waspish background. Her own background had been fairly affluent but not waspish. Her father was a Jew, Henry Rothschild, and her mother had died when she was a girl, leaving her to endure life with a step-mother.

A broken brutal childhood had given her a deep self-centredness, protected by a whiplash wit cracking down on friends and enemies alike, anyone within striking distance, and when no one was around it burst onto paper in short fragments of prose (colloquial to a degree) and verse. She was God's gift to magazine journalism, a founder-member of an aggressively articulate sisterhood. Crownie promoted her from *Vogue* to *Vanity Fair*, of which in April 1918 she became dramatic critic. Her fearless lashing of the current Broadway offerings soon gained her notoriety. Unfortunately her job ended abruptly when she cut down to size the talents of Billie Burke who happened to be married to Florenz Ziegfeld, the great impresario. He conveyed his – and his wife's – displeasure to Condé Nast, who passed the message on to Crownie; and he, to his eternal shame, fired Dorothy Parker (from now on she stuck to her married name even though her marriage rapidly disintegrated). Robert Benchley was so outraged that he resigned in sympathy.

By the time the *New Yorker* began, that sacking episode was all in the past and Dorothy Parker had become celebrated, the much dreaded, much loved lady-about-town whose carefully calculated off-the-cuff-isms were retailed by newspaper gossip-writers while her stories and poems appeared in widely read magazines such as *Life* and the *Saturday Evening Post*. She was re-employed as a theatre critic by a less prestigious journal than Crownie's and in 1927 she had a great success with her book of verse, *Enough Rope*; it sold as many copies as a best-selling novel. Then Ross got her to write the theatre criticism for his first two numbers. 'The present theatrical season has been a great little year of sex', she told readers. But by now her heart was no longer in the regular dramatic critic's nightly toil and her contributions to the magazine's two earliest years were afterwards confined to occasional verses and stories that well fitted Ross's term for the fiction published – 'casuals'. Herman J. Mankiewicz (whose career would be in screen-writing) took over the theatre reviewing for a while, to be succeeded by the novelist Charles Brackett. Dottie's heart was not really in regular book reviewing either, but under pressure from her bank manager, and officially divorced from Eddie in 1928, she took it on with the tremendous commitment that characterised everything Dorothy Parker did.

From 1 October 1927 'Constant Reader' led the New Yorker's book section most weeks, with around fifteen hundred words on two or three new books of her choice. The rest were listed or fully reviewed underneath her article by another hand. Her début was an awkward one with three ill-assorted books, two fiction and a topical book about Alfred E. Smith, a candidate for the presidential election, which someone higher up must have insisted she reviewed. ('This isn't the old *Dial*', Ross is reported to have said about the paper's early literary content.) One of the novels was

Caste by Cosmo Hamilton, concerning a society lady who marries a
Jew – and CR is not quite sure whether to be funny or angry about
the author's kid-gloved treatment of the theme – and the other
was May Sinclair's new novel, *History of Anthony Waring*. Here CR
let rip in the style that she would sustain throughout her two year's
incumbency:

> another of the short novels [May Sinclair] must be able to write, by
> now, with one hand tied behind her and buttered crumpet in the
> other ... [The novel] follows her formula with slightly ridiculous
> faithfulness. Her style has become, and I wish I were lying when I say
> it, a reduction to absurdity.

That 'I wish I were lying ...' was typical of CR's constant pose as
her readers' intimate buddy. She adopted the same matey. solipsis-
tic style in her reviews as in her stories, where she describes the
daily, or rather nightly, calamities that befall her; she is always
being martyred; whether by getting into the inextricable clutches
of a monumental bore at a dance, or by a bust garter ('Thank
God, I was sitting down when the crash came'), or now by a truly
terrible book to review. 'A few more of these young mezzo-
Hemingways, and I am going to put on black bombazine and go
Henry James,' she says, noticing Robert Hyde's novel *Crude*.
Confronted by James Branch Cabell's *Something About Eve*, she
appears to agree with the consensus view that his novels make him
the American 'master of prose in our day'. Then she pulls the rug
away from under her reader's feet: 'And I couldn't read all the
way through one of them to save my mother from the electric
chair.' With Sinclair Lewis's *Dodsworth* she admonishes the reader:
'May Heaven help you, as it assisted me, through the travelogues,
the debates, and the grotesquely over-drawn figures that clutter it.'
When Elinor Glyn's *It* lands on her desk she asks: 'Do you wonder
that I am never going to read anything else?' On 10 March 1928
she confesses defeat: 'The past seven days must live in the memory
of this department as Start 'Em and Shut 'Em Up Week. Not a
book finished – that's my record.' Then Parker feels unwell, a pain
in the abdomen. Instead of going to a doctor she gets hold of a
medical book written for the lay reader:

> I fall into a dead dreamless slumber bought on by my reading of a
> book called 'Appendicitis' ... the work of Thew Wright, AB, MD,
> FACS – 'to bring an understanding of appendicitis to the laity'. And

it really is terribly hard to keep from remarking, after studying the pictures, 'That was no laity; that's my wife'. It is hard but I'll do it if it kills me.

But she was soon laughing the other side of her face. She really did have appendicitis and had to go into hospital to have the damn thing out. She was off for three months. Then on 25 August Constant Reader returned to work:

> Well, well, and how have you been all this time? Oh, that's fine; as a matter of fact, I don't think I ever saw you looking better. Why, I've been pretty well, thanks. You know how it is – everybody seems to have a cold this treacherous weather. That's all has been the trouble with me; just a bothersome cold in the head, and a case of acute appendicitis.

CR may have recovered her spirits but the books remain as dreary as ever. 'The latest acquisition of the Constant Reader Memorial Library' is *The Lion Tamer* by E. M. Hull, author of *The Sheik*, the novel that was made into a silent film starring Rudolph Valentino. If it 'doesn't put me back into the hospital again, I shall know that I am completely well and start going out at nights.'

CR's most famous hatchet-job was the one she performed on A. A. Milne. She enjoyed pitching into him so much that she had two goes, one at the end of 1927 when *Now We Are Six* appeared. Milne's book was coupled with a new volume of light verse by Christopher Morley (a New Yorker contributor), *I Knew A Secret*. Both get it in the neck, especially Milne, who prompted the comment: 'Not since Fay Bainter played East is West have I seen such sedulous cuteness.' But the *coup de grâce* was reserved for *The House at Pooh Corner* the following year. Milne's widespread popularity in the United States at this time, not just as a children's writer but also as a playwright and author of the detective story *The Red House Mystery*, justified such attention. CR picks up on Milne's twee use of the word 'hum' as Pooh hums his way along: 'In fact so Good a Hum did it seem that he and Piglet started right through the Snow to Hum It Hopefully to Eyore. Oh darn, – there I've gone and given away the plot. Oh, I could bite my tongue out.' This leads up to her pay-off inspired by the turning of 'hum' into an adjective: 'And it is that word "hummy", my darlings, that marks the first place in *The House at Pooh Corner* at which Tonstant Weader Fwowed Up.'

She reminds me of Nigel Dennis, choosing a book as an excuse
for a knockabout turn rather than for its intrinsic merit. Many
review-worthy novels of more than fleeting importance appeared
during her tenure of office – *Dusty Answer* and *Death Comes for the
Archbishop*, for example; she ignored them, preferring books on
Happiness, Bridge, Etiquette (Emily Post) and Comic Strips.
Apropos Elinor Wylie's *Mr Hodge and Mr Hazard* and Samuel
Hoffenstein's *Poems in Praise of Practically Nothing* (oddly, a
bestseller) mock modesty prompts an ironic aside: 'My books this
week are too good for the likes of me to write about.' And she
pretends to nervousness about her cool reaction to Ford Madox
Ford's *The Last Post*. It might get her the sack, she implies. She
tells the reader: 'If you yourself haven't any spare jobs for a
retired book-reviewer, maybe some friend of yours might have
something.'

Yet when she does review an important book like *The Last Post*
or Hemingway's *Men Without Women* she is perfectly able to rise to
the task, still using her confidential idiom:

> After all the high screaming about *The Sun Also Rises* I feared for
> Mr Hemingway's next book. You know how it is – as soon as they all
> start acclaiming a writer, that writer is just about to slip downward.
> The littler critics circle like literary buzzards above only the sick
> lions.
>
> So it is a warm gratification to find the new Hemingway book,
> *Men Without Women*, a truly magnificent work. It is composed of
> thirteen [in fact fourteen] short stories, most of which have been
> published before. They are sad and terrible stories; the author's
> enormous appetite for life seems to have been somehow appeased.
> You find here little of that peaceful ecstasy that marked the camp-
> ing trip in *The Sun Also Rises* and the lone fisherman's days in Big
> Two-Hearted River in *In Our Time*. The stories include The Killers,
> which seems to me one of the four great American short stories.
> (All you have to do is drop the nearest hat, and I'll tell you what
> I think the others are. They are Wilbur Daniel Steele's Blue
> Murder, Sherwood Anderson's I'm A Fool, and Ring Lardner's
> Some Like Them Cold, that story which seems to me as shrewd a
> picture of every woman at some time as is Chekhov's The Darling.
> Now what do *you* like best?) The book also includes Fifty Grand, In
> Another Country, and the delicate and tragic Hills Like White
> Elelphants. I do not know where a greater collection of short stories
> can be found.

Here she is generous in her praise of a writer who celebrated male experience; many of her reviews concern works by other women – women who, like her, have elected to stand alone against the world. Some inspire in her a mocking derision and a tiny band arouse heartfelt admiration. Margot Asquith and the evangelist preacher Aimée Semple Macpherson are examples of the former, Isadora Duncan and Katherine Mansfield of the latter: 'That gifted entertainer, the Countess of Oxford, author of *The Autobiography of Margot Asquith* (four volumes, neatly boxed, suitable for throwing) reverts to tripe in a new book deftly entitled *Lay Sermons*.' The Aimée Semple Macpherson review is headed 'Our Lady of the Loud-Speaker': 'It is difficult to say whether Mrs McPherson is happier in her cackling exclamations or in her bead-curtain-and-chenille-fringe style. Presumably the lady is happy in both manners. That would make her two up on me.' Of Isadora Duncan in a review of *My Life* she comments: 'They [her lovers] were lucky men, they were. But she was not a lucky lady.' When Constant Reader writes about Katherine Mansfield's posthumous *Journal* – 'the saddest book I have ever read' – we feel that at last she has complete sympathy with the author under review:

> Only in its pages could she show her tragically sensitive mind, her lovely quivering soul. She was not of the little breed of the discontented. She was of the high few fated to be for ever unsatisfied. Writing was the precious thing in life to her, but she was never truly pleased with anything she had written. With a sort of fierce austerity, she strove for the crystal clearness, the hard bright purity from which stems perfect truth. She never felt she had attained them.

As a journalist Dorothy Parker was what is known in the trade as a 'deadliner', someone whose copy is delivered at the last possible moment; frequently after the last possible moment. Before the days of faxes and modems the copy's mysterious non-arrival was often blamed on the postal service. 'Not come yet? How odd! I'll see if I've got a black of it and send you that.' Nowadays that excuse does not wash any more.

Eventually Constant Reader procrastinated herself out of a job and she was reluctantly fired; by the spring of 1928 the book section was inhabited by less egocentric, less exciting, but more punctual writers.

In 1933 Ross was much impressed by a piece he was shown in the *Nation* over the signature Clifton Fadiman. It was about Ring Lardner, one of a series of critical appraisals of contemporary American writers by Fadiman. Ross asked Fadiman to have lunch with him and in the course of it said he wondered if Fadiman would care to review books regularly in the *New Yorker* and if so, would he like to send some sample pieces pitched to the readership of the magazine. Fadiman, confident in his journalistic skill, refused to submit sample pieces and said he would like to be judged by his work for the *Nation*. After which Ross capitulated and a deal was concluded.

'Kip' Fadiman was a friend and contemporary of Trilling and like him had been one of the most able pupils in Mark Van Doren's literature class at Columbia. Had there been room at that period for two Jews on the English faculty at Columbia University, Kip would have joined Lionel there after graduation. Instead he became a literary journalist of great ability. He was the first *New Yorker* book-reviewer to sign his reviews with his own name:

> What has happened roughly [he wrote in 'The Book-Reviewing Business'] is that the old type of book-reviewer, to whom the job was a game, has gradually been replaced by a new type to whom the job is a job. In the days of Laurence Stallings and Heywood Broun, you would on occasion get superb pieces of enthusiastic journalism, but more frequently sickening examples of hullabalunacy. Today book-reviewing is staider, duller, but unquestionably juster and more serious. It has a professional touch. It has grown up.

If Constant Reader had been the book-reviewer for the era of Prohibition, when literature was one of the more legitimate intoxicants on offer, Fadiman settled into the job during the Depression, when literature reflected the social malaise. Amidst all the economic turbulence and gloom America was discovering its own literature, its own recent past, its own ugly present. In 1942 Alfred Kazin would give a summing-up of this situation in *On Native Grounds*, where he studied what had happened to the American novel after the realist era of W. D. Howells. He discovered American writers who, if their technique owed a long-term debt to Zola, were essentially the products of their own native American environment: Steinbeck, Sinclair Lewis, Dos Passos, Saroyan, Nathanel West, Upton Sinclair, Dreiser, Sherwood Anderson *et al.*

The more immediate impact of the discovery of the home-grown product may be felt in Fadiman's reviews; in April 1934 he wrote of Faulkner's *Sanctuary*: 'Even those who call Mr Faulkner our greatest literary sadist do not fully appreciate him, for it is not merely his characters who have to run the gauntlet but also his readers. One does not so much finish *Sanctuary* as come through it in good shape.' The following year he was reviewing an American novel by a frequent contributor to the New Yorker, *Butterfield 8* by John O'Hara. Fadiman thought it was disappointing, the people reminded him of 'animated puppets' for which O'Hara never forgave him or the magazine, though he did write for it again after some time had elapsed.

Not that Fadiman restricted himself to work by American writers. He alternated in his lively genial manner between reviewing American books and those that arrived from Britain and the continent of Europe; but whatever the book, Fadiman invariably aimed his comments at an essentially *American* Common Reader. The *New Yorker* books page was not yet looking beyond that putative individual.

'I do not know', Fadiman wrote on 7 September 1935 recommending *The Root and the Flower* trilogy, 'how many American readers are familiar with the beautiful books of L. H. Myers'. Later that month he considered T. E. Lawrence's *Seven Pillars of Wisdom* and concluded that, 'For Americans, I think, the historical interest is limited. It is as a work, uneven but unforgettable, that *Seven Pillars* will be remembered.' Come October and he is having to deal with the latest instalment in translation of Jules Romains' long chain-novel *Les Hommes de Bonnes Volontés* (*Men of Good Will*), titled *The World From Below*. The following week he leads with the young British anthropologist Geoffrey Gorer's *Africa Dances*.

At the end of his career Fadiman reflected: 'For about a quarter of a century I have been one of that small, unimpressive army of American communicators who act as middlemen of thought and opinion . . . I do not apologise for this. It is the best I and my many peers can do.' He was being over-modest, as his published articles reveal and as, I am sure, he inwardly knew.

It was admiration for the work of Cyril Connolly and his wartime journal *Horizon* that prompted Edmund Wilson to make a business proposal to Harold Ross in 1942. Wilson felt that America sadly lacked a magazine of comparable scope and distinction – *Harper's* and the *Atlantic* had become 'stuffy and second-rate'; only *Partisan Review* 'in its small way' (he thought) filled the *Horizon* role. Why not start an American *Horizon* which he (Wilson) would edit? Ross considered the proposal but said it was not something he could initiate: he was an editor not a financier, but he would mention the idea to Raoul Fleischmann, the *New Yorker's* publisher. Fleischmann, whose relations with Ross were always strained to say the least (they were barely on speaking terms) turned down the idea. However, while all this was being discussed, Fadiman, after a decade of writing the book article decided the time had come for a rest from weekly reviewing. The way was open for Ross to offer the *New Yorker* book-critic job to Wilson.

At first Wilson hesitated, then he insisted on a salary and stipulations concerning space, holidays, and choice of books that no other chief book-critic from Sainte-Beuve downwards has enjoyed. Ross, who was in a position however reluctantly to pay, now that the magazine after its difficult early years had become enormously profitable, agreed and in 1943 Wilson came in on his own terms.

Wilson was then forty-eight, at the mid-point of an industrious writing life; in addition to his early verse, fiction and plays, he had behind him two seminal works of cultural history and criticism, *Axel's Castle* (1931) and *To the Finland Station* (1940), two among several substantial critical books on which his reputation as America's leading man of letters was based; and he would complete some half a dozen more detailed works of literary history, including the magisterial *Patriotic Gore* (1962), before his death at the age of seventy-seven.

In Wilson we have therefore a rare example of a regular weekly reviewer who himself wrote many substantial books. Like Dr Johnson and other eighteenth-century essayists of whom he was the heir, Wilson made his living primarily as a journalist. His critical books were off-shoots of weekly journalism. His period as chief reviewer of the *New Yorker* needs to be put in the framework of his earlier career as a journalist to understand his development and outlook. By the end of the 1920s he was already a major force in American cultural journalism, leading light of a reviewing clerisy in the inter-war period in New York; this clerisy writing in the daily and weeklies may be compared to the one I have identified during the same period in London. The big difference between them was that these American literary journalists were as much concerned with society as they were with literature; as much concerned about the trend towards mass unemployment as with trends towards modernism; as much concerned with politics as with literature.

After he had graduated from Princeton in 1916 Wilson joined the Intelligence Corps, returning to civilian life in 1919. That was six years after the Condé Nast organisation had purchased *Vanity Fair* and two years after the start of the liberal weekly, the *New Republic*. Wilson was managing editor of *Vanity Fair* from 1920 to 1921. Then he left to become literary editor of the *New Republic* in 1925 and associate editor from 1926 to 1931. Wilson's work for the *New Republic* in the 1920s and 1930s included journeys to places where the Depression was biting, where there was controversy over human rights. In 1931 he went to Chattanooga, Tennessee, to cover the Scottsboro case where nine young black men were threatened with electrocution for allegedly raping two white girls, a *cause célèbre* exploited by the American Communist party. Wilson's strength as a critic of literature stemmed as much from his powers as an observer of life in the raw as from his omnivorous reading.

His Marxism was never as whole-hearted as that of John Chamberlain, the book-reviewer of the *New York Times*, or of Malcolm Cowley and Matthew Josephson, his colleagues on the *New Republic*, both reacting from the spell of surrealism and dadaism they had come under when they were living in Paris. The manifest evils of the Depression forced all these critics to descend from the lofty palace of art and come down to earth. Cowley, back home in Connecticut after life among the Hemingways, Fitzgeralds and Crosbys in Paris, wrote *The Exile's Return*, and would go through a long invovement with Marxism, as would Josephson, the American writer who made Zola, France's great novelist of the masses, accessible in a major biography, and who would write that popular anti-entrepreunial work of financial history, *The Robber Barons*. Daniel Aaron in his study, *Writers on the Left*, says that when Wilson began his series of reports on the Depression in 1930, 'his socialism changed from pink to red, but the Communists who hoped to capture him for the party in the late twenties did not yet realise that Wilson's qualified acceptance of the Marxist view of society in no way signified an intention to join them.'

Wilson's boss was Herbert Croly, editor of the *New Republic* since its inception in 1914, who had announced that the magazine's purpose was 'less to inform or entertain its readers than to start little insurrections in the realm of their convictions'. Wilson's pieces frequently did that and always gave readers a basis on which to form their own opinions. When Croly died in 1930, the magazine was run by an editorial board consisting of Bruce Bliven, Edmund Wilson, R. M. Lovett, George Soule, Stark Young and Malcolm Cowley, who had taken over from Wilson as literary editor.

Later Cowley would combine editorial responsibilities with weekly reviews, of which he wrote hundreds during his long career, but for the moment Wilson's reviews were the star-turn each week. They were billed in much larger type than the other contributions on the elegantly designed non-pictorial cover. In the Fall Literary Number of 22 October 1930, his piece was called 'The Nietzschean Line' pegged to a new book from Norman Douglas, *Goodbye to Western Culture: Some Footnotes on East and West.* Wilson used the occasion as the pretext to launch a full-scale attack on other fashionable gloom-and-doom merchants, Clive Bell in his essay *Civilisation* and his own hero H. L. Mencken for some recent pessimistic utterances in the *Baltimore Sun.*

Other reviewers in the same issue were John Crowe Ransom, Louise Bogan, Newton Arvin, Howard Coxe, Michael Gold and T. S. Matthews. Arvin, an associate professor at Smith College, tackled Freud's *Civilisation and Its Discontents.* Matthews, future boss of Nigel Dennis on *Time* magazine, reviewed Siegfried Sassoon's *Memoirs of an Infantry Officer* and found the account of Sassoon's 'lone mutiny' the most interesting part of the book. Coxe struggled over Maugham's *Cakes and Ale.* These reviews were all intellectually challenging but the one that caused an uproar was Michael Gold's piece on Thornton Wilder, headed 'Wilder: Prophet of the Genteel Christ' and dealing compositely with *The Cabala, The Bridge of San Luis Rey, The Woman of Andros, The Angel that Troubled the Waters.*

> Mr Wilder remains the poet of a small sophisticated class that has recently arisen in America – our genteel bourgeoisie. His style is their style; it is the new fashion. Their women have taken to wearing his Greek chlamys and faintly indulge themselves in his smart Victorian pieties. Their men are at ease in his Paris and Rome.

Gold was one of the editors of the *New Masses* and the author of a controversial novel, *Jews Without Money* (1930). He damned Wilder for his escapism, his cult of the past, his indifference to the unemployed. He recommended readers to turn to Veblen's *Theory of the Leisure Class* and 'study it like the Bible'.

In following weeks the *New Republic* was deluged with correspondence from outraged readers, of which this letter was typical: 'Sir: The review of Thornton Wilder's works by Michael Gold is as shallow, unreasonable and spiteful thing as I have ever seen. May I ask what critical value comes from having a third-rate author review the works of a first-rate author?' In the end, after the controversy had continued unabated for several weeks, Wilson intervened in an unsigned editorial, 'The Economic Interpretation of Wilder'. He pointed out that the *NR* had no grudge against Wilder, whose books it had often praised, but that it also considered Gold an important writer because he was the only American critic of any ability who wrote about books from a Marxist viewpoint. Wilson questions the assumption underlying Gold's approach that 'the character of literature produced by any period is determined by the economic position of the class for which it is written'. But he concludes that although literature must ultimately be judged by its intrinsic worth, the social factor cannot be ignored: 'The pathos in Proust, after all, is merely the more presentable side of the impotence, the creeping corruption, the lack of the will to live. And so in Wilder the pathos and the beauty derived from the exotic lands of the imagination may be, as Michael Gold suggests, a sedative for sick Americans.'

Wilson did not spend the whole of the 1920s among the workers. His journals are full of incisive portraits of his contemporaries and their quirks of behaviour. He went in 1923 to a gathering given by Thomas Seltzer for D. H. Lawrence. Seltzer was a radical journalist who had been editor of *Masses* before Max Eastman, and who was now moving into publishing: he was D. H. Lawrence's third American publisher, coming between Huebsch and Knopf. His star-guest startled the company by suddenly launching into a hysterical attack against book-reviewers: they were all prostitutes, he screamed. Wilson calmly observed Lawrence's performance and wrote it up in his journal:

> He was lean but his head was disproportionately small. One saw that he belonged to an inferior caste – some bred-down unripening race of the collieries. Against this inferiority – fundamental and physical – he must have had to fight all his life: his passionate spirit had made up for it by exaggerated self-assertion. (I have never seen this physical aspect of Lawrence mentioned.) On this occasion he suddenly became hysterical and burst out in childish rudeness and in a high-pitched screaming voice with something like: 'I'm not

enjoying this! Why are we sitting here having tea? I don't want your tea! I don't want to be doing this!' The Seltzers, rather stodgy in their bourgeois apartment, sat through it and made no reply, and nobody else took any notice of it. Mrs Lawrence – whom I have more or less described as Mrs Grosbeake in *I Thought of a Daisy* – also sat silent, her feet in rather large shoes or sandals, one beside the other and flat on the floor, as if she were the anchor that held him down, the Mother *Erde* on whom he depended. The furious fit soon passed, and he presently came over and began to talk to me in a conventional British way. I don't remember what he said except to ask me a question or two about myself. I had earlier been rather antagonised by his denunciation of Dante as a writer who had tried to intellectualise love.

Wilson made a discovery as a critic that is very common. A piece he thought was favourable gave great offence to the author appraised; this discovery occurred when he reprinted a magazine article about Hemingway in a book of essays:

> The book contained an essay about him which had already appeared in the *Atlantic Monthly* and which, as a whole could not possibly be called either unfavorable or unsympathetic. But I had prodded the publicity Hemingway, and the publicity Hemingway was bellowing. When I found out that he had written his lawyer a letter of many pages, in which he claimed that about every other sentence was libellous (the publishers had sent him proofs), I concluded that he was not quite sane. His objections were eventually all boiled down to two trivial errors of fact and one error about an incident in one of his books, which of course I should have been glad to correct if he had simply written to me about them.

By the time he had joined the *New Yorker*, Wilson had gone back to the more sedentary life of full-time literary criticism. To the task of weekly reviewing he brought an uncompromising severity, facility in several languages and the broadest of outlooks. It was derived from his Princeton professor, Christian Gauss, who had first encouraged him to see a work of literature in the widest possible context; Romanticism, for example, cannot be contained within frontiers; Gauss's students studied its German, French and Italian manifestations alongside those in the English language. In addition, Wilson had a working knowledge of Latin and Greek literature. Later he added Russian to his stockpile of languages. In the 1940s, when he came to study the Dead Sea Scrolls about which he wrote a book, Wilson would add Hebrew to the list and finally he became conversant with Hungarian. Such polyglottery and accompanying literary appetite make the Raymond Mortimers, Cyril Connollys and even the Middleton Murrys of this world seem somewhat provincial.

Wilson's journalistic heroes when he was young were De Quincey, Poe, Bernard Shaw, James Huneker and H. L. Mencken. De Quincey's life is a cautionary tale for anyone who aspires to live by writing for literary periodicals, but in spite of spending so much time in a debtors' prison he did leave behind one or two essays that even now illuminate the works they examine. Poe was America's first and greatest literary journalist, along with his better-known claims to fame. Wilson said of Poe's career: 'The masterpieces excreted like precious stones by the subterranean chemistry of his mind were sprinkled like [in?] a rapid stream of news letters and daily reviewing that was itself made to feed his interests and contribute to his higher aims.' Poe took on the Bostonian clerisy who dominated the *Atlantic Monthly*, challenged them through analysis and ridicule (notably in his reviews of Longfellow) and liberated the reading public of his day for fresh artistic experience. The young Bernard Shaw performed a similar service for London opera-goers and theatre-goers when he exposed them to the winds of change from Norway and Germany. These critics continued 'that work of "Enlightenment" of which the flame had been so fanned by Voltaire'.

When Wilson turned to the French sages of the nineteenth century it was not Sainte-Beuve that he emulated but the historians Michelet and Taine. The first fifty pages of *To The Finland Station* are devoted to these two writers, and when Wilson enumerates the qualities in Michelet that he admires we feel inclined to substitute his own name for that of the Frenchman:

> It is an essential part of Michelet's strength and charm that he should seem less like a nineteenth-century scholar than like the last great man of letters of the Renaissance. In his early years he mastered Latin and Greek with a thoroughness which was at that time already rare; and he later acquired English, Italian and German and devoured the literature and learning of these languages. With small means, he succeeded in travelling pretty much all over Western Europe, and those regions, such as the Slavic East, to which his actual

travels did not penetrate, his insatiable mind invaded. The impression he makes on us is quite different from that of the ordinary modern scholar who has specialised in some narrowly delimited subject and got it up in a graduate school: we feel that Michelet has read all the books, been to look at all the monuments and pictures, interviewed personally all the authorities, and explored all the libraries and archives of Europe; and that he has it all under his hat. The Goncourts said that Michelet's attractiveness lay in the fact that his works 'seem to be written by hand. They are free from the banality and impersonality a printed thing has; they are like the autograph of a thought.' But what Michelet really goes back to is an earlier stage of printing before the journalistic or the academic formulas had come between first-hand knowledge and us. He is simply a man going to the sources and trying to get down on record what can be learned from them; and this role, which claims for itself, on the one hand, no academic sanctions, involves, on the other hand, a more direct responsibility to the reader.

In January 1944, under the title 'Through An Embassy Window', Wilson wrote an appraisal of the work of Harold Nicolson, his opposite number as the writer of the most influential weekly *causerie* in Britain. It was prompted by Nicolson's second volume of family memoirs that concerned his eighteenth-century ancestor Hamilton Rowan, a member of Ireland's Protestant Ascendancy. Before turning to the book, Wilson gives one of those comprehensive views of an author typical of his *New Yorker* articles, and standing as a model for reviewers who succeded him on the magazine. In it Wilson sees Nicolson as the victim of his singular upbringing; a diplomat's son protected always from 'the mob' and the ordinary pressures of life. It limited his understanding of Verlaine and Swinburne in previous books as it does his view of his great-great grandfather's remarkable career in this one. Yet Wilson is determined in this damaging assessment to be absolutely fair: he praises Nicolson as a critic of verse and above all as the author of *Some People* (1927):

It is at once his most candidly personal and his most irresponsible production, and it succeeds in touching off as none of his other books does the memories of his diplomatic experience into something like artistic ignition – because he has here turned *in* on this experience instead of trying to see the rest of the world *through* it.

Nicolson is left off lightly compared to the treatment given to such writers as Louis Bromfield, Anya Seton and Kay Boyle. Boyle's wartime novel *Avalanche* Wilson sees as a product of the commercial Hollywood school of fiction-writing and of the literary atmosphere of the *Saturday Evening Post* which serialised it. This vacuous novel makes Wilson nostalgic for the Parisian avant-garde magazines of the 1920s that he used to read and to which Boyle, as part of that expatriate Parisian society, once contributed.

Turning to Britain in subsequent weeks, Wilson was full of praise for the 'audacity' of Evelyn Waugh's wartime novel *Put Out More Flags*. Reviewing it prompts a thorough, admiring appraisal of this author's early work, though later he had grave reservations about *Brideshead Revisited*. Wilson confessed he could never get much out of Waugh's contemporary Anthony Powell's *The Music of Time*, or the work of Henry Green, but he was prompt in recognising the merits of Angus Wilson and Kingsley Amis. *The Wrong Set and Other Stories* was published in America in 1950. Wilson tells readers of the *New Yorker* that in this first book there has emerged a successor to Evelyn Waugh. He notes in Angus Wilson a singular absence of any 'noble value' in his portrait of post-war British society. Even Chekhov who, like Angus Wilson, is a 'clinician for a failing organism, is sad as well as sardonic and has some sense of a human dignity he hopes will emerge from the mess', whereas Wilson's people 'have sunk almost out of the reach of pity'. However 'the talent displayed seems so firm and bold, so rich in invention and wit, that it stimulates these comparisons'.

When *Lucky Jim* and *That Uncertain Feeling* were published in America, Wilson asks 'Is It Possible To Pat Kingsley Amis?' and as an Amis-admirer he concludes that these books are in the Waugh-Wilson tradition; but by now 'the class structure is breaking up' and in Amis 'we see everything from the point of view of baseless . . . unoriented young people. That uncertain feeling may be said to be the theme of *Lucky Jim* as well as of the book to which it gives its title.'

While I was in the United States, Wilson reviewed *Dr Zhivago* in the *New Yorker* of 15ᵗʰ November, 1958 under the heading 'Dr Life and his Guardian Angel', occupying nearly 8,000 words and reversing the usual order whereby a reviewer deals first with the work and then with the translation. He had read the book in the original

and had harsh things to say about the version by Max Hayward
and Manya Harari, taking around 1800 words over this (as many
words as a reviewer normally would give to the complete review).
Wilson enumerated the peculiar difficulties involved in translating
Pasternak:

> This writer has an enormous range of idiom – he makes all kinds
> of people talk, each in the language of his milieu and time – and an
> immense literary vocabulary. He is also an extremely idiosyncratic
> writer, a 'difficult' modern poet who has taken to prose, in which
> medium, despite his eloquence, his brilliance and the exactitude of
> his observation, he is somewhat less at home than with verse. There
> are passages of subjective impressionism in the early part of the
> book, where the characters are children or adolescents, which
> present the translator with difficulties of a somewhat similar kind
> to those which would be encountered in translating, say, Virginia
> Woolf.

Wilson's animadversions on the translation are a prelude to his
view of the novel as a whole: 'it is a book about human life and its
main theme is death and resurrection'. He sees it as fable of
contemporary history that is also a religious parable. It is ultimately, 'One of the great events in man's literary and moral
history'. He finds a rich symbolism both in the novel and in the
poems printed at the end. They communicate the sense of
resurrection that the reader is left with. The symbolism extends to
the names of the hero: Zhivago, Wilson explains, is a form of the
Russian word for life and living and Yury is the Russian for George.
Pasternak is not only the 'peer of Faulkner, Malraux, Auden' but
also – in his punning allusiveness – of Joyce.

   In spite of the length of Wilson's *New Yorker* review of *Dr Zhivago*,
he returned to the book for further commentary in another essay,
this time published in the *Nation* in April of the following year. He
went now more fully into what he saw as the sub-text involving St
George's legend, viewed by the light of the teaching of the Russian
Orthodox Church; he explained the sea-imagery that pervades the
novel, and he tried also to solve the mystery of why Stalin never
had Pasternak locked up. Wilson makes an ingenious but implau-
sible connection between the novel's narrative and Stalin's rever-
ence for his dead wife.

   By now Wilson's interpretation of *Dr Zhivago* had come to the
attention of Pasternak who, in an interview with a professor of

Russian at Princeton, also in the *Nation*, said that his novel owed nothing to Joyce, its imagery was intended to be purely descriptive, and no symbolism was intended in the names of the hero. Here then was Wilson as a critic expounding a work significantly at variance with the one intended by the author. Most critics who penetrate the 'hermeneutic' significance of literary works tend wisely to wait until the authors of them are dead, but Pasternak's denial did not upset Wilson, who said in reply that the author was probably not aware of the hidden layers of meaning in his work and that, given the situation in Russia, was probably not anxious to have his total meaning explicated.

During Wilson's weeks off the book-review in the *New Yorker* would sometimes be written by a migrant Englishman, Anthony West, who had joined the staff of the paper after working during the war for the BBC's Far Eastern Service. As mentioned before, he had lived his life in a state of hostility to his mother, Rebecca, who consistently blocked his attempt to write a life of his father. When West's biography of H. G. Wells appeared after her death, one tended to see her point. West's frustration over access to his father's biographical archive was book-reviewing's gain. It was to this that West turned, starting with some sparkling performances in the *New Statesman*. West inherited his father's passion for military history, shown in reviews in the *New Yorker* of Churchill's *Triumph and Tragedy*, Dos Passos' *The Head and Heart of Thomas Jefferson*, T. Harry Williams's *Lincoln and His Generals*, Richard Aldington's *Lawrence of Arabia* and *My Mission to Spain* by Claude G. Bowers, United States Ambassador from 1933 to 1939. West had an expert knowledge of military logistics and strategy unusual in a man of letters.

From his mother West inherited a willingness to lay down the law with great vehemence about writers living or dead. Confronted by Edgar Johnson's life of Dickens – hailed universally in 1953 as a standard work – West praises the biographical account but condemns as a 'pious absurdity' Johnson's rating of Dickens as superior to Dostoevsky and as the equal of Shakespeare and Balzac. George Eliot's letters edited by Gordon Haight received equally forthright treatment, provoking a rebuttal from Dr Haight. A translation of Zola's *La Curée* that had an introduction from Angus Wilson was notable for West's efforts to cut Zola down to size, along with a side-swipe at 'the aridity of the new school of English novel-writing of the Kingsley Amis and John Wain persuasion'. Ivy Compton-Burnett at the other end of the social register, and another flourishing British reputation at this time, fared no better.

West showed in his reviews a particular sensitivity to those writers whether of fact or fiction who suffered from emotional damage in childhood, as he believed he had. They include George Orwell and the Brazilian novelist Machado de Assis. He is especially sympathetic to Vyvyan Holland's *Son of Oscar Wilde* which, 'if not a particularly elegant piece of writing', has nonetheless 'considerable literary value'. In recalling what Holland and his brother had to suffer as boys, West seizes an opportunity to have a tilt at his father's old enemy, Henry James:

> What was done to Vyvyan and Cyril Holland [Oscar Wilde's sons] was the kind of thing that went on in the society from which Henry James gathered the material for his fragile webs of hint and suggestion; the contrast between the thin gruel of mystifications in *The Turn of the Screw* and the evil of the deliberate grinding away by this large group of hearty middle-class people at the happiness and the natural, instinctive appetite for life of Wilde's children is an enlightening one.

He does not mention what a privileged and in many ways happy childhood Vyvyan Holland had, in spite of the tragedy. But West could always be relied upon to be provocative as well as informative, to provide a valuation worth heeding.

The two reviewers who have carried Edmund Wilson's *New Yorker* torch into the present are John Updike and George Steiner. In his essay 'Edmund Wilson's Fiction: A Personal Account' (1975), Updike described the youthful avidity with which he read the sections of *Memoirs of Hecate County* in his local Pennsylvania public library while the book was still banned in New York: 'My first and to this day most vivid glimpse of sex through the window of fiction'.

When Wilson's *The Thirties* volume appeared posthumously in 1980, Updike reviewed it in the *New Yorker* and gave what a lit ed normally warns a reviewer against doing, a review not just of the book but of the other reviews as well. Apart from the invidious nature of the operation, it draws attention to the lateness of the writer's review; but Charles McGrath (as I write editor of the *New*

York Times Book Review, but then the *New Yorker* editor who worked closely on the book review-section under William Shawn) explains that Shawn did not like the magazine to review a book too close to its publication because he felt it smacked of commercial practice, of angling for publishers' advertisements. Updike was therefore free to discuss the reception of Wilson's Diary by other reviewers:

> Alas, a certain testiness has been noticeable in the reviews of *The Thirties*. Morris Dickstein, in the *Times Book Review*, found the writing bland and gray and the sexual episodes depressing. Gore Vidal in *The New York Review of Books*, complained of Wilson's foot fetishism, boring landscape descriptions, and nervous if not derisive attitude toward male homosexuals. and Harry Levin, whose every review nicely approaches the definitive, concluded in the *Saturday Review* that 'the volume adds a little – not very much – to the record, and nothing at all to his stature as a writer'.

But in noting that, 'There is something here to offend everyone' – puritans, gays, blacks – Updike is merely clearing the deck for his own positive assessment, seeing the whole decade as the crucial one in Wilson's life. This Updike/Wilson review preceded another, of the *Letters* between Wilson and Nabokov. Both show how thoroughly Updike had mastered the work of his predecessor. From Updike's reviews read in bulk one has the the sense that since the days of Wilson the battle for the appreciation of serious demanding contemporary literature, the war against the mindless 'booboisie' (as Mencken described it) has been well and truly won. We are now in a period of 'post-ness'. The 1930s and 1940s were still heroic decades, when intrepid prospectors like Wilson went out and opened up an exciting new country, the republic of Modernism. Now the same territory, teeming with old and new settlers, is in chaos through over-population and over-use of resources. Updike is an accredited guide to this vast region in whose hands we feel safe.

George Steiner began reviewing for the New Yorker in 1966 and like Updike has continued to the present time. He was recruited by Shawn on the strength of his critical books on *Tolstoy or Dostoevsky?* (1958) and *The Death of Tragedy* (1960). After he had signed a contract, Steiner went to see the ageing Wilson as an act of homage; it was mid-afternoon but the bottle of Bourbon at Wilson's elbow had, he says, already been quite severely punished.

'You think you're going to become rich,' Wilson told him. 'Well, don't do what I did and waste it all on f . . . ing alimony.'

Shawn was closely involved in any important decisions about what Steiner reviewed. If the paper had a books section supremo at this time it was Shawn, doubling with his other responsibilities, and it was Shawn who chose Steiner's first book, Randolph Churchill's life of his father. After that Steiner was free to come forward with suggestions about what he should review, based on a persual of publisher's lists, and he says that ninety per cent of these were accepted. Steiner has written more than 150 *New Yorker* reviews, only one of which was not published – a review of Hannah Arendt's book on Rahel van Hagen which Steiner had torn into. Shawn told him that Arendt was gravely ill and he did not wish to hasten her death.

Wilson was replaced by a rotating band of regular book reviewers, of whom Steiner and Updike are but two. A look at one arbitrarily chosen year – the year 1981 – will give an impression of how this system of rotation worked in practice. We find that in 1981 the two chief reviewing-stars, Updike and Steiner, have been comp- lemented by a third from across the water, V. S. Pritchett, who appeared in those days more often in the *New Yorker* than in any British journal; no doubt for the soundest of finanancial reasons. 'Chip' McGrath has his own explanation for the predilection of American editors for British writers as book-reviewers. Because of their financial need to review while they are establishing their reputations, young British writers get a much more rigorous training in the discipline of reviewing, he says, than their American counterparts, who tend to supplement their incomes by teaching creative-writing courses in a university or college. Hence the pool of Britons from whom American lit eds like to draw.

The book-reviewing 'policy' on the *New Yorker* at this, time in so far as one may be discerned, was that of targeting certain authors or 'schools' for extended appraisal and deploying the regular reviewers to this end, rather than attempting to give readers any broad account of the general publishing output. One of these targets was Nabokov who, since his death in 1977, had been received into the company of American greats and whose work was now being afforded much posthumous respect and critical discussion. Thus on 19 January we find VSP reviewing his *Lectures on Literature*, a book with an introduction by Updike.

Then in November, when the companion volume *Lectures on Russian Literature* came out, that is also reviewed at length, this time by Updike. And the following week when Updike's novel *Rabbit Is Rich* appears, that is reviewed at length by VSP with an appraisal of the whole Rabbit cycle up to that point, lauding its portrayal of provincial life in modern America. A slightly unfortunate game of box and cox, played by Pritchett and Updike with hints of back-scratching, seemed to escape Shawn's normal vigilance.

Another target is the Latin American novel. In late January the appearance of *In an Evil Hour* by Gabriel García Márquez gives Alistair Reid, the Spanish expert and translator, the opportunity to spread himself in an account of the explosion of fiction by South American writers, a phenomenon known as 'the Boom'. Reid suggests that had the present book been submitted in 1956, when it was written, its fortunes might have been rather different: 'if it had crossed the publisher's desk on its own feet . . . it would probably have been summarily ushered out'. The theme is taken up by VSP in a review of Borges's *Six Problems for Don Isidoro Parodi.*

Another enigmatic foreign writer, a lover like Borges of the ludic, Raymond Queneau, was given two innings from Updike, one in June for a reissue of his *Exercises in Style*, and again in December (when literary books are scarce) for his *We Always Treat Women Too Well*. Updike also has two shots at Calvino, one in February for his *Collection of Italian Folktales*, where the reviewer's enjoyment was muted, and again in August for *If On A Winter's Night* . . . where Calvino gets around five out of ten for ingenuity but nought for the book as a whole.

Contemporary American women novelists get a showing during off-weeks for Pritchett and Updike: in April Susan Lardner writes appreciatively of Mary Gordon's *The Company of Women* and in June of *Tar Baby* by Toni Morrison, whose major gifts were by this time recognised in America. It is Updike who has the task of reviewing new work by Muriel Spark, *Loitering With Intent*, and it is compared to its disadvantage with her first novel, *The Comforters*. Iris Murdoch's *Nuns and Soldiers* receives one of Updike's analytical reviews that salutes the narrative energy but concludes:

> By the final page (505) of the book we have lost patience with *all* the characters who if not stiff and sterile seem to be spoiled and selfish and the connection at the plot's heart, the female friendship

between Gertrude Openshaw and Anne Cavidge, no longer holds current and breaks off without a spark.

Here we have a dialogue between reviewer and novelist conducted across the Atlantic Ocean, something that was now frequently happening. This sense of an extended republic of letters embracing London, Dublin, New York, was noticeable especially in September, when the *New Yorker's* poetry critic, Helen Vendler. reviewed Seamus Heaney's *Poems: 1965–75* and *Selected Prose 1968–78*, a measured, knowlegeable piece putting Heaney in the context of the current Irish situation and the romantic tradition, 'The Keatsian harvest is corrected by a harsh history...', and starting to pave the way for Heaney's award of the Nobel Prize for Literature in 1995, which she hailed with another *New Yorker* article about him.

The year's fiction included Rushdie's *Midnight's Children*. VSP, the *New Yorker's* reviewer, was in the vanguard of the Rushdie fan club when he wrote:

> India has produced a glittering novelist – one with startling imaginative and intellectual resources, a master of perpetual storytelling. Like García Márquez in 'One Hundred Years of Solitude' he weaves a whole people's capacity for carrying its inherited myths and new ones that it goes on generating – into a kind of magic carpet.

The only novel Steiner reviewed in 1981 was Anthony Burgess's *Earthly Powers*, but what a novel! It gave Steiner the opportunity for a look at the totality of Burgess's work, its creative, parodic and musical elements all of which he goes into with that sweeping, fluent, stimulating allusiveness that is Steiner's trademark, concluding that the novel represents 'a feat of imaginative breadth and intelligence which lifts fiction high'.

Steiner is in discursive form as he was in February, reviewing a book that seems to have been written in order that he should review it, *The Victorians and Ancient Greece* by Richard Jenkyns, an Oxford classics don. In a soaring peroration to the review, the penetration of every aspect of modern life by Hellenic culture is unfolded; within the space of a few hundred words Steiner has mentioned Cicero, Plato, Phidias, Herodotus, Winckleman, Goethe, Nietzsche, Frazer, Joyce, Sir Karl Popper, adding that, 'We are Hellenic in our myths that dominate our sense of self – Narcissus, Oedipus, Prometheus, Hercules, Orestes, the beauteous

Helen'. As for the book it is 'alert and entertaining' but 'it could have been much better'. It is 'a young man's book'.

Scholarship is something this reviewer relishes, and the more wide-ranging or exotically remote the better. Philippe Ariès's *The Hour of Our Death* and the abstruse works of Guy Davenport, professor of English at Kentucky, are both bases for reviews of essay-like proportions. Steiner tells me that what he remembers most vividly about his reviews is that moment in 1974 when a book arrived with the title *Zen and the Art of Motorcycle Maintenance* by Robert M. Pirsig. He thought it must have been sent in error, but after reading it at a sitting he rang Shawn to tell him that it must be given major treatment.

There were weeks when these big guns – Steiner, Updike and Pritchett – were silent and reviews were quieter in tone, and there were even weeks when books were only 'Briefly Noted' with no lead review to enjoy at all. Naomi Bliven, another regular, competently reviewed what came her way, be it Isak Dinesen, Amos Elon, or Stassinopoulos's *Callas*. Whitney Balliett – the jazz critic but also a nimble book-reviewer – reviewed the new Peter De Vries and the latest in the Boswell story *The Applause of the Jury 1782–1784*. There were weeks when the decks were cleared for a major political book as when Daniel Patrick Moynihan reviewed Kenneth J. Galbraith's Memoirs or when a distinguished member of the musical London old guard, Desmond Shawe-Taylor, reviewed the massive new edition of *Grove's Dictionary of Music*.

At the time I write – some fifteen years later – Updike and Steiner have become elder statesmen, with Updike coming full circle as a regular reviewer of new fiction. Under Tina Brown and her literary editor Bill Buford, formerly editor of *Granta*, a new pluralism prevails. A British novelist like Peter Ackroyd may be asked to review a book rooted in British soil such as Juliet Barker's *The Brontës*, or Jeremy Treglown to do a ninetieth birthday assessment of Anthony Powell; but American reviewers occupy the pages as of right. With Paul Berman (on Whitman), Adam Gopnik (on Lewis Carroll), James Wolcott (on Raymond Chandler in the Library of America), Edward Hirsch (on Emerson) to mention a few reviewers at random, the targeting is more American and the tendency to cross the water for book-reviewers seems less compulsive than it once was, an accurate reflection of the change that has occurred in book pages generally. Under Edmund Wilson the *New Yorker*

book-review columns had a critical authority extending to both
sides of the Atlantic; now they have become merely one more
place the British or American reader turns to for thoughtful book-
reviews.

13

Baltimore, Hollywood, Edinburgh and Booker

M y view of American reviewing was by no means confined to New York. I travelled from the East to the West Coast, meeting many book-page colleagues. I spent several days with the lit eds of the *Christian Science Monitor* and of the *San Francisco Chronicle*. Their pages had more pull with readers than, say, the *Scotsman's* or the *Birmingham Post's* books pages back home because their readers did not feel the need always to turn to the New York newspapers for reviews; whereas their British counterparts normally read the London-based reviews in addition to those nearer to hand. One of the most fruitful of my talks was with Philip M. Wagner of the of the *Sunpapers*, as Baltimore's morning and evening papers are collectively known.

Wagner, as the editor of the *Baltimore Evening Sun*, had succeeded the great H. L. Mencken whose loud greeting he recalled as 'at once gay and gruff'. When Mencken died in January 1956, Wagner saw him laid to rest. 'The funeral of an unbeliever', he wrote, 'is more sombre than most, since the usual remarks about life everlasting are out of bounds.' The small group of relations and friends who had gathered in the funeral parlour to pay their respects included Alfred Knopf, his publisher, and the crime novelist James M. Cain.

Mencken, a Baltimorean whose iconoclastic wit and rhetoric travelled across the entire country, rarely moved from his native city. He had no desire to live in New York or anywhere other than Baltimore. It had been one of the chief ports of large-scale German immigration to America in the mid-nineteenth century. Mencken's grandfather had come from Germany to America, where he had prospered in the tobacco trade, founding a family fortune.

His grandson had no taste for commerce and refused after
college to enter the family business. Repeated reading of *Huckle-
berry Finn* provided the bookish youth with a stylistic model, a sense
of the possibilities of a purely American language about which as
an adult he wrote a major work. In 1911, in his early thirties,
Mencken started to write a regular column in the *Evening Sun*
called Free Lance, much of it later reprinted as *Prejudices* – Series
One to Five – one of the most famous opinion-columns in the
history of journalism. Contemporary novelists such as Bennett,
Wells and W. D. Howells, the dramatists Sudermann, poets such as
Witter Bynner and Amy Lowell, the editors Harriet Monroe, and
other modish people were all savagely put down. The reputation-
breaking prose reads freshly even now. Here is a man talking
passionately, inflammatorily, about matters of the utmost concern
to him personally. Of the *The Theory of the Leisure Class* and its
author Professor Dr Thorstein Veblen, the fashionable academic
guru, Mencken writes:

> Though born, I believe, in These States, and resident here all his
> life, he achieves the effect, perhaps without employing the means, of
> thinking in some unearthly foreign language – say, Swahili, Sumerian
> or Old Bulgarian – and then painfully clawing his thoughts into a
> copious but uncertain and book-learned English. The result is a style
> that affects the higher cerebral centers like a constant roll of subway
> expresses. The second result is a sort of bewildered numbness of the
> senses, as before some fabulous and unearthly marvel. And the third
> result, if I make no mistake, is the celebrity of the professor as a
> Great Thinker. In brief, he states his hollow nothings in such high
> astounding terms that they must inevitably arrest and blister the
> right-thinking mind. He makes them mysterious. He makes them
> shocking. And so, flinging them at naive and believing minds, he
> makes them stick and burn.

In such rhetoric we can discern the master of Kenneth Tynan,
of Nigel Dennis. Mencken wrote books about Shaw and Nietzsche,
his two early heroes. He became in 1914, with the dramatic critic
George Jean Nathan, the co-editor of the magazine *Smart Set*,
essential reading for anyone who wanted to be in the artistic swim.
Mencken was pro-German when the war broke out and that
resulted in the termination of his Free Lance column. He also
acquired a reputation for bursts of anti-Semitism; he refused to

accept that there should be any ban on racist remarks in print and in public.

It was in the period of the Depression that Mencken exerted his greatest influence. With the backing of Alfred Knopf, Mencken and Nathan founded the monthly journal *American Mercury*, of which he became sole editor in 1925. It was a riposte to the hegemony of the Bostonian *Atlantic Monthly* and it became not only the organ for Mencken's bellicosity and contempt for the Average American reader's taste – *homo boobiens* of the *boobosie* he called him – and the pretensions of *bozart (beaux arts)*, but also a platform for those contemporary writers whom Mencken did admire: Dreiser, O'Neill, Sherwood Anderson, Cabell, Hergesheimer, Sandburg, Van Vetchen, Sinclair Lewis and Edgar Lee Masters; the American realists.

Mencken's contribution to literary journalism was seminal, although in his latter years he tired of literature altogether and turned his mind to social and political matters. Before he became incapacited by a massive stroke he wrote memoirs of his Baltimore childhood in the *New Yorker*, pieces reprinted as *Happy Days*.

The tradition of books coverage in the *Sunpapers* continued. After lunch I was taken by Wagner to the office where I met A. D. Emmert, their book expert who lectured at Johns Hopkins University on contemporary literature. For half an hour he deplored the present standards of American literary journalism but I could not help feeling that his presence as guide and mentor to the citizens of Baltimore about new books in the *Evening Sun* was a rebuttal of his own argument.

After a marathon drive on my own across the continent from New York, I did not find much newspaper literary journalism of distinction in Southern California but I enjoyed the experience of being there enormously. I was there from mid-March for three months, working on Gissing material at the Huntington Library, alongside Cambridge academics on sabbatical leave: Peter Laslett, the Cambridge historian, and Muriel Bradbrook, the future Mistress of Girton. I stayed at the Atheneum on the campus of Cal Tech (the California Insitute of Technology) and sometimes drove along the Los Angeles Freeway into LA and beyond to look up Oxford contemporaries such as Gavin Lambert and Alan Cooke who had made good in Hollywood. Sam Behrman had suggested I

ring his friends Leonore and Ira Gershwin. My call to Mrs
Gershwin resulted in an invitation to dinner the following evening.

I rang the bell of their white Spanish-style house in North
Roxbury Drive, a few streets away from Sunset Boulevard. A smiling
butler, the black man in a spotless white coat from a pre-war B
movie, opened the front door. 'Mrs Gershwin is in the pool,' he
explained. Then he led me through a long room on the walls of
which I glimpsed some post-Impressionist French paintings. No
time to study them as we passed through glass doors to reach a
paved terrace, beyond which I saw a gleaming swimming-pool as if
waiting to be painted by David Hockney, and beyond it an asphalt
tennis-court. In the pool a number of people were standing in the
water chatting, laughing.

My hostess greeted me the water up to her waist. 'Behri' – their
name for Behrman, prononuced like 'Berry' – 'told us you were
coming. Now before I do any introductions you must get cool. It's
so *hot!* Go and strip.' She pointed to the cabanas at the side of the
pool. A selection of floral swimming trunks of different sizes –
several extra large – were hanging above a pile of freshly laundered
towels. Suitably attired I made my way to the pool where I was
introduced to the other bathers; any self-consciousness I might
have had was soon dispelled. They all seemed delighted to meet
someone new from Britain. At least one, an actor, was British, or
had been way back. Lee (as everyone called her) said she was not
swimming or even moving much because she had just had her hair
done. After a while a small, stocky, tight-lipped man in white casual
clothes, a few strands of black hair plastered across his bald head,
appeared from the house. It was Ira Gershwin. He halted pool-side
and studied me closely through his thick-lensed glasses as if we
might have met before.

'When I knew you were coming,' he said, 'I looked to see what I
had by Gissing. I found I had *New Grub Street* and *Tales of Mean
Streets*.' 'That's most impressive,' I replied. It really was impressive.
Would, for instance, Noël Coward have even heard of Gissing?
Perhaps just – through Tynan's joke that Gissing was the present
participle of Gosse. I forebore to say to Gershwin that the latter
book was not in fact by Gissing but by Arthur Morrison. (Chandler,
surely, must have read it when he was a young man in England
and the phrase 'mean streets' lodged in his mind for use later.)

I clambered out and when I had changed we went into the
house where Ira now showed me some of the collection of pictures
including three Rouaults, a Vlaminck and various mementoes of

his brother. Some of these were in a games-room downstairs, dominated by a pool table and a pinball machine. 'My brother was an artist as well as a composer,' he said, 'a very fine portrait-painter.' Yes, George had been talented in that way as well, as surviving portraits he drew of his relations and colleagues attest. He did a portrait of Schoenberg, who had been in Hollywood in the 1930s and with whom he played tennis. They had a great respect for each other both on the court and off. There was a sense of the lost one over the whole house, I felt, of that terrible moment in 1937 when George died of a brain-clot and the great flow of creativity stopped. But it is a mistake to think of Ira's reputation as wholly dependent on the lyrics he wrote for his brother's compositions. Other composers with whom Ira collaborated were Harold Arlen, Vernon Duke, Jerome Kern and Kurt Weill.

By now everyone was out of the pool and drinks were being served on the terrace where we sat in canvas chairs. A Chinese chef was moving among us offering savoury crêpes straight from his frying pan. I wondered if this perhaps was the start of dinner, but no, it was merely canapés. There were eight or nine fellow-guests who all seemed very much at their ease, as if they came here for this kind of sumptuous hospitality two or three nights a week. Some of them were powers in the industry in their own right; others were more modest talents but all had clearly been adopted as honorary members of the Gershwin family. Both Ira and Lee had been raised as members of large Jewish familes in New York. Lee (née Strunsky) had married Ira in 1926, George being then on the crest of his first wave of success. Then in the summer of 1936 when they became involved in movie-projects they all moved to Beverly Hills. In 1937 when George died, Lee and Ira stayed and remained there until their own deaths half a century or so later.

The person that night whom I found most accessible was a man of my own age, Lawrence (Larry) D. Stewart, a member of the English Department at UCLA. He had published a book on an obscure eighteenth-century author, and just finished another on Scott Fitzgerald (he was having difficulty placing it; everyone in LA seemed to be writing books about Scott Fitzgerald). He explained that he came to the Gershwins' most afternoons to assist Ira with his work on the Gershwin papers. He had unearthed some pieces by George deemed irrecoverably lost, co-written *The Gershwin Years*, and helped Ira put together a collection of his songs,

Lyrics on Several Occasions, to be published later in the summer. They were now working on sorting out the immense but chaotic Gershwin archive. It was the beginning of a tidying and cataloguing operation that led to all George and Ira's librettos, drafts, and other material being deposited in the Library of Congress to form the Gershwin Collection, from which several of the early musicals have recently been revived on CD with the original orchestrations.

Another guest was Irene Sharaff, the costume designer and her female partner, both looking stunning, and also delightfuly easy to talk to. Sharaff had originally made her name with costume-designs for *Meet Me in St Louis* with Judy Garland and since then had done the costumes for a string of Hollywood musicals. She was awarded an Oscar for her costume-designs for *An American in Paris* in 1951. That movie was a Gershwin triumph, receiving the award for the best motion picture of the year. If the director Vincente Minnelli and the star, Gene Kelly, were not chez Gershwin that night, the producer of it, Arthur Freed was, accompanied by his wife. The Freeds were neighbours of Lee and Ira and among their greatest friends.

Like Ira, Freed began life as a lyricist. Among his many successful lyrics was the title song of *Singin' in the Rain*. He had then become a producer, a master-mind of movie-musicals while the genre was at its peak. He had produced almost every major musical made by MGM until the late 1950s. He was on a high now because of the success of *Gigi* at the Oscar award ceremonies. We talked about musicals currently on in London like *Irma La Douce*. 'It's *The Guardsman*,' said Freed, cryptically. I did not pursue this *aperçu* and I am still not clear what he meant. Then he asked me: 'Did you ever read a book called *The Once and Future King*?' 'Yes,' I said, 'T. H. White, all about King Arthur.' 'We bought it,' he explained. 'We're going to make a musical out of it.' 'Are you!' I countered. 'It's terribly long, isn't it?' 'Oh,' he made a gesture with his hand, 'we're not going to make the whole of it. We'll cut it.' Thus *Camelot* was conceived. It was Alan Lerner and Fritz Loewe who formed their own production company to make it, first into a play and then a movie made by Warner Brothers. Even so, Freed seemed to be involved.

Lee asked me what I had been doing with myself while I was in California. I said I had been to the degree-giving ceremony at Cal Tech where the address had been given by Solly Zuckerman. 'Solly!' she cried. 'You heard Solly! He's one of our oldest friends. He always comes to see us when he's in this part of the world. As a matter of fact he was here the other night until very late playing poker.'

Solly had been born in Cape Town and then came to England for his BSc at London University. He had as a young graduate gone to Yale to do research on the nervous system. This was in the late 1920s, the era of Prohibition, when the Gershwins were living in New York. They often went to a speakeasy, Tony's, where Harold Ross, Sam Behrman, Lillian Hellmann, Dashiell Hammett and other now household names were to be seen. Solly used to go to Tony's regularly and made friends with all these people but especially the Gershwins. 'I went to rehearsals and to plays with Lee,' Solly wrote in his memoirs, 'and became enamoured of the stage. In a quiet way she dominated whatever room she was in.' I could vouch for the truth of that.

Solly went with Lee and Ira to the opening performance of *Let Them Eat Cake* in October 1933, and to *Porgy and Bess* directed by Rouben Mamoulian in 1935. Neither show was commercially successful at the time. *Porgy* (a folk opera about disadvantaged blacks but the brain-child of two non-blacks) survived its initial commercial failure and reviews like that of Joseph Wood Krutch in the *Nation* – 'to my lay ear Mr Gershwin's music though pretentious enough, seemed lacking in both memorable melodies and real dramatic effect' – to reach an apotheosis in the Glyndebourne production of 1986, which Lee attended. She had refused permission for a British revival for years. It has eclipsed *Let them Eat Cake* but, as the recording in 1987 from the Brooklyn Academy of Music showed, that piece has some of Ira's wittiest lyrics. During work on *An American in Paris* Alan Lerner used to visit the Gershwins and play Scrabble with Ira; bouts that had an intensity comparable to a confrontation between two grandmasters at chess.

Ira asked me what I written and I had to confess it was mainly reviews. 'It's the worst paid of all writing,' he said, at which I nodded my complete agreement. He had been a critic in his youth but had wisely got out of journalism before it was too late. Lee interrupted to say that there was one other guest whom they were waiting dinner for – Oscar Levant. Did I know him? I hesitated and Lee explained. Oscar had in his youth been a remarkable pianist and had made himself indispensable to George at rehearsals; when George made arrangements of his work for two pianos, Oscar in his early twenties would play opposite him on the second piano.

Ira said that on account of his association with George, Oscar

would always be welcome at Roxbury Drive. '*Always*,' he repeated
with great emphasis, nodding his head. Unfortunately Oscar's
early musical triumphs had not led anywhere and his gifts had
become diffused; he became an actor, a writer, a dancer, a wit and
layer down of the law on the model of his Irish namesake. Oscar
had appeared in several of the Arthur Freed-Gershwin film musicals, such as *The Barkleys of Broadway* in 1949, where he had
performed a dance number with Ginger Rogers and Fred Astaire,
and in *An American in Paris.*

Currently Oscar had his own television show twice a week on
one of the LA channels, where he chatted with guest celebrities
and members of the audience on anything that cropped up. As
soon as Oscar had finished recording that night's programme he
would be along for dinner. He had become unpredictable and
could sometimes be very difficult, and even insulting to their other
guests. 'But *you* needn't worry,' she added touching my arm, 'He'll
adore you.'

In the event he did not; nor I him. It was as if Oscar feared I
might be going to usurp his role as the house literary expert,
however briefly. Larry Stewart, who possessed a Zen-like calm in
the face of Oscar and everyone else, posed no threat to him. The
trick was to let Oscar monopolise the conversation, which I did,
but I found it difficult to hold fire when the talk turned to Tynan,
whom of course they all read. 'New York spoiled Tynan,' Freed
said. You should have known him at Oxford, I felt like saying.

After dessert and before coffee, Oscar got up and left with a
curt nod of general farewell. 'I hope I have not driven him away,'
I said to Lee when he had gone. 'Oh no, it's nothing to do with
you. His programme is through. Now it is safe for him to go back
home.' The conversation after dinner in the drawing-room turned
to Judy Garland and I sensed concern. She was close friend of Lee,
who always gave her great support during her recurrent crises.
Judy was currently on the road on a long tour doing 'all the old
numbers' Lee said, shaking her head ruefully.

I felt sadly it was time for me to go before I out-stayed my
welcome. 'You must come again,' Lee said, taking my hand. She
looked me full in the face. 'It's hard being your age,' she said. She
was the most gracious woman I met during the whole year in
America.

It passed very rapidly. It was now August and time for me to
leave. My departure was hastened by the news that Alan Pryce-
Jones was standing down as the editor of the *Lit Supp* and that

Arthur Crook was taking over. This information came from Arthur himself, who hinted that my job-prospects would be enhanced by my returning sooner rather than later. Before I left New York for home I had time for a visit to Broadway to see Ethel Merman in *Gypsy*. In the event, my second period on the *Lit Supp* proved to be brief. Before long I was attending my own leaving party in Printing House Square, and, as we have seen, moving down Ludgate Hill to Fleet Street to start work on the book section of the new *Sunday Telegraph*.

As a lit ed I came to know many leading publishers one of whom, John Calder, invited me to attend a press conference for three of his authors, exponents of *le nouveau roman*, Marguerite Duras, Nathalie Sarraute and Alain Robbe-Grillet. To have arranged for three leading French novelists to leave their native Paris and tour Britain in a series of discussions about the aesthetics of a new kind of novel was something unprecedented in 1961.

Calder opened the conference himself. His underlined his three novelists' subordination of narrative interest to rigorously exact description from which the reader might infer such narrative as the text warranted. In retrospect, the three novelists seem to have had rather divergent aims and Robbe-Grillet – an engineer by training – to be the only practitioner of the *nouveau roman* in the way that Calder described. But they were all three forthcoming about their artistic credos and, in spite of the language-barrier, put across their reasons for their mistrust of narrative and sense that the novel needed a new discipline if it was to survive. Someone asked Robbe-Grillet if there were any living English novelists who fulfilled his criteria for a novel. He thought for a moment and, surprisingly, said Henry Green.

The trio went on tour with Calder and attracted big audiences, especially at the University of Birmingham. The Earl of Harewood was at this time the artistic director of the Edinburgh Festival. He remarked to Calder on this impressive turn-out by the young to listen to the French novelists. Literature had always been the least well-represented of the arts at Edinburgh. 'Why don't we put that right and have an international conference of novelists at the Festival?' he suggested. The result was that Calder arranged two conferences at the Edinburgh Festival, one the novel, in 1962, and one the following year, chaired by Kenneth Tynan, on the current drama.

With the help of Sonia Orwell, then at the peak of her friendship with Mary McCarthy, Calder persuaded eminent writers from all over the world to come to Edinburgh and appear there in public discussion in the summer of 1962. Ironically, the one country not represented was France. 'The French wouldn't dream of going north in August,' explained Calder. But the English and the Welsh have no such inhibition. Even Richard Hughes left his fastness in Merioneth, where for the past decade he had been at work on his chain-novel *The Human Predicament*, to come along and make an intervention. He declared that the novel was fighting for its life in the literary arena, like the early Christians thrown to the lions. Stephen Spender, then co-editor of *Encounter*, was much in evidence trying to give some direction to the sessions. During five days of public meetings there were discussions on the present state of the novel; a Scottish day; a session on Commitment; one on Censorship and one on the Novel of the Future. The Festival had never before – or since – hosted a literary event of this order. The attendance by the paying public for each session was at capacity level.

The occasion was revealing but not perhaps in the way intended by Harewood and Calder. Novelists are unused to speaking in public to vast audiences and tend to ramble unless they prepare their texts carefully in advance, and they are even worse in the chair. True, the Scots on their home ground provided some lively skirmishes, especially those between Hugh MacDiarmid and Alexander Trocchi, a British experimenter with the *nouveau roman* as well as with drugs. But the platform discussions tended to be notable only for nebulous, ill-expressed thoughts leading nowhere. Rebecca West, brought up in Edinburgh, swept out three-quarters of the way through, with apologies to Calder; she was incensed by the Americans who tended to hog the limelight. 'Yesterday finished me,' she said. 'I thought the dialogue between Mailer and Mary McCarthy the essence of idiocy.'

I put up at the Caledonian Hotel where both Malcolm Muggeridge and Claud Cockburn were staying. Some of the funniest moments were over drinks with them after the main business of the day was completed. They were amused at the standing ovation with which the audience had welcomed Henry Miller to the platform, after which the smiling Miller proved to be totally inarticulate. I groaned over this Edinburgh Festival assignment at the time; but now I'm glad that McLachlan made me go. I was required to phone through an article summing everything up for the next *Sunday Telegraph*. If the reader will forgive me, I will reprint the short piece I filed:

'Is that Iris Murdoch?' a woman asked her friend, pointing at Muriel Spark. Place: McEwan Hall, Edinburgh. Time: a wet afternoon in August, 1962. Event: the International Writer's Conferencer on the novel today. In other words, the moment when writing along with the Tattoo became one of the performing arts.

The conference was by no means a total disaster, but what was badly needed was a much firmer direction of the proceedings by the rather shadowy organisers. Like all performances, it badly needed producing.

Perhaps in future years if the experiment is to be repeated, Wimbledon should be the model and some form of seeding introduced, whereby the really good players could get to grips with each other on the centre court at different times during the week, and the rest be relegated to a side-show.

As it is one is left with a long series of regrets. If only Henry Miller and Lawrence Durrell could have been drawn into the thing a bit more ... If only Mary McCarthy could have developed one or two of the interesting ideas she threw out and then retreated from with a curt 'that's all' ... If only some clear-headed antagonist could have cut into Norman Mailer's obscurities as soon as they were uttered and led him back to meaningfulness.

If only one of the Dutchman could have said a bit less and the brilliant delegate from Ceylon a bit more ... If only William Burroughs could have talked about drugs and not about censorship ... If only Angus Wilson and Dame Rebecca West could have got together and thrashed out their disagreements about the origin of the English novel.

From all this it will be clear that the main tenor of the conference was Anglo-American. Little local difficulties like nymphet-love, kept occurring which could not have meant much to some of the delegates. 'In India,' as Kushwant Singh never seemed to tire of saying, 'we are up against much bigger problems.'

A propos 'Lolita' Miss McCarthy singled out this work and Nabokov's 'Pale Fire' (soon to be published in this country) for special praise.

The absence of any representation from France (apart from Maurice Girodias, Henry Miller's first publisher) was badly felt throughout but especially during the session on Commitment, which achieved the remarkable feat of pursuing its entire course without a single reference to Sartre (who after all invented the term).

Here, indeed, was discovered the perfect recipe for an interminable afternoon: take a once fashionable word, about the meaning of which no one has ever been clear, and then invite a dozen writers from different countries to talk about it without once defining it.

By contrast the session on Censorship had for its starting-point something about which everyone was clear, and which several writers present had been greatly bothered by in their careers. This provided some of the liveliest discussion of the whole conference.

Yet it took the the interruption of a self-confessed, one-time professional pornographer from the audience to get the delegates to consider the question of whether there are in fact some written things that are harmful and ought not to be disseminated in a civilised society. He in his simplicity provoked what they in their wisdom had evaded. Dame Rebecca West made a memorable intervention here. But such illumination was rare.

Still it was something to stare at the greatest goldfish bowl of literary talent ever exposed to public view. Words die on the air almost as soon as they are uttered, especially in the great spaces of the McEwan Hall, but who present will ever forget Hugh MacDiarmid's kilt, Richard Hughes's beard, Henry Miller's benign bespectacled grin, Mary McCarthy's twitching smile, Muriel Spark's own pale fire, Lawrence Durrell's rotund geniality, Kushwant Singh's blue headdress, Angus Wilson's vivid shirts?

I have now forgotten all those things; but what I do still remember is Mary McCarthy's intervention on the state of the novel which she afterwards developed into a lecture published in 1972, 'A Guide To Exiles, Expatriates and Internal Emigrés'. Her point was that whereas many of the major pre-war novelists had been expatriates (Henry James, Hemingway, Scott Fitzgerald, Djuna Barnes), the major novelists of the present exemplified by Nabokov were exiles. The distinction she made was this: the expatriate leaves his country voluntarily and is essentially a hedonist in search of the good life. He is able to return home at any time – as Malcolm Cowley's book *The Exile's Return* proved. Cowley's Parisian contemporaries were not real exiles; they were expatriates in search of a happy life. The real exile is a political figure; he has left the country of his birth because of its political regime which would imprison him and/or censor his novels. His residence abroad is enforced. Joyce and Beckett are dubious cases of writers adopting the mantle of exile who could – had they so desired – have returned to Dublin with impunity. By contrast are those Russian writers Pasternak and (at the time Mary McCarthy was adumbrating her thesis) Solzhenitsyn and many South Africans; the latter were 'internal exiles'. 'This might be a definition of the internal exile: a man who has taught himself to behave as if he had already crossed a frontier while refusing to leave his house.' As with much of Mary McCarthy's critical writing, one could go on discussing the points she raised for hours.

Calder and the egregious Girodias were not the only publishers present. Anthony Blond, an old friend and Oxford contemporary, had come along in his white American coupé, which he drove majestically along the streets and squares to parties in the New Town. 'It's my one self-indulgence,' he told me (meaning the car). He had two of his authors with him, Simon Raven in the front seat and in the back Jennifer Dawson, a shy young woman who had written a compelling novel about madness, *The Ha-Ha*. Raven spoke at one of the sessions, his main point – one that Dr Johnson and Somerset Maugham had made on earlier occasions – was that no man unless he were a blockhead ever wrote except for money. The audience but not the panel seemed shocked by this.

Rosamond Lehmann and J. R. Ackerley were also in Edinburgh for some of the time. I do not remember either of them on the platform, but I do recall overhearing a conversation between them in the Festival Club where we all used to go for drinks. The subject under discussion was ways in which one might communicate with the dead; in Ackerley's case, this related to the dead in the animal world. The other memory I have is of the over-flowing hospitality accorded to us by the native Edinburgh writers, led by the poet MacDiarmid (Christopher Murray Grieve), a founder of the Scottish National Party from which he was expelled in 1933, after which he joined the Communist Party, from which he was also expelled and which he rejoined in 1956. He was not an internal exile in any of McCarthy's senses; he was thoroughly at home to judge by the way he proudly showed us around the ancient town. During one of these get-togethers there was a discussion of Simon Raven's point, that the chief consideration in writing a novel was the money. 'I couldn't disagree with him more,' said a locally-born

Scottish writer: 'For Heaven's sake! We're all smart enough to make a living in other ways, aren't we?'

Some novelists, the Bellows, the Amises, do make a substantial sums of money but many do not. 'I don't know why *anyone* writes a novel,' I once heard Isabel Colegate remark. There is always the chance for a serious novelist of a windfall through the award of a prestigious literary prize. Fiction prizes – the Booker, the W. H. Smith, the Whitbread – funded by those modern Maecenases, the big corporations, have mushroomed since I first became a lit ed; it is not only the prize money that is significant but also the increased sales accruing to the winning novels because of the publicity generated by the award.

The first Booker Prize panel in 1969, chaired by the literary editor of the *Guardian*, William Webb, with Rebecca West, Stephen Spender, Frank Kermode and David Farrer, gave the prize to P. H. Newby for *Something To Answer For*. The award to this writer, who had held down a top job at the BBC for much of his working life, established the prize in the way it intended to continue – as an award to the best novel in absolute terms; not necessarily the one likely to give the greatest happiness to the greatest number, the benchmark that the publishing industry and booksellers would have preferred. But how do the judges decide among so many contenders which novel truly is best? Can any *one* novel honestly be judged to be indisputably better than *all* the others ? These are questions that if we thought them through seriously would make a nonsense of the Prize. In that early period the London literary editors had a considerable role in the award: Webb was followed in succeeding years as chairman by David Holloway the (*Daily Telegraph*), John Gross (*TLS*), and Ion Trewin (*The Times*). The Prize became, and has in essence remained, the festive climax, the Open Night, of the year's work in the writing and reviewing of literary fiction.

Each London lit ed is invited to the award dinner (the invitation is for him alone and has not since the early days included his partner, who is reduced to watching the proceedings at home on television). The six novelists short-listed receive invitations for themselves *and* their partners; and so do the judges. The contending novelists are placed strategically at separate tables, buoyed up by their agents and editors, and shot in close-up as they eat, joking and joshing to hide their anxiety; they make six opposing camps;

a brief speech of acceptance lies concealed in a hand-bag or dinner-jacket pocket. Just in case.

The dinner is now a very grand affair, held in mid-October at the Guildhall with a fanfare of trumpets, flood-lights and tv cameras. Two-thirds of the guests are clients of Booker – nowadays a food distribution company – that uses the occasion for corporate entertaining. My memories go back to the period when it was held in places like the Café Royal, without benefit of television. In those days it was a less pretentious event but more fun. In 1972, when John Berger received the prize for his novel G – a historical *tour de force* using Serbian nationalism at the time of the First World War as a background – the prize got a great deal of gratuitous publicity through Berger's speech of acceptance – or rather, non-acceptance. Proclaiming his disgust at Booker's involvement in the sugar trade in the Caribbean, their exploitation (he alleged) of the labour force, he seemed to be turning down the prize. In the end he said he would take the prize and donate it to the Black Power movement.

Sir Michael Caine, the Booker director who was our host at the dinner, remained politely impassive at this outburst; but when Berger sat down there was a furore among the guests. The critic George Steiner, one of the judging panel – the chairman was Cyril Connolly, a lead-reviewer this time rather than a lit ed – turned to me: 'There's an old saying – "When you're invited out to dinner, don't spit in the soup".' If Berger's aim had been to damage the reputation of the Prize, he could not have been hoist more completely with his own petard. After that the Prize went from strength to strength to reach its present eminence; today it holds its own for the prestige and exposure it gives the winner with the Prix Goncourt and even the Nobel Prize for Literature.

When my turn came to be a judge in 1984, lit eds had ceased to be chairpersons and were merely invited to be members of the panel. My chairman was Richard Cobb, Professor of Modern History at Oxford since 1973 and just about to retire. Apart from his high reputation as a historian, he had another one as a writer and broadcaster. His *Still Life: Sketches From a Tunbridge Wells Childhood* is a classic of anecdotal writing. Cobb's wide knowledge of the regional French novel – writers such as Giono, Ramuz, Mistral – whom the average British Francophil up to his eyes in Balzac, Stendhal, Flaubert, Zola and Proust tends to ignore, seemed to be an added qualification for him to chair the Prize.

Before we met for the first of our lunches, none of my fellow judges was known to me personally. By the end they were all good friends. There was another Oxford don among us, John Fuller, tutorial Fellow in English at Magdalen College, son of the poet Roy Fuller, himself a distinguished poet as well as being the author of a 'gothicky' novella, *Flying to Nowhere*, which had been short-listed for the prize the year before. Fuller and I discovered we shared a love of chess and have been playing each other (by post) ever since. Polly Devlin, the journalist and writer, and Ted Rowlands, the Labour MP for Merthyr Tydfill and Rhymney since 1983, were the other two.

The first lunch was in May at Book House in Clapham, where our host was Martyn Goff, the Director of the National Book League (soon to become the Book Trust). Goff has been admin-strator-in-chief of the Prize from the outset and, together with Caine, was crucial to its survival. We were all present except for Rowlands, whose parliamentary duties prevented him from attend-ing on this occasion.

'Where are the books?' we asked Goff over sherry; like Noahs praying for rain.

'Ah *books* . . .' said Goff, as if the concept were new to him. 'Don't worry there'll soon be books . . . Actually this year we're trying to cut down the number submitted.'

Goff explained the then rules of submission: each publisher was able to submit up to four novels and draw the attention of the judges to another four and any one of the judges had the right to 'call in' any novel published within the time-span but not submit-ted. Hence the importance of reviews. Publishers who had, say, six or more novelists, each of whom hoped that his or her novel might be a contender for the prize, had the invidious task of deciding which four to submit; one way out of the dilemma was for them to submit the weaker ones. reckoning that the stronger would almost certainly get called in. It meant that the conscientious judges, obliged to read every book submitted (there is no preliminary sifting), would have to wade through a number of novels that did not stand a ghost of a chance of winning the Prize. As Angus Wilson put at the 1975 dinner, when he was chairman of the judges: 'I do wish that publishers would realise that this is a Miss World contest and refrain from submitting Miss Bexhill-on-sea and Miss Lytham St Anne's . . .' (or something rather like that). Goff also explained to us the geographical area covered by the Prize. It included novelists writing in English in countries like South Africa and Ireland that had once been part of the Commonwealth or British Empire.

I asked him if the Prize had ever been won by a volume of short stories. Goff said that it hadn't, but that there was nothing in the rules to prevent the judges from giving it to one if they wished, as its then full title, the Booker McConnell Prize for Fiction, made clear. He also said that there was nothing to prevent us from giving the Prize to a novelist who had won it in a previous year. Considerations like that were to be put out of our minds. Each book should be judged entirely on its merits and not on the track record of the writer. If we wanted to, we could give it to a first novel or just as properly to a hundredeth novel. It was not until 1997 that a first novel was declared winner, Arundhati Roy's *The God of Small Things*. So far no novelist has ever won it twice.

Goff assured us that his role was a completely impartial one. He was there simply to advise us over any problems we had with the rules, a benign Clerk of the Court, and he would be present at all our meetings for consultation. He also warned us about leaks to the Press in advance of the final meeting. Such leaks had in previous years marred the judging process. They continue so to do.

Soon there was hardly a day without the postman arriving at my front-door with his arms full of jiffy-bags. I counted a hundred and seventy novels by the time they were all in.

It was useful to me as a lit ed to have this advance knowledge of what was being published in fiction in the autumn and reminders of what we had reviewed on our pages or overlooked in the spring. It was also tremendous fun. *Pace* Angus Wilson, there is no cause to feel sorry for Booker Judges: they have the time of their fiction-reading lives. *And* they get paid; not as much as the prize but quite generously.

The second lunch at Book House, with Ted Rowlands joining us, was in July. By this time we were all stuck into the task of reading and were sounding each other out informally over what we had read. As the wine circulated around the long cool basement room where we ate, we threw names of novelists at each other. 'Have you read X yet?' 'Yes: surprisingly good.' 'What about Y . . .?' 'It only arrived this morning.' 'I'm afraid I just couldn't get on with Z.' 'Oh couldn't you! I *loved* it.'

By the end of this lively lunch the 'bonding' process of the jury was fairly complete. Ted suggested we might like to go back with

him to the House of Commons where further refreshment would
be available but alas, I had, to return to the office. Fuller had
brought his car and he gave Cobb and me a lift back into central
London. As we went through the Hyde Park Underpass, it emerged
that Cobb had not been to that part of London since the tunnel
had been built some ten years earlier.

Our next lunch in September was a crucial one to decide on the
short-list of six novels; the list to be released immediately after our
deliberations were concluded. By now we were required to have
read every single novel at least once. The lunch was served not in
the cheerful basement room but in Goff's more headmasterly
office upstairs, where in an adjoining room was a copy of every
novel submitted.

There is no formal procedure for the Booker judges to follow in
making their decisions. Each panel looks to its chairman for
guidance. Cobb was a good chairman and our discussions pro-
ceeded smoothly, but at the same time were full of fascinating
disgreements. People's core attitudes emerge in all sorts of interesting ways when you ask them to make definitive judgements about
the novels they have been reading. It was, for instance, quite
noticeable how certain loyalties, especially ethnic ones, came to
the surface: Polly Devlin making a strong case for Irish Clare
Boylan and Ted Rowlands for Welsh Emyr Humphreys.

We decided, as probably every panel does, that we would draw
up a pre-short-list consisting of all the novels that one or other of
us thought should be considered for the final short-list. Then in
reviewing that list, eliminate those novels that only had partial
support leaving in (say) twelve novels from which we would choose
the final six. Our first list contained twenty-five novels. Here it is:
Kingsley Amis, *Stanley and the Women*; Martin Amis, *Money;* J. G.
Ballard, *Empire of the Sun*; Julian Barnes, *Flaubert's Parrot;* Anita
Brookner, *Hôtel du Lac;* Anita Desai, *In Custody*; Howard Jacobson,
Peeping Tom; Penelope Lively, *According to Mark*; Angela Carter,
Nights at the Circus; Caroline Blackwood, *Corrigan*; William Boyd,
Stars and Bars; Dirk Bogarde, *West of Sunset*; William Golding, *The
Paper Man*; Emyr Humphreys, *Jones*; Catherine Heath, *Behaving*;
Beryl Bainbridge, *Watson's Apology;* Fred Uhlman, *Reunion;* André
Brink, *The Plague*; Elaine Feinstein, *The Border*; Alan Massie, *One
Night in Winter;* David Hughes, *The Pork Butcher*; Teresa St Aubin
de Teran, *The Tiger*; David Lodge, *Small World*; Namila Golkhale,
Paro; Clare Boylan, *Last Resorts.*

It was a strong preliminary list. Devlin put forward fourteen nominations; Curtis thirteen; Cobb and Fuller both eleven and Rowlands ten. We were going to have to relinquish half of our own nominations for a start. At this point the arbitary nature of the whole operation had begun to dawn upon us. The next step was to see whether any novels had overwhelming support. In the event, the only novels that all of us agreed unanimously should be on the list were *Empire of the Sun* and *According to Mark*. Both went through to the final short-list without further ado.

Next, with four votes apiece, came *Peeping Tom*, *Small World*, *Hôtel du Lac*, *Flaubert's Parrot*. If we had been working strictly to number of preliminary votes cast, they would have been the four remaining novels to be short-listed and we could have packed up and gone home. But it did not work out like that. It was not a strict ballot: the nominations were recorded on a rough chart I had drawn up in my notebook while we were talking and expressing our preferences; possibly fallibly recorded in some instances. Rowlands found himself in an isolated position, as he dearly wanted Dirk Bogarde on the list and we could not see eye to eye with him. But then nor could Devlin and I persuade him, or Fuller or Cobb, of the merits of Angela Carter's *Nights at the Circus*. Cobb's guillotine came down sharply at that and even more sharply at any mention of Martin Amis's *Money*. Both *Circus* and *Money* (even though there were three of us behind it) dropped out at this point; and so did Amis *père's Stanley and the Women*. However, his turn came in 1986 when *The Old Devils* won the Prize.

As the discussion began to repeat itself, Goff, the silent smiling man, looked pointedly at his watch. We reached the stage where if I could get a minimum of two or three novels I wanted for the prize into the final six, I was prepared to bow to the consensus of rejection on the others. If at this stage a Booker judge feels that his/her best novel has been omitted or that one included is *wholly* unworthy of the prize, then this is the moment to resign – as sometimes happens. I did not feel like doing that, even though I could not see *Flaubert's Parrot* as being anything more than a *New Statesman* competition entry that had gone on a bit. To my mind it was not a novel. But I was over-ruled. It was 'fiction' wasn't it (they said), so why was I quibbling? It appealed greatly to Cobb, who relished the spectacle of Dr Enid Starkie, Flaubert's biographer, and a one-time sacred monster of the Oxford French School being cut down to size.

Our short-list, then, on which we all agreed at the end of an exhausting meeting was: *Empire of the Sun* by J. G. Ballard; *Flaubert's*

Parrot by Julian Barnes; *In Custody* by Anita Desai; *According to Mark*
by Penelope Lively and *Small World* by David Lodge. I sometimes
wonder what would have happened if at that point we had broken
up for a cup of tea and then gone back into solemn conclave to
declare the winner. I think it would have gone to the Ballard,
which was then uppermost in everyone's mind. But, as Goff said
prophetically after the meeting ended: 'So often the favourite at
this stage is not the eventual winner.'

The Booker Award is orchestrated so that after the short-list is
announced there is a month's pause before the dinner. The hiatus
generates excitement, controversy and gives members of the public
a chance to read the books and the judges the chance of reading
them over again.

The final meeting to decide the winner takes place not in Book
House but at the headquarters of Booker plc, which in 1984 were
at Bucklersberry House in the City, a short taxi-ride away from the
Guildhall. The judges arrive at three-thirty p.m. with their suitcases
and each is allotted a changing-room. They then proceed to the
board room where they are greeted by Goff. Tea or fresh orange
juice is offered. Then, sitting around the long board-room table
with writing-pads and finely sharpened pencils in front of each
place, they get down to business. It was generally assumed that our
meeting would be a shortish one and that we would soon declare
Empire of the Sun the winner. Ladbroke's, whose 'book' on the
Booker has become an integral part of the whole event, were
quoting it at two to one.

Ballard's novel describes the experiences of a small boy who
becomes interned by the Japanese when they occupy Shanghai
during the Second World War. Taken to a huge open prison
camp, he becomes separated from his parents, who were part of
the city's pre-war international community, and after suffering
many hardships, he survives the ordeal thanks to his pluck,
resourcefulness and good fortune.

While the novel was *sub judice* for the Booker, two readers who
had themselves been interned in Shanghai during the war wrote
to the *Listener*, after the novel had been reviewed there, to say that
much of the novel did not 'bear the remotest resemblance to what
happened' to them. It also became known that, unlike his young
hero, Ballard had not been separated from his parents. We did
not let that influence us; fiction is fiction and fact is fact, we said;
though again it is not quite that simple, is it? For instance, is
Schindler's Ark, which won the Booker in 1982, under the chairman-

ship of John Carey, Merton Professor of English at Oxford, fact or
fiction? Would it be less considerable if it did not happen to be
true historically? However the faction argument was certainly not
what torpedoed *Empire of the Sun*. Its defeat was due to more subtle
causes.

After some general discussion, I sensed that the tide of support
for Ballard's novel was going out. Artistic criteria became uppermost in the judges' minds; form rather than content. The only one
of us who was whole-heartedly in favour of Ballard now was
Rowlands. He was, if he will forgive me, the plain man on the
panel, innocent of literary criticism and literary in-fighting, and to
him, having lost his brief for Bogarde, the Ballard with its powerful
story-line and revelation of a harrowing aspect of the Second
World War not previously brought to public attention, seemed the
obvious choice. But although the rest of us had passed it through
on the nod for the short-list, I could see that at this stage Cobb,
Fuller and Devlin had begun to have their reservations about it.
They were articulated most clearly by Fuller, who felt that parts of
it – he quoted one short passage – were over-written. But it was
not anything very specific against Ballard's book or even the desire
to defeat general expectation (though I suppose that cannot be
completely ruled out); it was a strong positive preference all three
of the above-mentioned had for wanting to make *Hôtel du Lac* the
ultimate winner. That became abundantly clear when they started
talking about it, the wonderful artistry of it and so forth. We all
have a concept of what we most demand from a novel and in their
case Brookner's realised their ideal requirements wholly. They felt
it was a near-perfect book and that the Ballard, for all its force,
was in artistic terms less than perfect.

Here we come up against the ultimate absurdity and invidious-
ness of the Prize. How do you choose between chalk and cheese?
Apples and pears? There is no way except quite arbitrarily.
Ballard's novel and Brookner's novel have both enjoyed an
enormous success commercially and artistically; both have
enhanced their writer's reputations; both have been filmed; both
are good novels. But only one got the Prize.

I was amused after the award was made to *Hôtel du Lac* to find
myself type-cast as a champion of the novels of Anita Brookner
and asked speak about them on radio as each new one appeared.
True, I admired *Hôtel* but it was not my choice at that last meeting
of the judges. Like Rowlands, I was an odd man out. I wanted to
give the prize to David Lodge for *Small World*. It seemed to me to

be a much more ambitious novel, breaking new territory as well as being hugely, hilariously enjoyable.

I went on and on about it at that last meeting – Rowlands seemed surprised by the zeal of my advocacy – but to no avail. Cobb, Fuller and Devlin still preferred *Hôtel du Lac* and I could have gone on praising *Small World* till I was blue in the face but it would not have made a scrap of difference. In the end it was Fuller who said: 'Well, you're not going to resign if we give it to Brookner.' Put like that I had to admit I wasn't, and to Goff's relief I caved in, and we had a winner, *Hôtel du Lac*.

As soon as the winning novel is known, Goff's highly efficient staff from Book House, who are standing by, go into action. Officially the winner is not announced until the end of the dinner, and as a judge you are enjoined to keep the name secret from the soup to the speeches. In fact all the lit eds present know who the winner is when they arrive at the dinner because they have a hotline to the Book House staff who tell them in advance of the dinner so that they can carry the Booker award story that night in all editions. Programmes on the World Service, like their arts magazine 'Meridian', also get advance warning of the winner. Also the television crews whose news programmes carry the announcement live know who the winner is; but all are sworn to secrecy so that to the winner and to the majority of guests, it comes as a surprise. It was nonetheless disconcerting when I arrived at the dinner, bursting with self-importance, to be told by Philip Howard, the lit ed of *The Times*, 'I think you've made a very wise choice.'

The Booker dinner is in two parts. Part one consists of the four-course dinner. During coffee the Booker host, then Caine, rises to call upon the chairman of the judges to announce the winner. This he/she does for the television cameras with a minimum of explanation and the winner then receives the prize and makes a brief speech of acceptance, while the losers crunch theirs up. Anita Brookner seemed genuinely surprised when she heard that she had won and went up to receive the award from Cobb; her eyes widening to such an extent that they seem to cover most of her face. She said that as an art historian, her earlier profession, she was only prepared for making speeches that went on for three-quarters of an hour with slides. Polite laughter.

After that there is an interval. The television coverage moves to a panel in the studio whose members give their reaction to the award just announced; this discussion is viewed by the home audience but not the guests in the Guildhall. (It was on one occasion; that proved to be a complete disaster by greatly holding up proceedings at the dinner.)

Everyone returns to his or her table and part two begins. The host stands up again. He formally thanks the judges, Goff, the Book House staff, and anyone else who has in the course of the year made a significant contribution to the administration of the award. He mentions the names of the most eminent of his guests and he presents the losers with leather-bound copies of their novels, to much sympathetic applause. Then he asks the chairman to return to the platform and to talk at greater length about the current year's award.

It gives the chairman not merely an opportunity to elaborate on the difficulty he and his colleagues had in making the award and to mention several of the novels that made the cut but not the final short-list; but, if he feels up to it, also to deal with state of fiction at the present time. The best such speech I heard was made by David Daiches in 1980 after they had given the Prize to William Golding for *Rites of Passage*, an account of the novel in what he called the post-heroic age.

Following tradition, Cobb returned to the rostrum after the interval. As he spoke I found my eyes focusing on the handsome profile of Kilmartin, who was sitting at a table in my direct line of vision to the speaker. Cobb first of all said what a happy ship we had been as judges and how much he would miss our lunches; then he said that in awarding the prize this year we had wanted to give it to a novel that people would enjoy and actually read, not one by a novelist like Proust whom anyway he had not read. At this Kilmartin's face jerked smartly ceiling-wards in reflex-action, as if responding to the impact of an upper-cut.

I never had the opportunity of asking Cobb why he went out of his way to repudiate Proust, and none of the printed explanations seem at all satisfactory. I think he must have felt guilty about one or two of the more difficult novels on the list to which he had given rather short shrift in our discussions and wished to cover himself.

It is rare for a year to go by without some controversy in the awarding of the prize but the tradition of spitting in the soup by the prizewinner has been in abeyance since J. G. Farrell followed suit from Berger when he received the prize for *The Siege of Krishnapur* in 1973 and had some harsh things to say about our hosts. As chairperson in 1983, Fay Weldon in awarding the prize to J. M. Coetzee for *The Life and Times of Michael K* used her state-of-the-art speech to pitch into publishers as a body and their treatment of novelists on whom they are so dependent. That is one opportunity given to some novelists to let off steam about the way novels are marketed and reviewed. Another, more generally available and lastingly effective, is through the novel itself. I have dealt with the reviewing of fiction but what about the fiction of reviewing? A rapid look at the way over the years novelists have handled reviewers and literary editors in their novels may prove to be illuminating.

14

Pen and others

All authors suffer from the the bias, the prejudice of reviewers. They have a few means of redress, the crudest being to seek out the reviewer and punch him the face, a response implemented, rumour has it, on at least one occasion by Roy Campbell. Another is to pursue the offending reviewer through the courts, but this can prove expensive; reviewers have a wide latitude in law to say what they think about an author's work provided it is presented as an honest *opinion* of the work and is factually accurate. Occasionally, though, a novelist may feel that a reviewer's robustly expressed opinion has crossed the boundary into defamation, as did L. P. Hartley when T. C. Worsley slammed into his novel *Poor Clare* in the *Evening Standard*. Hartley started proceedings for libel which lasted for many months until it was settled out of court, most distressing for the highly strung Worsley.

A less costly means for an author to let off steam about reviewers is to put them into a novel or a poem, showing them up as the glorious asses they are. Dickens put Leigh Hunt into *Bleak House* as Harold Skimpole. Aldous Huxley put Middleton Murry into *Point Counterpoint* as the loathsome Burlap; and Mary McCarthy based her story 'Portrait of the Intellectual as a Yale Man' on John Chamberlain in his parlor-pink Marxist days.

This kind of creative backlash begins in the eighteenth century as a part of the same drive that produced the art of caricature. Pope was dealing mainly with authors not reviewers as literary dullards in *The Dunciad*: he gave a deadly portrait of Addison in his role as a judge of his contemporaries' literary work – 'Willing to wound but not afraid to strike' – in *The Epistle to Dr Arbuthnot*. A generation later Sheridan pilloried, in *The Critic*, the corrupt manipulation of the public prints in their reports on the theatre. Reviewers acquired even greater power in the next century as they pitched ferociously into the likes of Wordsworth and Keats. The counter-attack from the poets' side was Byron's poem, 'English Bards and Scots Reviewers', naming the chief reviewers and covering them in ridicule.

In the next century Tennyson was no happier about reviewers than Byron as he showed in a short poem published in the *Cornhill* in 1863.

Hendecasyllabics

O you chorus of indolent reviewers,
Irresponsible, indolent reviewers,
Look, I come to the test, a tiny poem
All composed in a metre of Catullus,
All in quantity, careful of my motion,
Like the skater on ice that hardly bears him,
Lest I fall unawares before the people,
Waking laughter in indolent reviewers.
Should I flounder a while without a tumble
Through this metrification of Catullus,
They should speak to me not without a welcome,
All that chorus of indolent reviewers.
Hard, hard, hard is it, only not to tumble,
So fantastical is the daily metre,
Wherefore slight me not wholly, nor believe me
Too presumptuous, indolent reviewers.

Thackeray felt less hostile to reviewers than Tennyson, no doubt because he had been one himself; for many years he reviewed books in *Fraser's Magazine*, the *Morning Post*, and *Punch*. Gordon N. Ray described the novelist at this period, before his fiction became self-supporting, as a Victorian equivalent of Edmund Wilson, capable of reviewing anything whether it was fiction by Dickens or Disraeli, biographies of Hume, Beau Brummell, Dr Arnold, Madame D'Arblay's *Diaries*, Horne's *New Spirit of the Age*, Dr Carus's *Travels in England*, Haydon's *Lectures on Painting*, or Alexis Soyer's *Gastronomic Regenerator*.

Thackeray was master of the the spoof as well as the straight review. This talent emerged in 1837 when he was asked to review a manual of 'silver fork' etiquette by one James Henry Skelton,

entitled *My Book; or, The Anatomy of Conduct.* Thackeray pretended
he was Charles James Yellowplush, 'sometime footman in many
genteel families'. He wrote a mock-deferential account of the book
in a spelling that mimicked Yellowplush's pronounciation of the
English tongue, aping that of the aristocracy. In the event Yellowplush proved far too good a comic invention to waste on a single
book-review. He became the presiding genius of an entire book,
The Yellowplush Papers.

Thackeray's autobiographical novel *Pendennis* gives us insights
into the world of Victorian book-reviewing. When Arthur Pendennis arrives in London by the stage-coach to start work as a law-
student, a fellow-passenger, a newspaper reporter, points out the
Cyril Connolly of the day: 'Mr Hurtle, the reviewer, walking with
his umbrella . . . Pen thought it was quite an honour to have seen
the great Mr Hurtle, whose works he admired. He believed fondly,
as yet, in authors reviewers and editors of newspapers.' Pen settles
in chambers where his life-style is such that his money soon runs
out; another pupil, George Warrington (based on Thackeray's
contemporary at Charterhouse, G. S. Venables), confesses that he
keeps his bank balance in credit by writing articles for the legal
journals. He says that he feels sure that Pen with his literary flair
and social connections would be able to earn a modest competence by literary journalism. He takes him to Paternoster Row, to
meet the booksellers who own and run the literary periodicals.
Pen meets Mr Bungay and Mr Bacon, who before they quarrelled
and split up were partners in the well-known publishing firm,
Bacon and Bungay. Now they have become rivals. Bungay publishes the *Londoner*, to which Bacon responded by publishing the
Westminster Magazine. Bacon has just started a new journal, the
Whitehall Review, and Bungay, as he explains to them, is proposing
to counter this by bringinging out the *Pall Mall Gazette*. The
adversarial politics of Parliament extended to these journals. If the
Tories were championed in one sheet the views of the Whigs
would be represented in another.

The person Bacon has in mind to edit the *Pall Mall Gazette* is an
Irish journalist at present in the Fleet Prison because of unpaid
debts. Pen accompanies Bacon on a visit to him there. During
their visit, Captain Shandon dashes off a prospectus for the *Pall
Mall Gazette* – 'it will be written for gentlemen by gentlemen' (the
whole satirical screed is a fascinating statement of journalistic
intent) – for which Bungay pays him on the spot with a five pound

note 'eagerly clapped into his pocket'. Shandon was based on William Maginn, the aboriginal Lunchtime O'Booze, who founded *Fraser's Magazine.*

Pen reflects to Warrington on the plight of Shandon,

> 'of accomplishments so multifarious, and of such an undoubted talent and humour, an inmate of a jail for half his time, and a bookseller's hanger-on when out of prison.'
> 'I am a bookseller's hanger-on; you are going to try your paces as a hack,' Warrington said with a laugh. 'We are all hacks on some road or other.'

Pen's chance to show his skill as a reviewer comes soon after this conversation. The servant of the chambers hands Warrington a bulky brown-paper parcel:

> 'Pen, you beggar!' roared Warrington to Pen, who was in his own room.
> 'Hello!' sung out Pen.
> 'Come here; you're wanted,' cried the other, and Pen came out. – 'What is it?' said he.
> '*Catch!*' cried Warrington, and flung the parcel at Pen's head, who would have been knocked down had he not caught it.
> 'It's books for review for the *Pall Mall Gazette*. Pitch into 'em,' Warrington said. As for Pen, he had never been so delighted in his life. His hand trembled as he cut the string of the packet, and beheld within a smart set of new neat calico-bound books – travels, novels, and poems.
> 'Sport the oak, Pidgeon,' said he. 'I'm not at home to anybody today.' And he flung into his easy-chair, and hardly gave himself time to drink his tea, so eager was he to begin to read and to review.

Like his creator, Pen soon proves himself to be one nature's reviewers and in a short while he has earned himself a place among the magazine's regular contributors:

> He worked away hard every week, preparing reviews of such works as came into his department, and writing his reviews with flippancy certainly, but with honesty, and to the best of his power. It might be that a historian of threescore, who has spent a quarter of a century in composing a work of which our young gentleman disposed in the course of a couple of days reading at the British Museum, was not

altogether fairly treated by such a facile critic; or that a poet who
had been elaborating sublime sonnets and odes until he thought
them fit for the public and for fame, was annoyed by two or three
dozen pert lines in Mr Pen's review, in which the poet's claims were
settled by the critic, as if the latter were my lord on the bench, and
the author a miserable little sinner trembling before him.

Pen's journalism brings him in an income of four guineas a
week from the *PMG* alone; with contributions to other periodicals
he is soon knocking up nearly four hundred a year, a pleasant
enough stipend for an unattached man about town in mid-
Victorian days. He is read avidly by his fellow clubmen, not least
by that arch-snob Major Pendennis, his uncle, whose whole life is
centred on clubs and country houses and who gets a reflected
glory from his brilliant nephew, whom he had hitherto tended to
write off as a ne'er-do-well.

For all his smartness and success as a reviewer, Pen always plays
fair. Indeed Pen gets a wigging from his editor for praising a book
published by the rival firm. To which he retorts heatedly:

'. . . I would rather starve, by Jove, and never earn another penny
by my pen' (this redoubted instrument had now been in use for six
weeks, and Pen spoke of it with vast enthusiasm and respect) 'than
strike an opponent an unfair blow, or, if called upon to place him,
rank him below his honest desert.'

'Well, Mr Pendennis, when we want Bacon smashed we must get
some other hammer to do it,' Shandon said with fatal good nature;
and very likely thought within himself, 'A few years hence perhaps
the young gentleman won't be so squeamish.'

Thackeray's novel, with its fictitious *Pall Mall Gazette*, appeared
in serial form in 1848–50. In 1865 the real historical *Pall Mall
Gazette* was founded in emulation of it by Frederick Greenwood
and George Smith, the publisher of Charlotte Brontë, proprietor
of Smith, Elder and Co. and the *Cornhill*. The *PMG* was a new
evening paper, 'written by gentlemen for gentlemen' (to be read
in their clubs) with a notably strong literary half. John Morley
became its editor and his friends Leslie and Fitzjames Stephen
were among contributors, as were both Trollope and Matthew
Arnold whose essays, later published as *Friendship's Garland*, first
appeared in its pages. It was initially a bastion of Liberalism.
Morley was succeeded by W. T. Stead whose sensational article,

'Maiden's Tribute', on the white slave trade it ran; after him came
Edward Cook, and towards the end, when it had turned Tory, it
was edited for a time by that Edwardian Lothario and 'Soul', Harry
Cust, who signed up Henry James to write for it and appointed
H. G. Wells as dramatic critic. Wells then had the awkward job of
writing about James's disastrous excursion into the West End
Theatre, *Guy Domville.*

Victorian reviewers were often single men who lived in chambers
like Pen and Warrington; after university they became articled as
lawyers and ate their dinners at an Inn of Court but they spent
much of their time writing reviews and articles for the periodical
press, as practitoners of the higher journalism. There is a full-
length portrait of such a literary man in our next exhibit, Hardy's
early novel *A Pair of Blue Eyes.* In Henry Knight, formerly a fellow
of an Oxford college, the enthusiasm and generosity of Pen as a
book-reviewer have disappeared and been replaced by a tone of
pained censoriousness. His dreary chambers in one of the dimmer
Inns, cluttered with piles of review copies, are a cheerless male
preserve into which the sun rarely penetrates; a tank of aquatic
plants and fish suggests an amateur interest in science as well as
literature.

But like Pen's, Knight's reviewing mandate is a catholic one and
it includes current fiction. He has recently been particularly hard
on a historical novel he has been sent for review, *The Court of King
Arthur's Castle, a romance of Lyonesse.* He reviewed it in the *Present,*
the learned monthly journal for which he reviews regularly. Under
the cover of a pen-name, Knight discerned 'the hands of some
young lady hardly arrived at the years of discretion'.

And he was right. The book Knight reviewed was the pseudonymous work of Elfride Swancourt, the heroine of Hardy's novel
(she of the pair of blue eyes), the daughter of the Reverend
Christopher Swancourt, rector of Endlestow on the coast of
Cornwall not far from Tintagel Castle. Mrs Swancourt, her step-
mother, tries to talk the mortified Elfride out of the badness of the
review. 'Now, my dear ... It proves you were clever enough to
make him think of Sir Walter Scott, which is a great deal' – a
chapter that no one who has ever lived with a writer can fail to
warm to.

Knight turns out to be the nephew of Mrs Swancourt, who

invites him to stay with them in Cornwall. When the invitation is accepted the identity of the anonymous reviewer is revealed, as is that of the pseudonymous author. Masks off, the novelist and her reviewer confront each other in the drawing-room. Knight remains inflexible in his opinion but that does not prevent Elfride from being attracted by him:

'You made me very uneasy and sorry by writing such things!' she murmured, suddenly dropping the mere *caqueterie* of a fashionable first introduction, and speaking with some of the dudgeon of a child towards a severe schoolmaster.

'That is rather the object of honest critics in such a case. Not to cause unneccessary sorrow, but: "To receive damage by us in nothing," – that was what I think a powerful pen once wrote to the Gentiles. Are you going to write another romance?'

'Write another?' she said, 'that somebody may pen a con-demnation and "nail't wi' Scripture" again, as you do now, Mr Knight?'

'You may do better next time,' he said placidly: 'I think you will. But I would advise you to confine yourself to domestic scenes.'

'Thank you. But never again!'

'Well, you may be right. That a young woman has taken to writing is not by any means the best thing to hear about her.'

'What is the best?'

'I prefer not to say.'

'Do you know? Then, do tell me, please.'

'Well' – (Knight was evidently changing his meaning) 'I suppose to hear she has married.'

The model for Henry Knight was Hardy's friend, Horatio Mosley Moule, one of the sons of the Reverend Henry Moule of Fording-ton in Dorset to whose family Hardy became attached. Horace, who left Oxford and then Cambridge without taking a degree, advised Hardy to continue with his architectural training when he was thinking of abandoning it for the study of Greek tragedy; advice that the young Hardy heeded. Robert Gittings in his Hardy biography cautions his readers against identifying Moule too closely with Knight who, he says, in spite of a depressive strain in his nature, liked to dwell on the bright side of things in the books he reviewed. Moule's articles appeared frequently in the *Saturday Review*, founded in 1855, where some of the highest reviewing standards of any Victorian periodical were in evidence and to which Hardy himself contributed.

A Pair of Blue Eyes came out in 1873; eighteen years later Gissing's *New Grub Street* appeared containing various specimens of that by now prolific and largely pathetic genus, *homo auctor*, man (and woman) as author; the novel portrays an industrious group of professional scribblers from the middle rank of society. Alfred Yule and Edwin Reardon, the two main ones, represent aspects of the writer of the book: Yule is Gissing the classical scholar and essayist; Reardon, Gissing the prolific three-decker novelist.

Gissing depicts the literary profession here as a death-trap; destructive of the domestic happiness, health and in the end the minds of its practitioners. Dire poverty is the norm; a job as a clerk in a hospital at £1 a week, unwisely given up by Reardon on the strength of a modest success with a novel, is a better option financially than authorship. It is the womenfolk, the wives and daughters, who bear uncomplainingly the brunt of this condition. They have to put up with husbands and fathers who are congenitally ill-tempered and full of sulky self-pity. The older women are reduced to domestic drudgery; the younger ones slave away as reseachers in the reading-room of the British Museum. Panizzi's golden Bloomsbury dome may have represented a secure haven of work in progress for Karl Marx, but Gissing shows market forces grinding down many of its regular denizens as they work against the clock on shilling lives and popular histories.

Literary journalism and reviewing, with its making and breaking of reputations, plays a crucial part in this world. The novel's anti-hero, the manipulative literary journalist Jasper Milvain, describes his working day:

> 'I got up at 7.30, and while I breakfasted I read through a volume I had to review. By 10.30 the review was written – three quarters of a column of the *Evening Budget.*'
>
> 'Who is the unfortunate author?' interrupted Maud caustically.
>
> 'Not unfortunate at all. I had to crack him up; otherwise I couldn't have done the job so quickly. It's the easiest thing in the world to write laudation; only an inexperienced grumbler would declare it was easier to find fault. The book was Billington's *Vagaries;* pompous idiocy, of course, but he lives in a big house and gives dinners. Well, from 10.30 to 11, I smoked a cigar and reflected, feeling that the day

wasn't badly begun. At eleven I was ready to write my Saturday
causerie for the *Will o' the Wisp*, it took me till close on one o'clock
which was rather too long. I can't afford more than an hour and a
half for that job. At one I rushed out to a dirty little eating-house in
the Hampstead Road. Was back again by quarter to two, having in
the meantime sketched a paper for *The West End*. Pipe in mouth, I
sat down to leisurely artistic work; by five, half the paper was done;
the other half remains for tomorrow. From five to half-past I read
four newspapers and two magazines, and from half-past to a quarter
to six I jotted down several ideas that had come to me whilst reading.
At six I was in the dirty eating-house, satisfying a ferocious hunger.
Home once more at 6.45, and for two hours wrote steadily at a long
affair I have in hand for *The Current*. Then I came here thinking
hard all the way. What say you to this ? Have I earned a night's
repose?'

'And what's the value of it all?' asked Maud.

'Probably from ten to twelve guineas, if I calculated.'

'I meant what was the literary value of it?' said his sister with a
smile.

'Equal to that, of the contents of a mouldy nut.'

'Pretty much what I thought'.

'Oh but it answers the purpose' urged Dora, 'and it does no one
any harm.'

'Honest journey-work!' cried Jasper. 'There are few men in
London capable of such a feat. Many a fellow could write more in
quantity, but they couldn't command my market. It's rubbish, but
rubbish of a very special kind, of fine quality.'

A new genus is emerging, the literary careerist. Milvain triumphs
and Yule and Reardon go under: the shape of things to come. A
much better way of making a living than reviewing in the 1890s
for a man of letters was for him to bend his talent to the literary
form that had become all the rage, the short story, as that 'infant
prodigy' Rudyard Kipling, was doing. At this time Gissing kept
body and soul together, not by reviewing which he abhorred, but
by writing short stories for journals like the *London Illustrated News*.

Long after it was all over Kipling looked back on the world of
the literary hacks of the 1890s in the story 'Dayspring Mishandled'
in *Limits and Renewals:* 'In the days beyond compare and before
the Judgments, a genius called Graydon foresaw that the advance
of education and the standard of living would submerge all mind-
marks in one mudrush of standardised reading-matter, and so

created the Fictional Supply Syndicate to meet the demand.' One
of the hacks pressed into service to meet the demand, 'a man-
nered, bellied person called Alured Castorley', escapes from such
work to become an authority on Chaucer and a critic, writing
reviews 'in which calling he loyally scalped all his old associates as
they came up'. Another of the hacks, James Andrew Manallace
becomes a successful novelist pandering to the popular craving for
tales of the olden times. Castorley goes out of his way, 'to review
one of Manallace's books with an intimacy of unclean deduction
(this was before the days of Freud) which long stood as a record.'
The two men were, as it happens, at one time paying court to the
same woman and thus doubly motivated Manallace plans his
revenge by forging a fragment from a lost Canterbury Tale which
Castorley, in his latterday eminence as the world's leading authority on Chaucer, authenticates.

Kipling has some cruel fun with these characters. It culminates
in the movement led by Manallace to secure his duped rival
'recognition' for his Chaucer discovery in the form of a knighthood (the story bears more than a vague resemblance to an
episode in the career of Edmund Gosse, whose scholarly reputation was destroyed by a devastating review from Professor Churton
Collins). But here Manallace delays the *coup de grâce* and his victim
escapes exposure through an early death. Many of Kipling's stories
encompass a sadistic hoax, a merciless drive for revenge; this one
is unique in having the world of literature and literary scholarship
as its base.

Henry James was another novelist who began life as a literary
journalist. Even at the height of his periods of creativity, he never
abandoned the writing of appraisals of his English and French
contemporaries. The world of the Edwardian reviewer and literary
journal, the author-reviewer relationship, is reflected most directly
in his tale, 'The Figure in the Carpet'.

James depicted a young reviewer confronting an elderly novelist
at a Friday to Monday house-party after his review of the great
man's latest novel has just appeared in a fashionable literary
journal. Has the great man read the review? And if so, what did he
think of it?

Yes, he tells their hostess, and it is 'the usual twaddle'. The great
man then learns to his horror that the reviewer is present as a
fellow-guest. A gentleman as well as a novelist, he takes him aside
to make amends. All he meant, he explains, was that in his

estimation *no* reviewer has ever succeeded in penetrating to the essence of his work.

But where does that essence lie? The rest of the tale traces the reviewer's attempts to answer this unanswerable question. It is an intricate paper-chase: the trail takes him into the domestic life of the novelist and of several of his fellow-reviewers and literary editors, all of it leading back to the mind of the novelist where the elusive information remains hidden. At the end of the story, when the novelist is dead, the narrator-reviewer begs a colleague whose late wife knew another colleague who was in the confidence of the novelist to let him have the precious *information* (my italics).

> 'As an older acquaintance of your late wife's than you were,' I began, 'you must let me say to you something I have on my mind. I shall be glad to make any terms with you that you see fit to name for the information she must have had from George Corvick – the information you know that had come to *him* poor chap, in one of the happiest hours of his life, straight from Hugh Vereker.'

Did Martin Amis read this? If so, did it come to mind when he recycled the Jamesian notion of information in his book about a novelist and a reviewer (see below)?

Somerset Maugham was a writer who complained that he was never taken seriously by reviewers and that the fashionable ones ignored him. It was not entirely true, but he determined to have his revenge on the metropolitan literary world in 1930 in *Cakes and Ale*, where Maugham shows us how reputations are cultivated in London drawing-rooms by hostesses who take up writers in one season and then – oh so gracefully! – drop them in the next. He was thinking of Ford's mistress, Violet Hunt, with her salon on Campden Hill rather than those really grand circles, the houses and mansions of the nobility, to which only the most fashionable novelists were on occasion of their greatest moments of glory invited. Their fickle patronage was the theme of Beerbohm's story, 'Maltby and Braxton'. Maugham shows how a writer (Edward Driffield, based on Hardy) may peak his reputation and become known as a Grand Old Man simply through having lived a very long time. And with exceptional malice he shows us the Novelist as a Fixer, ensuring friendly reviews by the simple process of taking hostile reviewers out to lunch and flattering them, that London literary world where everyone knows everyone. In Alroy Kear, based on Hugh Walpole, who when he read an advance copy had a minor nervous breakdown, Maugham exacted supreme revenge. Why? No one is quite sure. They were both pupils of the same public school, The King's School, Canterbury, and both gay men, but there must have been more to it than that.

The novelist-hero of Graham Greene's *The End of the Affair* resigns himself to being placed somewhere below Maugham by reviewers, who grudgingly grant him a measure of technical competence as a craftsman. His attitude to reviewing emerges when his mistress's husband comes home one evening and narrowly misses catching them making love. Trustingly unaware of what has been going on, the cuckolded husband offers Bendrix, the novelist, a drink:

> I said I wouldn't have a drink; I had work to do.
> 'I thought you said you never worked at night.'
> 'Oh this doesn't count. A review.'
> 'Interesting book?'
> 'Not very.'

Towards the end of the novel, when the invisible hound of heaven is bearing down upon the novelist for the kill, we meet the free-lance reviewer and literary critic, Peter Waterbury, whose questions to Bendrix are a tedious, if professionally unavoidable, distraction. Greene's novelist's contempt for literary journalism is focused on this critic, whose girlfriend the novelist threatens to steal, just to rub the critic's inferiority home. He is prevented by from doing so by divine intervention – or so it seems to him at the time. Waterbury has the lowest rating of any professional reviewer described by a novelist; someone so far away from the reality of either creativity, belief or unbelief, that only 'emptiness lies ahead'.

I once quoted Bendrix's opinion that reviewing did not count as work back at Greene when trying to inveigle him into doing a review; he replied: 'I am afraid that unlike Bendrix I always find only too much work in a . . . review, so I must still resist temptation as I really intend to have a holiday for a long time.'

Martin Amis's *The Information* is the latest example of this incestuous genre: it restates in terms of the literary situation of the late
twentieth century many of the themes concerning the nature of
reviewing and literary life that we have observed in this cursory
look at the fictional reviewers and novelists of the nineteenth.
Gwyn Barry and Richard Tull, who met as undergraduates at
Oxford, remain friends in London, both hell-bent on a literary
career; but now at this mid-point and crisis-point (they are both
about to become forty) Gwyn's career has suddenly taken off so
that he can do no wrong with the reading public, while Richard's
has remained grounded in endless reviewing.

It is in sleep, the novel begins by affirming, that the flow of
inspirational information is cycled through the writer's brain;
Richard's sleep is troubled, broken, fitful; he wakes in tears as the
information fails him; whereas Gwyn's sleep seems (in Richard's
eyes) undeservedly peaceful, serene: 'For *him*, either there would
be no information, or the information, such as it was, would be all
good.'

No success hurts quite as much as the success of a close
contemporary. Richard hits one of his children the day that Gwyn's
novel *Amelior* is number nine on the bestseller list. Here is Amis on
Richard as a reviewer:

> Like most young reviewers Richard had come in hard. But instead
> of getting softer, more catholic, more forgiving (heading towards
> elderly impartiality and, beyond that, journey's end: a gurgling
> stupor of satisfaction with everything written), Richard had just got
> harder. There were personal reasons for this, of course, which
> everyone eventually sensed. As a reviewer he wrote forcefully – he
> had an individual voice and an individual memory. But he subscribed
> to the view of the Critic as Bouncer. Only geniuses were allowed in
> Richard's speakeasy. And the real trouble with all those novels he
> was sent was that they were *published*. And his weren't . . .

The world of the little magazine of which Richard is a literary
editor and of the endless stream of literary biographies that land
on his desk for review, of the vanity publishing houses of which he
becomes an employee, of radio interviews and television chat-
shows, of signing-sessions and public readings, of the promotional
American tour, of literary awards and charitable foundations, the
whole contemporary literary circus, is unfolded with marvellous

energy and accuracy in a prose that blends the precious with the colloquial, the high style with the low. And there is the underlying Kiplingesque revenge motif, the perpetration of a hoax by one writer on another. Amis, not content with merely professional aggression, posits a link between literature and the underworld and takes us into areas of grievous bodily harm that represent a new element in the novel of literary rivalry and reviewing.

Amis knows the world he is writing about from personal experience. He served his term as a literary journalist and editor on the *TLS* under Arthur Crook in 1974, and on the *New Statesman* when Claire Tomalin was in charge of the arts and books. Then he became its lit ed in 1977 through to 1979. His own career up to now conforms in part to that of both characters. Amis's novels have the deliberate 'difficulty' of Richard's (though I found myself sailing through *The Information*, despite its length) and they enjoy the acclaim of Gwyn's. Nor has he altogether ceased to be a reviewer.

15

The continuation

I am often told by people who grew up in the period covered by this book that reviewing is in decline. That is not the impression I get when the weekend arrives and on Saturday *The Times* and *Telegraph*, the *FT*, the *Independent* and the *Guardian* with their arts and books supplements land on the mat, to be followed next day by the *Sunday Times*, the *Observer*, the *Independent on Sunday*, the *Sunday Telegraph*. Nor is it the impression I get when I read the *TLS*, the *London Review of Books*, the *New York Review of Books*. Nor is it the impression when the monthlies, the bi-monthlies and the quarterlies, the *London Magazine*, the *Literary Review*, *PN Review*, *Poetry Review*, *Prospect* and many more publications carrying general book-reviews arrive.

Nowadays newspaper book-reviews are often part of a separate review section in a magazine-format and not integral with the news part of the newpaper; or some quality newspapers offer readers a mid-week 'serious' books page and a lighter one in the magazine on Saturday. Magazine books pages rather than broadsheet books pages in newspapers mean that reviews and reviewers have more space than they used to have, and designers have bigger and better opportunities for deploying large illustrations alongside reviews, some of which, even I have to admit, do work wonders. But the *Sunday Times* supplement, *Books*, to take but one example, seems to my elderly eyes – in spite of these spatial advantages – to lack the authority of Jack Lambert's books pages that were such an integral part of the main paper. By contrast *Books* is integral with the *Funday Times*, a comic for children, inserted in the middle of it. Yet if space is the name of the game – and for a lit ed it must be – this format does give additional scope for the kind of book-feature McLachlan was always urging me to include in my wretched page and a half; book-review sections now regularly include a page for paperbacks and children's books and several are embellished by diarist's gossip, featurettes about books treasured by the great and good, poems, bestseller lists and reviews of the other reviews.

If one were to measure the column inches devoted each week to book-reviews in national newspapers circulating in Britain at the present time, the total would, surely, surpass that for any previous period. And if I had to chose between publishing a novel in the 1930s and publishing one now, purely on grounds of it getting reviewed by someone likely to understand what I was trying to do, someone given adequate space to discuss it, I think I would chose the present time. The lit eds of my generation, now put out to grass, or the several who, sadly, are attending that last great launch party in the sky, must look enviously at the sheer amount of space the literary editors of today have at their disposal. Were they still alive, Lambert and Kilmartin could not, surely, conclude that *overall* standards have declined and would they not also have to concede that today's reviewers are on the whole a good deal less self-indulgent than their predecessors? The proliferation of university professors means that the reviewing-pool for lit eds to fish from is larger than ever before.

A new, diverse breed of reviewer has taken over from the omniscient reviewing clerisies and their star-performers. To be sure, one misses one's Sunday dialogue with Cyril Connolly the hedonist, Philip Toynbee the mystic, Nigel Dennis the wit, Rebecca West the literary diva, Anthony Burgess the musicologist and numerologist. There is no one at present I turn to with anything like the same eagerness; no one whose reviews provoke the same amount of controversy, of 'feedback', no one whose personality is stamped on his or her reviews in the way theirs was. Nowadays one tends to read a review because one is interested in the book rather than the reviewer.

But is that necessarily such a bad thing? The star has been replaced by the ensemble; it is a part of the same levelling process that has occurred in the theatre. The sons and daughters of Jim Rose's 'new men' and women are now in charge. They do not know Latin as their grandparents did, and if they quote in a foreign tongue, they are obliged to give an English translation in brackets. But they know infinitely more about American literature, about Latin American literature, about African literature and they know about sociology, feminism, filmography, cybernetics, linguistics, ethnology, ecology, disciplines of which their forebears were largely ignorant. They are less insular, less self-consciously bookish; indeed they are less well-read in the by-ways of literature, and even some of the highways, but not less well-informed in more worldly terms or less conscientious as reviewers.

Survivors belonging to the old guard are still around; like the Law and the Stage, reviewing is one of those professions where if you are lucky you can stay in work until you reach the grave and sometimes – if you are a prompt deliverer of copy – a week or two beyond it. Several elderly British reviewers of today belong to a transatlantic reviewing-network which includes the *TLS*, the *London Review of Books*, the *New Yorker* and the *New York Review of Books*; these journals are our most prestigious platforms of reviewing, where eminent academics may be found reviewing alongside ex-ambassadors, ex- and present MPs, museum directors, actors, poets, novelists, biographers. Each of these publications has its clerisy, its ethos; but they are not mutually exclusive; we now have an interchangeable reviewing community; the big boys and girls crop up here, there and everywhere. John Updike may be in the *New Yorker* one week and the *NYRB* the next, likewise George Steiner will be in the *New Yorker* one week and the *TLS* the week after. John Bayley seems to shuttle between the *TLS*, the *NYRB* and the *LRB* with a regularity that is breathtaking, and Frank Kermode and P. N. Furbank are almost as ubiquitous. In the same week Rosemary Dinnage will be fielding Melanie Klein in the US and Isak Dinesen in the UK. All four journals circulate widely on both sides of the water, and in order to know what is going on in the world of books, you need to read all four fairly regularly. This represents an investment of time and money that few of us are able to make.

Frank Kermode's review of Philip Roth's *Sabbath's Theater* in the *NYRB* of 16 November 1995 was headed 'Howl', after Ginsberg. 'It seems essential [wrote Kermode] to understand the seriousness of Roth's transgressive imaginings.' That is a professor of literature speaking; it is not a sentence that a Cyril Connolly or a Rebecca West could conceivably have written. To transgress is to go beyond defined or acceptable limits; in a biblical context it meant to sin (cf. the rebel angels, Adam, Eve, transgressors all) punishable by exclusion. Now it has become in reviewers' eyes the badge of inclusion. Kermode compares Roth's transgressive imaginings with those of Shakespeare in *King Lear*. In the same number of the

NYRB Joyce Carol Oates, a novelist on the faculty at Princeton, reviewed Susanna Moore's novel *In the Cut.* The last word in the title is argot for the female pudenda. The heroine works in a downtown bar, Pussy Cat, where all the waitresses are topless and one of them, Tabu, has mastered the knack of 'lifting paper money, from the bar-top, with her vagina'. '*In the Cut* [writes Joyce Carol Oates] is advertised by its publisher as an "erotic thriller" which seems harshly reductive for a work of serious literary ambition.'

In the plastic arts transgressive seriousness can still occasionally run into difficulties with the law, as in the case of the photographer Robert Mapplethorpe. The next review in this same issue of the *NYRB* (by Luc Sante) is of posthumous collections of Mapplethorpe's photographs and interpretive books on him. Sante referred to the notorious 'X Portfolio', printed on special red paper, 'so that, perhaps, cautious parents can tape them shut' and subject of legal proceedings in Cincinnati. He described the photographic study, 'Jim and Tom, Sausalito, 1977':

> a leather-hooded man urinating into the open mouth of another man, evokes for Danto [Arthur C. Danto, author of *Playing with the Edge: The Photographic Achievement of Robert Mapplethorpe*, University of California Press] the classical theme of 'Roman charity' (the daughter offering her breast to her shackled and starving father). It might more simply be said to refer to holy communion: the standing donor, half-extending his arm, stands over the supplicant who kneels and presents his upturned face, eyes reverently closed. The two are surrounded by darkness but streaked with a light that comes from above. Whatever one's visceral or acculturated reaction to the act depicted, there is no denying the picture conveys a hush, a powerfully concentrated peace that overrides the menace of the leather hood and the sordidness of the grimy bunker.

Transgressive seriousness is but one among many themes to be found in the on-going discourse of contemporary reviewing. Although the *NYRB* and *LRB* are at heart literary journals, without any regular section devoted to politics or current affairs, they do in practice use books (or at moments of international crisis they waive the requirement of a suitable book altogether) to publish pieces by reviewers like Timothy Garton Ash on eastern Europe, Misha Glenny on the former Soviet Union and the former Yugoslavia, Edward Said on Israel and the Palestinians. These articles often have the same topicality as straight reports in *Time* and *Newsweek* while being much more provocative and *engagé*. Nowhere in Britain has the Palestinians' case been put more forcefully than in the *London Review of Books*.

By contrast the *TLS* usually has to wait for the right book to come along before taking the plunge into the political arena. However, under its present editor Ferdinand Mount (a former political leader-writer and aide to Margaret Thatcher, as well as being a novelist and social historian) it has certainly not lost its power to generate controversy through its reviews and correspondence columns. At heart it still remains what it always was, 'an . . . organ of literary criticism' at a time when there are widely divergent and hotly debated views about the nature of the discipline known as literary criticism.

Stanley Fish's *Professional Correctness: Literary Studies and Political Change* and Terry Eagleton's review of it (*TLS*, 24 November 1995) defined the central issue. Fish sees literary work as 'a distinctive enterprise' and literary criticism as 'characterised by a limited set of concerns.' The attempt to change society lies outside these concerns. Fish has an old-fashioned respect for the author and he believes that such things as the author's intention, the tradition to which the work belongs, its historical occasion, all come into play in a reading of it. He gives us a demonstration of criticism in action by examining the following three words, 'Yet no more . . .' when penned by Milton at the opening of 'Lycidas'. It was a demonstration of the Happy Critic at work, sticking to his last, and it occupied much of the first of the lectures on which the book is based. The venue of the lecture was Oxford University, the university where Eagleton is Thomas Warton Professor of English. The invective with which he repudiated Fish's thesis reveals the deep divisions about the nature of the subject that currently exist among those who teach literary criticism at university level.

The critic, Eagleton claimed, has his right to a transgressive seriousness just as much as the artist. The activities that Fish wishes to exclude from the distinctive enterprise of criticism are put emphatically back in by Eagleton:

> In any case, he [Stanley Fish] fails to see that political criticism is
> not something opposed to literary criticism but a particular species
> of it, not something different from literary criticism but a different
> kind of literary criticism. He does not see either that all literary
> criticism is a specific kind of literary criticism, that there is no

Platonic Form of literary criticism to be contrasted with its political, semiotic, philological and other varieties. And he does not recognize that political criticism may – must – be read as closely as the style of analysis he himself prefers.

Certainly, as I hope I have demonstrated, there is no Platonic Form of literary editing either. The job is what each individual makes of it, within the limits imposed on him or her by the scope and aims of the publication he or she serves. When I look around now at all the journals that run books pages, each of them employing a lit ed, I wonder whether we might not begin to think of it not merely as a job in journalism but as a profession.

For someone of a bookish turn of mind who is prepared to put up with, indeed positively enjoy, the hurly-burly of newspaper journalism, it is a profession I would recommend entering. I found the role of working with a clerisy of reviewers I nursed a rewarding one. If there were many intensely frustrating moments, there were very few dull ones. Sir William Haley was right. As the lit ed you have to create the occasion for lively reviews even when the material for them is hard to seek, and that was a task I found most enjoyable. If I was frequently to be heard grumbling about the poverty of the books on offer from the publishers, viewing my time in retrospect it seems to have been a period of some importance for literature, when the novel on both sides of the water renewed itself after the heroic age of modernism; when the art of biography gained exciting new territory and when contemporary poetry underwent a quiet revolution, with many significant new voices making themselves heard. I was privileged to have a job that enabled me to observe and participate in all this; to continue after leaving university to work on what meant most of all to me – literature. If I did not succeed in living by it, I did succeed in living off it. And if the reader is inclined to think that that is an easy option, may I, with the greatest respect, suggest he or she try it some time?

Notes

(Place of publication of all books mentioned is London unless otherwise stated).

1 Journalist and literary man

7 Worsthorne: see Peregrine Worsthorne, *Tricks of Memory* 1993.

9 Halifax: *The Life of Lord Halifax* by the Earl of Birkenhead, serialised in the *Sunday Telegraph*, 4–18 July 1965; Attlee's review, 'Lord Halifax as I Judge Him' appeared on 25 July. It began: 'In *Halifax* the Earl of Birkenhead gives us a long, perhaps excessively long, biography of a very curious character . . .' and it went on to make the point that 'you will not find in this book any reference to any social problem.'

13 Frederic Warburg, *An Occupation for Gentleman*, 1959; also *All authors are equal: the publishing life of Frederic Warburg 1936–71*, 1973.

13 VG to AC, 5 June 1963, author's collection.

14 LW to AC, nd, author's collection.

2 'Because we are too many . . .'

16 Eliot's review, *Monthly Criterion*, June 1927, p. 359.

17 Dick Francis review by C. P. Snow, *FT*, 19 July 1973; *Bookseller*, 4 August 1973. 'Mr Francis is wonderfully good.'

3 Star wanted

26 *Diary of Philip Henslowe*, edited by R. A. Foakes and R. T. Rickert, Cambridge, 1961, reviewed in the *Sunday Telegraph*, 2 April 1961.

28   Nigel Dennis's review of *New Maps of Hell*, *Sunday Telegraph*, 12 February 1961.

33   Nigel Dennis's review of *The Complete Ronald Firbank* and *Ronald Firbank: Valmouth and other Stories*, *Sunday Telegraph*, 30 April 1960.

34   Theodora Bosanquet (1880–1961), literary editor of *Time and Tide* from 1935 to 1958, and author of *Henry James at Work*, 1924.

34   Phyllis Bottome (1884–1963), *Alfred Adler Apostle of Freedom*, 1939.

34   Nigel Dennis, *Jonathan Swift: A Short Character*, New York, 1964 (UK, 1965), p. 32.

35   Wilson told Nabokov: see *The Nabokov-Wilson Letters 1940–1971*, edited by Simon Karlinsky, 1979, p. 38.

35   James Stern: see *The Hidden Damage: A Personal Pilgrimage with W. H. Auden to Post-War Germany 1945* (New York, 1947; London, 1990).

36   Whittaker Chambers; *Witness*, New York, 1953.

37   Dennis reviewed Emlyn Williams's book on the Moors murders, *Beyond Belief* in the *Sunday Telegraph*, 4 June 1967. Taking its cue from Williams's earlier autobiography, the review took the form of a letter to Williams from his grandmother. It began: 'My darling little George ... ' and sustained, in this burlesque voice, a withering demolition of the book.

37   *The Letters of Oscar Wilde*, edited by Rupert Hart-Davis, 1962. Dennis's review, 'At last we can sum up Wilde', appeared in the *Sunday Telegraph* on 24 June 1962, after selections from the letters had been running in the paper for the previous three weeks. Dennis began: 'In only one respect do *The Letters of Oscar Wilde* fall short. They do not explain why 62 years after Wilde's death nearly 1000 pages of them should have deserved to be the object of eight years editorial labour.'

37   Mary McCarthy's review of Tynan's *Curtains*, in the *Observer*, 22 October 1961. Alan Pryce-Jones wrote the second review. See *The Life of Kenneth Tynan* by Kathleen Tynan, 1987, p. 183ff.

4   Enter the Dame

40   Anthony West, *Heritage*, New York, 1955 and *H. G. Wells: aspects of a life*, 1984.

40   'I don't think anybody...': Rebecca West interviewed by AC, BBC Radio 3, on her 80th birthday; extracts printed in the *Listener*, 15 February 1973,' Dame Rebecca West talks to Anthony Curtis about social improvements and literary disasters'.

41   'I have had an unpleasing...' RW to AC, 4 December 1961, author's collection.

42   'There was acre after acre...': *Listener*, 15 February 1973.

42   'I gave evidence...': ibid.

43   'I think first-rate editors...' ibid.

43   *The New Humpty Dumpty*, *English Review*, September 1912; see *Ford Madox Ford: The Critical Heritage*, ed. Frank MacShane, 1972, p. 40.

43 Violet Hunt (1866–1942), novelist, feminist and for many years mistress of Ford Madox Ford.

43 *Marriage* review, *The Freewoman*, 19 September 1912

44 Vassall tribunal, *The Vassall Affair* by Rebecca West (a *Sunday Telegraph* pamphlet), 1963.

44 'He gave you ten ideas . . .': RW to AC in conversation.

45 'I am worried . . .': RW to AC, 3 February 1961, author's collection.

45 'I have been looking . . .': RW to AC, pc nd, author's collection.

46 'I have known Charlie . . .' RW to AC, pc nd, author's collection.

46 'I really could not bear . . .': RW to AC, 20 September 1961, author's collection.

46 'If we *must* have a religion . . .' Nigel Dennis, *Two Plays and a Preface*, 1958, p. 53.

47 Father Matthew Prior: see Victoria Glendinning, *Rebecca West A Life*, 1987, p. 144. Prior was a Jesuit friend of RW's mother and an authority on St Augustine.

47 Rebecca West, *The Court and the Castle: A Study of the Interactions of Political and Religious Ideas in Imaginative Literature*, 1958.

48 *Ulysses*: the first Paris edition was in 1922; there were various Paris editions throughout the 1920s; copies were frequently smuggled into England, the first English edition appearing in 1936.

48 I. P. Pavlov, *Conditioned Reflexes*, translated and edited by G. V. Anrep, 1927.

49 'All our youth . . .': 'Uncle Bennett' in Rebecca West, *The Strange Necessity: Essays and Reviews*, 1928 (reprinted Virago, 1987).

50 'the thing is a lie . . .': Gordon N. Ray, *H. G. Wells and Rebecca West* 1974, p. 177.

50 'After weeks of dreariness . . .': RW to AC, April 1964, author's collection.

51 Invitation to lunch with Trillings: RW to AC, February 1965, author's collection.

51 Diana and Lionel Trilling: see also Chapter 11.

51 'The world's worst driver . . .': Merlyn Holland to AC, May 1995.

51 The Warren Commission Report on the assasination of President Kennedy, 1965.

52 'I do intensely . . .': *Listener*, 15 February 1973.

52 'I wrote novels . . .': ibid.

5 From Greene to Snow

54 James Pope Hennessy, *Robert Louis Stevenson*, reviewed by Graham Greene in the *Observer*, 10 November 1974. He attacked the book for perpetuating the romantic myth of RLS and neglecting to re-assess the work. 'It is difficult indeed to understand why this biography was written at all.'

54   'I am afraid . . .': GG to AC, 10 April 1961, author's collection.

56   'Return to Cuba', *Sunday Telegraph*, 22 September 1963.

56   'Nightmare Republic', *Sunday Telegraph*, 29 September 1963.

56   'I am sorry to say . . .': EW to AC, 4 July 1962, author's collection, in *The Letters of Evelyn Waugh* edited by Mark Amory, 1980, p. 558. Firbank, *The New Rhythum and other pieces*, 1962.

56   Mitford review in the *Sunday Telegraph*, 28 April 1963, of *The Sphinx and Her Circle: A Memoir of Ada Leverson* by her daughter, Violet Wyndham, 1963.

57   'Sorry, but I've written . . .'; CSL to AC, 7 December 1962, author's collection.

57   'How are you, Jack?' Dyson to AC. H. V. D. Dyson (1896–1975) was a Fellow and Tutor in English of Merton College from 1945 and a member of the Inklings.

57   'While I appreciate . . .' TSE to AC, 18 September 1963, author's collection.

58   TSE review, 'Language of New English Bible', *Sunday Telegraph*, 16 December 1962.

58   'Thanks very much, but what I thought from . . .': WE to AC, 1 October 1962, author's collection. Vladimir Nabokov, *Pale Fire*, 1962.

58   'Thank you for your letter but I mustn't let myself . . .': FRL to AC, 18 September 1964, author's collection.

58   'I'm afraid it would not be possible . . .': Harold Wilson (Baron Wilson of Rievaulx) to AC, 22 March 1963, author's collection.

59   'I was very interested . . .': Harold Macmillan to AC, 1 June 1965, author's collection. 'Macmillans on the Move' by AC, *Sunday Telegraph*, 6 June 1965.

61   Crossman review of Brian Gardner's *The Wasted Hour: The Tragedy of 1945*, in the *Sunday Telegraph*, 17 November 1963.

62   'Bob Ardrey's plays . . .': Michael Redgrave to AC, 21 June 1968, author's collection.

62   (Sir) Donald Wolfit (1902–1968) review of *Macready* by Alan Downer, *Sunday Telegraph*, 25 June 1967; holograph Garrick Club library.

64   Alan Hodge and Robert Graves, *The Long Weekend, a social history of Great Britain, 1918–1939*, 1940, and *The Reader Over Your Shoulder: a handbook for writers of English prose*, 1943.

64   Peter Quennell's review of Boswell, *The Applause of the Jury 1782–85* edited by I. S. Lustig and F. A. Pottle [Yale editions of the Boswell Private Papers], 1982. 'Bozzy in a tizzy or two', *FT*, 20 March 1982.

66   'I was particularly interested . . .': PQ to AC, 7 April 1984, author's collection.

66   William Cooper, *Scenes From Provincial Life*, 1959.

68   'I should have loved . . .': CPS to AC, 14 January 1966, author's collection.

68   'May I brood . . .': CPS to AC, 28 October 1969, author's collection.

69   Lord Drogheda: see his *Double Harness: Memoirs*, 1978.

69   Harold Acton, *More Memoirs of An Aesthete*, 1970; Snow's review in, *FT*, 23 April 1970. 'He feels more than his fair share of social guilt'.
70   'rugged moralist...': FRL to OU English Club, 1949.
71   Stephen Spender, *World Within World*, 1951; Roy Harrod, *The Life of John Maynard Keynes*, 1951.
71   R. G. Cox, 'The Great Reviews', in two parts, *Scrutiny*, Vol. VI, 1937; reprinted in *A Selection from Scrutiny* compiled by F. R. Leavis, Vol. 2, (Cambridge, 1968), p. 241ff.
74   'I shall be most grateful...': CPS to AC, author's collection.
74   C. P. Snow, 'The Case of Leavis and the Serious Case', *TLS*, 9 July 1970.

6 Jim and Terry

75   J. L. Garvin: see David Ayerst, *Garvin of the Observer*, 1985.
77   E. J. B. Rose, conversation with AC, 18 January 1994.
80   Sir Allen Lane (Lane Williams), 1902–70, founder and chairman of Penguin Books and other publishing imprints.
81   Orwell on Leavis's *The Great Tradition*, *Observer*, 23 January 1947.
82   Orwell, 'Confessions of a Book Reviewer', *The Penguin Essays of George Orwell*, 1984, p. 375.
82   Harold Nicolson: see the biography in two volumes by James Lees-Milne, 1980 and 1981.
82   'In 1949, without informing his father, Nicolson's son...'. Nigel Nicolson to AC, 8 September 1994.
83   HN on Leigh Hunt, *Observer*, 13 March 1949.
83   HN, *Observer* reviews in 1949: Fulford, 20 March; Weizmann, 27 March; Gooch, 13 April; Alun Lewis, 17 April; Bloch, 27 April; Ruskin, 15 May.
83   'At home in half-a-dozen...': Nigel Nicolson's introduction to *Harold Nicolson Diaries*, New and Condensed Edition, 1980, p. 8.
84   HN's early books: *Paul Verlaine*, 1921; *Tennyson*, 1923; *Byron*, 1924; *Swinburne* (English Men of Letters series), 1926.
84   'He was a scrupulously fair critic...': Lees-Milne, *ibid*, Vol 2 p. 295.
85   'an Englishman overlaid...': Virginia Woolf, 4 July 1927, *The Diary of Virginia Woolf* (1980), vol. 3, p. 145.
85   Edwin Muir: see *An Autobiography*, 1954 (earlier version, *The Story and the Fable*, 1940); *First Poems*, 1925.
87   Muir *Observer* reviews in 1952: Leavis, 20 January; Gogol, 24 January; Hugh Walpole, 2 March; Malraux, 20 April; *Hemlock and After*, 13 July.
88   Terence Kilmartin: see Philip French, 'A Literary Life', *Observer*, 28 December 1986.
88   Other reviewing talents in the *Observer*, in 1952: Auden, 6 January; Isherwood, 27 January ('Back to Berlin', 23 March); Mann, 23

February; Angus Wilson on Edmund Wilson, 9 March; Raine, 23
March; Greene, 31 August.

89 'Why do I . . .': John Osborne, *Look Back in Anger*, 1957, p. 10ff.
89 'his mind was exercised . . .': Anthony Sampson to AC, December
    1995.
90 *Friends Apart: A Memoir of Esmond Romilly and Jasper Ridley in The
    Thirties*, 1954 (reprinted 1980).
90 Philip Toynbee: *Tea With Mrs Goodman* (1947); *Pantaloon* (1961); *Two
    Brothers: The Fifth Day of the Valediction of Pantaloon* (1964); *Part of a
    Journey: An Autobiographical Journal 1977–1979* (1981); *End of A
    Journey: An Autobiographical Journal 1979–81* (1988).
91 'out of the pulpit': Polly Toynbee to AC, 24 February 1994.
91 Nicolson reviews in the *Observer* in 1960: Grousset, *Chinese Art and
    Culture*, 3 January; Moers, *The Dandy*, 28 February; Hilles ed. *New
    Light on Dr Johnson*, 6 March; Gide, *Pretexts*, 13 March; Gilbert Murray,
    Unfinished Autobiography, 20 March; Sprigge, *The Berenson Story*, 27
    March; Stanley Unwin, *The Truth About a Publisher*, 3 April.
92 Nicolson on Margery Ross (ed.) *Robert Ross: Friend of Friends, Observer*,
    6 April 1952; Violet Trefusis, *Don't Look Round, Observer*, 9 November
    1952.
92 Nigel Nicolson's *Portrait of a Marriage* 1973 contains Vita's diary of
    her love-affair with Violet.
92 Toynbee, Camus obituary, *Observer*, 10 January 1960.
92 Toynbee, *Observer* reviews in 1960: R. W. B. Lewis, *The Picaresque Saint*,
    17 January; *X and NLR*, 24 January; Hansen, *My Poor Arthur*, 31
    January; Durrell, *Clea*, 7 February.
93 Durrell profile, *Observer*, 28 February 1960.
93 Toynbee on Green's *Doting, Observer*, 27 April 1952; on Beckett's
    Molloy, 18 December 1955.
93 'Re-reading yesterday's review . . .': 10 October 1977, *Part of a Journey*,
    p. 51.
94 'Moral problems . . .': 23 August 1977, ibid, p. 26ff.
95 For Taylor's early life and journalism, see Adam Sisman, *A J. P.
    Taylor, a biography*, 1993.
96 A. P. Wadsworth was editor of the *Manchester Guardian* 1944–56.
96 Taylor, Kilmartin and Beaverbrook: see Sisman, *op cit*, p. 255ff and
    Anne Chisholm and Michael Davie, *Beaverbrook A Life*, 1992, p. 501ff.
96 A. J. P. Taylor, *From Napoleon to Stalin*, 1950; *The Origins of the Second
    World War*, 1961.
96 Taylor *Observer* reviews in 1960: Lewis, *Jolly Jack Tar: A Social History of
    the Navy 1793–1815*, 24 January; Pakenham, *The Jameson Raid*, 31
    January; De Gaulle, *Mémoires de Guerre: le Salut 1944–46*, 5 February;
    The Fall of Parnell, 6 March; *The House Built on Sand – German Policy to
    Russia*, 13 March; Lord Derby, 10 April; Minney, *The Private Papers of
    Hore Belisha*, 24 April.
97 'the wonder grew . . .': Goldsmith, *the Deserted Village* 1770, I. 215.

98   A. Alvarez, *The Shaping Spirit*, 1958.
99   Alvarez, review of *Honour'd Shade*, *Observer*, 10 January 1960; G. S. Fraser, letter, *Observer* 17 January 1960.
99   Alvarez on Edith Sitwell, *Collected Poems*, *Observer*, 28 July 1957, reprinted in *Beyond All This Fiddle* (1968), p. 69: 'I have always found it difficult to know what all the fuss was about.' Connolly had acclaimed the Sitwell volume in the *Sunday Times*. Philip Toynbee told Alvarez: 'I know which side I'm on!' (Alvarez to AC, September 1997).
100 Alvarez on Pound, *Thrones . . .*, *Observer*, 6 March 1950.
100 Karl Miller on Snow's *The Affair*, *Observer*, 10 April 1950.
100 John Davenport on Dennis's *Cards of Identity*, *Observer*, 30 January 1955.
100 Toynbee on *Cards of Identity*, Books of the Year, *Observer*, 18 December 1955.
100 Marghanita Laski on *Women at Oxford, Observer*, 24 January 1960; *This Is my God, Observer*, 28 February 1954.
100 Kathleen Nott, *The Emperor's Clothes*, 1954.
101 Beatles article: David Astor to AC, August 1995.
102 Terry and Angus as colleagues: see Margaret Drabble, *Angus Wilson a biography* 1994.

7   Leonard and Jack

105 *The Saturday Book*, founded in 1941 by Leonard Russell and edited by him until 1951.
105 *Parody Party*, 1936; *Press Gang*, 1937; *English Wits*, 1940, all edited by LR.
105 'Where Engels Fears To Tread' in *Parody Party*, reprinted in *The Condemned Playground: Essays 1927–1944*, 1945.
106 Harold Hobson, Philip Knightley and Leonard Russell, *The Pearl of Days: An Intimate Memoir of The Sunday Times*, 1972.
106 'He had no duties . . .': *Pearl of Days*, p. 185ff.
106 'Russell explained . . .': ibid., p. 187.
107 'Rees [felt] rightly . . .': ibid., p. 151.
107 *Books on the Table*, 1921. Heywood's 'The Hierarchie of (Blessed) Angels', p. 47; 'Wine & Mr Saintsbury', p. 193.
109 'For a good many years . . .' *Pearl of Days*, p. 114.
109 'Russell didn't particularly . . .': ibid., p. 199.
110 'On Friday afternoons . . .' ibid., p. 221.
111 'How terrible about Desmond . . .': CC to J. W. Lambert, nd [June 1952], J. W. Lambert Archive, Bodleian Library (henceforward JLA).
112 Serialised books: Somerset Maugham, *Ten Novels and Their Authors*, 1954; Montgomery of Alamein, *Memoirs*,1958; Joy Adamson, *Living*

Free: the story of Elsa and her cubs, 1961, and *Forever Free: Elsa's Pride*, 1962; William Manchester, *Portrait of a President*, 1962 and *Death of a President November 20–25 1963*, 1967.

112   John Pearson, *The Life of Ian Fleming, creator of James Bond*, 1966.

113   'My wife and I . . .' *Selected Letters of Raymond Chandler*, edited by Frank MacShane, 1981, p. 321.

113   J. W. Lambert, youth and early career, Catherine Lambert to AC, May 1995.

114   *The Cadet-Ratings' Farewell* by Nelson Division, HMS. King Alfred (L), Words by C/R J. W. Lambert, Lancing, 4 December 1941. JLA.

114   Katina Paxinou played Jocasta and Hecuba in the London World Theatre Season, prompting JWL's article 'The Lady From the Sea', *Sunday Times*,10 April 1966.

115   Agatha Christie's letter of thanks. JLA.

116   Estoril: pc, nd. CC to JWL, JLA.

117   'Weather good . . .': CC to JWL, JLA.

117   'Greece is . . .': CC to JWL, JLA.

117   Whites, Monday: CC to JWL, JLA.

117   CC's seventieth birthday, letters, JLA.

117   Lambert tribute to CC, *Encounter*, May 1975.

117   S-B's career: see A. G. Lehmann, *Sainte-Beuve: a Portrait of a Critic 1804–42*, Oxford, 1962.

118   'A man who has read . . .': Harold Nicolson, *Sainte-Beuve*, 1957, p. 218.

120   'Chamfort detested humanity . . .': *The Unquiet Grave: a word cycle by Palinurus*, 1944, revised edition with an introduction by Cyril Connolly, 1951, p. 218 (of the 1973 edn).

120   Connolly's review of Nicolson's Sainte-Beuve, *Sunday Times*, 9 June 1957.

121   'a curious amalgam . . .': *By Way of Sainte-Beuve*, 1954, p. 2.

8   Printing House Square

124   N. B. C. Lucas: see his *An Experience of Teaching*, 1975.

124   T. H. Aston: see Kenneth Dover, 'The Aston Affair 1980–85', *Marginal Comment*, 1994, p. 222ff. .

125   Edmund Blunden: see Barry Webb, *Edmund Blunden. A Biography*, New Haven, 1990, p. 239ff.

125   L. H. Rice-Oxley: see Theresa Whistler, *Imagination of the Heart: The life of Walter de la Mare*, 1993. R-O. had first come to know the poet as an Oxford friend of his son, Richard.

126   C. S. Lewis, *A Preface to Paradise Lost*, based on lectures delivered at University College, South Wales, was published in 1942, and much discussed in Oxford at this time.

127   'Mathew was a printer by trade . . .': see Oliver Woods and James

Bishop, *The Story of The Times: Bicentenary Edition 1785–1985*, 1985, p. 328.

127   Fr Gervase Mathew (1905–76), Dominican monk and Oxford Byzantinist, who lectured in the university on various subjects including England in the fourteenth century.

129   (A) Patrick Ryan, 1900–72, assistant editor of *The Times* from 1948 to 1965. He also had the title of literary editor until 1968.

129   Michael Swan, *A Small Part of Time. Essays on Literature, Art and Travel*, 1957.

129   'Oliver Edwards' (Sir William Haley), *Talking of Books*, 1957.

134   'God from a cloud . . .': *The Letters of T. S. Eliot Volume 1 1898–1922* edited by Valerie Eliot, 1988, p. 345.

134   'He was amazingly fluent.' Alan Pryce-Jones, *The Bonus of Laughter*, 1987, p. 56.

135   AP-J on Ionesco, *TLS* leader 'Fresh Fantasies', 31 December 1954; *Observer* 17 January 1960, on *The Rhinosceros*.

138   Charles Morgan (1894–1958) was dramatic critic of *The Times* from 1926 to 1939. See Chapter 9 for his writing as 'Menander' during the war for the *Lit Supp*.

9   Richmond's realm

140   For the origins of the *TLS*, see 50th Anniversary article, 15 January 1952. Harold Child was the anonymous author.

141   Moberly Bell: see *The Life and Letters of C. F. Moberly Bell* by his daughter, E. H. C. Moberly Bell, 1927. 'Well the scheme . . .', p. 251; and see F. Harcourt Kitchen, *Moberly Bell and His Times: An Unofficial Narrative*, 1925.

144   'my old Winchester friend Bruce Richmond': see Harold Child, *A Poor Player: The Story of a Failure*, Cambridge, 1939, p. 47.

145   'our literary copy boy . . .': Heren to AC, March 1994.

146   'There is still . . .': T. S. Eliot, 'Bruce Lyttelton Richmond', *TLS*, 13 January 1961.

146   'I am firmly convinced . . .' ibid.

147   'I am realising . . .': *The Letters of Virginia Woolf Volume 1, 1891–1912* edited by Nigel Nicolson and Joanne Trautman, 1975, p. 180

147   Review of Howell's *The Son of Royal Langbirth* by VW, *Guardian*, 14 December 1904; reprinted in *The Essays of Virginia Woolf Volume 1 1904–1912*, edited by Andrew McNeillie, 1986.

148   'Don't you think . . .': *Letters*, I, p. 317.

148   'Well, going through it again . . .': ibid.

149   'Nay, my dear Miss Stephen . . .' and 'I really believe . . .': ibid., p. 327.

149   VW reviews of *Letters from Catalonia* etc. are all re-printed by McNeillie, *op. cit.*, to whose notes I am much indebted.

150   'She gives us . . .': *Essays*, I, p. 68.
150   'My dismissal is revoked.' The *Diary of Virginia Woolf, Vol. 1 1915–1919*, edited by Anne Olivier Bell, 1977, p. 128.
151   'St Loe was . . .': James Strachey, Preface to *Spectatorial Essays* by Lytton Strachey, 1964, p. 9.
152   'Bacon discusses' . . .: ibid., p. 83. 'Bacon as A Man of Letters', *Spectator*, 24 October 1908.
153   'Not one of us . . .': Clive Bell, *Pot-Boilers*, 1918, p. 5.
153   'He gives . . .': *Diary*, 1, p. 151.
154   'In my judgement . . .': Bell, *op. cit.*, p. 11.
154   Review of Solomon Eagle, *Books in General, TLS*, 21 November 1918.
155   'A book in the best of taste . . .': quoted by Michael Holroyd in *Lytton Strachey: A Critical Biography Volume 1: The Unknown Years*, 1967, p. 259.
155   'His book comes out . . .' and 'I couldn't promise. . . .': VW, *Diary* 1, p. 138.
155   'I wrote to ask . . .': VW, *Letters*, II, p. 223.
156   Gosse letter, *TLS*, 27 June 1918.
156   Strachey reply, *TLS*, 4 July 1918.
157   Sanderson letter, *TLS*, 18 July, 1918.
157   Mary [Mrs Humphry] Ward letter, *TLS*, 11 July 1918.
158   'Unlike George Eliot, who had returned the two volumes . . .': Henry James, *The Middle Years* 1917, p. 82 ('Ah those books – take them away, please, away, away!').
158   'We feel it . . .': *TLS*, 19 March 1914, expanded as 'The New Novel' in *Notes on Novelists*, 1914, the last of James's four collections of literary criticsm.
159   'So far . . .': Wells lecture, reprinted in *An Englishman Looks at the World*, 1914, as 'The Contemporary Novel'.
159   'Nearly all the novels . . .': ibid.
159   'Driven by curiosity . . .': Arnold Bennett, first in *New Age*, 25 May 1911, then in *Books and Persons*,1917, p. 315.
160   *Spectator* on *Ann Veronica*: 'A Poisonous Book', 20 November 1909.
160   'what are we to say of Mr Wells . . .': *TLS*, 2 April 1914.
161   For the 'pacifist effort' see Caroline Moorehead, *Troublesome People Enemies of War 1916–1986*, 1987.
161   'The first sense . . .': *Fortnightly Review*, August 1917; reprinted, *Within the Rim*, 1918.
161   'I do hope . . .': *Boon*, 1915.
163   For the *New Age* see John Carswell, *Lives and Letters: A. R. Orage, Katherine Mansfield, Beatrice Hastings, J. Middleton Murry, S. S. Kotelian-sky 1906–1957*, 1978.
163   Leeds Art Club: see Carswell, p. 23ff.
165   Bennett was regular book critic on the *Evening Standard* from November 1926 until his death in March 1931; see Drabble, p. 313ff.
165   Ford, who had edited the *English Review* since it started in 1908, was

replaced as editor in February 1910 by Austin Harrison. *The New Machiavelli* ran there serially from May to November 1910, and was published as a book in 1911.

165 'Astounding width . . .' Bennett, *Books and Persons*, p. 297.
166 'It is art . . .': see *Henry James & H. G. Wells: A Record of their Friendship, their Debate on the Art of Fiction and their Quarrel*, edited with an introduction by Leon Edel and Gordon N. Ray, 1958.
166 'what the public square': see Elfrida Vipont, *Arnold Rowntree: A Life* 1955, p. 33.
167 Middleton Murry: see F. A. Lea, *The Life of John Middleton Murry*, 1959.
168 'This collection . . .' *Rhythm*, March 1913.
168 Murry and Mansfield: see *Katherine Mansfield: The Memories of L.M.* (Ida Baker), 1971; Anthony Alpers, *The Life of Katherine Mansfield*, 1980; Jeffrey Meyers, *Katherine Mansfield: A Biography*, 1978; Claire Tomalin, *Katherine Mansfield A Secret Life*, 1987.
169 'She looks ghastly ill . . .': VW, *Diary I*, I, p. 150.
170 'A Soldier's Declaration': Stanley Jackson, *The Sassoons: Portrait of a Dynasty*, 1968, p. 164; Jon Stallworthy, *Wilfrid Owen: A Biography*, 1974, p. 206.
171 Murry, 'The Sign-Seekers': reprinted in *Evolution of an Inellectual*, 1920, pp. 1ff. 'We are conscious . . .' and 'I mumbled . . .', ibid.
171 Bennett, 'On Writing Novels', *op. cit.*
172 'Mr Sassoon's verses . . .': *Nation*, 13 July 1918, reprinted in *Evolution*, p. 70ff; 'a gallant and distinguished author' and Philalethes (Russell) letter, *Nation*, 20 July 1918; Sassoon on Murry, Ottoline Morrell, *Memoirs*; Mansfield to VW, 23 July 1918; these reactions to Murry's review quoted by Alpers, *op. cit.*, pp. 282ff and 443ff.
173 'Success has . . .': VW, *Diary I*, p. 257.
174 'doesn't one . . .': *Athenaeum*, 9 July 1920.
175 'love to linger . . .' and 'it is true . . .': *Athenaeum*, 21 November, 1919; reprinted in *Virginia Woolf: The Critical Heritage*, 1975, p. 80.
176 'A decorous elderly dullard . . .': VW, *Diary I*, p. 314.
176 'The truth is . . .': VW, *Diary*, ibid.
176 'Today the reviewers . . .' and 'Oh the relief': VW, *Diary*, V, p. 61ff.
176 'I am in such a twitter . . .': *ibid.*, p. 67.
177 'Now this is one of the strangest . . .': ibid., p. 70.
178 VW, *Reviewing*, published 2 November 1939 in the Hogarth Sixpenny Pamphlets with a Note by LW, reprinted in *The Captain's Death Bed*, 1950.
179 'a short, slim, elegant man . . .': Rupert Hart-Davis, *The Power of Chance*, 1991, p. 75.
180 'Mr T. S. Eliot's Confession': *TLS*, 14 September 1940, reprinted in *The Modern Movement TLS. Companion*, edited by John Gross, 1992, p. 80.

180   Leavis letter: *TLS*, 21 September 1940, reprinted in *F. R. Leavis: Letters in Criticism*, 1974.
180   Charles Morgan, see *Reflections in a Mirror*, 1944.
181   'I hear . . .' [Murray reported sacked]: Arthur Crook to AC, 26 April 1995.
181   Stanley Morison's, six-point memorandum: see Nicolas Barker, *Stanley Morison*, 1972; SM on Carr, NB to AC, July 1995.
182   'it is clear . . .': *TLS*, 10 June 1949.
183   Labedz on Carr: *TLS*, 10 June 1983; reprinted in *Communism TLS. Companion*, edited by Ferdinand Mount, 1992, p. 189.
185   MacDiarmid review: *TLS*, 31 December 1964 and letter, 21 January 1965.

10   Cuthbert, Janet and John

186   'The *New Statesman* was started by the Webbs . . .': main sources are 'Early Days' by Clifford Sharp, *NS*, 14 April 1934 (the 21st birthday number); *The Diary of Beatrice Webb Volume Three: 1905–1924, The Power to Alter Things*, edited by Norman and Jeanne MacKenzie, 1984, p. 183ff; Edward Hyams, *New Statesman: The History of the Fifty Years 1913–1963*, 1953, and Adrian Smith, *The New Statesman: Portrait of A Political Weekly 1913–1931*, 1996, a scholarly account of the power struggles on the periodical until Kingsley Martin took over.
187   'Of course to some extent I was a fish out of water . . .': MacCarthy, 'What the New Statesman Has Meant To Me', *NS*, 14 April 1934.
188   'You know . . .': Bernard Shaw, *Collected Letters*, vol. 3, edited by Dan H. Laurence, p. 178.
188   'Clifford Sharp possessed . . .': MacCarthy, ibid.
189   Bland *ménage*, see Julia Briggs, *A Woman of Passion: The Life of E. Nesbit 1858–1924*, 1987.
189   Bland on A. C. Benson; *NS*, 18 October 1913.
189   Gould review of Conrad: *NS*, 31 March 1917.
190   'Recent Verse' (Pound) review; *NS*, 6 January 1917.
190   'Reflections on *Vers Libre*' by T. S. Eliot: *NS*, 3 March 1917 – 'the so-called *vers libres* which is good is anything but free.'
191   'The Awakening of Women' supplement: *NS*, 1st November 1913; 'Women in Industry' supplement: *NS*, 21 February 1914.
191   GBS on *Caesar and Cleopatra*: *NS* 3 May 1913; on Almroth E. Wright: *NS*, 18 October 1913.
192   'The notion of the supposed intellectual inferiority of women . . .': Affable Hawk made Arnold Bennett's book *Our Women* the subject for a 'Books in General' (*NS*, October 1920) in which MacCarthy agreed with Bennett that women 'are inferior to men in intellectual power, especially in that power which is described as creative'. It prompted a withering response from VW the following week (*NS*, 9

October 1920) and another one replying to his reply the week after (*NS*, 16 October 1920). Finally Ethel Smyth joined in on women and music (*NS*, 30 October 1920).

192   'Had Zimri . . .': editorial, *NS*, 9 December 1916.

192   'Common Sense About The War': 'On 14 November [1914] it appeared as a monumental supplement to the *New Statesman*', Michael Holroyd, *Bernard Shaw 2: The Pursuit of Power*, 1989, p. 349.

193   'He and Woolf had a harsh argument . . .': see exchange of letters, September 1923, between Henderson and Woolf in the Henderson papers, Box 21, Nuffield College Library, Oxford.

193   MacCarthy as Affable Hawk on Beerbohm: *NS*, 7 October 1922; on *The Criterion*, *NS*, 4 November 1922.

194   'They steal each other's reviewers . . .': VW, *Diary*, II, p. 252.

194   Mortimer's review of *The Dove's Nest*,: *NS*, 7 July 1923.

194   Quennell's review of *Rossetti*: *NS*, 12 May 1928.

195   Edward Sackville-West: see Michael De-la-Noy, *Eddy The Life of Edward Sackville-West*, 1988.

195   Connolly on MacCarthy: see *A Romantic Friendship: The Letters of Cyril Connolly to Noel Blakiston*, 1975, p. 161 ff.

196   Morand: although Connolly told Blakiston how pleased MacCarthy was with a review he had written of a book by Paul Morand (12 August 1926, *op. cit.* p. 162), no trace of it can be found in the files of the *NS*. Connolly's first *NS* review, of the works of Sterne, was on 25 June 1927.

196   A. E. Housman article and follow-up: reprinted in *The Condemned Playground, Essays 1927–1944*, 1945, p. 47ff.

196   'What we meant . . .': 'The Twenties', *The Evening Colonnade*, 1973, p. 23.

197   *A Family of Friends*: review in the *Sunday Times*, 1960; reprinted in *The Evening Colonnade*, p. 43.

197   'Desmond has offered . . .': CC to Blakiston, *op. cit.*, p. 299.

198   'The reviewing of novels . . .': ibid., p. 90.

198   'knew that they had been "had" . . .' *Enemies of Promise*, 1938; new edition 1948, p. 42.

199   *The Village*, I, 63; *Enemies*, p. 85.

199   'A writer . . .': ibid., p. 91.

200   'a fat soft cooing priest': see V. S. Pritchett, *Midnight Oil*, 1971, p. 192.

200   *NS* merger with *Nation*, see D. E. Moggridge, *Maynard Keynes: An Economist's Biography* 1992, p. 508 ff.

201   Kingsley Martin: see C. H. Rolph, *Kingsley: The Life, Letters & Diaries of Kingsley Martin*, 1973, and Martin's own *Father Figures, a first volume of autobiography 1897–1931*, 1966, and *Editor, a second volume of autobiography 1931–45*, 1968.

201   Harold Nicolson rejects offer: see H. N. *Diary*, 19 October 1932.

202   *Lady into Fox* in Flyte's room: *Brideshead Revisited*, 1945, p. 54. DHL:

'That *Lady into Fox* stuff is pretty piffle – just playboy stuff', to Middleton Murry, 17 September 1923, *The Letters of D. H. Lawrence* (Cambridge, 1987), p. 500.

202   'There were sets...': Frances Partridge, *Memories*, 1982.

203   'I found...': Garnett, *The Familiar Faces: the third part of an autobiography*, 1962, p. 149 ff.

204   T. E. Lawrence, *The Odyssey of Homer*, Oxford, 1932. Bowra review: *NS*, 8 April 1933.

205   'Shorter Notices...': Garnett, *op. cit.* p. 151.

205   Garnett, 'Books in General', *NS*, 1933–39 *passim*.

206   'I wrote only...': Garnett, *op. cit.* p. 149.

206   RM asks VW to write 'Books in General': VW, *Diary*, V, p. 240.

207   'many characteristics...': Raymond Mortimer, Autobiographical Preface to *Try Anything Once: Selected Writings*, 1976.

207   'an at times delightful burlesque...': Betjeman, *An Oxford University Chest*, 1938, p. 185.

207   'patient tutorials': RM on 'Desmond MacCarthy', *Try Anything*, p. 13.

209   RM on *Suicide; a social and historical study* by Henry Romilly Fedden (later books as Robin Fedden): *NS*, 14 May 1938.

209   The Competition: see *New Statesman Competitions* edited by G. W. Stonier, 1946.

210   Maclaren-Ross, 'Week-end Competitions': reprinted in *The Funny Bone*, 1956, p. 146.

211   General Knowledge Paper: set in *NS*, 25 December 1937; letter from Lancelot Hogben attacking the GKP, *NS*, 1 January 1938; essay by YY (Robert Lynd), 'A Wicked Paper', and D. W. Brogan letter, *NS*, 8 January 1938; letters from Barbara Wooton, E. M. Forster and a poem-letter from W. J. Turner, 15 January; letters from Ruth Adam, V. S. Pritchett and a group of Oxford students, 22 January; final letter from Hogben, 29 January 1938.

212   Dachau article: *NS*, 13 November 1937 and one follow-up letter, 27 November 1937. The author of the anonymous article may have been Oliver Woods, the *Times* man in Germany, whose own newspaper spiked his report on Dachau.

212   Pritchett: for his early career see *A Cab at the Door: Early Years*, 1968, and *Midnight Oil*, 1971.

213   *The Best Short Stories of 1927*, edited by Edward O'Brien, 1928. VSP's contribution was 'Tragedy in a Greek Theatre' (from the *Cornhill*), p. 154ff.

214   V. S. Pritchett: *The Complete Short Stories*, 1990, and *The Complete Essays*, 1991, comprising *In My Good Books* (1942), *The Living Novel* (1946), *Books in General* (1953), *The Working Novelist* (1965), *The Myth Makers* (1979), *The Tale Bearers* (1980), *A Man of Letters* (1985), *Lasting Impressions* (1990).

215   '*Dead Souls* belongs to that group of novels...': VSP, *Complete Essays*, p. 42.

215 T. C. Worsley, *Flannelled Fool: A Slice of Life in the Thirties*, 1966.'What did you say . . .': p. 114ff.

216 TCW theatre reviews, reprinted in *The Fugitive Art: Dramatic Commentaries 1947–1951*, 1952. 'Schoolmasters seem . . .': p. 42.

217 TCW reviews *Variation on a Theme*. *NS*, 17 May 1958. 'It is Mr Rattigan's best play so far.'

217 'a leading book-reviewer . . .': *In Praise of Love*, Duchess Theatre, London, 1973. Sebastian Crutwell is based in part on TCW and in part on John Clements, the actor, and his marriage to Kay Hammond.

218 Anthony Curtis, *New Developments in the French Theatre: a critical introduction to the plays of Jean-Paul Sartre, Simone de Beauvoir, Albert Camus and Jean Anouilh*, 1948, reprinted New York, 1950.

220 *Imaginary Conversations: Eight Radio Scripts by Michael Innes, Rose Macaulay, Seán O'Fáolain, V. S. Pritchett, Herbert Read, G. W. Stonier and C. V. Wedgwood*, edited with an introduction by Rayner Heppenstall, 1948. Ackroyd, *Dickens*, 1990, contains a conversation between Dickens and Ackroyd while walking through London, p. 306 ff, and 'a true conversation between imagined selves' (Chatterton, T. S. Eliot, Wilde and Dickens) on the nature of inspiration, p. 472ff; 'while the novelist . . .': 'Lively Ghosts', *NS*, 9 October 1948.

220 Joad on Sartre: *NS*, 28 August 1948.

224 Ackerley: see Peter Parker, *Ackerley: A Life of J. R. Ackerley*, 1989, for his long career as lit ed and his battles with Reith.

225 'As for dedication': *Abinger Harvest*, 1936.

226 'The amount of cleverness . . .': *Listener*, 24 March 1949.

227 Woolf's silence to colleagues about VW's suicide: Jeremy Potter, deputy chairman of *NS* 1951–69, to AC, June 1994.

227 'he mocked her stream-of-consciousness technique . . .': Drabble, *op. cit.*, p. 151 and ff, for Wilson's later opinion of Woolf's fiction.

227 Greene on Forster and VW: 'An English View of François Mauriac', *The Windmill*, No. 1, 1946, p. 80; reprinted as 'François Mauriac', *Collected Essays*, 1969.

228 Walter Allen: see his *As I Walked Down New Grub Street: Memories of A Writing Life*, 1981.

228 *Night and Day*: see the anthology from it edited by Christopher Hawtree with a preface by Greene, 1985. Walter Allen's column on football, 'High Seriousness and Aston Villa', is given on p. 245.

228 *To Beg I Am Ashamed*: *NS*, 21 November 1953. Greene thought it was difficult to see why the book had been suppressed before the war. This review has not been reprinted.

229 'So to the question . . .': Preface to *The Anathemata*, 1952; reprinted in *Introducing David Jones: a selection of his writings*, edited by J. Mathias, 1980, p. 116.

230 Raymond's review of *Helena*: *NS*, 21 October 1950.

232 Angus Wilson, *Such Darling Dodos*, 1950.

233 'I was a Bloomsbury . . .': *Rebecca's Vest*, 1993, p. 30, *Doubles: Studies in Literary History*, 1985.
234 Sir Frank Kermode and *Encounter*: see *Not Entitled: A Memoir*, 1996, p. 221ff.

11   Open doors

237 *The Bodley Head Saki*, edited with an introduction by J. W. Lambert, 1963.
237 J. W. Lambert and M. Ratcliffe, *The Bodley Head 1887–1987*, 1987. The book was not reviewed in the *Sunday Times*!
238 Watergate Classics: see Anthony Curtis, 'Gissing and the Betjeman Circle', *The Gissing Journal*, (Bradford), January 1997.
238 'A Portrait of George Gissing' by AC, produced by Sasha Moorsom (later Young), BBC. Third Programme, 27 November 1957.
239 Alfred Kazin, *Starting Out in the Thirties*, New York, 1965.
240 'Only in the case . . .': Hiram Haydn, *Words and Faces*, New York 1974, p. 74.
241 Snow on 'log-rolling': untraced.
241 Brooks Atkinson, dramatic critic of the *NYT* from 1925 to 1960, with a break during the Second World War.
242 *The Dial*: see James D. Hart, *The Oxford Companion to American Literature*, Fifth Edition, 1983, p. 199ff.
244 'I make haste . . .': Mark Van Doren, *The Happy Critic*, New York, 1961.
244 'Van Doren was unforgettably the poet . . .'. Kazin, *op cit.*, p. 39.
245 'No-one who has followed . . .' Trilling, 'Another Jewish Problem Novel', review of *The Disinherited* by Milton Waldman in the *Menorah Journal*, April 1929; reprinted in *Speaking of Literature and Society*, edited by Diana Trilling, Oxford, 1982, p. 16ff.
248 TSE on Humanism: reprinted in *Selected Essays*, 1932, p. 343ff and p. 443 ff.
249 'Our Critics, Right or Wrong': in the *Nation*, I: 23 October 1935; II: 6 November 1935; III: 20 November 1935; IV: 4 December 1935; V: 18 December 1935.
251 'It is not to be imagined . . .': *Nation*, 18 December 1935, p. 126ff.
252 Stephen Marcus, *The Other Victorians – a study of sexuality and pornography in mid-Victorian England*, 1966.
252 'the ideal reviewer': reprinted in Marcus, *Representations*, 1976, p. 121.
253 *Studies in a Dying Culture*, with an introduction by John Strachey, 1938; *Further Studies*, 1949. Tynan on Caudwell, see 'Culture in Trouble', *Tynan on Theatre*, 1964, p. 186.
253 John Reed: see *inter alia* his *Red Russia*, 1919; *Ten Days that Shook the World*, 1919; the biography by Granville Hicks, 1936, the movie *Reds*,

1981; for J. R. clubs, see Daniel Aaron, *Writers on the Left: Episodes in American Literary Communism* New York, 1961 (new edition, 1992); and for Rexroth at JR conference, see Linda Hamalian, *A Life of Kenneth Rexroth*, New York, 1991, p. 61ff.

254 'these two radical impulses . . .': Irving Howe, 'This Age of Conformity', 1954.

254 Rahv: see Mary McCarthy's obituary tribute, 'Philip Rahv 1908–1973', reprinted in *Occasional Prose*, 1975, p. 3ff.

256 'Calverton's house . . .': Kazin, *op. cit.*, p. 66.

257 *Partisan Review:* quotations from January/February 1947.

258 *I'll Take My Stand*, 1930. A manifesto in the form of a symposium by twelve Southern writers, affirming their regionalism.

258 'The man of letters . . .': *Sewanee Review*, Summer 1945, p. 336.

259 'The population should be homogeneous; where two or more cultures exist in the same place they are likely to be either fiercely self-conscious or both to become adulterate. What is still more important is unity of religious background; and reasons of race and religion combine to make any large numbers of free-thinking Jews undesirable.' *After Strange Gods*, 1934. For Eliot and Maurras, see Anthony Julius, *T. S. Eliot, Anti-Semitism and Literary Form*, Cambridge, 1996, p. 214ff.

259 Bollingen Prize: see Partisan Review issues for 1949; also Julius, *op. cit.*, p. 205.

262 S. N. Behrman, *The Worcester Account*, New York, 1954; dramatised in part as *The Cold Wind and the Warm*, 1958.

262 Wolcott Gibbs: dramatic critic of the *New Yorker*, 1940–58.

262 Kenneth (Peacock) Tynan (1927–80): in his Oxford production of *Hamlet* in 1949, the 1603 'Bad Quarto' text was used. It was given first at the Malvern Festival, where Rosencraft (in this version) was played by Lindsay Anderson, and then at the Rudolf Steiner Hall (now demolished) Baker Street, London W1, where R. was played by AC. Hamlet was played by Peter Parker (later Sir), Horatio by John Schlesinger, Polonius by Jack May, Marcellus by Robert Hardy, Laertes by Alan Cooke. Ophelia was not Shirley Catlin (later Baroness Williams) as is sometimes said but Evelyn Arengo-Jones. Tynan was the Murderer in the play scene.

263 'To think that a man should live on pea-nuts in a town called Troy!': *New Grub Street*, chapter xxviii.

263 bowdlerised letters: *Letters of George Gissing to His Family*, edited by Algernon and Ellen Gissing with a Preface by His Son, 1927.

264 book villain: *An enquiry into the nature of certain 19th century pamphlets* by John Carter and Graham Pollard, 1934.

265 greatest coup: see T. S. Eliot *The Waste Land: a facsimile & transcript of the original drafts including the annotations of Ezra Pound*, edited by Valerie Eliot, 1971.

266 fellow Gissingite: *The Letters of George Gissing to Eduard Bertz* (1961),

edited by Arthur C. Young, one of the trio of editors of the award-winning *The Collected Letters of George Gissing* in nine volumes, Ohio, 1990–7.

268   Quentin Anderson, *The American Henry James*, New Jersey, 1957; 'The Mature James', *TLS*, 14 June 1957.
268   Alfred A. and Blanche W. Knopf: see *The Company They Kept: An Exhibition Catalog* tracing the development of Knopf Inc., compiled by Cathy Henderson, Austin, Texas, 1995.
269   'beloved Ben': Rumer Godden to AC, 1995.
270   Ed Murrow: see *In Search of Light: The Broadcasts of Edward R. Murrow 1938–1961, New York*, 1967.
270   Tynan, *Sweet Bird* review, *New Yorker*, 21 March 1959.
270   *Act One An Autobiography* by Moss Hart, New York, 1959. Reviewed *New Yorker*, 28 November 1959.

12   Ross and Wilson

272   Ross: see James Thurber, *The Years With Ross*, New York, 1959; Brendan Gill, *Here at the New Yorker*, 1975, revised edn 1990; Thomas Kunkel, *Genius in Disguise: Harold Ross of the New Yorker*, New York, 1995.
273   talent for light verse: see 'The Titans' by Fillmore Hyde, *New Yorker*, 25 February 1928.
274   Dorothy Parker: see *The Collected Dorothy Parker*, with an introduction by Brendan Gill, (Penguin) 1989 (an enlarged version of *The Portable Dorothy Parker*, New York, 1944). Many but not all of Constant Reader's reviews may be read there.
276   *Caste* and Waring reviews, *New Yorker*, 1 October 1927.
276   monumental bore, 'The Waltz' *CDP* p. 47. 'crash came', 'The Garter' *New Yorker*, 8 September, 1928
276   'A few more . . .': Parker on *Crude, New Yorker*, 22 October 1927.
276   Cabell, *Something About Eve* review in *New Yorker*, 29 October, 1927.
276   Lewis, *Dodsworth*: review in *New Yorker*, 16 March 1929; reprinted in *CDP*, p. 522.
276   Glyn, *It*: review in *New Yorker*, 26 November 1927; reprinted in *CDP*, p. 464.
276   Wright, *Appendicitis*: review in *New Yorker*, 24 March 1928. reprinted in *CDP*, p. 504.
277   'In fact so Good . . .': *New Yorker*, 20 October 1928, reprinted in *CDP*, p. 517.
278   'My books this week . . .': *New Yorker*, 31 March 1928.
278   Ford, *The Last Post*: review in *New Yorker*, 4 February 1928; reprinted in *CDP*, p. 487.
278   'After all the high screaming . . .': 29 October, 1927; reprinted in *CDP* p. 458.

279 Margot Asquith: *New Yorker*, 22 October 1927; reprinted in *CDP*, p. 455.
279 Aimée Semple: *New Yorker*, 25 February 1928; reprinted in *CDP*, p. 496.
279 Isadora Duncan: *New Yorker*, 14 January 1928; reprinted in *CDP*, p. 479.
279 Katherine Mansfield: *New Yorker*, 8 October 1927; reprinted in *CDP*, p. 451.
280 Fadiman: 'Ring Lardner and the Triangle of Hate', *Nation*, 22 March 1933. His other appraisals in the *Nation* were of Hemingway (18 January), Joseph Hergesheimer (15 February) and James Branch Cabell (12 April 1933).
280 'What has happened...': 'The Book-Reviewing Business', *Party of One: the selected writings of Clifton Fadiman*, New York, 1955, p. 305 ff.
281 'Even those...': *New Yorker*, 21 April 1934.
281 O'Hara, *Butterfield 8*: reviewed in *New Yorker*, 19 October 1935.
281 Myers, *Root and Flower*: reviewed in *New Yorker*, 7 September 1935.
281 Romains, *The World from Below*: reviewed in *New Yorker*, 5 October 1935.
281 Gorer, *Africa Dances*: reviewed in *New Yorker*, 12 October 1935.
281 'For about a quarter of a century...': Fadiman, *Party of One*, quoted by Peter Green in an introduction to *Appreciations*, 1962, selections from Fadiman's writings.
283 Malcolm Cowley: *The Exile's Return: A Narrative of Ideas*, 1934, revised 1951.
283 Matthew Josephson: *Zola and his Time* (1928), *The Robber Barons* (1934); see also the biography David E. Shi, *Matthew Josephson: Bourgeois Bohemian*, New Haven, Connecticut, 1981.
283 'his socialism changed...': Aaron, *Writers on the Left*, p. 81.
285 Wilder letter: *New Republic*, 29 October 1930; Wilson's summing-up is reprinted in *The Shores of Light*, p. 503.
285 'He was lean...': *The Twenties*, 1975, p. 120.
286 'The book contained...': *The Bit Between My Teeth*, New York, 1965, p. 523.
287 Edmund Wilson, *The Scrolls From the Dead Sea* (1955), revised as *The Dead Sea Scrolls 1947–69* (1969).
287 'that work of "enlightenment"...': 'Thoughts on Being Bibliographed' in Edmund Wilson, *Classics and Commercials: A Literary Chronicle of the Forties*, New York, 1950, p. 110 ff.
287 'It is an essential part...': *To the Finland Station*, 1940, p. 20.
287 Wilson, 'Through an Embassy Window: Harold Nicolson': *New Yorker*, 1 January 1944, reviewing Nicolson, *The Desire to Please* (with the Rowan portrait), 1943. See *Classics and Commercials*, p. 121 ff.
289 Ibid. for reviews of Boyle, 15 January 1944 (p. 128 ff.); Waugh, 4 March 1944 (p. 140 ff.); and see *The Bit Between My Teeth*, for reviews

of Angus Wilson, 15 April 1950 (p. 270 ff.) and Kingsley Amis, 24
March 1956 (p. 275 ff.).

289   Review of *Dr Zhivago*, 15 November 1958, reprinted in *The Bit
Between My Teeth*, p. 428 ff; and Wilson with Barbara Demming and
Eugenia Lehovich, 'Legend and Symbol in *Dr Zhivago*', *Nation*, 25
April 1959.

291   Anthony West see *Principles and Persuasions: The Literary Essays of
Anthony West* (1957), on Edgar Johnson's *Dickens*, p. 106ff; on Zola,
p. 126ff; and on Vyvyan Holland, p. 141ff.

292   John Updike on *Memoirs of Hecate County*: reprinted in *Hugging The
Shore: Essays and Criticism*, New York, 1983 p. 196; on *The Thirties*,
ibid., p. 206.

292   Shawn's attitude to publication date and Britons as book-reviewers:
Charles McGrath to AC, November 1995.

294   Wilson and alimony: Steiner to AC, September 1995.

294   Randolph S. Churchill, *Winston S. Churchill*, reviewed *New Yorker*, 5
November 1966.

297   Pirsig review: *New Yorker*, 15, April 1974.

13   Baltimore, Hollywood, Edinburgh and Booker

299   'at once gay and gruff': see Philip Marshall Wagner, *H.L. Mencken*,
Baltimore, 1966; H. A. Williams, *Mencken*, Arizona, 1977; and for
historical background G. W. Johnson, F. R. Kent, H. L. Mencken
and H. Owen, *The Sunpapers of Baltimore*, New York, 1938.

300   'Though born . . .': *Prejudices: First Series*, 1921, p. 66.

302   George and Ira Gershwin: see Edward Jablonski, *Gershwin A Biography*, New York, 1987; L. D. Stewart & Jablonski, *The Gershwin Years*,
New York, 1958 (revised 1977); *Lyrics on Several Occasions* by Ira
Gershwin, Gent, New York, 1959; Robert Kimball, *The Complete Lyrics
of Ira Gershwin*, New York, 1993; Philip Furia, *Ira Gershwin: The Art of
the Lyricist*, Oxford, 1996.

304   Solly Zuckerman was chairman of the British government's advisory
committee on scientific policy; see his *From Apes to Warlords*, 1978,
p. 82, for the Gershwins.

305   J. W. Krutch review of *Porgy and Bess: Nation*, 30 October 1935.

305   Ira v. Lerner at Scrabble: Alan J. Lerner to AC, London, 1973.

305   Oscar Levant: see Jablonski, *passim*.

308   Hughes' project for a chain-novel: the first part of *The Human
Predicament*, *The Fox in the Attic*, had been published in 1961. I stayed
with Hughes and his wife at their house Mor Edrin on the coast of
Merioneth in late September, before publication, to interview him
for the *Sunday Telelegraph*. He completed only the second part of the
work, *The Wooden Shepherdess* (1973), before his death in 1976.

308   '. . . essence of idiocy': RW to AC, nd, author's collection.

309 'Is that Iris Murdoch?' *Sunday Telegraph*, 26 August 1962.
310 Mary McCarthy's 'Guide to Exiles . . .': reprinted in *Occasional Prose*, 1985, p. 69.
312 Isabel Colegate: acceptance speech at W. H. Smith book award lunch for *The Shooting Party*, 1980.
318 *Empire of the Sun*: Ballard review by Richard Jones, *Listener*, 20 September1984. Letters on internment in Shanghai, *Listener*, 11 October 1984.

14   Pen and others

323 Campbell's assault: untraced, but the recipent seems to have been Stephen Spender.
323 Richard Lister (T. C. Worsley) L. P. Hartley, *Poor Clare*: review by *Evening Standard*, 29 October 1968. The heading was 'Summing up Myra . . . the most flavourless, colourless, characterless, featureless, passionless, bloodless woman in modern fiction . . . to say nothing of Edward.'
324 'Hendecasyllabics': *The Poems of Tennyson*, edited by Christopher Ricks, 1969, p. 1155.
324 Thackeray as reviewer: see first volume of the biography by Gordon N. Ray, *Thackeray, The Uses of Adversity*, 1955, p. 190ff.
325 Mr Hurtle: *Pendennis*, 1850, chapter XXIX.
325 *PMG* prospectus . . . five pound note: *Pendennis*, chapter XXXIII.
326 *Fraser's Magazine* (1830–82): Thackeray was a frequent contributor (see Ray, *op. cit.*). It was notable for the quality of its book-reviews.
326 'of accomplishments . . .' and 'Pen, you beggar!': *Pendennis*, chapter XXXIII; 'he worked away hard . . .': *Pendennis*, chapter XXXVII.
327 'I would rather starve . . .': ibid.
327 *Pall Mall Gazette*: for the historical journal, see J. W. Robertson Scott, *The Life and Death of a Newspaper*, 1952.
328 Wells on *Guy Domville* and on Cust: see Wells, *An Experiment in Autobiography: Discoveries and Conclusions of a Very Ordinary Brain (since 1866)*, vol 2, 1934 (p. 535 of the 1984 edition).
329 Hardy, *A Pair of Blue Eyes*, 1873. 'You've made me . . .': Chapter XVII.
330 Gissing, *New Grub Street*, 1891, see 'Recruits': Chapter XIV.
331 Kipling, 'Dayspring Mishandled', *Limits and Renewals*, 1932.
332 Gosse and Churton Collins: see Ann Thwaite, *Edmund Gosse: A Literary Landscape*, 1984, p. 277ff.
332 'The Figure in the Carpet': published first in *Cosmopolis*, January and February 1896, one of the group of tales described by HJ as 'scenes of the literary life'; see *The Complete Tales of Henry James*, edited by Leon Edel, Vol. 9, 1946, p. 273ff.
333 Maugham: for reviews of his work, see *Somerset Maugham The Critical Heritage*, edited by Anthony Curtis and John Whitehead, 1987.

334   'I said I wouldn't...': *The End of the Affair*, 1951; p. 45 in the
      Collected Edition, 1974.
334   'I am afraid...': GG. to AC, 10 April 1961, author's collection.
335   Martin Amis, *The Information*, 1995, p. 67.

15   The continuation

341   Fish, *Professional Correctness*, Oxford, 1995; a revised and expanded
      version of Fish's Clarendon Lectures, delivered in Oxford in May
      1993.
341   Eagleton on Fish, *TLS*, 24 November 1995.

Further reading

[This list contains a selection of books not previously mentioned that are relevant to reviewing. In addition, easily located, there are collections of reviews by individual reviewers, and the Routledge Critical Heritage volumes where a selection of reviews for a given author is chronologically presented.]

Richard D. Altick, *The English Common Reader: A Social History of the Mass Reading Public, 1800–1900*, Chicago, 1957.

Victor Bonham-Carter, *Authors by Profession: Vol. 1 From the Introduction of · Printing to the Copy right Act 1911*, 1978; Vol. 2 1911–1981, 1981.

Margaret Cooter and others, *Reviewing the Reviews: a woman's place on the book page*, 1987.

Nigel Cross, *The Common Writer: Life in nineteenth-century Grub Street*, Cambridge, 1985.

Walter Graham, *The Beginnings of Literary Periodicals*, Oxford, 1926; *English Literary Periodicals*, New York, 1930.

John Gross, *The Rise and Fall of the Man of Letters: Aspects of English Literary Life Since 1800*, 1969. A major contribution.

Sylvia E. Kameran (ed.), *Book Reviewing*, Boston, 1978.

Stephen Koss, *The Rise and Fall of the Political Press in Britain: Vol. 1 The Nineteenth Century: Vol. 2 The Twentieth Century*, 1984. Not concerned with literary journalism as such, but invaluable background reading for its account of newspaper affiliations, their owners and editors.

Q. D. Leavis, *Fiction and the Reading Public*, 1932. A seminal work.

George Moore, *Avowals* (limited edition 1919), 1924. Contains dialogues between Moore and Gosse.

S. P. Rosenbaum, *The Early Literary History of the Bloomsbury Group*, 2 vols: *Victorian Bloomsbury*, 1987; *Edwardian Bloomsbury*, 1994. A comprehensive study of the reviewing and other writing of the Bloomsbury clerisy.

Nicholas Spice (ed.), *London Reviews: A selection from the London Review of Books, 1983–1985, with an introduction by Karl Miller, 1985.*
Morton D. Zabel, Literary Opinion in America, revised edition 1951. By a Professor of Literature at the University of Chicago, who was also a literary journalist and editor.

Index

Index

Index

374

Index

Wagner, Philip M. 299
Walkley A. B. 138, 144
Walpole, (Sir) Hugh 32, 87, 160, 227, 334
Walter, Arthur 142
Warburg, Frederic 13
Ward, Mary (Mrs Humphry Ward) 157
Ward, Thomas Humphry 143
Warde, Beatrice 181
Warner, Marina 103
Warshow, Robert 257
Wass, Sir Douglas 239
Watson, William 190
Waugh, Evelyn 32; reviews in *Sun Tel* 56; 77,
    78, 93; *Rossetti* 194–5; 228, 230, 289
Webb, Beatrice & Sidney 186–8, 191
Webb, William, lit ed *Guardian* 236, 312
Weidenfeld, George (Lord Weidenfeld) 103
Weightman, J. G. 95
Welch, Colin 55–6
Weldon, Fay 20, 321–2
Wells, H. G. 40; *Marriage* 47; angry with RW
    49; 74; 'Scope of the Novel' 159; dispute
    with James 160–6; 187–8, 328
West, Anthony 40, 206, 291
West, Dame Rebecca (Cicily Isabel Fairfield,
    later Andrews) 39–53, 60, 107, 194, 223
Wharton, Edith 148
White, E. B. 257, 273
White, Katherine 273–4
Wilde, Oscar 32, 37–8, 174
Wilder, Thornton 249, 284–5
Wilkinson, Clennel, lit ed *NS* 200

Williams, Emlyn 13, 37
Williams, Patricia 103
Williams, Tennessee 270
Wilmers, Mary-Kay, editor *London Review of
    Books* 235
Wilson, Angus 24, 78; *Hemlock and After* 87;
    lead-reviewer *Observer* 101–2; attacks VW
    227; 232, 289, 291, 314
Wilson, Edmund 34, 120, 281–94, 297
Wilson, Harold 67
Wiskemann, Elizabeth 184
Wodehouse P. G. 32, 81
Wolfit, Sir Donald 62
Woolf, Leonard 14, 72, 147, 178, lit ed
    Nation 193–4, 225, 227, 231
Woolf, Virginia (VW) 40, 85–6, 134, 147–79,
    189, 192, 196, 202, 227; *Diaries* sold to
    Berg 265
Woollcott, Alexander 241, 274
Wordsworth, William 71, 83, 324
Worsley T. C. (Cuthbert), lit ed *NS & N* 63,
    99, 207, 216–22, 228, 323
Worsthorne, Peregrine 8, 27, 130
Wyndham, Violet 56

Young, Arthur C. 266–7
Young, B. A. 63

Ziegler, Philip 115
Ziman, H. D. (Zed), lit ed *Daily Telegraph*
    28–30
Zola, Emile 74, 283, 291
Zuckerman, Lord (Solly) 304–5